RSAC

SEP 2003

D0208192

GETTYSBURG

Jim Weeks

GETTYSBURG

★ ★ ★ ★ ★ ★ ★ ★ ★ ★ ★ ★ ★ ★ ★ ★

MEMORY, MARKET, AND AN AMERICAN SHRINE

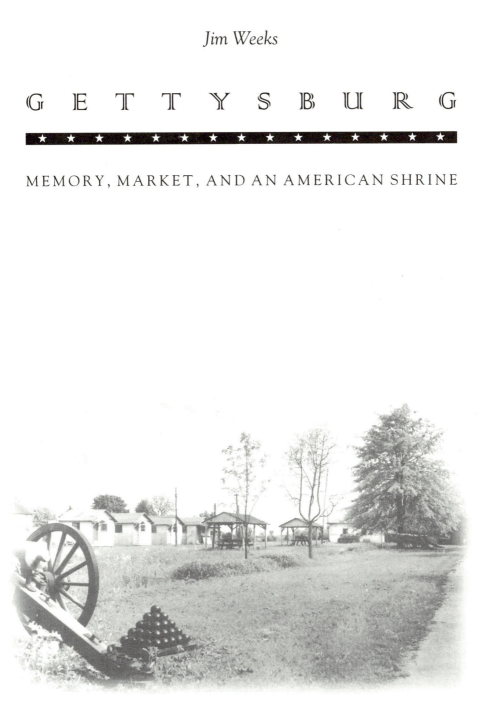

PRINCETON UNIVERSITY PRESS • PRINCETON AND OXFORD

Copyright © 2003 by Princeton University Press
Published by Princeton University Press, 41 William Street, Princeton, New Jersey 08540
In the United Kingdom: Princeton University Press, 3 Market Place,
Woodstock, Oxfordshire OX20 1SY

ALL RIGHTS RESERVED

Library of Congress Cataloging-in-Publication Data
Weeks, Jim, 1950–
Gettysburg : memory, market, and an American shrine / by Jim Weeks.
p. cm.
Includes bibliographical references (p.) and index.
ISBN 0–691–10271–6 (alk. paper)
1. Gettysburg National Military Park (Pa.)   2. Gettysburg, Battle of, Gettysburg, Pa.,
1863.   3. Tourism—Social aspects—Pennsylvania—Gettysburg.   4. Heritage
tourism—Pennsylvania—Gettysburg.   5. Memory—Social
aspects—Pennsylvania—Gettysburg.   6. Historic sites—Economic
aspects—Pennsylvania—Gettysburg.   7. Pennsylvania—History—Civil War,
1861–1865—Monuments.   8. United States—History—Civil War, 1861–1865—Monuments.
I. Title.
E475.56 .W44 2003
973.7′349—dc21   2002074911

British Library Cataloging-in-Publication Data is available

This book has been composed in Goudy
Printed on acid-free paper. ∞
www.pupress.princeton.edu

Printed in the United States of America

1   3   5   7   9   10   8   6   4   2

973.7349 W418g 2003
Weeks, Jim, 1950-
Gettysburg : memory, market,
and an American shrine

★ ★ ★ ★ ★ ★ ★ ★ ★ ★

A GETTYSBURG SOUVENIR

FOR GARY S. CROSS

Contents

☆ ☆ ☆ ☆ ☆ ☆ ☆ ☆ ☆ ☆ ☆

Illustrations

☆ ☆ ☆ ☆ ☆ ☆ ☆ ☆ ☆ ☆ ☆

Acknowledgments

☆ ☆ ☆ ☆ ☆ ☆ ☆ ☆ ☆ ☆ ☆

ALONG the pilgrimage route that ended again at Gettysburg, I met many a friend without whose aid the journey would not have continued. The Department of History provided generous support through a Hill Fellowship in 1997, and subsequently funded travel to deliver papers at national meetings. In search of research material I traveled as far south as Durham, as far north as Worcester, and as far west as Chicago. Although it is not possible to individually thank those who contributed to my research, all were most cordial and helpful in spite of often straitened circumstances. Many doggedly tracked down materials and took time to discuss my project far beyond the requirements of their institutions. These people include, in alphabetical order, Louise Arnold, U.S. Army War College, Carlisle, Pennsylvania; Fred Bauman, Jr., Manuscript Division, Library of Congress, Washington, D.C.; Woody Christ, Adams County Historical Society, Gettysburg; Robert Sayre Cox, and Brian Dunnigan, Clements Library, University of Michigan; John Coski, Museum of the Confederacy, Richmond; Sue Hamburger, Penn State Special Collections; Scott Hartwick, Gettysburg National Military Park; David Hedrick, Gettysburg College; Randy Roberts, Western Historical Manuscript Collection, University of Missouri-Columbia; Paul Romaine and Sandra Trenholm, Gilder-Lehrman Collection, New York; Jane Sferra, Ohio Historical Society; Chris Dupin, Princeton University Library Department of Rare Books and Special Collections; Mark Van Ells, Wisconsin Veterans Museum, Madison, Wisconsin; Steve Wright, Civil War Library and Museum, Philadelphia; and Helena Wright, Smithsonian Institution. Kathy Georg Harrison of Gettysburg National Military Park and her colleague Winona Peterson deserve special thanks for allowing me access to the park's archives. They graciously accommodated my presence in their cramped quarters off and on for nearly a year.

I also take this opportunity to thank a number of helpful employees of the following institutions whose names are unknown to me: Chicago Historical Society; College of William and Mary Special Collections, Williamsburg, Virginia; Historical Society of Pennsylvania, Philadelphia; Na-

tional Archives and Records Administration, Washington, D.C., and Philadelphia; National Library of Medicine, Bethesda, Maryland; Newberry Library, Chicago; Pennsylvania State Archives and Library, Harrisburg;
Perkins Library Special Collections, Duke University, Durham; Southern
Collection, University of North Carolina, Chapel Hill; University of Wisconsin Special Collections; and Wisconsin Historical Society, Madison.

Thanks also to Gettysburgians Jackie White, Thelma Dick, and Vera
Culver, who shared family papers, photographs, and reminiscences. Carleton Smith and Katie Lawhon of the Gettysburg National Park Service
and Susan Robertson of Friends of the National Parks at Gettysburg most
graciously allowed me to borrow photographs. David Meskers of Strasburg,
Pennsylvania opened his extensive collection of Gettysburg materials for
my use. The staff of Penn State's Interlibrary Loan cheerfully provided innumerable reels of microfilm and other research materials month after
month. I owe both thanks and apologies to the student employees of the
microforms department, whom I often delayed after closing time. Some
students even thought I worked there.

Several fine minds provided motivation and helped refine the ideas in
this study. David Blight of Amherst College as well as William Pencak and
Anne C. Rose of Penn State contributed valuable suggestions in spite of
their often frenetic schedules. Gary Gallagher of the University of Virginia
not only provided much advice during the project's early stages, but aided
access to several archives and historical societies. His encouragement and
comments often kept the fires burning. To Gary Cross of Penn State, I
apply President James Garfield's remark that his idea of an education was
Mark Hopkins, president of Garfield's alma mater, Williams College, "on
one end of a log and me on the other." Gary continuously nurtured this
project with inspiration as well as invaluable ideas from his fertile mind.
Nevertheless, I will repeat the second biggest cliché cited in books built on
the kindness of others, that none of those who assisted along the journey
are in any way responsible for technical or judgmental errors.

Finally, my family kept me going materially and spiritually. Moose, Alice,
and Phil graciously shared space while offering companionship. My wife,
Beth, often turned drudgery into fun, proved a model traveling companion,
and needless to say demonstrated much patience. My mother-in-law, Teddy,
supported this effort in several important ways, not the least of which was a
keen sense of humor when levity seemed in short supply. Jack, Jay, and Bess
accompanied me on trips to Gettysburg, and their observations proved most
insightful. I also owe much to Boots and Judi, who were part of the initial
pilgrimage to Gettysburg over forty years ago and, although we cannot escape beings relatives, are still my friends. Most of all I owe a debt to my
mother and father, Catherine Weeks and L. James Weeks. They not only
continually provided spiritual and material sustenance, their belief in the
culture of aspiration encouraged curiosity about the world, cultural capital
for which I am much indebted.

Introduction

☆ ☆ ☆ ☆ ☆ ☆ ☆ ☆ ☆ ☆ ☆

"YA GOT ME, AGHHHHH!" Lurching from the imaginary bullet fired by my finger, cousin Jack tumbled off the stone wall on Gettysburg's Cemetery Ridge. On that summer noon in 1959, the heyday of family touring, other tourists near the High Water Mark ignored the killing. War as play occupied baby boomers at all of this national shrine's place-names, which had been fixed in the gazetteer of Americana—the Wheatfield, Devil's Den, Little Round Top, the Angle. Whether or not children and parents pondered Gettysburg's lessons of national sacrifice that day, they visited on family time. After driving over the battlefield, families might have relaxed at a motel pool, shopped for souvenirs, or visited a proprietary tourist attraction. As had Gettysburg visitors before and since, most combined commemoration with play, reaffirming allegiance to country while on leave from everyday routine.

With a view that the American landscape had something to teach, Mom and Dad packed the black '53 Ford every summer in the late fifties and the sixties and drove us to places claiming significance in American history: Plymouth Rock, Valley Forge, Bunker Hill, Williamsburg, and Gettysburg. Of all the historic sites we visited prior to Gettysburg, and all those explored long after the '53 Ford expired, Gettysburg produced not just the most vivid memories, but a transformation in me akin to religious conversion.

The family stayed at an eight-dollar-a-night tourist cabin that proved a bit cramped for six. When the proprietor told my father the next larger cabin cost thirteen dollars, Dad hesitated and, as if it were the only possible response, whistled one long blast. We drove the battlefield avenues from one monument to the next, gaping at the sculptural variety as if we were on a scavenger hunt. Occasional waysides explaining the battle broke the stones' mesmerizing effect and reminded us of the event this park memorialized. At the Soldiers' National Cemetery, we stumbled through the Gettysburg Address memorized in school. Our patriotic thoughts may have been inchoate, but we understood Gettysburg's place in the struggle for liberty at home and overseas. Tourists could not escape references to this notion. Peering down at President Dwight David Eisenhower's farm from a nearby observation tower was as much a part of Gettysburg touring as Ike-and-Mamie teacups, pincushions, and postcards. Only at Gettysburg did the Free World's leader merge in a comforting omnipresence with the Civil War leader who here reaffirmed America's destiny. Lincoln in bronze, Lincoln in ceramic, and Lincoln in wax reinforced our reverence for the mythical hero whose portrait hung alongside George Washington's and the flag we saluted in our school. Together at Gettysburg, Ike and Abe exuded assurance of the nation's glorious past and an even more glorious future.

Gettysburg's carnivalesque sights, crowds, and kitsch enchanted the puerile mind. The Civil War forage caps, toy guns, and Confederate flags we purchased in town assumed talismanic powers, inspiring us to scramble, charge, and retreat over ground that once hosted mass carnage. Our boyish imaginations were stimulated by a mammoth circular painting of the battle, the cyclorama—a relic of preautomobile, preelectrified entertainment the likes of which P. T. Barnum once displayed. Museums of an earlier day, stuffed with macabre, grotesque, and ghoulish curiositites, titillated us even in the age of television and atoms. Along with providing soft drinks, ice cream, and souvenirs, these ma-and-pa emporiums displayed battlefield-dug bones, teeth, bullets gathered in geometric shapes, and, in one case, what appeared to be a whitewashed chicken coop labeled mysteriously General Longstreet's Headquarters.

While my mother and sisters patronized the Hall of Presidents—an old-fashioned waxworks collection of American presidents and first ladies—we visited a museum that included a diorama and "slave hideaway" from which frightful mannequins stared. A short walk brought us to a museum opened in an old orphanage by Cliff Arquette, folksy NBC television personality Charley Weaver. Even though Arquette used his television aura to attract customers, the museum reflected the nineteenth-century fondness for pot-pourri. Among the bric-a-brac blending Civil War with television themes, the museum featured an optical device through which one could see the figure of an orphan chained in the building's basement. When I arrived home, the topsy-turvy exhilaration of carnival swung to fear, producing sleepless visions of staring dummies, children chained in dungeons, rattling bones, and, worst of all, the memory of a photo showing a bayonet rammed through a human skull. But terror from the trip quickly gave way to an emotional response that has lingered ever since, manifesting itself in a variety of ways.

A fresh perspective on that visit, evolving over the intervening decades, produced several key reflections that served as the origin of this book. One is that the permanent imprint Gettysburg left on my imagination, the reason for its enduring attraction, lay in the way the place simultaneously shattered time and offered entertainment. On the one hand, Gettysburg broke through the humdrum of my suburban life by cheating the present.

Its soldiers' cemetery, panoramic views, expansiveness, and abundance of oversized funereal monuments evoked a sense of grandeur that lured one into a distant time. On the other hand, the carnival aspects of Gettysburg—sensuous, strange, full of possibilities—offered a hyperreal sense of the here and now. Gettysburg combined extremes of the worldly with the otherworldly, simultaneously overwhelming, thrilling, entertaining, amusing, and frightening. More than commemorating the site where something had happened, Gettysburg seemed a place where something *was happening*. My experience, like those of other tourists, replicated a medieval pilgrimage: we stepped out of everyday life and encountered the wondrous through extraordinary sights, amusements, and magical goods.

Another observation evolving from my initial visit is that Gettysburg, one of America's most important shrines, is its continual state of transformation. Objects on the landscape, including the cemetery, monuments, fencing, cannon, interpretive signs, and tourist attractions, can be read as texts revealing the cultural standards of those who built and visited the shrine. Even the absence of structures removed in recent decades communicates much about the current era of heritage tourism. At the time of my first trip, over forty years ago, Gettysburg showed signs of a different era of touring. Tourist cabins, gas stations, family attractions, garish signage, as well as ma-and-pa museums and refreshment stands, dotted town and battlefield. These tourist services have vanished in an attempt to replicate the ambience of 1863, a trend likely to accelerate. Similarly, the 1950s Gettysburg differed from its 1900 manifestation, which catered to railroad tourists, and was in turn dramatically different from its immediate post–Civil War counterpart, which served genteel tourists. This slow, imperceptible transition from one landscape to another opens a window not only on visitors but on the succession of reigning aesthetics involving memory and market.

A third reflection surfaced with the transformation of Gettysburg after Vietnam and the rise of reenacting as an appropriate form of commemoration. When I visited as a kid, I remember standing near a crowd at the great bronze, open-book monument on Cemetery Ridge while a guide referred to the High Water Mark. I puzzled later over what Gettysburg had to do with the ocean, straining to imagine a tide flooding the sloping farmland ahead. But I did not dwell on this enigma nor on any of the other symbolic imponderables I encountered, for my imagination had been stirred by the diorama, cyclorama, souvenir toys, and props on the landscape such as fencing and cannon. Together they provided a graphic narrative of the battle, aiding my quest to see advancing Rebel battle lines whenever I looked out over the battlefield. Although I did not realize it at the time, commercial culture—from guided tours to stereographs and movies—always had provided a subtext to Gettysburg's larger historical meaning. Indeed, these graphic forms, expressed in recent years through reenactors and restored landscape, could thrive apart from the historical significance of the battle.

These observations that began with a childhood trip are addressed in the following pages: the apparent paradox between Gettysburg as both a site of commemoration and an object of commerce, and the evolution of both memory and tourism. Arguably, Gettysburg's significance rests as much in its stature as a cultural icon as in the battle's historical outcome. Civil War historian Fletcher Pratt once remarked that "Gettysburg" and the "Civil War" were virtually synonymous terms. Yet bigger armies had faced off during the Civil War; grander and costlier assaults were made elsewhere; equally significant turning points occurred. So why has Gettysburg's memory not only overshadowed other Civil War battles, but many other American historical events as well? And why has a battle described by participants as "awful beyond description" with upwards of fifty thousand casualties served as a significant source of leisure for Americans? A town that without the battle would be today as effaced as most other nineteenth-century market towns is instead a byword for Americana. A short list of celebrity visitors to this national crossroads includes Lucille Ball, Henry Ward Beecher, Menachem Begin, William Jennings Bryan, William "Buffalo Bill" Cody, Frederick Douglass, Thomas Edison, David Lloyd George, U. S. Grant, Joseph Hooker, Nikita Khruschev, John L. Lewis, George C. Marshall, Mary Pickford, Frederick Remington, Jacob Riis, Lillian Russell, Anwar Sadat, Philip Sheridan, William T. Sherman, Adlai Stevenson, Billy Sunday, Owen Wister, and most presidents since James Buchanan.

Judging from Gettysburg's infusion into American life, the battle's twenty-odd hours of combat action represent perhaps the most powerful moments in American history. Indeed, its power appears to grow instead of diminish as the battle recedes in time. Attempting to thoroughly list the diverse ways Gettysburg appears electronically, in print, and in plastic is almost hopeless. Television and movies have referred to Gettysburg in comedies, drama, documentaries, and in cable series. *Gettysburg*, a movie based on Michael Shaara's 1977 best-seller about the battle, *The Killer Angels*, played nationwide beginning in 1993 and became a television feature. One of the film's heroes, Joshua Lawrence Chamberlain, launched a subindustry that peddled Chamberlain books, beer, T-shirts, mugs, and credit cards. Chamberlain's hometown in Maine went so far as to construct a public park resembling Little Round Top, the site where Chamberlain achieved cinematic immortality.

But Gettysburg in celluloid is only one form of its pervasiveness. In 1984, a magazine devoted to the battle, *Gettysburg*, was launched, while Thomas Publications, a publisher located in Gettysburg, prints a variety of books and pamphlets devoted to the battle. Gun manufacturers market commemorative Gettysburg firearms. Toy merchants produce Gettysburg board games and a Gettysburg Barbie doll. Computer users may purchase Gettysburg screen savers and computer games, or access Gettysburg Listservs and Gettysburg Web sites. Until demolition of the National Battlefield

Tower in 2000, a television camera mounted atop the structure provided a continuous view of the battlefield.

Nearly two million tourists visit the battlefield annually, requiring services provided by hostelers, restaurants, impresarios, and fast-food operations. Gettysburg passes as a kind of Civil War Canterbury, where shrine and festival merge. Tours, seminars, and institutes abound, from tactical studies to explorations of the haunts of tortured soldierly spirits. Air-conditioned buses provide audiotape tours around the battlefield, while a small army of licensed guides offer the same service live and privately. Beyond the standard fare, a variety of historical organizations sponsor specialized tours that last several days and sometimes focus on only a few hours of fighting. Wax museums, relics of bygone commercial amusement, continue to attract tourists, as do other catchpenny operations. Of recent origin are costume shops offering uniforms and paraphernalia for reenactors who seek vicarious entry into the past. Most ubiquitous, perhaps, are the souvenir shops, which sell not only traditional ceramic dinner bells, cedar boxes, and teacups, but innovative mementos such as T-shirts featuring creative Gettysburg themes, Civil War ties, boxer shorts, and bric-a-brac related to the movie *Gettysburg*. Several of the largest tourist shops, including the National Park Service's bookshop, position television monitors above the shopping floor and play *Gettysburg* in endless loops in spite of the film's sentimental dramatization of history.

But Gettysburg is not only consumed. It is also a consuming place, engulfing aficionados in a number of ways. Like holy men, some zealots drawn into Gettysburg's vortex renounce life elsewhere and attempt to survive off of the tourist industry. The more realistic may satisfy themselves with Gettysburg-related activities and frequent visits. Thousands of Gettysburg enthusiasts nationwide belong to organizations dedicated to studying the battle, perpetuating its memory, preserving battlefield land, and restoring the site to its 1863 appearance. These organizations offer not only fellowship for the like-minded through E-mail and periodic meetings, but public education seminars about the battle, preservation and restoration advocacy, and group works projects on the battlefield. Reenactors find Gettysburg the most desirable battle to re-create, staging annual dramatized and sanitized versions of the original carnage. Over ten thousand participated in 1998. Historical writing about the Gettysburg campaign has absorbed the attention of many talented individuals, both academic and nonacademic, who delve into increasingly minute aspects of the battle. Thus Gettysburg boasts the largest corpus of literature of all Civil War campaigns, while other potentially enlightening topics about the Civil War remain unexamined. One might also argue that highly organized Gettysburg preservation, rehabilitation, and construction efforts divert resources and attention from other significant but less-publicized historical sites.

One of the many ironies of Gettysburg is that while it is one of America's most popular sites of memory, the memory of the site itself has been largely ignored. Few articles and no books in the twentieth century have been dedicated to Gettysburg's development as an American shrine. The articles and book chapters have merits, but tend to read the past backward. They applaud nineteenth-century efforts to create the park as "preservationist" and drive an artificial wedge between "commercial exploiters" and self-effacing "memorializers." Like a morality play, this rearview reading of history has plucked certain groups and individuals from the stream of Gettysburg's development and sorted them out as "good" or "bad" according to contemporary standards. In addition, the literature ignores tourism altogether other than to condemn it as the shrine's bugbear. But shrines require pilgrims, and pilgrims in modern societies are consumers of images and services. Gettysburg has been part of a cultural marketplace ever since the shooting stopped, and its memory has spread with the growth of consumer culture. In other words, the cultural context in which Gettysburg earned its niche as a national icon and sustains that status has been neglected. Seen from a larger cultural perspective, Gettysburg takes on new significance— not just as a site of a pivotal Civil War battle, but as a shrine shaped by an evolving consumer culture. Its story sheds light on the nature of modern pilgrimage, including trends in leisure activities, commemoration, public behavior, mass culture, and merchandizing of the past.[1]

Unfortunately, the memory gap in the shrine's multisided history has worked ill for charting its future. In the absence of historical knowledge, myths became either a shield or a bludgeon in fights over custodianship of contemporary Gettysburg. This book resurrects a forgotten past that can inform ongoing controversy. Much of the contribution made here results from a departure in the use of source material. The backbone of evidence has been built not from documents generated by official custodians, but from serials that reveal Gettysburg as a process of interaction between producers and consumers.

Important questions about Gettysburg are addressed in this book. How, for example, was such a horrific field of slaughter transformed into a major site of commercial leisure? Why is such a renowned tourist trap so fiercely defended against commercialization? Why is Gettysburg more like Gatlinburg or Niagara Falls than other Civil War battlefields? Why does Gettysburg have more monuments than any other battlefield on the planet? Why has Gettysburg become such a great cultural icon—indeed, an American cliché invoked in popular mediums such as television comedies, crossword puzzles, and quiz shows? These and other questions find answers through the book's central idea that Gettysburg is much more culturally significant than simply a Civil War battlefield, and only recently has it been narrowly defined as such.

In addition to coming to terms with fundamental questions, the following chapters also challenge key assumptions about Gettysburg. First, Gettysburg did not emerge as a shrine simply by popular will. Entrepreneurs, promoters, and boosters have labored to attract pilgrims since the battle ended. Second, Gettysburg never was at odds with the marketplace, which instead played a major role in constructing and reconstructing the shrine. A third assumption confronted here is that African Americans have ignored Gettysburg because they were not considered part of the battle's significance nor included in commemorative celebrations. As will be seen, African Americans used Gettysburg extensively for communal celebration near the turn of the twentieth century. Fourth, the present perspective that certain enterprises associated with the battlefield transcended the marketplace (avenues and monuments) while others desacralized (observation towers, the electric trolley) is reconsidered. Finally, the teleological view of Gettysburg's development—that the present era of visual purification represents the culmination of progress in preservation—will be challenged. I argue, rather, that the present era is simply the latest in a series of transformations driven by cultural, economic, and social change, and that, furthermore, simulacra aid co-optation of the sacred by heritage tourism.

Too often battlefield preservationists observe an uncomplicated dichotomy between the shrine and profanation by the marketplace. Gettysburg enthusiasts—some of whom, paradoxically, earn a livelihood from Gettysburg's popularity—view commercial threats to Gettysburg as the Beast of the Apocalypse. In 1998, enthusiasts were "aghast," according to USA Today, over a partnership between the National Park Service and a private enterprise to construct a new visitors' center. "They see visions of Disney World marring the battlefield landscape," the article concluded. The Boston Globe early in 1999 quoted a Washington consultant as stating "the crown jewel of American battlefield parks is going to get honky-tonked up" over the project. History, however, reveals a more complex process: Gettysburg has long been an emporium and, more recently, a themed mall of cultural goods. Indeed, Gettysburg is hardly Disney World's antithesis, and in fact is much more akin to Orlando's shrine of global Americanization than enthusiasts would care to admit.[2]

Yet the preservationist response is understandable. After all, contemporary life is so permeated by commercial interests that people yearn for sacred space that they believe lies beyond commercialism's profaning influence. Gettysburg provides an opportunity to pin faith in the sacred to a tangible place, whose borders the faithful assume they are defending against the barbarians of commercialization. Yet we only have to reflect on how Gettysburg has been experienced to begin to see the situation differently. The making of Gettysburg transpired as the nation underwent dramatic change in an industrializing America. Within little over three decades after the battle, the United States became the world's greatest industrial power and soon turned the corner from producer to a consumer nation. A new commercial culture penetrated the heart of American life, combining merchandising with intangibles such as holidays, religion, and national purpose. The unfolding of this commercial culture paradoxically created sacred space to escape it. Like Christmas or civic celebrations, it was precisely Gettysburg's perceived transcendence of the marketplace that both enhanced and masked its position as a commodity. In other words, the making of Gettysburg into an icon did not simply happen because a great Civil War battle had been fought there. Rather, a commercial web often entwined with ritualistic activity packaged it for a consuming public and continually repackaged it for new generations. Its chief producers in the marketplace have been not only entrepreneurs, but those organizations dedicated to perpetuating the battle's memory, including federal, state, and local government, Civil War veterans, reenactors, and preservation groups. To achieve its central position in American culture, Gettysburg had to be brought within the cultural hub of American life, the marketplace.[3]

Reflection on Gettysburg's power in contemporary culture suggests this mix of the sacred and secular. If *sacred* refers to the transcendent beyond time, and *secular* means its opposite, the quotidian including commerce, then these two apparent opposites knit into a helix. As my own family's initial experience at Gettysburg suggests, a glance at the way people experience Gettysburg shows how the secular and sacred blend: the reenactor who dresses in an eight-hundred-dollar costume; the enthusiastic viewer of the movie *Gettysburg* who places flowers on the 20th Maine regiment monument; the double-decker bus tour over "sacred ground" that plays canned narration and the Gettysburg Address; a stroll through the cemetery followed by a "ghost tour"; guides and shop owners who decry profanation by the market yet depend on it for a living; and battlefield preservation promoted by the same organization that sells Gettysburg T-shirts, caps, and mugs and conducts lotteries to "save Gettysburg." This book intends to show that blending these opposites, the sacred and the secular, animates Gettysburg's popularity.

Even more convoluted is the way both the sacred and the secular have shifted over time. While the packaging of Gettysburg has evolved with changing technologies and social change, so has the sense of the sacred. Viewed from today's perspective, for example, what makes Gettysburg different from a tourist attraction like Niagara Falls is that it marks a special slice of historical time worth recalling in the present. Yet during its early stages of development as a tourist site, Gettysburg shared with Niagara Falls the timeless, "sublime" qualities that defined American shrines in the nineteenth century. Obversely, the Gettysburg cyclorama displayed by the National Park Service today as a sacred inheritance originated as entrepreneurial-driven, urban mass entertainment in the late-nineteenth century. Monuments, trees, and carriage avenues intended to evoke contemplation about sacrifice and national purpose for nineteenth-century genteel culture intrude on sacred sensibilities in the twenty-first century's desire for authenticity. Similarly, the Gettysburg National Military Park (GNMP) visitors' center, designed as a memorial to human freedom during the Cold War, today violates the equation of the sacred with visual purity. Former abstractions about the sacred have transmogrified into the re-creation, Disney-like, of the battlefield as it appeared in 1863. To the cultural elites who built the memorial park, the pure, unsullied view of the past we demand today would have been an ineffective and inappropriate vehicle of remembrance. The meaning of the event, then, has changed along with aesthetics. What would have been relegated to the market fair a century ago is today inside the pilgrim cathedral.

Examining this shift opens a window on leisure activities of Americans. The sense of the sacred at Gettysburg initially had been fixed by the aesthetics of genteel tourism. Understandably, postbattle developers shaped Gettysburg for the mid-nineteenth-century group possessing the means and time to travel. By late in the century, however, working-class people began taking vacations—even "day trips"—as incomes increased, work hours decreased, and transportation improved. Facilities then were added at Gettysburg to meet the more spontaneous behavior of working-class visitors. By the mid-twentieth century, with the arrival of a homogenous public traveling by auto, the place of play for the genteel became the sacred ground. Play moved outside the park on garish strips of commercial attractions, motels, diners, and souvenir shops. In the most recent era of heritage tourism, play has moved into the sacred space with reenactor encampments and the drive to restore the battlefield to an appearance of 1863. Tourists who once conquered space now conquer time, too, and yesterday's play is today's commemoration. Reenactors wage sanitized versions of Gettysburg's combat at nearby stage sets, where onlookers pay admission to watch history "being made."

To demonstrate the shifting sands of sacred and secular, memory and market, this book is divided into four parts of two chapters each. The arrangement is chronological, with each part defined by the way my research unveiled discrete developmental phases. The dates bracketing each part of the book provide orientation but are in some cases approximate and not exact fissure points. (For example, while I used 1920 to mark the end of the railroad era and the beginning of the automobile era, automobile tourists had been arriving at Gettysburg since after the turn of the century but had displaced horses by 1920.) Phases might be primarily driven by social change or technologies or both. "Phase One: 1863–1884," which catered to the genteel market, gave way to "Phase Two: 1884–1920," with the confluence of increased commercial leisure and revived interest in the Civil War. "Phase Three: 1920–1970" developed with the triumph of the automobile and mass culture, but the final "Phase Four: 1970–2000" took shape as mass markets segmented along with deflation of national pride in the post-Vietnam era. As these four phases rest on cultural production and consumption, the first chapter of each part is devoted to manufacture and marketing of the shrine during that period, while its companion chapter explores why consumers purchased the product and how they experienced it. Because images and their increasingly sophisticated delivery have so powerfully defined, furnished value, and shaped expectations for the shrine, each phase integrates a discussion of Gettysburg-related representations circulating at the time. Hopefully the structure achieves its intent of moving away from elitist perspectives of Gettysburg, instead exploring the way Gettysburg has been manufactured and experienced.

This book attempts not to judge the variety of ways Gettysburg has been sold and consumed. But I do intend to suggest that the shrine has a much subtler and more intricate relationship with the marketplace than an adversarial one. In the process I reassess the presumption that Gettysburg's sacrality is immutable and unchanging. If this book simply informs current enthusiasts that they too cannot escape the marketplace any more than their predecessors, it will have served its purpose. As with all shrines, Gettysburg and the history of its development, revealed in the following pages, tell us more about the American people than about the battle Gettysburg memorializes.

PHASE ONE

☆ ☆ ☆ ☆ ☆ ☆ ☆ ☆ ☆ ☆ ☆

1863-1884

A Genteel Summer Resort

The interest in it will continue to increase, and in the lapse of years, when distance not only lends enchantment to the view, but its great historic event will be mellowed by the dim, uncertain light of the past, it will be visited by thousands. Some will come out of veneration for the dead who lie buried on its fields and upon its hills; others to view the spot where the Great Rebellion culminated, and dashed itself upon a rock; while others again will come from idle curiosity, to cut walking sticks on the battlefield, and try to find mouldering bullets to carry away as mementoes of the three days of July.

COLONEL W.W.H. DAVIS, *Gettysburg Star and Sentinel*,
August 13, 1869

Chapter One

☆　☆　☆　☆　☆　☆　☆　☆　☆　☆　☆

A Grand and Holy Work

BATTLE-FIELD VIEWS

A full set of our Photographic Views of the Battle-field of
Gettysburg, form a splendid gift for the Holidays. The finest
yet published can be seen at the Excelsior Gallery.

TYSON BROTHERS, Gettysburg

JUST FIVE MONTHS after the titanic battle and shortly before Christmas, Charles J. and Isaac Tyson placed the above advertisement in a Gettysburg newspaper. Their enterprise was one among many that had descended on the battlefield that summer to photograph, draw, write, and engrave; the photographers no doubt imagined Christmas might stimulate demand for their images. There was nothing new about commercializing the Christian holy day, but the Tysons' daring lay in conflating Christmas with what would become a national shrine and linking both with commerce. The ad prophesied a complex commingling of the sacred and secular at Gettysburg.[1]

The great battle that claimed fifty-one thousand casualties ended July 3, leaving charred pastures, foul odors, polluted wells, and broken soldiers who overwhelmed the town of twenty-five hundred. A Union combat veteran, haunted a month later by the "indescribable terrors" of the battle, termed the fighting "awful beyond description" and told his wife, "I think you would not care to read the details of the fight as it was." Yet despite the frightful carnage, Northern states breathed a sigh of relief as the Confederate invaders withdrew southward and the danger to Northern cities ebbed. Many Northerners grown war-weary with repeated Union failures now took heart at the news of an invigorated Army of the Potomac's determined stand. In a religious nation, Gettysburg lent sacred purpose to the war's slaughter. Newspapers described the battle within the providential sweep of history, labeling it an American Waterloo, Thermopylae, or Armageddon.[2]

Gettysburg's divine purpose infused the meadows, woods, and rocky ridges where fighting occurred. Just three weeks after the battle, on July 24, 1863, the *New York Herald* predicted that Gettysburg "will, in the future, be one of the nation's altars." The people of a nation claiming divine inspiration but hosting a variety of Christian sects required unifying sacred sites. But beneath Gettysburg's sacred endowment stirred hordes of curiosity seekers who arrived to gape at the destruction. These two different ways of seeing the battlefield presaged endless conflict over how to remember the sacrifice and the difficulty of sorting the sacred from the secular.[3]

From the beginning, commercial interests as well as cultural authorities transformed the horrific event into a memorial that would provide both a contemplative atmosphere and pleasure. Purveyors produced a variety of goods for personal consumption with Gettysburg themes, while artists attempted to interpret the fighting on canvas for public edification and entertainment. Local promoters, reaping the benefit of the battle's cultural capital, attempted to fashion Gettysburg into a summer resort and spa. As early as 1875, Confederate Major John W. Daniels remarked that Gettysburg already had been "projected into a conspicuousness which belongs to no other field" due to "Northern painters, sculptors, essayists, orators, and historians [who] have exhausted the resources of art and language in picturing its actors and scenes."[4]

At the time of the battle a cultural marketplace peddled memory as part of the goods and experiences sold to aspirants of gentility. *Gentility* and *genteel culture* refer to the broad, common culture of the nineteenth century that filtered downward from the apex of society to affect individual behavior as well as public space. Communicated through an aesthetic of refinement involving appropriate objects, manners, and taste, gentility appealed in a shifting society where appearances mattered. Tangible hallmarks of gentility were readily available, thanks to transportation, printing, and other technological products of industrialization. Curious about the world opening around them yet concerned with stability, the middle-class proponents of gentility simultaneously turned outward through travel and images and inward to the sacred space of family life. Yet underneath the dominance of genteel leadership seethed impulsive urban and rural working-class pastimes the genteel never penetrated. Moreover, behind a patina of self-restraint and uplift, the genteel themselves harbored a fascination for the exotic, the grotesque, the racy. Impresarios such as P. T. Barnum and other cultural vendors profited by offering exotic, violent, and sensational attractions and literature under the guise of edification.[5]

Religious and political leaders earlier had fretted over the menace of abundance and purchased pleasure. Ironically, Protestantism served as a lever prying middle-class Americans loose from a producer ethic that disparaged luxury and leisure. Protestants' self-scrutiny to in the hopes of attaining salvation and their desire to emotionally touch God produced longings in them for a more abundant life. Perhaps because Victorians by the time of the war often found faith and work wanting, commercial venues more and more satisfied yearnings for regeneration. Reversing the opinion that moral degeneration resulted from nonproductive time and indulgence, religious leaders increasingly viewed appropriate experiences and goods as important ways to restore spiritual life threatened by industrializing society.[6]

Nature provided genteel aspirants one of the most important venues for aesthetic enrichment and edification. Inspired by the commercial art of romantic landscape painters, writers, and poets, the refined individual sought transcendent experience in scenery. By gazing at vistas or strolling among trees, brooks, and meadows, one might encounter the sublime in God's handiwork. Nature thus facilitated a regeneration missing in faith alone. An article in the *Philadelphia Public Ledger*, for example, termed such leisure a "religious duty" that could "purify, refine, and elevate . . . by its calm and rational enjoyment in the service of virtue and religion."[7]

The most accessible public spaces for reflection on nature were rural cemeteries, commercial ventures that often featured tours and guidebooks. Characterized by dramatic landscaping, ponds, and winding promenades, the cemeteries emerged along with other civic reforms of industrialization. On the one hand, they were businesses that aimed to reward shareholders; on the other, they offered people release while teaching them civic values, social unity, and the divine in nature. Cemetery directors encouraged "pilgrimages" to the grounds and welcomed visits from the working class, although directors often despaired over inappropriate visitor behavior and took steps to control conduct. Still, some cemeteries attempted to pamper visitors with refreshment stands and other comforts in an effort to compete with amusements outside the gates.[8]

Establishing rural cemeteries became a vogue project for the reform-minded boosters of small towns as well as cities. In 1854 Gettysburg, for example, a town of fewer than three thousand, dedicated its own Ever Green Cemetery, designed by a Baltimore architect. With seventeen acres featuring avenues, fencing, and exotic species of trees, the cemetery replaced cramped churchyards with the heights above town that featured sweeping views of the Blue Ridge. Within a year Ever Green Cemetery corporation had sold 300 shares of stock as well as 270 lots, and required tickets for Sunday admission. Nearly a decade later these heights, known locally as Cemetery Hill, earned additional significance as a scene of desperate fighting.[9]

Although the proximity of rural cemeteries enabled all classes to benefit from nature, before the war largely the middle and upper classes toured the choicest scenic places. Around 1820, the transportation improvements that promoted industrialization also facilitated leisurely travel. The imprimatur of gentility transformed travel from simply a medium for overcoming space into an aesthetic experience that coaxed industrious Americans away from the workplace. Touring natural wonders became as essential for the genteel as owning uplifting goods such as pianos and books.[10]

In a young country focused on progress but devoid of antiquities, the quest for the sublime in scenery helped establish national identity. American tourists found the equivalent of ancient ruins in the natural splendors of Niagara Falls, the White Mountains, the Hudson River Valley, or the mineral waters of spas. Combining scenery with symbols of the country's progress, such as mines, bridges, colleges, prisons, and asylums, touring in effect transformed natural attractions into shrines.[11]

Yet the sacred associations of nature masked commercial staging. Paradoxically, at the same time the genteel traveled to escape the commercial world, they purchased a commodity promising rejuvenation and an encounter with the sublime. Guidebooks, which appeared in quantity as soon as the transportation revolution began in the 1820s, played a key role in packaging the genteel tour. With industrial efficiency, some offered "skeleton tours" for the time conscious and daily itineraries advising the time increments one might expend at noteworthy places. Significantly, guidebooks created expectations by defining sites, evaluating their popularity, and informing readers of the cultural value of each. A guidebook published in 1828, for example, noted that Mount Vernon was "consecrated ground [where] every American recurs with the most enthusiastic devotion." But the guidebooks that manufactured romantic wonderland also appealed to baser instincts with the titillating or frightening, just as genteel travelers might duck into a sideshow or view a macabre scene at Niagara Falls, the White Mountains, or Mammoth Cave.[12]

Guidebooks were only one part of the travel industry that marketed scenic Americana. Beginning about 1840, a graphic revolution in printing and photography enabled widespread dissemination of prints, stereographs, poetry, and travelogues considered essential for the cultivated. Recognizing the successes of artists such as the Hudson River School painters to popularize travel, railroads by the 1850s hired photographers to shoot scenes along their lines. Photographs of renowned vistas and cemeteries were converted to stereographs, a collection of which nearly every parlor contained as the century progressed. Traveling panoramas of landscapes, some biblical, provided entertainment and uplift.[13]

As representations of the sublime, scenic prints and images took on even greater religious significance when introduced into middle-class parlors. In the middle-class "cult of domesticity," the parlor functioned as the heart of the home, where religious and moral instruction took place. Like nature and the "separate sphere" for women, the parlor occupied a paradoxical position. Ostensibly above the quotidian world of commerce, in reality the parlor was tied to the marketplace. Its furnishings and bric-a-brac, defined and reinforced by popular literature, reflected the family's refinement and moral character. Even the raucous street celebration of Christmas was brought into the parlor and tamed, with a boost from commerce, into a sacred family holiday. Poetry, pianos, books, stereographs, plants, and natural specimens brought the outside world into the parlor and mingled them with treasured family mementos. By connecting the family to the world in miniature, the parlor functioned like the classical "memory palace," which linked imaginary objects with specific spaces. But the meaning cast on parlor goods both shaped and represented the owners' religious values, transforming the parlor, a relatively new social space, into hallowed space.[14]

With its new methods of representation, the market disembodied scenic places and delivered them as vivid images. A combination of stereoscopes, prints, guidebooks, travelogues, newspapers, books, journals, panoramas, observatories, and railroads offered glimpses of the divine while connecting Americans to their country. In turn, through the dissemination of images in the cultural marketplace, the market not only created anticipations about places, but determined their cultural salience. This transformation of landscapes into commodities with sacred associations would prove more than adequate for packaging a great American battlefield.[15]

Gettysburg and the Genteel Impresarios

Two years after the battle, a reporter wandering across the scene of conflict wrote, "It is difficult to say anything new on a theme already hackneyed." By 1865, Gettysburg already had achieved preeminence among many sanguinary struggles to save the Union. In the weeks after the battle, its appeal swelled, with newspaper columns describing Gettysburg in the verbal brush strokes of a romantic panorama. A joint project of Northern states carved a Soldiers' National Cemetery out of a pivotal site on the battlefield to honor the republic's fallen heroes. The superintendent of burials asserted that no Confederate remains polluted the sacred soil of this Valhalla. Dedicated less than five months after the battle, the cemetery received appropriate sanctification from President Abraham Lincoln and Edward Everett.[16]

That fall, a seemingly different form of memorializing also appeared. A variety of Gettysburg-related goods, including booklets, maps, sheet music, photographs, and stereographs, entered the cultural marketplace. Some of these commemorative items represented the fruits of those photographers, artists, correspondents, and relief workers who had arrived in Gettysburg after the battle. Gettysburg relics went on display at Philadelphia's Christian Commission offices, the Historical Society of Pennsylvania, and the Massachusetts Historical Society. Presaging Gettysburg's materialization later in the century at the era's great exhibitions, Baltimore's Sanitary Fair and Philadelphia's Great Central Fair displayed and sold battle debris as well as natural specimens from the battlefield the following spring. Margaretta G. Meade, chairwoman of the Arms and Trophies Committee for the Great Central Fair, wrote that Gettysburg curiosities, "coming from a place which will always be memorable in the history of our country, will be an object of great interest."[17]

It is tempting to view these ostensibly different approaches to commemorating the Union victory at Gettysburg as the origin of a pattern that has continued ever since—one transcendent and the other trivializing. Yet on closer inspection, the polarity disappears and the distinctions blur. Gettysburg-related products offered in the marketplace—music, print, and images—were edifying goods designed to instruct and improve. Linked to a providential event, these items brought sacred associations into parlor space and enhanced the inviolability of both. On the other hand, the cemetery, for all its solemnity, hardly transcended the market. After all, by combining edification and entertainment, cemeteries counted among the most popular tourist attractions. The site possessed sacred meaning for its panoramic views as well as its use as a mausoleum for fallen warriors. In his explanation of the cemetery's design, landscape architect William Saunders hoped to "realize a pleasing landscape and pleasure ground effect" for contemplative strolls. Saunders not only prescribed serpentine avenues and arboreal variety, but small, uniform gravestones instead of ornamentation that might overpower nature. With appreciation of the vistas available on Cemetery Hill, he hoped to achieve an awe-inspiring effect analogous to the sublime sought by tourists at the mountains or ocean.[18]

But the battlefield eclipsed the cemetery as a tourist attraction from the time the fighting stopped. Even as Gettysburg reeled from the battle's frightful aftermath, local attorney David McConaughy moved to transform the battlefield into a landscape appropriate for genteel touring. McConaughy has been viewed as a provincial but unambiguous preservationist who struggled at the local level to save a national treasure. In fact, McConaughy's role is more complex and nuanced. Along with John Badger Bachelder, discussed below, no individual worked harder to package Gettysburg for the genteel touring market than McConaughy did.

Born in Gettysburg and a graduate of the local Pennsylvania College, McConaughy represented the era's quintessential town booster. The Republican attorney brought the YMCA to Gettysburg, helped found the Gettysburg Railroad Company, and at the time of the battle served as director of the Ever Green Cemetery Association. When the war began producing corpses of local youth for burial, McConaughy displayed his enterprising spirit. To refine an even more attractive garden for reflective leisure, McConaughy proposed erecting "a handsome and imposing shaft of marble" around which would be placed Adams County's "martyred dead." McConaughy's scheme failed to mature, but a year later the cemetery director improved on it after the unanticipated windfall of carnage.[19]

While Pennsylvania Governor Andrew Curtin appointed David Wills, another Gettysburg attorney, to deal with the thousands of Union dead, McConaughy initiated his own plans to benefit Ever Green Cemetery. Perhaps for reasons explained by the competitive social and business environment of town life, the two Republican lawyers disliked each other. While Wills shopped for land, McConaughy offered the governor "the most liberal

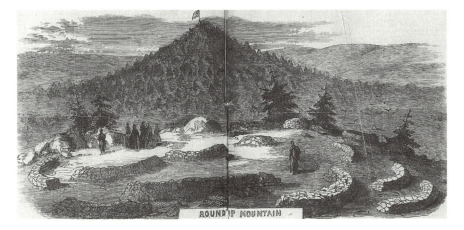

FIGURE 1. Tourists on Little Round Top, 1863 (*Frank Leslie's Illustrated Newspaper*, December 5, 1863)

arrangements" for Union burials on land adjacent to his cemetery. McConaughy, in an added bit of hustling, informed the governor that he had purchased "the most interesting portions of this illustrious Battlefield," including Round Top, with its "wonderful stone defenses," and Culp's Hill, "embracing the extensive timber breast works, & the equally wonderful exhibition of the withering effects of our musketry fire." Nor was that all. The cemetery association, he told Curtin, had agreed to erect on the grounds "a noble National Monument in memory of the battles and the dead." While offering the governor an attractive solution to the burial crisis, McConaughy outlined plans for a complete genteel pleasure ground: heroic landscape, panoramic views, and his cemetery enterprise thrown in as the central attraction.[20]

Wills, however, secured a resolution from other states' burial agents that the soldiers' cemetery should be independent of Ever Green. Not to be outflanked, McConaughy agreed to sell land next to the Ever Green for the soldiers' cemetery, but stipulated that "to enhance the interest of our grounds with the glorious memories of these Battles, and the ashes of the heroic dead," no wall should separate the burial grounds. After Wills threatened to move the cemetery elsewhere, the imbroglio ended when a number of "patriotic citizens," including prominent members of Ever Green's board of directors, persuaded the governor that the commanding site next to Ever Green could be purchased with no restrictions.[21]

McConaughy, with only part of his plan shattered, was not yet through. Although an acquaintance wrote that "McConaughy has been in a bad way ever since Wills outgeneraled him in the Cemetery matter," McConaughy tried another approach, this one beyond Wills's grasp. Days after the cemetery board reached an agreement with the governor, McConaughy announced his plan for the battlefield in the *Adams Sentinel*. Repeating his earlier overture to the governor, McConaughy called for incorporation of the battlefield and the creation of statewide committees to drum up support. Shares of the Gettysburg Battlefield Memorial Association (GBMA) would be limited to ten dollars, and McConaughy explained he would seek an incorporating act from the state legislature similar to that of a cemetery association. Not surprisingly, a group of influential citizens endorsed the plan. Already, less than six weeks after the battle, the burghers of Gettysburg viewed the battlefield as a rural cemetery writ large—as they termed it, a "standing memorial" with civic and didactic purpose.[22]

Well aware of the media's value to his cause, McConaughy employed the press to enhance the fledgling project's stature. Immediately he cultivated connections with Philadelphians, both to boost the GBMA and to avoid the stigma of an exclusively local project. Perhaps because of the organization's prestige, McConaughy established strong relations with the Historical Society of Pennsylvania, whose president, Joseph R. Ingersoll, he importuned to serve as chairman of the GBMA. Son of Jared Ingersoll, Federalist candidate for vice president in 1812, Ingersoll had served as minister to England during the Pierce administration. McConaughy surely understood the pragmatic value of attaching famous names to his project. He wrote in 1864 that he wanted to enlist on the board of directors key Union heroes of Gettysburg, Major Generals George G. Meade and Winfield Scott Hancock, to "give us some influence." Appreciating the ability of romantic writers and painters to transform rustic landscape into coveted scenery, McConaughy urged Henry Wadsworth Longfellow and John Greenleaf Whittier to consider applying the pen to Gettysburg. In his letters to the popular American poets, McConaughy romantically described Gettysburg's landscape and concluded, "I cannot repress the thought that the poet would find here much material awaiting the baptism of his genius to render it immortal in verse."[23]

As McConaughy promised, his incorporating act resembled that of a rural cemetery when signed into law in 1864. It provided the GBMA with complete control over the battlefield, empowering the new corporation to issue shares, create a board of directors, and erect "*works of art and taste*" (italics added). A supplement passed by the legislature two years later allowed the GBMA to establish avenues, plant trees, and regulate visitor behavior. Most notably, in deference to the genteel touring market, the seventy acres McConaughy purchased by 1864 focused only on the most dramatic battlefield landscapes and ignored less-scenic locations where significant fighting occurred.[24]

In his role as rural cemetery director and Gettysburg booster, McConaughy realized that ornamental memorials both sacralized landscape and drew visitors. Not only did he express the need for "works of art and taste," but he later proposed a large monument for Cemetery Hill, "which shall attract the eye of the traveler and visitor to this Citadel of Liberty." He also considered the possibility of enclosing the GBMA land with an iron fence. McConaughy revealed his vision for an adorned battlefield at an 1866 meeting of teachers in Gettysburg, where he tried to sell GBMA certificates. There he summarized the GBMA objectives to purchase "all the points of greatest interest around Gettysburg; to open a broad avenue along the main lines of battle; to erect an observatory on Round Top; and also to erect everywhere low monuments and enduring structures," thus making Gettysburg "the Mecca of the American patriot."[25]

After the war, a combination of circumstances—a desire to forget the conflict, competing postwar charitable causes, and depression in the 1870s—accounted for apathy toward McConaughy's plans. Nevertheless, he kept fighting. From a state senate seat won in 1866, McConaughy lobbied for the GBMA and other Gettysburg projects. In 1866 and 1868 he wheedled three thousand dollars for the GBMA out of the state legislature after reciting the association's intent to erect "shrines of loyalty, patriotism and liberty, whither, in all times, will come the sons of America, and the pilgrims of all lands." Other legislators suspected his rhetoric about "sacred ground" masked financial motives. For example, when in 1866 springs purported to contain miraculous healing properties were "discovered" on the battlefield, McConaughy introduced a bill in 1866 to incorporate the Gettysburg Lithia Springs Association, with himself as an incorporator. The corporation managed a bottling works and planned to construct a hotel connected with the springs. When Senator McConaughy argued for a monument to Pennsylvania Major General John F. Reynolds and a home for disabled veterans near the springs, an opponent charged that McConaughy "has been working all winter to fix up a new battle of Gettysburg," as "he wants a monument, a hotel, and now a soldier's home."[26]

Although parsimonious Northern state legislatures failed to finance Gettysburg monuments through the 1870s, even when prodded by a GBMA lobbyist, the GBMA did improve the landscape for tourists. With McConaughy in charge through the decade, the GBMA rebuilt Union defense works, placed wooden placards at important points, and positioned several dozen condemned cannon in time for the 1876 United States centennial. Thus a tamed and bucolic version of the 1863 battlefield landscape served as an inexpensive solution to the absence of monuments. The GBMA also appealed to Southern visitors by resolving in 1872 "to exclude partisan and sectional spirit from the indications," an example of the market's ability to soften sectional enmity.[27]

Perhaps tiring of the lack of support for his grand memorial plan, McConaughy lost the spark that fueled his fervor for the GBMA. In the late 1870s, the Pennsylvania department of the Grand Army of the Republic (GAR), a veterans' organization, purchased a majority of stock shares in the GBMA. By 1880, the GAR had erased GBMA debts and dominated the election of officers to the board. Thus displaced, McConaughy departed

FIGURE 2. "A Genteel Pleasure Ground": Soldiers' National Cemetery in background, East Cemetery Hill in foreground, showing GBMA improvements for visitors, including restored lunettes and cannon barrels (Tipton Photograph, ca. 1878, Sample Book 1:18, no. 736, Adams County Historical Society, Gettysburg, Pennsylvania)

the organization he had founded and directed for sixteen years. The *Gettysburg Compiler* rejoiced that "new life in the management" would "make the Battle-field one of the grandest parks in the country." That, of course, had been McConaughy's goal all along.[28]

By 1900, driven by an invigorated regard for the war's memory, the GBMA had realized McConaughy's initial vision of monuments and carriage avenues. McConaughy himself had acquired 120 acres of battlefield land, initiated improvements designed to please genteel Northern and Southern tourists, and established a flexible organization dedicated to memorializing the battlefield. At the same time he looked backward to the rural cemetery model, he anticipated, with his appreciation of publicity and images, newer forms of promotion and display. Paradoxically, as he profaned the sacred by bringing it into a commercial enterprise, he also turned the battlefield into a special and sacred place. In doing so he not only helped open Gettysburg to the services required by modern pilgrims, but he initiated the battlefield's transformation from the hell experienced by participants into a landscape of edifying views infused with the heroic.

Complementing McConaughy's effort, a photographer and illustrator

named John Badger Bachelder also fashioned Gettysburg for genteel consumers. Titled "colonel" by Pennsylvania's governor for once serving as
principal of a military school, Bachelder earned his living as an artist, print-
maker, photographer, and man on the make. Arriving in town just three
days after the battle, Bachelder believed Gettysburg represented the climactic struggle he had been anticipating since attaching himself to the Army of
the Potomac the previous year. Unlike other photographers and bohemians
who recorded Gettysburg and then departed, Bachelder spent the remaining three decades of his life promoting Gettysburg as the focal point of his
trade in images. In the process, he shaped public perceptions of Gettysburg
as both a shrine and a tourist site. And in the end, he assumed McConaughy's role as manipulator of the battlefield landscape itself.[29]

Initially Bachelder sketched scenes of town and prominent landmarks
such as John Burns's residence, Devil's Den, Round Top, and General
George Meade's headquarters. To some of these sketches he added watercolor as well as his conception of what combat on the spot might have
looked like, especially during the Confederate assault on the third day. But
at some point early in his sojourn, Bachelder decided to create an "isometrical" map of the Gettysburg—a panoramic scene of the entire battlefield
illustrating, as he explained, "everything that could effect the tide of battle
or be of interest to the public." Like P. T. Barnum, Bachelder valued newspapers and other forms of print to stir public interest. Even before the
print's 1864 publication, Bachelder had distributed free copies to army officers hoping to use their favorable comments in advertising blurbs. To give
the map additional legitimacy, Bachelder offered veterans disabled in the
battle preference as sales agents.[30]

The map sold thousands of copies. Bachelder's design, depicting Union
and Confederate troop positions set against imaginary three-dimensional
scenery, gave it aesthetic value. Like the popularity of mountaintop views
or panoramas, it addressed the quest to literally broaden one's horizons. In
the accompanying descriptive key, Bachelder invited viewers to "[I]magine
yourself in a balloon, two miles east of the town." Bachelder later wrote
that the map "is well adapted to framing and forms a suitable ornament for
the Library—Hall—dining or sitting room." In effect, the map transformed
the monstrous conflict into an edifying image appropriate for the parlor.[31]

With its portrayal of troop positions shorn of sectional rancor, Bachel-
er's map became a popular souvenir for veterans both North and South. For
some, it jarred loose memories branded on the mind by the battle's pandemonium. "Your 'Isometrical map' hangs in my office here within reach of
my hand," wrote a former lieutenant to Bachelder. "The battle is a huge
nightmare to me . . . a terrible panorama of tremendous events piled up in
that 36 hours." Just as the GBMA took steps to create a landscape devoid
of lingering war passion, the map demonstrated how the marketplace could
soothe sectional bitterness. A former Confederate wounded at Gettysburg

asked Bachelder in 1867 for his "true map" and added, "I know of fifteen or twenty persons who will send for maps also when they see mine." Another from Mississippi ordered a map and inquired about a job as an agent to sell them. How many former Confederates purchased Bachelder maps is of course unknown, but evidence suggests that Robert E. Lee owned a copy. Aside from the maps potential to accelerate national healing, widespread dissemination stimulated interest in Gettysburg.[32]

The map's success encouraged Bachelder to pursue additional Gettysburg enterprises. At the end of the war he planned a grand illustrated history of the battle, no doubt prompted in part by the notebooks of information he collected for the map. Beginning in 1865, Bachelder regularly invited officers to meet him at Gettysburg and relate the disposition of their troops during the battle. He later boasted that over a thousand officers accepted his invitations. Those who could not attend responded with written accounts. Every one of these meetings called attention to the battlefield and underscored its importance. Although driven by Bachelder's business interests, such events along with his traveling lectures about the battle helped earn Bachelder and Gettysburg a reputation for impartiality.[33]

Bachelder's other Gettysburg projects reflected an ambitious scope. His envisioned *Illustrated History of the Battle of Gettysburg* never came to fruition because of his stereographic business and other concerns. One parlor piece that did emerge from the effort, however, was James Walker's 1870 painting *Repulse of Longstreet's Assault*, which Bachelder used to illustrate his Gettysburg lectures and later transformed into a parlor engraving. Depicting the moment of the nation's salvation, the panorama of smoking fields roiling with shadowy figures blazed with ethereal light in its center. Bachelder also tailored Gettysburg for the genteel market through guidebooks such as *Gettysburg: What to See and How to See It* (1873) that infused nature with hoary associations: "The traveler now studies the towering eminences, the rocky ravines, the woody coverts, the open fields, the meandering waters, and all the vast region over which destruction and death held carnival for three long days, with an intensity of interest which the simple charms of nature never would have aroused." Rather than views of the battlefield, woodcuts of romantic scenery from Longfellow's *Poems* embellished a text that viewed Gettysburg as a special place where North and South could celebrate common valor.[34]

After he had sculpted an image suitable for the genteel, Bachelder moved on to accomplishing McConaughy's dream by shaping the battlefield itself. About the same time David McConaughy left the GBMA, in the 1880s, Bachelder attained a position on the board of directors. As Northern states moved to erect memorials on the field, Bachelder's knowledge of the battle proved highly useful. Appointed Superintendent of Tablets and Legends in 1883, Bachelder ensured each monument contributed to a complete historical narrative for visitors. Policies he suggested for inscribing and positioning

FIGURE 3. Romantic landscape from John B. Bachelder's guidebook *Gettysburg: What to See and How to See It*, 1873

monuments—such as placing monuments at the point where attacks were launched— significantly influenced the way visitors experienced the battlefield. It was Bachelder who envisioned and designed the High Water Mark monument, the holy of holies at the shrine, and insisted that the adjacent copse of trees be protected by an iron fence. Yet at the same time he established this crowning monument to Union victory, Bachelder furthered the appeasement he demonstrated in his other Gettysburg ventures by urging the opening and marking of Confederate lines. In supervising monumentation, Bachelder in effect managed the battlefield's memories.[35]

Bachelder's packaging of Gettysburg as a sublime place suitable for the parlor or escape from the quotidian gave the battlefield value in the cultural marketplace. In the process, he transformed horror into pleasure and, like McConaughy, eased sectional reconciliation. Appropriately, the citizens of Gettysburg feted Bachelder in 1886, presenting him a small cannon fashioned from shot and shell—a suitable gift for one whose combined enterprises enriched the town's economy.[36]

New Industry, Sacred Springs

Although tourism to the battlefield grew steadily in the late-nineteenth century, tourists were no strangers to Gettysburg even in the antebellum years. Often falsely characterized as "a sleepy little village," Gettysburg, with its almost twenty-five hundred citizens, ranked in the upper one-quarter of the country's population centers. The county seat's public institutions and amenities had attracted genteel travelers before the battle. In addition to a railroad facilitating the flow of goods and people, Gettysburg boasted gas lighting with street lamps, a public water service, a bank, three newspapers, a college, a theological seminary, a women's academy, a rural cemetery, an almshouse, a county prison and courthouse, and several hotels.[37]

Still, the town was hardly prepared for the deluge of July 1863. In addition to twenty thousand wounded soldiers and eight thousand dead rotting in the heat, thousands of curiosity seekers and soldiers' relatives clogged the town immediately after the battle. Yet for some enterprising citizens, the throngs meant business opportunity. Reports circulated in the press and army that locals tried to profit from the national crisis by exploiting both armies. Charges flew that greedy citizens sold whiskey, water, and bread to Union troops at exorbitant prices. Charles Francis Adams, Jr., of the First Massachusetts Cavalry complained that southern Pennsylvanians "make money out of their defenders by selling soldiers bread at twenty-five cents a loaf and milk at fifteen cents a canteen." Most damaging were charges that Gettysburg farmers forced the wounded to pay for transportation and sustenance.[38]

The accusations haunted Gettysburg periodically in the following decades as the town transformed the temporary economic opportunity into a permanent bonanza. At the twenty-fifth anniversary of the battle in 1888, for example, the New York Times commented that "[n]owhere else in the wide world is the art of squeezing so thoroughly understood and so harshly practiced as at Gettysburg," reminding readers that townspeople had charged soldiers a nickel a glass for water during the battle. But the same newspaper noted less vindictively in 1865, "The battle is proving a great source of benefit to Gettysburg," predicting "it will become one of the most popular places of resort, that is, if the means of getting there are improved." On the one hand, circumstances forced responsibility on the town to serve as steward of a national memory. On the other, townspeople could control their own destiny by shaping the site for the market, as McConaughy demonstrated. In many ways, Gettysburg's stigma reflected the age-old fissure between the medieval shrine and fair, God's time and the merchant's time. Led by a progressive press and enterprising boosters, the Gettysburg community both helped transform Gettysburg into a pleasure spot and supplied services and experiences expected by modern pilgrims. Some even dreamed of transforming Gettysburg into a resort where one might find spiritual and physical rejuvenation.[39]

Townspeople knew their town had made history, and that history as displayed on an epical landscape could be packaged and sold. An open letter "to the people of Adams County" by the *Adams Sentinel*'s editor in 1865 saw the battle, "one of the chief events in recorded history," as an opportunity that "the providence of God has put within the power of the people of this county." But God helps those who help themselves. Applauding the GBMA's efforts to preserve evidence of destruction, he advised fellow citizens to add monuments, markers, and better railroad connections, because "[w]e should have ten times the travel stopping here to visit the battlefield."[40]

Town boosters responded to Gettysburg's popularity by organizing to improve visitor services. As early as the cemetery dedication in November, they formed committees for special events both to manage visitor hospitality and to publicize the town. At the Soldiers' National Cemetery dedication just five months after the battle, for example, a committee encouraged citizens "to throw open their houses . . . for compensation" and then booked visitors at the residences. A spirit of mutual ownership often pervaded the town's new industry. Community initiative not only hosted tourists but also improved attractions by helping rebuild lunettes, redoubts, and breastworks, and constructing a Round Top lookout in 1881. Townspeople also hoped to profit from the new industry by purchasing stock in the GBMA or investing in such enterprises as an observatory for tourists on East Cemetery Hill.[41]

The popularity of the panoramic sweep available from landmarks of the Union triumph such as Cemetery Hill, Little Round Top, and Round Top inspired McConaughy's father-in-law, merchant George Arnold, to improve the scenic gaze for tourists. Perhaps with McConaughy's encouragement, in 1878 he financed the fifty-foot wooden observatory with help from local stock subscription and charged twenty-five cents for admission. Three years later another tower embellished the gaze from Big Round Top, constructed by the local GAR post with local support. Both towers brought to fruition an unrealized scheme by the Soldiers' National Cemetery board of managers in 1868 to erect an observatory in the cemetery. In promoting the Big Round Top lookout, the local press laconically summed up the combination of memory, nature, and boosterism that made Gettysburg tourism hum. "Visitors would thus be afforded a commanding view of the entire battle-

FIGURE 4. Observatory erected on East Cemetery Hill in 1878, photographed during a Department of Pennsylvania Grand Army of the Republic encampment, 1885 (5E-5002A, Gettysburg National Military Park)

field, as well as one of the most extensive and charming landscapes in the country. Up with the observatory!"[42]

Townspeople quickly realized the battle's legacy meant more than simply trampled crops and damaged property. The stream of visitors requiring orientation motivated some locals to offer themselves as guides. Later in the century several earned excellent reputations, but in 1869 a *Philadelphia Inquirer* correspondent claimed the guides had "many cock and bull stories to relate." To improve business efficiency, guides linked with the hack rental business and hotels within a few years. Obviously, progress and past went hand in hand. Community-spirited citizens suggested improvements to the town's new industry or bristled when it faced threats. A citizen advised in 1868 that "[w]hen improvement seems to be the order of the day," town street names should be changed to the names of Union generals such as Reynolds, Howard, and Meade. Another complained in 1878 about the removal on Culp's Hill of "old bullet marked trees which had been regarded with such interest by battlefield visitors."[43]

Many townspeople whose property had the misfortune of being defaced by gunfire carefully preserved these stigmata and zestfully pointed them out to visitors. Two years after the battle, a visitor at the Globe Inn who in-quired about the battlefield's whereabouts was informed by the innkeeper that he stood on the battlefield at that very moment. To prove it, the proprietor escorted him outside and pointed to a Confederate shell embed-ded in a brick wall. With some sarcasm, the visitor added, "The battle-field was put into the bill." Townspeople learned that tourists were just as eager to possess detritus of death as to gaze at it. Relics and souvenirs had for centuries possessed a Christian pedigree allowing pilgrims to carry home a coveted, tangible reminder of a sacred journey. A cottage industry quickly emerged in Gettysburg to satisfy tourists' obsession for relics, and by 1865 a newspaper correspondent could report that "relics, of course, are now a staple commodity in the town." Just five months after the battle, during the cemetery dedication, townspeople sold relics from tables set up on the side-walks. A *Philadelphia Inquirer* correspondent wrote in 1869 that relic dealers "hawk their wares around the streets or sell them at stands, where their business is announced in prominent letters." He added that the vendors "attach considerable humbug" to their goods by selling each bullet as "the agency by which some prominent Union or Confederate officer was sent to eternity." One dealer, Joel A. Danner, amassed enough relics to open a museum in the mid-1870s on the town square.[44]

As battle debris grew increasingly scarce, townspeople manufactured sou-venirs for tourists. Although in later decades townspeople crafted sophisti-cated souvenirs such as miniature cannon and monuments, early handmade mementos for the genteel traveler emphasized nature. Women assembled baskets of dried flowers gathered from the battlefield, while enterprising townsmen cut walking canes from battlefield wood, which they packaged in lots and sold as wood from particular battlefield place-names. McConaughy promoted the GBMA by sending battle-scarred tree trunks to historical societies. Local photographer William H. Tipton, who sold photographs and snapped tourist photographs as souvenirs, advertised "The Finest Views of Gettysburg *Scenery*" in the early 1870s rather than the "battlefield views" promoted earlier. Locals thus demonstrated another clever dimension to their transformation of the dreadful event into a desirable commodity.[45]

Some townspeople realized that if they could not add value to the battle's memory, the battle's memory could add value to their enterprise. Locals selling real estate promoted their properties' historic value, usefulness as a hostelry for tourists, or propinquity to the national cemetery. A boarding house advertised accommodations for battlefield visitors as early as 1863. The Cumberland House Hotel near the Soldiers' National Cemetery changed its name to the Battle-field Hotel in 1865, promoting itself as "one of the relics of the Battle of Gettysburg," where one might purchase "Ice Cream and all kinds of refreshment, at all hours, to accommodate promenaders." George Rose, the owner of a farm that had suffered damage July 2, nev-ertheless realized the historical associations of the site outweighed his loss.

In attempting to sell the farm in 1866, he termed the property "the cele-brated Rose Farm"—capitalizing on engravings and stereographs of dead on his property—and emphasized its location "on that part of the Battle-field where the fiercest of the conflict raged, giving it a historic interest which may be of great value to the owner."[46]

The idea of transforming Gettysburg into a summer resort emerged from the 1865 "discovery" of springs west of town whose water purportedly healed wounded Confederates. A professor of physical science at the local Pennsylvania College declared samples he examined "to be like the cele-brated Vichy Springs of France." According to further scientific examina-tion the water contained "lithia," a coveted therapeutic substance "as rare among minerals as gold and silver among metals," according to the Get-tysburg Compiler. A history of the springs published in 1872 cited the first documented instance of healing, when a victim of "rheumatic gout" hob-bled into town on crutches hoping the water might cure his infirmity. A few weeks later the invalid returned a healthy man, "the distortions of limbs and the enlargement of joints had disappeared, and the hitherto in-dispensable crutch had been thrown aside." Word quickly spread of the miraculous water, prompting a rush of visitors in search of thaumaturgy. The Gettysburg Star early in 1866 declared the springs attributable only to "supernatural agency, and for a providential purpose," and that their appear-ance on the decisive battlefield of the war was "a sign of national deliv-erance and regeneration." Soon known as the Katalysine Springs (a euphe-mism for laxative, literally "loosening below" in Greek) or Lithia (mineral) Springs, the springs received widespread attention and praise in publica-tions such as the Druggist's Circular and Chemical Gazette and Medical and Surgical Reporter."

The Gettysburg waters joined a long list of medicinal springs, called "wa-tering places," scattered throughout the country. Water in Christian tradi-tion offered a source of regeneration and healing. In nineteenth-century Europe, revived interest in the salubrious effects of water, combining Chris-tian belief with Roman legacy, spread to the rising middle class. Like the American cult of romantic nature followed the European example, water-ing-place resorts sprang up in the United States to indulge genteel travelers seeking self-renewal from industrializing society. Spas such as Saratoga Springs, New York, or Poland Springs, Maine, offered an appropriate arena for wealthy socialites. As the century progressed, watering places increas-ingly promoted themselves as resorts rather than asylums for invalids.[48]

Visitors had frequented several watering places in the Gettysburg neigh-borhood long before the Civil War. But with the "discovery" of the Ka-talysine Springs, boosters quickly grasped the potential of hosting a tripar-tite attraction for genteel tourists consisting of a epochal historic site, a romantic landscape, and regenerative waters. One enterprising spirit re-marked that the springs offered "combined attractions" for a hotel site where "the lover of the beautiful in nature" could spend the day sauntering on the battlefield's "holy ground" and return "in time for the evening's amusements." Furthermore, he noted, if Gettysburg produced a medicated lozenge similar to the Vichy Springs' lozenge, it would "crowd its trans-Atlantic rival from the markets of the world, as a memento of the great battle-field on which was fought the decisive battle of the gigantic American civil war."[49]

A cabal of boosters envisioned grand possibilities for the medicinal springs. Its proprietor, Emanuel Harmon, wrote early in 1866 to Edward McPherson, clerk of the U.S. House of Representatives and owner of Gettysburg property, asking for publicity for the springs to "have it go the rounds of the press." Another scheme surfaced in 1866 to construct a veterans' home at the springs, where the gestalt of healing waters and shrine of national salvation might soothe crippled heroes. An acquaintance of McPherson's who pushed the scheme informed him, "I think you own a farm, you told me once, in that vicinity, and if such a scheme as this is properly carried out, it would quadruple the value of every inch of ground in the immediate vicinity." Other plans included buying and enlarging the nearby Theological Seminary buildings for tourists, constructing cottages for invalids, and even developing an entire planned community with a park. The latter's objective was "to transform Gettysburg into one of the most popular summer resorts in the country," the *Gettysburg Compiler* commented.[50]

Despite the dreams of boosters and investors, peddling the water itself initially proved more successful than developing a resort. A New York company leased the springs in 1867, erecting a bottling works that employed thirty hands and shipped out 240 dozen bottles a day. The Gettysburg Spring Company published promotional material affirming the water's power to cure all ailments including rheumatism, kidney stones, constipation, impotence, bronchitis, and the pains of puberty. Big-city newspapers in New York and Philadelphia praised the water's miraculous properties. The *New York Times* in 1868 published the outrageous statement that the water "possesses very wonderful curative properties, if it does not actually possess the power of imparting perpetual youth." Acclaim for the water's properties invariably turned to its famous source of origin. The *New York Herald* stated that "the remarkable cures that this water has made of chronic diseases, the historic associations of the place, and its beautiful scenery, seem to promise that Gettysburg will soon become famous as a great American watering place." Over a year later, the *New York Times* even claimed that Gettysburg, "famous in the national annals as a field of glory . . . promises to rival Saratoga as a watering place."[51]

Thanks to McConaughy, an incorporation act to develop a watering place at the springs passed the state legislature in 1866, with himself, Edward McPherson, and David Wills, among others, as incorporators. Although progress stalled for want of capital, outside pressure mounted to construct a resort. By 1868 one hundred members of Congress, including James A. Garfield. John A. Logan, Roscoe Conkling, and James G. Blaine, signed a memorial endorsing a summer hotel for "the thousands of visitors who will gladly seek opportunities to visit these now historic scenes." Governor Curtin grasped the reality of a resort at Gettysburg when he approved "a place of entertainment, near its medicinal springs, for the accommodation of those who may resort thither to renew their patriotism and physical health at these respective fountains."[52]

The *Gettysburg Star and Sentinel* confidently predicted that a resort at the springs would be "one of the best paying enterprises on American soil." A reorganized local company, with David Wills as one of the directors, constructed a four-story, three-hundred-occupant hotel in 1869, complete with a cupola for observing the battlefield, a horse-drawn railway from the depot, and a Western Union telegraph line. Echoing the *New York Times's* observation that the springs "is fast becoming as famous as the battle itself," the *Gettysburg Star and Sentinel* commented, "Instead of being hereafter chiefly notable as a former scene of the wholesale destruction of human life, it is to be distinguished as the theatre of modern miracles, rivaling if not surpassing anything of which we have any authentic record, whereby human life and health are to be saved and human suffering relieved." No one hinted at incompatibility between a genteel resort and the battle's memory. On the contrary, the hotel, intended for healing the fractures of industrialism, augmented the image of Gettysburg as an edifying center for leisure.[53]

To boosters such as McConaughy, the battlefield and hotel were entwined enterprises. Less than two months after the hotel opened, McConaughy invited dozens of both Union and Confederate officers to the hotel. Enlisting Bachelder's aid, McConaughy ostensibly aimed to tap the officers' memories to follow through on his design to mark the battlefield. Although only a few Confederates showed up—Robert E. Lee begged off because he felt it prudent "not to keep open the sores of war"—but over a hundred Union officers attended. McConaughy secured free rail passes for participants and guaranteed low rates at the hotel. For what transpired as a media event, townspeople decorated the streets in festive raiment and provided the pomp of a military escort for the returning heroes. Correspondents from New York, Philadelphia, Washington, and illustrated weekly newspapers and the Associated Press descended on the town. With a shorthand correspondent trailing behind, groups of officers followed Bachelder around different parts of the battlefield for five days, while Bachelder listened and drove wooden stakes to mark the positions. At midweek, the Springs Hotel hosted a "grand hop" that continued "until the small hours of the morning."[54]

The press saw through the event as a promotional gimmick. Agreeing with the intended outcome, a *New York Herald* correspondent admitted that "it will be an enduring first-class advertisement to the Gettysburg springs as a summer resort." The event put another correspondent in a foul mood. "Those most interested in the affair," the *New York Tribune* man wrote, "are gentlemen identified with certain money-making projects in this vicinity, whose investments require more than ordinary watering to insure profitable returns." Even attendee Brigadier General Alexander S. Webb wrote of his suspicions "that the arrangements looked rather toward the interests of those interested in the Springs and also toward the personal interests of Col. Batchelor [*sic*] in the Battle of Gettysburg."[55]

Some Northerners also found McConaughy's gesture of inviting former Confederate officers distasteful, especially in light of the common assumption that Gettysburg stood as a symbol of national salvation. Perhaps the Springs Hotel serves as an another example of how the marketing of Gettysburg acted as a leveler of old animosities. In discussing tourists just two months after Appomattox, in fact, the *Gettysburg Compiler* noted "the number seems to be increasing daily," and "they come from all parts of the country, North, East, West, and of late not a few from the South." Before the gathering of officers in 1869, a letter to the *Gettysburg Star and Sentinel* signed "Southerner" stated that "[a] casual estimate of the visitors now at the Gettysburg springs shows that by far the larger number are from the South." Because, he went on, Gettysburg would likely become the nation's "greatest resort" for invalids and summer tourists, both Union and Confederate positions should be marked "for the observation of all men." In the interest of their enterprises, McConaughy and Bachelder abandoned partisanship for a product with intersectional appeal. Bachelder also may have may have had financial interest in the hotel in addition to his books and prints. Both his *Gettysburg* and *Popular Resorts* guidebooks included an engraving of the springs hotel in the frontispiece.[56]

Neither other hotels nor villages and parks ever rose alongside "this modern pool of Siloam," as the *Gettysburg Star and Sentinel* predicted, but the Gettysburg Springs Hotel thrived season after season through the 1870s and the 1880s despite frequent ownership shifts. Featuring landscaped grounds, an artificial lake, a billiard room, a bowling alley, and bathing rooms, it housed famous visitors to the battlefield and served as a social venue for cotillions and balls. Although the springs initially attracted the infirm to the establishment, the Gettysburg Springs Hotel was more a setting for social exchange than for therapeutic water cure. The hotel served middle-class patrons too impecunious for more fashionable resorts such as Newport or Saratoga. Fantastic claims for the water's curative powers faded with the rise of scientific medicine, while the hotel declined with the growth of seaside resorts and a trend toward travelers pursuing more physically vigorous vacations. Plans to transform the hotel into a sanitarium at the turn of the century fizzled, as did a scheme to remodel the building as a Masonic home. Four years after its last use as a hostelry during the battle's fiftieth anniversary in 1913, the abandoned structure burned to the ground.[57]

Despite its relatively brief history, the springs and hotel well illustrate a step in Gettysburg's development as a tourist site. It was no accident that the hotel's emergence and decline parallel the development and transformation of genteel touring at Gettysburg. The "discovery" of the springs surfaced from the battle, and by the time the hotel's popularity waned, Gettysburg catered to a new type of visitor—more peripatetic, more carefree, more interested in amusement than reflection. In its heyday, the hotel captured the expectations of mid-nineteenth-century refinement while offering psychological and physical therapy, sociability, and fashion set against an epical landscape. The cupola with its observation platform allowed patrons to focus outward on the surrounding scenery of the battlefield, providing viewers a commanding perspective of the landscape like other observatories in Gettysburg or like Bachelder's map.[58]

Along with development of the battlefield, the Springs Hotel demonstrated the impulse by Gettysburg boosters to transform Gettysburg into a genteel touring site. If Gettysburg used the springs to enhance tourism, so the springs used the scenic battlefield for the same end. An 1881 advertisement for the hotel listed all the edifying attractions available to visitors, including "superb" drives "over this beautiful and romantic country"; the Soldiers' National Cemetery, "beautified by art and nature"; a "fresh, cool, invigorating atmosphere"; and Pennsylvania College and Lutheran Theological Seminary, which "impart to the place an intellectual and moral influence." The advertising copy devoted the most space to the battle, "the marks of which are still visible on the walls of many houses, fences, trees, etc." Tourists were assured that the battlefield offered plenty to fill their gaze: "The lines of battle are kept intact, having been purchased by the Battlefield Memorial Association; the breastworks, trenches, and lunettes are still standing, with scores of cannon mounted, which present the appearance of a battlefield after the conflict."[59]

Like the battlefield itself as both a pleasure ground and a shrine, the springs possessed a sacred quality that enhanced Gettysburg's providential associations. More, the miraculous, restorative springs, "discovered" at the sanguinary place where the American drama played out, served as a metaphor for national restoration. As Bachelder noted in his 1873 battlefield guidebook, veterans North and South would "interchange generous courtesies" primarily at Gettysburg because "there gushes healing water, said to possess wonderful virtues, to which the feeble, the sick, and the weary resort for strength and rest." Gettysburg would be the site where an infirm nation might be restored to health.[60]

By the 1870s, Gettysburg resembled a traditional religious shrine complete with relics, sepulcher, and a holy font, all of which beckoned middle-class pilgrims seeking spiritual rejuvenation, moral improvement, and an encounter with the sublime. Gettysburg boosters realized that Providence might will battles and healing springs, but shrines required worldly effort.

McConaughy's plans for "memorial stones" stalled due to closefisted legislatures, but according to the May 27, 1873, *New York Times*, the Katalysine Spring Company planned to sell bonds secured by its property to raise funds "for placing indication stones on the battle-field." In other words, the battlefield and springs were not different sides of the same coin, but the same side of the coin. Boosters considered the combined enterprise essential to the success of a genteel touring site. "As the great multitude hasten to Gettysburg for health or pleasure," Bachelder commented in his guidebook, "the renowned battle-field will come to be as much a part of their aims as it would be if it was the plunging Niagara."[61]

Not until the 1880s did the GBMA's plans to create a great memorial park at Gettysburg come to fruition. At that time a revived interest in the war, a new railroad into town, and other circumstances ended the first era of Gettysburg's development and launched the second phase, during which Gettysburg's popularity skyrocketed. But the first phase clearly set the stage for more sophisticated marketing of the past. Images, tourist guides, medicinal springs, and the battlefield itself made Gettysburg conform to genteel expectations. Town boosters were eager to tailor Gettysburg for the cultural marketplace, launching the town's new industry with élan. When McConaughy founded the GBMA, he not only created an official custodian to acquire and sculpt landscape, but produced an organization capable of later coordinating construction of a memorial park. Just six years after the battle, a *New York Times* correspondent returning to Gettysburg wrote, "If this quiet little village could, only seven years ago, have seen itself as it now is, it would have rubbed its eyes with as much wondering perplexity as did Rip Van Winkle when he first awoke from his long dream in Sleepy Hollow."[62]

By the end of the 1870s, an ineffable scene of human wreckage, described with adjectives such as *revolting*, *sad*, and *ghastly*, had been turned into a pleasant site for genteel touring. Yet while masking war's reality, sublime scenery helped transform the carnage into an instrument of God's holy purpose for a destined nation. At the same time, as evidenced in Bachelder's projects, McConaughy's memorial landscape, and the springs hotel, ignoring sectional bitterness to secure the widest market for Gettysburg aided reconciliation. And the fact that Gettysburg had leisurely uses meant it would not be confined to the fusty pages of history, but could exist as an organic idea. As a source of pleasure and commemoration, Gettysburg's memory would be transformed again and again.[63]

Chapter Two

☆ ☆ ☆ ☆ ☆ ☆ ☆ ☆ ☆ ☆ ☆

A Stream of Pilgrims

LESS THAN four months after the battle, Mrs. Cornelia Taylor, her husband, and a few friends left Lansboro, Pennsylvania, to visit some soldiers in the Army of the Potomac near Washington, D.C. Because the group failed to obtain passes into the lines, they visited instead sights of interest to genteel tourists: the Capitol, the East Room of the White House, the Treasury Building, the Post Office Building, and the Smithsonian Institution. But in addition to these edifying places, the group also sought evidence of the war convulsing the nation. They walked about Alexandria's soldiers' cemetery, inspected the hotel where Union hero Colonel Elmer Ellsworth was killed, and visited hospitals where soldiers of both armies recuperated. Then, as if designing their own Grand Tour of patriotism, they decided to finish the sojourn with a convoluted train ride eighty miles north to the town that recently had made news, Gettysburg. There the Taylors and friends meandered through the tents of Camp Letterman General Hospital, where both Union and Confederate wounded seemed happy to greet the strangers and chat about the war. Then the group went on to inspect the battlefield, "the saddest sight I ever saw," Mrs. Taylor recalled at the number of graves, some only partially covered. "On the whole it looked as if it had been a hard fought and dear [sic] gained victory."[1]

Mrs. Taylor exemplified the genteel tourist who would dominate Gettysburg for the next generation. Curious about their country, genteel travelers visited institutions that provided moral lessons and insight about civic and cultural life. Self-consciousness about their aesthetic sensibility led genteel tourists to scenic areas they viewed as sacred places evoking inspiration and emotions characteristic on the refined individual. Unlike their bourgeois European counterparts, however, American antebellum travelers lamented the "the want of intellectual and poetic associations within the scenery," as Sarah Josepha Hale commented. A correspondent on the battlefield in 1865 reflected, "Not a few American writers and tourists have plaintively deplored the utter absence of all historic recollections connected with the scenery of our varied beautiful country." But at Gettysburg, Americans could view a panoramic landscape fit for antiquity and equaling Sir Walter Scott's romanticizing. Thoreau wistfully mused that the American republic could revive the heroic ages, and many viewed Gettysburg as the occasion. Allusions to providential, heroic, and mythical events in press accounts prompted pilgrimages and encouraged travelers to anticipate an American Armageddon or Thermopylae.[2]

Genteel consumers were lured by publicity that prompted a Philadelphia journalist to term Gettysburg "a theme already hackneyed" by 1866. Nevertheless, the abundance of published word pictures and illustrations produced an image that infused the battlefield with value and created anticipation. Two years after the battle, German immigrant and scholar Francis Lieber wrote to Gettysburg native and Clerk of the House of Representatives Edward McPherson asking for directions to Gettysburg, stating, "Some day, in returning from Washington to New York I must take Gettysburg and see the far-famed field." A year later, the Reverend Theodore Culver expressed delight after finally visiting the battlefield he had heard so much about. "For three years I have been hungering and longing for a sight of this wonderful battle-region," Culver wrote, "and now 'mine eye seeth it.'" The uses to which the battlefield was put, as a morally edifying place, ensured that the memory of the battle might grow distorted, but not faded. "You cannot overestimate the interest taken up by the people everywhere in the battle field of Gettysburg," battle veteran General S. Wylie Crawford wrote in 1869.[3]

Nineteenth-century genteel tourists often referred to themselves as "pilgrims" wayfaring to America's sacred places. The *Adams Sentinel* predicted the new Soldiers' National Cemetery "will be the point of many a pilgrimage," and at the cemetery's dedication, the Reverend T. H. Stockton prayed that "the pilgrims of our own land and of all lands will be thrilled with its inspiration." Indeed, tourists to Gettysburg had much in common with medieval pilgrims to holy sites. Both were forms of ritual travel whose expectations were shaped by literature and graphic art. Because genteel travelers were the only significant group that regularly traveled for leisure in the mid-nineteenth century, it is not surprising that boosters and entrepreneurs of Gettysburg shaped tourism around their expectations.[4]

As clerics had despaired centuries before, however, pilgrims to shrines often stray from the prescribed path to pursue folk pastimes and pleasures. Pilgrims in industrial societies too expect extraordinary experiences during their release from routine. For them, trash from the battle took on miraculous power, and they used methods of the unrefined to obtain them. Groups dedicated to moral improvement used the rituals of patriotic touring as an excuse for carefree merrymaking. As shown by the experience of Mrs. Taylor, the well bred might peek at sights ordinarily considered inappropriate. At the time Mrs. Taylor visited, genteel travelers had not yet established their dominance, and they commingled with common folk who arrived on the shattered scene without desire for or pretense of uplift.

A Vast Concourse of Onlookers

No sooner had the thunderous conflagration ended on July 3 than Gettysburg faced new challenges. Thousands of human and horse carcasses rotted in the heat, putrefying in a smoking scene of trampled crops, damaged fences, burned barns, and war debris. To a townsman's understatement that "[I]t seemed as if a furious hurricane had passed over our town," a visitor on July 7 more expressively gasped, "My God, what a sight!" Representatives of dozens of benevolent societies rushed into town to succor the wounded, along with inquisitive relatives and friends of dead and dying soldiers. "As soon as the battle was over," young Oliver Blocher of Gettysburg remembered, "the people come flocking in like sheep." The new floodtide of visitors so strained the town of twenty-four hundred that many slept in the street and "had to go hungry gut and empty belly," according to Blocher. "The streets were a perfect Babel, filled with vehicles of every description and thousands of wounded Union soldiers," a newspaper editor recalled of the pandemonium.[5]

Hideous sights, smells, sounds, and clouds of flies plagued the town for weeks after the battle, exacerbated by visitors digging up graves in search of dead relatives. Despite the heat, residents shut their windows at night when putrefaction grew particularly noxious. Townspeople who fled before the fight now returned to find charred ruins, missing property, or homes and outbuildings converted into hospitals. "The country for forty miles around seems to have turned out to view the sad relics of one of the fiercest battles of the war," noted the *Gettysburg Compiler*. Some like Bachelder, Brady, or latecomer journalists arrived on business, hoping to profit by producing images of the disaster area or publishing stories about it. Some of those stirred by press accounts expressed shock when they confronted a horrific battlefield instead of the anticipated romantic imagery. A New Jersey woman who volunteered to help the wounded felt the frightful sights "robbed the battlefield of its glory." Another, after wandering the lugubrious fields with companions wrote, "The desolation is sickening," adding, "Suffice it to say that we soon had our fill of it," and the group hastily departed. A startled correspondent for the *Philadelphia Public Ledger* vented his disgust on those ultimately responsible for the carnage. "Oh, the horrors of this cruel war," he despaired. "It beggars the descriptive energies of language, to convey an adequate conception of them!"[6]

Yet the awful sights seemed to attract rather than repel the crowds, and entrepreneurs profited. "Every conceivable wheeled vehicle which can carry passengers is dragged to the battle-field," the *Gettysburg Compiler* commented. Genteel travelers and common folk both strained to gape at the spectacle. The juxtaposition of the sublime hand of Providence with the rawest of realities heralded the unfolding of a shrine at Gettysburg. A Philadelphia woman nursing the wounded persuaded families of dead soldiers to leave the remains of loved ones in Gettysburg. On July 29 she wrote to her husband that Gettysburg was "the most honorable burying-place a soldier can have," and predicted that, "Like Mount Vernon, it will be a place of pilgrimage for the nation." Professor Michael Jacobs of Gettysburg's Pennsylvania College concurred, remarking that not mere "idle curiosity," but "a laudable, a patriotic interest in the country's rejoicings" motivated most spectators. From Jacobs's genteel perspective, everyone could "have their patriotism and gratitude to God kindled anew" by witnessing the sacrifice of "blood-stained fields, those freshly made graves, and the mangled limbs and bodies of their fellow citizens."[7]

Other observers were not as sanguine about the presence of spectators or their motivations. The distinction between genteel visitors and tasteless gawkers proved difficult. Even among the genteel, acceptable forms of mourning swung easily into obsession with morbidity. A wounded Confederate prisoner, amazed at the ghastly field's entertainment potential, sneered that even though "the big show was gone," sightseers gaped at the ground where it had occurred. "A torn and bloody garment would attract a crowd, which would dispense [sic] only to concentrate again to look at a hat perforated by bullets," the Southerner recalled. He himself became a spectator of the "vast concourse" of spectators, which included "whole families with the baby." Fascinated both by the crowd's intensity and "the habiliments of the men and variegated plumage of the women," he sketched a mixed-class group consisting of "the typical farmer, the German costumed in clothes of the last century, the village belle and the country housewife, all moving in pursuit of the same object and animated only by idle curiosity." The *Philadelphia Public Ledger* on July 15 welcomed to Gettysburg all who might minister to the wounded, but excoriated voyeurs who came "for the simple purpose of seeing." The editorial pointed out that such a visitor was "a consumer" who leeched resources from wounded heroes of the republic. Not to waste an opportunity, the author instructed readers that gawking affronted genteel culture. "To come here, merely to look at the wounded and dying" the paper went on, "exhibits a most vitiated and disgusting taste."[8]

Although sightseers of all classes dwarfed the number of humanitarians, Union Colonel Charles Wainwright condemned the locals who fled before the Southern tide, refused to help the wounded or bury the dead, and then "came down in their waggons to see the sights, to stroll over the ground, and gaze and gape at the dead and wounded." Similarly, Provost Marshall General Marsena Patrick complained about "curiosity hunters" and stated he was "thoroughly disgusted with the whole Copperhead fraternity of Gettysburg." But Patrick's irritation focused not on gaping yokels, but on battlefield vultures who "came in swarms to sweep and plunder the battle grounds." Rifles, ammunition, blankets, swords, harnesses, and other flotsam of the struggle disappeared in their wagons. Captain William W. Smith, one of the officers left in charge of securing government equipment, wryly informed a superior that at the rate scavengers pilfered U.S. property, "three or four days would clear the field."[9]

A Rage for Relics

Patriotic concerns or investigating the welfare of acquaintances in the army could mask curiosity about the unspeakable. Battlefield articles might be pilfered for their value as souvenirs or stolen for profit. In the aftermath of the battle, newspaper accounts invariably mentioned the cornucopia of wasted goods strewn about the battlefield. A correspondent for the *Berks and Schuylkill Journal*, for example, remembered "pieces of clothing, tattered shelter tents, spoiled cartridges, canteens pierced by bullets, torn haversacks, broken muskets, sabres, bayonets, soldiers' equipments—all were mingled in confusion." Yet for the genteel, the detritus of war immediately took on enchanting qualities because of its link to an event made epical by the press. A Philadelphia woman who nursed wounded soldiers stalked the battlefield and picked up bullets, belt buckles, a cartridge box, and a Bible. "These we shall carefully preserve as mementos," she wrote to her husband on July 18. The *Adams Sentinel* grasped the sacred aura the battle cast on its debris when it remarked in November that "[t]he ground in these vicinities is yet strewn with remains and relics of the fearful struggle—ragged and muddy knapsacks, canteens, cups, haversacks, threadbare stockings trodden in the mud, old shoes, pistols, holsters, bayonet sheaths, and here and there fragments of gray and blue jackets—mournful and appealing mementos of the civil strife whose victory would be shreds and tatters, like these rags, were it not so nobly purchased for so glorious a cause."[10]

Although it is easy to conclude that souvenirs profane the sacred and trivialize sacrifice, the *Adams Sentinel* in 1863 implied the opposite. After throngs swarmed the battlefield on dedication day searching for souvenirs, the paper noted, "Hundreds gathered up, to bear with them the spirit of Gettysburg to every quarter of the State, relics more eloquent than oration." Indeed, the paper had it right. Like fragments of bone and pieces of wood from medieval shrines, relics had value because of publicity but in turn helped spread the site's boundaries and confirm its aura. The power of

Gettysburg relics is perhaps suggested by one of the most unusual ever acquired. During the cemetery dedication, a native sharper assured a visitor he had hired the mount used by General Robert E. Lee.[11]

The popularity of Gettysburg relics provides a measure of the great esteem held for the place from the outset. According to some accounts, the rage for relics had nearly stripped all battle residue from the field within a few years. Others noted how tourists had hacked away at trees to obtain the popular souvenir of a bullet embedded in wood. "What war has spared," a *New York Times* correspondent noted while touring Culp's Hill in 1869, "the chisel and the knife of the relic hunter has destroyed, so that the whole place is a perfect wreck." The *Inquirer* correspondent confirmed that "hatchets, axes, and saws have been brought into requisition to recover balls embedded in wood." Such behavior was common at rural cemeteries, and besides, a bullet embedded in wood complemented collections of natural artifacts. Even if a furtive deed of the refined, landowners and the GBMA threatened legal action against slicing, cutting, and boring within a year after the battle.[12]

But tourists did not confine their purloining to battle debris. In a culture that miniaturized the world in the parlor, natural objects from Gettysburg could fuse nature, history, and private memory. Alongside the seashells, stuffed birds under glass, dried specimens, and live ivy trained to grow along cornices might rest part of the Gettysburg landscape. Sometimes battlefield flora were arranged in patterns and placed in shadow box frames or fashioned into moss baskets, pine-cone frames, moss crosses, leaf wreaths, as well as canes. War correspondent Whitelaw Reid, while covering the battle for the *Cincinnati Gazette*, stooped to gather a handful of roses, columbine, pinks, and cyprus from a war-torn grave at Ever Green Cemetery. "They are my only trophy from that glorious field," he wrote. *Philadelphia Press* correspondent George Gross, remarking that the red berries on a shrub at the embattled Sherfy Farm were "typical of the blood shed at its roots," was urged by the owner to take some home "as pleasant mementos of Gettysburg." A visitor from Erie, Pennsylvania, an acquaintance of Colonel Strong Vincent's father, found the rock on Little Round Top where Vincent had been killed and removed a small evergreen tree and three black raspberry bushes as mementos. By 1872, when the *Gettysburg Compiler* remarked that "[r]elic worship is a mania which seems to have as strong a hold on the popular affections now as it did in the Middle Ages," a mania for canes cut from battlefield trees appeared to match enthusiasm for pieces of the rood. The possession of a "natural" relic may have been as important to a genteel visitor as a piece of the true cross to a medieval pilgrim. It linked the sublime of nature with a transcendent event and brought them both into the private time of the possessor. The irony was that the genteel pilgrim in quest of a piece of transcendence behaved like a boor to get it.[13]

FIGURE 5. Souvenir basket of dried flora gathered from the battlefield, framed and placed under glass (author's collection)

The Genteel Tour

No exact date marks the beginning of tourism at Gettysburg other than the battle's immediate aftermath. A steady flow of visitors continued after the postbattle deluge. Until a new railroad facilitated access in 1884, Gettysburg's location at the end of a spur from Hanover made for slow travel. The *New York Times* on July 7, 1865, predicted that Gettysburg "will become one of the most popular places of resort—that is, if the means of getting there are improved." But visitors continued arriving, despite the inconvenience, "from all parts of the country," according to the *Adams Sentinel* in 1864, to view the battlefield and cemetery. Sacred associations emerged from both Gettysburg's bucolic scenes and its atonement for America's lamentable absence of antiquity. "Many thousands of visitors have come for the purpose of taking a view of this now sacred locality," wrote Professor Michael Jacobs of Gettysburg's Pennsylvania College in 1864, "passing from point to point for the purpose of impressing on their minds the scenes of deepest interest which were enacted here."[14]

It is possible that Jacobs's "many thousands" in the years after the battle arrived in groups. Immediately after the battle, organizations found didactic value in Gettysburg's landscape. Before the railroad companies themselves promoted excursions and "day trips" to Gettysburg later in the century, a variety of organizations—most within a hundred-mile radius—sponsored trips to Gettysburg. A county official noted in 1866 that since the battle, organizations had visited Gettysburg "almost without number." In succeeding years excursions by fraternal, professional, sectarian, and, beginning in the mid-1870s, veterans' organizations multiplied vastly. Dedicated to moral development, edification, and sociability, these groups sponsored a variety of activities during the year aimed at the improvement of their members. Excursions to scenic areas enabled members to absorb the uplifting qualities of nature, often while sharing a feast—the "pic-nic." But Gettysburg offered resources enriching to the genteel agenda beyond scenery, including seminary, college, battlefield, the springs "discovered" in 1866, and, after 1869, the Gettysburg Springs Hotel. Often Gettysburg served as a popular "side trip" for organizations holding meetings in nearby cities.[15]

Organizations typically observed a protocol of decorum when visiting, suggesting the genteel public regarded Gettysburg as a shrine early on. Through ritual performances these groups transformed Gettysburg into a shrine; in turn, Gettysburg legitimized and strengthened them, connecting members to the group and nation within the moral universe of the genteel. Beginning in the late 1860s, church and fraternal groups occasionally numbering over two thousand brought brass bands and military companies to stage ritualistic processions through town. After disembarking at the railroad station, groups often toured the battlefield in small squads or by using the guides' "big wagon." Afterward the band struck up martial airs to parade members on a prescribed route to the National Cemetery for prayers, music, speeches, and even baptisms. Then the procession wound on to Culp's Hill or the town's fairgrounds, where members enjoyed a picnic and speeches. In 1878, the Great Council of the Imperial Order of Red Men, with 150 "tribes" represented, paraded "in very handsome regalia" through the cemetery to the tunes of three brass bands. In contrast to the later focus on war that began with the surge of veterans, speeches often focused on peace as the lesson of Gettysburg. At one huge Sunday school gathering in 1875, for example, a local official told the group, "May you leave this field rejoicing that you are soldiers of the Prince of Peace, using your influence at all times in the interest of His kingdom until nations shall learn war no more." Following group activity, excursionists typically scattered to sites on the genteel itinerary such as the seminary, heights on the battlefield, or springs.[16]

Gettysburg's natural attractions ensured its immediate entry under the rubric of sacred places. It was no accident that both Wills's Soldiers' National Cemetery project and McConaughy's GBMA immediately purchased battlefield locations offering dramatic landscapes and superb views, including Cemetery Hill, Little Round Top, and Culp's Hill. After the battle, a group of women from Lancaster tried consoling a woman searching for the grave of her only son "by directing her attention to the peaceful scenery and quiet beauty that reigned around." Invariably, tourists commented about views they obtained from the battlefield's heights. General Joseph "Fighting Joe" Hooker, relieved of commanding the Army of the Potomac just before Gettysburg, found the battlefield "more grand and inspiring than I had anticipated" after attending a regimental reunion at the Springs Hotel in 1875. "It is vast, magnificent, sublime," Hooker added. Others found sunsets from the heights inspiring. "Nowhere on earth can such superb summer sunsets be found," a tourist wrote in the *Philadelphia Press*. The superintendent of the Soldiers' National Cemetery complained in 1875 about belligerent visitors who insisted on remaining after closing hours to watch the sun set. Even after they were allowed to linger until 8:00 P.M., they resisted. Importuners finally persuaded the War Department to keep the cemetery gates open until one half-hour past sunset during the summer season.[17]

Tourists discovered that Gettysburg offered a nostrum for the "neurasthenia" of modern life, an important justification for sojourning. "Its pure air and invigorating breezes would of themselves be sufficient inducements for a visit from the tired and heated denizens of the city," a *New York Times* correspondent wrote, "even if it had no health-giving spring." Standing on Cemetery Hill on a May day in 1867, Schuyler Colfax remembered a refreshing spring breeze "full of that electric vigor which braves nerves and sinews for the active duty of life." By providing therapy, nature attracted visitors in its own right. Accounts of visits often failed to mention the battlefield at all, emphasizing the salubrious compensations of nature Gettysburg offered. A visitor writing for the *Boston Transcript* found the vistas "an unbroken series of superb landscapes as restful and inspiring to tired city workers as they are beautiful to the lover of fine scenery." A tourist from Baltimore, "tired of the demands of business," took to the hills Gettysburg on foot and declared, "A ramble over them gives rest to the mind and vigor to the body." Release from the ailments of modern life through the purposeful, elevating charms of nature made Gettysburg a quintessential summer resort for pleasure seekers.[18]

To many seeking rejuvenation, the Gettysburg Springs Hotel from its opening in 1869 served as the linchpin of Gettysburg's attractions. For Northerners and sojourners below the Mason-Dixon line, the hotel with its cupola for viewing the battlefield, baths, and other amenities functioned as a center for genteel repose. Some commentators thought the hotel brought stature to Gettysburg by offering tourists features found at elite spas. At the same time, the absence of ostentation and luxury, appropriate for the spot commemorating salvation of the republic, recommended the hotel above comfort and appointments. Almira Lincoln Phelps, sister of Emma Willard, found the springs hotel appealing because it catered to a more sober clientele than did Newport or Saratoga. Phelps found social entertaining at the hotel, including masked balls, an Italian string band, and a production of Gilbert and Sullivan's *H.M.S. Pinafore*, satisfactory without being preten-

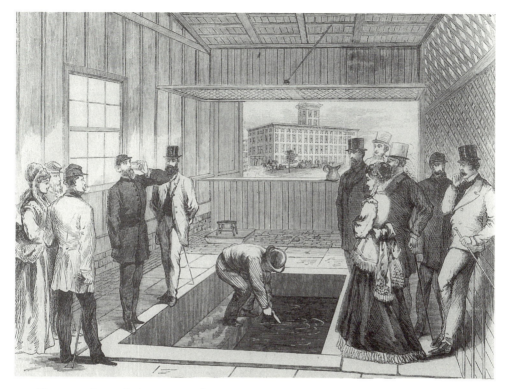

FIGURE 6. Spring house at Gettysburg Katalysine Springs with Gettysburg Springs Hotel in background (*Frank Leslie's Illustrated Newspaper*, July 24, 1869)

tious. After spending several weeks at the hotel, she contrasted elite spa patrons, the "would-be great or fashionable . . . the snobs of society" with the "good and sensible men and women" patronizing the Springs Hotel. At the springs, a site of national and personal rejuvenation, the sincerity of genteel culture could be assured without threat of hypocrisy. Patrons of genteel leisure quickly displaced those in search of thaumaturgy, although veterans sought cures for war wounds at the springs as late as the 1880s.[19]

Yet for the genteel visitor, what distinguished Gettysburg from other summer resorts was the fusion of landscape and epic into a single providential event. Gettysburg offered a new kind of attraction that enabled tourists to see the hand of God not only in nature but in the Union triumph as well. Gettysburg's combination of pastoral fields, rocky glens, and heights offering sweeping views seemed deserving of the great battle it had hosted. "Who shall ever stand on these heights which marked the highest tide of the invasion," a *Cincinnati Gazette* correspondent wrote, "without hearing the voice of the Lord, sounding above the din of the well remembered battle, saying: 'Hitherto shalt thou come, but no further.'" Other than Cemetery Hill, tourists found Little Round Top a point of interest for its spectacular views and significance in the divine triumph. According to Jacobs, by 1864 "[t]housands have stood upon its almost sacred summit," gazing out at "green fields and the wooded ridges that lay stretched out in the forefront, and the long line of blue mountains that skirted the distant sky." The dramatic, boulder-strewn landscape at this part of the battlefield represented God's lapidary inscription decipherable by the sensitive individual.[20]

Visitors could not resist comparing the enormity of the past with serenity of the present. A *Baltimore American* correspondent in 1867 contrasted the "carnival of death" with the bucolic scene five years later, where "naught but the mountain breeze is heard, and the busy hum of industry rising up in quietude from these bloody fields." Although the journalist found a literary device in counterposing war and nature, he added that the two were inseparable at Gettysburg. "Distance, in point of revolving years, lends enchantment to the scene," he wrote. This fantasy element expected by tourists gave Gettysburg its special appeal. For all the aesthetic stock placed in scenery, it also served as entertainment. When industrialization shattered time and space, entrepreneurs jumped into the new market for expansive views of the world with travelogues, images, stereographs, simulated environments, observatories, or great "panoramas" of scenery or events that enabled viewers to transcend time and place. In terms of illusion, the panorama provided a "time machine" effect through a sweeping, participatory view of the scene; metaphorically, it reinforced the middle-class sense of command and control. This heightened sense of escaping confinement and extending experience became a feature of genteel tourism at Gettysburg.[21]

Although a traveling panorama of the battle had been produced as early as the 1860s, and in the 1880s artists would paint commercially successful panoramas of the battle for urban entertainment, Gettysburg tourists in the 1860s and 1870s used their imaginations to produce the panorama effect. The term *panorama* that emerged out of this form of entertainment was even used by visitors to describe the amphitheater-like landscape at Gettysburg. Before the battle a Confederate soldier used the term to describe the southern Pennsylvania countryside as "one bright panorama for miles." Fields and dales seemed perpetually etched by the martial deeds that quickened at the tourists' gaze. A visitor looking out over the landscape in 1865 remarked that the famous features of the battlefield "are all before us again as natural as when they were bristling with the cannon and bayonets of the soldiers of the republic." Another gazing from the Soldiers' National Cemetery a decade later found inexpressible the thoughts "which come thronging upon the mind as I looked around upon the panorama."[22]

While Gettysburg possessed great symbolic value, by providing both enhanced perspectives and tangible reminders of the whirlwind of destruction it appealed to a desire to incarnate the battle. Tourists purchased a variety of prosthetic services in Gettysburg to enhance the battlefield's panoramic

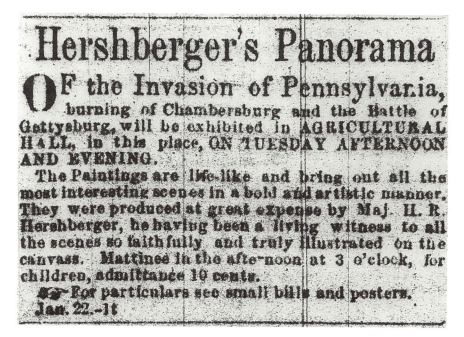

Hershberger's Panorama

OF the Invasion of Pennsylvaria, burning of Chambersburg and the Battle of Gettysburg, will be exhibited in AGRICULTURAL HALL, in this place, ON TUESDAY AFTERNOON AND EVENING.

The Paintings are life-like and bring out all the most interesting scenes in a bold and artistic manner. They were produced at great expense by Maj. H. R. Hershberger, he having been a living witness to all the scenes so faithfully and truly illustrated on the canvass. Mattinee in the afternoon at 3 o'clock, for children, admittance 10 cents.

For particulars see small bills and posters.

Jan. 22.-1t

FIGURE 7. Advertisement for early "panorama" of the battle, exhibited in Gettysburg (*Gettysburg Star and Sentinel*, January 22, 1869)

effect, including field-glass rentals, Bachelder's "isometric" map, guides, handbooks, stereographs, and visited observatories at the springs hotel, East Cemetery Hill, and Big Round Top. All helped transpose the story of the apocalyptic battle onto the landscape. "What grand pictures may be anticipated!" the *Gettysburg Compiler* mused during the planning of the Round Top observatory in 1881. Thanks in part to restorative work by the GBMA and preservation of battle scars by townspeople, tourists found it easy to experience the sense of omniscience attempted later by cycloramas and other visual entertainments. Enlisting a guide whom he termed "a walking encyclopedia" in 1867, Schuyler Colfax recalled "listening eagerly to the clear and vivid recital of the exciting scenes of those great days— the marching and countermarching of regiments and armies, the charge, the shock of the contending legions, the repulse, and the final victory." The previous year the Reverend Theodore Cuyler thrilled to the ubiquitous evidence of conflict in Gettysburg and reported gleefully, "I cannot write of a tithe of the intensely interesting objects around me." Even the wall of the room where he lodged possessed an "ugly scar" from a bullet that passed through the window. Sauntering over the battlefield, Cuyler reported an intense desire to relive the historical event. "I crouched down behind the stone wall that sheltered our boys in blue," he wrote of his experience on

Cemetery Ridge, "and tried to imagine how they felt on that terrible day of carnage." Visitors did not fail to mention the "small pox" of bullets on brick or shells protruding from walls. A correspondent for the *Philadelphia Times* noticed in 1878 how stone walls on the field had been "carefully kept as they were during the battle" and how the GBMA had planted cannon on Cemetery Hill "against which the Louisiana Tigers cast themselves." As this writer indicated, the whole had a tendency to plunge visitors back to 1863.[23]

Genteel tourists thus found in Gettysburg a new and entertaining approach to national self-identification, which Gettysburg cycloramas turned into profitable entertainment in the mid-1880s. Even while the battle was being fought, an eyewitness could not help commenting on the juxtaposition of martial splendor and scenery during the grand Confederate assault on the third day: "And yet as I sit here with the aid of a glass and drink in the beauty of the landscape where waving fields of harvest are already ripe for the laborer . . . I for the moment loose [*sic*] a realization of the fact that tis brother arrayed against brother in deadly conflict, and see only the grandeur, a beauty of the scene, which does surpass in awful sublimity aught I have *ever ever* imagined." This anonymous viewer attempted to paint with words a canvas of the martial grandeur that overwhelmed him. It was this monstrous scene of organized killing set against pastoral American abundance, mechanized death on a grand scale dovetailed with the amplitude of life, that tourists tried to imagine and impresarios tried to re-create in a variety of forms later on.[24]

The Bizarre, Sensational, and Macabre

Curiosity about the battle's awful panoply contrasted sharply to contemplations of sacrifice on a heroic landscape, but the sacred made battle voyeurism all the more acceptable. Yet it was not certain where edification left off and sensationalism began. Gettysburg, for example, challenged the genteel pursuit of God's handiwork in nature with landscapes mutilated by the thunderbolt of war. Some thought the destruction enhanced the sacred because the scale of damage manifested divine wrath much like an area devastated by flood, storm, or fire. "Entering upon the consecrated grounds," a *Baltimore American* correspondent wrote in 1867, "one cannot help feel a reverential awe—a sort of silent veneration, with sadness of heart—as the eye everywhere within visual range, falls upon some striking evidence of 'grim visaged war.'"[25]

Yet this same correspondent recommended displays of grotesque nature at Culp's Hill and Little Round Top as "the most interesting portions of the battle grounds for strangers to visit." Among the first purchases of the GBMA, these sites proved the most popular for tourists, who found them extraordinary. Visitor after visitor gaped at torn and dying foliage on Culp's Hill or pockmarked boulders on Little Round Top. A *Frank Leslie's* correspondent also linked the transcendent with the sensational when he labeled the desolate landscape at Culp's Hill "one of the most interesting of those spots made sacred by the blood of patriots." As if shocked by war's defilement of nature, another visitor surveying Culp's Hill noted, "Every tree was scarred and torn, a chilly blight resting upon its summer crown of beauty." While some visitors thus tied the damage to Gettysburg's sacred associations, the natural deformities drew a crowd as if they were a carnival freak show. A more typical assessment termed the trees "seamed, disfigured, and literally dying or dead from their wounds." In a sensuous description of the devastated timber, a newspaperman reported trees "scarred from base to limbs so thickly that it would have been impossible to place one's hand upon their trunks without covering the marks of a bullet." The hideous sight set his mind to wondering that "[t]he storm of bullets must have been as thick as hailstones in an ordinary storm." Even sixteen years after the battle, a correspondent for the *Boston Transcript* found that "the old scars yet remain in many cases as plain as when first made."[26]

For the genteel traveler, fractured nature sharply distinguished Gettysburg from other scenic places. In 1866 a Pennsylvania College student decided to use his few allotted leisure hours for a tour of the battlefield instead of the usual chess, reading, or baseball. In what he termed "an account of my rambols," the youthful spirit recorded pauses at both sacred and sensational spots. He and his chum first visited the cemetery, where they cursed the "rebel horde" after viewing "the hallowed resting place of the brave and noble dead." Then the youths "journeyed along the lines passing Meade's head quarters viewing shatered breast works intrenchments shatered trees that had been scard". As far as intriguing sights accessible to and appropriate for genteel tourists went, nothing could compare with Gettysburg.[27]

Enthusiasm for Gettysburg's attractions could quickly slide into a morbid fascination with death and decomposition common in Protestant America. The battle that could turn the effluvia of war into valuable relics also could make the ghoulish into a respectable memento. Samuel Weaver, in charge of burials at the Soldiers' National Cemetery, swore that no Confederate bodies polluted the sacred soil reserved as a Valhalla for national heroes. Confederate remains were accorded no more respect and propriety than were other souvenirs. Liberty Clutz, a Gettysburg woman who complained of "much to stir the feeling of horror" because of shallow burials, nevertheless appeared fascinated at a human hand her sister Annie brought home after a walk over the battlefield. "Dried to parchment so that it looked as though covered with a kid glove," Liberty remarked, "there was nothing repulsive about the relic, and we all remarked on the smallness of the fingers." She joked that the hand had been attached to "a Southerner who had never worked with his hands." In 1869, a *Philadelphia Inquirer* corre-

FIGURE 8. Tourists on Culp's Hill viewing scarred nature (*Frank Leslie's Illustrated Newspaper*, July 24, 1869)

spondent noted that officers invited to the Gettysburg Springs Hotel reunion had "barbarously carried away" bones from Confederate graves as souvenirs.[28]

Tourists could not resist the lure of the macabre. Four months after the battle, one who eagerly scrambled into the crevices at Devil's Den to gape at Confederate dead wrote, "I almost strangled from the effects of the smell caused partly by these decomposed bodies." Battlefield guides sensed what patrons really wanted to see and titillated them with gruesome sights. Isaac Moorhead, a railroad officer and bookstore owner visiting in 1864, enlisted Mr. Frey, "an excellent guide" who took him to the "Valley of Death" between Little Round Top and Devil's Den. Eyeing a skeleton among the rocks, Moorhead fingered the rib bones and found a bullet, which he surmised had caused the victim's death. Then, "moving aside a flat stone, Mr. Frey showed us the grinning face and skull of a rebel." Touring the same spot in 1866, a group from the Pennsylvania State Teachers' Association found a skull fixed upon a fence post, a grisly sight the group descriptively related in a report of the tour. Bones gradually disappeared on the battlefield, but suggestions of the macabre did not. W.W.H. Davis, summering in Gettysburg in 1869, inquired at a house pocked with hundreds of bullet marks on the plastering. Davis reported, "The owner told me that the dead were piled up along the fence three feet high, and I was shown where the blood of the slain still discolors the hard ground." Stimulating the senses and shocking sensibilities appeared to be part of the tourist regimen. A tourist in 1875 recalled how guides habitually took visitors to the place where Union General John Reynolds fell. "Several trees are pointed out, each the identical one under which he stood when he received the fatal shot," the visitor joked. Gettysburg entrepreneurs thus joined postmortem photography and sensational literature of the day in exploiting the macabre for profit.[29]

Celebration and Merriment

Despite gestures of decorum, visitors sometimes used Gettysburg as a venue for release of playful urges. A throng of twenty-five hundred arriving in August 1875, sponsored jointly by a band and military company, marched through town and the cemetery stepping to the tunes of four bands. Still in procession, the parade then moved to the fairground building, which quickly converted into a dance hall. While many participants buckled down to "industrious sight-seeing" in town and on battlefield, "the chief point of attraction," according to the *Gettysburg Star and Sentinel*, "was the Lager Beer Saloon improvised at the Agricultural Implement Shed." The paper especially noted that all but a half keg out of twenty brought by the group had disappeared by departure time. Entertainment for the afternoon consisted of a race between a "noted pedestrian" and a horse at the fairgrounds track. The man won, but the judges gave the nod to the horse after deciding the man cheated by breaking into a trot.[30]

Gettysburg encouraged a festive air among visiting groups by donning floral arches, bunting, and flags for large excursions or on civic holidays. When the Grand Council of the Improved Order of Red Men advertised "A Day of Enjoyment is Promised all Red Men and Pale Faces Who Attend," the advertisement did not intend to appeal to the pious. Decoration Day festivities at the cemetery drew larger numbers of excursionists throughout the 1870s; by the end of the decade, over ten thousand excursionists were disembarking at the depot from as far away as Philadelphia and Washington, D.C. The July 4 holiday attracted fewer excursionists but relied less on ritual. At the celebration in 1873, novel spectacles siphoned off many of the large crowd. Van Amburgh's Menagerie, a circus parked in Gettysburg especially for the Independence Day crowd, appealed to cultured tastes by advertising its "great study of natural history." But Van Amburgh's also featured the sight of performing dogs, "Russian athletes," aerialists, jugglers, and an "infant acrobat." In the afternoon, many of the day's visitors strayed to the fairground for a jousting tournament, where nine knights with names as banal as "Ivanhoe" and "Knight of Black Steed" competed in five tilts. The winner of the competition crowned a "Queen" from the "large number of ladies" whose "approving smiles incited the chivalrous Knights to their best endeavors."[31]

Within a decade after the battle, Gettysburg boasted an unusual combination of genteel allurements. The letter of a Cornell college student, J. C. Hendrix, who visited Gettysburg in 1871 illustrates how a trip to Gettysburg approximated a medieval pilgrimage for travelers. Enthusiastically summarizing his Gettysburg meanderings for a Dartmouth friend, Hendrix alluded to the providential nature of the two great armies meeting at such a "natural fortification." At the Soldiers' National Cemetery, he praised the grounds and "grand" monument, adding a textured word painting of the four "sublime" figures surrounding its central granite shaft. But then on his "jaunt" over the battlefield he remarked on its corporeal aspects, the "scars left by both armies" that caught his attention. "Shells are half buried in some housewalls, bones lie over the ground and here and there over the field you see a patch of grass more luxuriant than its neighbor, and then you know that some poor unfortunate affords a fertilizer to the soil." Hendrix claimed he "gathered relics from the graves of dead heroes," "fell in love a score of times," and "drank of the all-curing Katalysine water." Finally, after observing "a balloon ride the clouds," Hendrix ended up at "a round of dissipation" the evening before, where he "had a fair specimen of the cream of society of the country abouts."[32]

Hendrix writes to his friend as if he is recovering from a magical discovery. Like a medieval pilgrim, he experiences the transcendent, the sublime, and the strange in escaping from routine. Although he is evidently not an especially religiously minded individual, Hendrix sees the hand of Providence at work in setting the battle at such an impregnable outgrowth of nature. Battlefield mementos will allow him to take home tangible reminders of the famed soil and his memorable trip. Hendrix finds the sublime in art. He struts his aesthetic sensibility by singling out the monumental art as a symbolic expression of the moral and transcendent meaning of the battle. Yet he also is quick to note the exotica of Gettysburg, including scarred buildings and gruesome sights on the battlefield. Medieval shrines often featured sacred springs from which pilgrims sought miraculous cures. Hendrix's remark about the springs' healing power is perhaps sardonic, but he mentions the springs as if a drink were a mandatory part of a visit to Gettysburg. Finally, on holiday from routine, he flirts and frolics. For Hendrix, the trip offered release, an encounter with the extraordinary, and transformation that characterized medieval pilgrimages.[33]

The battlefield itself counted as only one of many attractions for edifying summer activity. *Appleton's Hand Book of American Travel* in 1867 suggested that visitors allow only one day to see the battlefield but two days to visit the springs, heights with "extensive views," and the seminary with its "fine library." On the tenth anniversary of the battle, the *Gettysburg Compiler* announced that "[v]isitors increase every day" because "the many attractions of this historic vicinage are not to be surpassed." Still, what set Gettysburg apart from other genteel pilgrimage sites was the romantic, translucent memory of the battle set on the landscape. The variety of means employed to aid the tourist quest for a commanding view of past and present landscapes helped transform the horror of the original event into an edifying pastime. And the reproduction of Gettysburg in the cultural marketplace, which transformed a historical event into a dynamic image, overshadowed other sacrifices of the Civil War. Just three years after the battle, a saunterer in the Soldiers' National Cemetery claimed his senses flooded with "an overwhelming sense of the wickedness of war." Yet he caught himself, recalling that the Union dead at Gettysburg "form but a small, single sheaf from that great recent harvest reaped by DEATH with the sickle of war."[34]

The fissure point between the sacred and secular at shrines is not always clear. As a new type of American sacred place that improved the genteel itinerary by grafting an event of classical proportions of the American landscape, Gettysburg helped lure the middle class away from work and into self-fulfillment through purchase. But Gettysburg also pushed the genteel agenda beyond educational institutions, watering places, scenery, and history. As impresarios like P. T. Barnum well knew, for all their advocacy of improving leisure, the middle class also loved exotica and would consume it voraciously if it were coated with a patina of refinement. Furthermore, patrons found Gettysburg a place that masked the impulse to have fun. Organizations used Gettysburg as an appropriate place to enact rituals, display civic pride, and enhance their stature, but Gettysburg also offered the opportunity for communal merriment.

In the years after the battle, tourists could make sense of Gettysburg only through cultural terms already established for other American sacred places through the marketplace. The sublime seen in such sites as Niagara Falls, the White Mountains, or the Catskills transferred easily to the bucolic Gettysburg landscape. The first souvenirs manufactured from battlefield flora reflected a reduction of the great event to understandable natural specimens, much as Niagara Falls could be taken home as a gypsum chunk. Tourists who had purchased an aesthetic appreciation of scenery in the decades before the Civil War set the stage for the visitor consuming Gettysburg after 1863. Unaware of the paradox of the commercialized sublime, tourists brought the same contradiction to Gettysburg that they had taken to other pilgrimage sites. At the same time they visited Gettysburg ostensibly to find transcendence, they did so with materialistic self-indulgence. While their objectives differed from those of later tourists, they established a pattern of veneration and play that has characterized Gettysburg ever since.

PHASE TWO

☆ ☆ ☆ ☆ ☆ ☆ ☆ ☆ ☆ ☆ ☆

1884-1920

A Mecca for Patriots

The popular estimate of its importance has been emphasized by the fact that, as the years roll by, the interest in it, instead of diminishing, is steadily increasing, as is attested by the constantly swelling number of visitors, and by the erection of memorial structures in commemoration of the great deeds of the heroes who here gave their lives.

—DAVID B. BUEHLER, Vice President, Gettysburg Battlefield Memorial Association, preface to J. Howard Wert's 1886 *A Complete Hand-Book . . . and Guide to the Positions on the Gettysburg Battlefield*

Chapter Three

☆ ☆ ☆ ☆ ☆ ☆ ☆ ☆ ☆ ☆ ☆

A Memorial of the Whole Struggle

GETTYSBURG'S streets rocked with the din of artillery on February 26, 1884. Added to the clamor of bells and cheering crowds fluttering red, white, and blue, the booming signaled festivity rather than martial panoply. Into the town irrevocably changed by war in 1863 steamed the bedecked locomotive *Jay Cooke*, bearing a beaming Cooke himself. Partially financed by this tycoon, the Gettysburg and Harrisburg Railroad dramatically improved on the existing Hanover railroad's connections to northern, eastern, and western population centers. The *Harrisburg Patriot* termed the celebratory cannonading "nearly as important to the town as that which occurred twenty-one years ago," and the railroad "another victory for Gettysburg" that "brings the historic battlefield within reach of the thousands who want to visit it." Appropriately, the locomotive stopped outside of town for a brief ceremony that included driving two golden spikes, one inscribed "1863" and the other "1883." But the spikes represented more than just corporate gimmickry exploiting historical memory. Rather, they suggested how much America had changed in the interim since the battle. In a country dramatically different from the one left behind in the Civil War, market forces once again courted the past to sire a shrine appropriate for the new order.[1]

Just as the railroad led the pace of postwar change in America, so too did the new line into Gettysburg spearhead development of the shrine. It was no coincidence that the Gettysburg icon grew apace with America's shift from a producer to a consumer nation. A new commercial society characterized by rapid communications, display, spectacles, images, and increased leisure needed shrines and created them. During the four decades bracketing America at the turn of the century, railroads exploiting a rage for the American past furiously promoted Gettysburg in a variety of ways. The steel carpet opened Gettysburg to a new class of travelers for whom tourism had earlier been unthinkable, including many veterans. The marketplace of genteel culture began a process of blurring into a commercial culture of popular taste that became mass culture in the twentieth century. Thanks in part to the railroad, the genteel resort of the immediate postwar years gave way to one that included a broad cross-section of America, genteel and plebeian, black and white. Separate spaces catered to both genteel and working-class tastes, yet the genteel accommodated the plebeian. While the genteel agenda for constructing a park much like a rural cemetery finally came to fruition, it appealed to the more plebeian tastes of returning veterans and less-cultivated citizens. It burst through genteel restraint and recalled the popular story of valor rather than genteel abstractions about salvation of the republic. The shift reflected broader trends as the idea of Gettysburg became part of the nationalizing of American culture. Gettysburg earned the nickname "Mecca of the Patriot" as both place and concept, a true shrine in the vanguard of mass culture forged from a ragged, heterogeneous society.

New Wonders on the Battlefield Every Day

A national transformation in the late-nineteenth century brought to a close the local initiatives that had created a genteel resort at Gettysburg. By the time World War I shattered the Victorian era's complacency, America boasted the world's most prodigious industrial output while its size, population, number of the foreign-born and of white-collar workers, and the GNP all had doubled since the Civil War. Burgeoning metropolitan areas began to dominate the countryside that had defined the antebellum nation. American life grew ever more uniform as national networks serving commerce sped the flow of information, images, goods, and people.[2]

Paradoxically, the vertigo induced by commercial culture sought therapy in the bygone. The Civil War era appeared all the more extraordinary when measured against progress and America's new challenges. On the fortieth anniversary of Gettysburg, the *Philadelphia Public Ledger* remarked that the United States of 1903—"rich, peaceful, prosperous beyond all dreams"— imagined the Civil War as a distant epoch. "The wartime conditions, remembered as of yesterday," the paper noted, "seem infinitely remote, as though they must have belonged to some elementary period of civilization with which we no longer have anything in common." Yet it was precisely this remoteness that underscored Gettysburg's value in the present. Veterans espousing genteel virtues as well as the genteel elite glanced back at the war as a golden age of selflessness and noble sacrifice. Although genteel control of culture had never been total, the new challenges posed by vulgar acquisitiveness, millionaire parvenus who dodged wartime service, and the dawn of a mass culture at odds with the genteel agenda seemed particularly disconcerting. In light of America's exceptional place in the world, increasing national might made moral fiber all the more important.[3]

To some, veneration for past accomplishments promised to straighten the backbone of Americans. History infused a civil religion that offered both an anodyne to change and compensation for religious doubt raised by science. Holidays and rituals of the new civic faith embraced by the public such as Memorial Day, flag worship, or pilgrimages accompanied the new commercial culture. Pilgrimages in particular were thought to be a particularly valuable approach to quickening the patriotic spirit. "The Historical Pilgrimage will stir the imagination of the average American, vivify for him a too monotonous existence, quicken his interest in an heroic past, and give him an appreciation of a fruitful present," a writer noted in 1893.[4]

Commerce harnessed and nourished civil religion just as it tamed, systematized, and promoted old festivals such as Easter and Christmas as holidays. Photography, mass markets, railroads, and mass spectacles enabled the past to be consumed as a form of leisure. With some irony, change itself became the chief vehicle for access to the past, which in turn eased the burden of change. The era's great fairs, for example, commemorated historic events such as the centennial of American independence or the quatercentenary of the Columbian encounter. At the same time, these fairs celebrated progress by displaying the latest consumer goods and technological marvels. Department stores used historical themes for pageants and parades, which bolstered both sales and civic pride. The new art of store window dressing used historical and patriotic tableaux to sell merchandise for civic holidays. These displays served as urban shrines that not only promoted the holidays and patriotism, but transformed the past into an entertaining visual feast.[5]

By the 1880s, progress had both evoked and enabled revival of the Civil War's memory. The Grand Army of the Republic (GAR), a Union veterans' order moribund in the 1870s, experienced a burst in membership that counted over 400,000 members by 1890. With thousands of posts across the North, and strength in large urban chapters, the GAR served as an instrument of national memory by synchronizing and popularizing reunions, civic holidays, and celebrations in innumerable hamlets and towns. Monument companies flourished from producing Civil War monuments, the greatest public patronage of art in the United States until the New Deal. In town squares North and South and on battlefields, the ubiquitous monuments capped by common soldiers guaranteed as much a continual reminder of the soldiers themselves as the war itself. The publishing industry too profited from Civil War reminiscences that appealed to the sentiments of both sections by ignoring political issues and substituting valor for mass killing. The popularity of publishing ventures such as the *Philadelphia Weekly Times's* "War Annals" or *Century Magazine's* "Battles and Leaders" series illustrated the public mood for wartime narratives of duty and courage over themes of treason and sacrifice.[6]

In the floodtide of books, articles, monument building, reunions, and pilgrimages celebrating the Civil War, Gettysburg represented the high-water mark. Finally the Gettysburg Battlefield Memorial Association (GBMA) obtained the support necessary to follow through on its founder's earlier vision of adorning the field with "works of art and taste." Demonstrated through monuments, avenues, and other embellishments, this aesthetic reflected in the rural cemetery aimed for civic instruction and moral uplift. Monuments provided a permanent solution to preserving memory, evoking reminders of a debt the present owed the past. Gathered together as in a cemetery, a collection of monuments staked out a sacred environment of thoughtful repose.[7]

Adornment of the bloodstained fields began in 1879, when the Pennsylvania Department of the GAR seized control of the languid GBMA. Paralleling the membership trends of its parent, the Pennsylvania GAR rose from 3,647 members in 1873 to 41,000 by 1887. The new GBMA leadership, opened to non-Pennsylvanians in 1883, galvanized the organization to sculpt a park from the battlefield. It solicited financial support by urging Pennsylvania GAR posts to buy stock subscriptions and successfully lobbying the legislature for ten thousand dollars. In a pamphlet designed to elicit public interest, the GBMA outlined its plans for laying avenues and placing monuments that would create "a Park, the diversified and natural beauty of which can hardly be excelled" and "a history, delineated upon the ground."[8]

To tame the pastoral landscape into a park, the GBMA bought properties, built carriage lanes, and directed state commissions in placing monuments. One by one, Northern states contributed toward land purchases and monuments for the regiments they fielded in the battle. But GBMA directors assumed ironfisted control over the field. Although state commissions submitted the designs chosen by regiments, the directors dictated the terms of placement, materials, and inscription, permitting no digressions from their vision of a formal park. A Committee on Legislation courted state assemblies for appropriations and whipped up interest among veterans. A less-direct method used a psychological technique of a type employed in modern public relations. In 1882, before the rush to erect monuments began, the GBMA placed signboards around the field noting the positions of Pennsylvania troops. "The placing of these cheap boards had the desired effect," recalled J. M. Vanderslice, a GBMA director. Non-Pennsylvanians touring the field "would inquire with indignation whether there were no other troops than Pennsylvanians engaged in the battle," and once home would encourage their state legislators to appropriate funds. "Public interest was thus gradually being awakened," Vanderslice recalled.[9]

By the time Congressman Daniel E. Sickles's legislation (the Sickles Bill) turned the battlefield over to the U.S. War Department in 1895, the

GBMA had purchased 600 acres of land, constructed 17 miles of avenues, and supervised the placement of 320 monuments, one for nearly all the Federal army's volunteer units. "The matter seems to be contagious," the *Gettysburg Star and Sentinel* noted early in the monument frenzy. After 1884, Northern states began providing monument funding for each unit they fielded at Gettysburg, although individual memorial associations often added their own contributions. For veterans, placement of a monument at Gettysburg represented public acknowledgment of their entire wartime activity. Some regiments erected more than one monument on the field, and others not engaged in the battle insisted on erecting a monument at Gettysburg even if they had experienced combat elsewhere. When Wisconsin dedicated its monuments in 1888, a Milwaukee newspaper urged all citizens to make a pilgrimage to Gettysburg for the ceremonies, even though only six regiments out of fifty-four fielded by the Badger State during the war fought at Gettysburg. Even swindlers cashed in on the craze. A scam artist posing as a government agent appeared in Montgomery County, Pennsylvania, assuring veterans that for a fixed fee he would inscribe their names on a monument at Gettysburg.[10]

Monuments in classical, Richardson Romanesque, and Beaux-Arts styles dotted the site. Returning to the battlefield for the first time in over two decades, Major General Abner Doubleday hailed Gettysburg as "one of the art-centres of America." It was more than the moral uplift of art that stimulated monument building, however. Everyone seemed to profit from the frenzy. Each dedication drew hundreds of visitors, and for years afterward many veterans would return again and again with their post or family members to visit the regimental monument. Monument production for Gettysburg and other Civil War battlefields boosted the monument industry significantly and stimulated new techniques for manufacturing memorials. The Van Amringe Granite Company of Boston, which touted its Gettysburg work as an entree for advertising, sculpted so many Gettysburg monuments that it published its own guidebook to the field. Monuments provided railroads with more to puff, tourists with more to see, merchants with more customers, monument companies with more business, and veterans with the feeling of a guaranteed place in public memory.[11]

Veterans realized that monuments answered the dilemma of fading memory, substantiating in stone the story of their heroism as the battle receded in time. Yet they also understood that objectifying memory with monuments made its own history. Veterans' groups competed for the biggest and most attention-getting memorials in the park, even if this distorted the historical record. As work proceeded, historian Jacob Hoke remarked in his 1887 book *The Great Invasion* that survivors' organizations "are vying with each other" to mark where they fought and "beautify" the park. In a letter soliciting funds, the monument committee of the 121st New York requested contributions "to erect a monument that shall reflect honor upon the peo-

FIGURE 9. Advertisement by the Smith Granite Company publicizing monuments the firm produced for the Gettysburg battlefield (WHi-2440, Wisconsin Historical Society)

ple of Otsego and Herkimer Counties. . . . [W]e want, and will have, as fine as any." The letter reminded readers that "the nation has selected this bat-tle-field as the grand mausoleum of our patriot dead," and therefore the monument "should be one of which your descendants will not be ashamed." A similar circular from the 17th Pennsylvania Volunteer Cavalry Associa-tion despaired that veterans "who were willing to make their breasts a barri-cade to the enemy" could not now afford a monument that would "compare favorably with others on the field."[12]

Others realized that not only monuments, but their absence, made his-tory. When Massachusetts, with twenty-one regiments in the battle, surged ahead of Pennsylvania, which had fielded seventy-three, the *Philadelphia Times* remarked that "the casual visitor, without any knowledge of the rela-tive number of troops engaged, would be forced to conclude that the Bay State did most of the fighting on the federal side." Reassuring Pennsylvania veterans that they would not be excluded in the race for memory, the com-mander of the Pennsylvania GAR promised members in 1886 they would be represented by "marble and granite shafts, not excelled in beauty and grandeur by any on the field."[13]

Display and the scramble for prominent spots often seemed to get the upper hand. "Each regiment seems to have the impression that it had the honor of saving the day," wrote a member of the GBMA. When the GBMA insisted that the 72nd Pennsylvania place its monument in the secondary line of battle it occupied during Pickett's Charge, and not at the "Bloody Angle" where the assault was repulsed, an irate officer of the 72nd pro-ceeded to dig a foundation at the famed spot. Although the GBMA ar-rested him, the monument association pursued the more prominent loca-tion in the courts. On a technicality, the association in 1891 won the case in the Pennsylvania Supreme Court and, gloating in triumph, placed a dra-matic bronze figure swinging a clubbed musket on the more celebrated site. Perhaps emboldened by the 72nd's success, an officer of the 20th Massa-chusetts monument association in 1896 asked if the regiment's monument near the Bloody Angle could not be moved "to the most advanced position occupied by the regiment during the battle." Were that not permissible, the officer queried, could the regiment not place "a more prominent marker" at its current location?[14]

The logic of monumental display encouraged officials to mark Confeder-ate positions at a shrine initially intended to symbolize republican triumph over treason. Southerners, however, faced postwar financial problems too severe to allow them to purchase memorials for a battlefield associated with Confederate defeat. "Gettysburg is too sad a field to attract many south-erners," a Confederate veteran of Pickett's Division wrote. Yet this veteran received an enthusiastic response from veterans of the Philadelphia Brigade after discussing a possible memorial to Pickett's Division near their monu-ments. "They think it is a mistake to exclude Confederate monuments," the

Southerner wrote, "as their presence there would add real interest to the spot." Union veterans realized that for their stones to speak of heroism, symbols of a worthy foe also must be present. Many who years earlier balked at the idea of Southern memorials were now eager to mark Confederate positions. John B. Bachelder, by this time Superintendent of Tablets and Legends for the GBMA, argued in an 1889 letter to Congress that marking Confederate lines "would increase the value of Union monuments" and improve the tourist experience. "How can I," a Union veteran wrote to Bachelder, "tell my boys, with any hope of their understanding, of the magnificent rush of panoplied humanity that attacked us that day unless aided by such a survey of the Confederate lines?"[15]

Although Southern states did not erect memorials on the battlefield until the twentieth century, Southern papers had urged them to fund Gettysburg monuments long before. "The truth of history, as well as the South's duty to herself, demands it," declared the *Nashville Banner*. A Confederate veteran who found "nothing to be ashamed of" at Gettysburg explained that Southern monuments would not only present the Confederate perspective to tourists, but add to the interest value of the battlefield by narrating Confederate valor. "The visitor to this battlefield," he wrote, "when he sees where the Confederates charged and fought, sometimes hand-to-hand with the Federals, when he learns from personal observation what a tremendous advantage General Meade had over General Lee as to position, will glory in the dash and dauntless courage of southern men." The tourist industry in Gettysburg agreed that Southern monuments would add to the battlefield's attractiveness. When a Pennsylvania legislator in 1903 proposed a monument to General Robert E. Lee jointly funded with Virginia, the *Gettysburg Compiler* urged monuments to Southern commanders as a stimulus to tourism. "To have this battlefield visited and studied by a constantly increasing number of Southerners would mean a continual benefit to the community through the increase such travel brings," the paper stated. Monuments helped transform Gettysburg into a shrine of national valor rather than Union victory, thus burying political issues in tons of marble and granite.[16]

When the War Department assumed control of the battlefield in 1895, it supervised additional monument construction and gradually added more avenues, fencing, tablets, cannon, trees, and observation towers. By that time, the ennobled poses of some artwork placed on the field oriented visitors toward the glory of combat and away from reflection about mass sacrifice. In the veterans' competitive quest to memorialize the role of common soldiers, many of the realistic bronze designs they chose entertained and evoked the senses instead of pensiveness. Finely detailed giant figures firing, kneeling with hammer cocked, or swinging clubbed muskets contrasted sharply to adjacent, older funerary models of Egyptian obelisks, Greek war trophies, or the classical mounted leader. "Everywhere upon that great, great battlefield one sees the soldier in action," a visitor in 1894 recalled.[17]

Thoughtful visitors realized the danger of display. Some found the popular monumentation vulgar. A *Baltimore Sun* writer in 1896 termed Gettysburg "our national museum of monstrosities or chamber of horrors." The sheer visual spectacle produced a distended memory of Gettysburg at the expense of greater sacrifices elsewhere. Frank Moran, a veteran and editor of the GAR newspaper *National Tribune* complained, "My soldier pride in Gettysburg and in this rich country too will be immeasurably augmented when I see a few drops of the favors now being showered on Gettysburg lovingly sprinkled over the swamps of the Peninsula, the jungles of the Wilderness, and the Carolinas; over Chickamauga, Shiloh, Stones River."[18]

Representing the culmination of genteel values, the battlefield's memorialization resembled nothing as much as that asylum for genteel repose, the rural cemetery. Complaints suggest that this model of memory was under attack even as it was being built. Some visitors found the rural cemetery environment too embellished and funereal. A *Century* contributor termed the battlefield "an unsightly collection of tombstones," while a veteran who made his pilgrimage in 1898 stated that the battlefield "reminded one of a great cemetery." "Think of a cemetery three miles long and a mile wide," wrote *Boston Globe* correspondent George Alfred Townshend, "with the fields full of cenotaphs, symbols, obelisks, and human figures, looking as if the stone and bronze ages had left over their graveyard to a miniature race." By the 1880s, the popularity of cemeteries as pleasure grounds for contemplation had waned in the rise of municipal parks and travelers' interest in greater physical activity. Still, a majority of visitors would agree with a veteran who wrote in 1886, "Gettysburg has now become the Mecca of America, and as the birthplace of Mohammed is the most holy city of Islam so has Gettysburg become the most sacred city in our land."[19]

In many ways, the shrine was consistent with the era's genteel aesthetic that built art museums, universities, symphony halls, and museums of natural history as monumental reminders of cultural order and civic improvement. Lauding the embellishment of the battlefield for visitors, the *Philadelphia Public Ledger* remarked in 1897, "At Gettysburg we are inculcating patriotism by an object lesson which should be made as impressive and enduring as possible." Yet cracks fissured the intent. The solemnity of the rural cemetery model contradicted Gettysburg's role in reflecting new aesthetics of memory and tourism. Many of the monumental objects on the battlefield displayed the new restlessness for action over contemplation and visual stimulation over uplift. Citizens of all classes, common people the genteel elite hoped to influence, contributed to the monuments of their hometown heroes through fairs and fund drives. Small wonder critics found the artwork tasteless and without edifying potential. "The old battlefield is a vast and wonderful graveyard of monuments built by the dollars and hearts of the veterans without any expenditure of aesthetic taste," complained one New Yorker.[20]

FIGURE 10. View of Hancock Avenue about 1912, taken from the tower in Ziegler's Grove, illustrating the similarities to the rural cemetery, below (author's collection)

Although ostensibly venerating the past, the shrine, like other products, was manufactured, promoted, stamped, and sent by the latest communication technologies. "New attractions are being added almost weekly," the *Gettysburg Star and Sentinel* commented in 1887. Karl Baedeker's 1893 U.S. guide, in fact, listed the monumental spectacle as the key Gettysburg attraction, noting, "There are nearly 400 monuments on the field . . . being of all designs," and "[o]ver $1,000,000 has been expended on the grounds and monuments." Not coincidentally, Gettysburg emerged as a popular resort just as department stores became urban shrines, with their interiors designed like cathedrals. By the turn of the century, the former scene of carnage had metamorphosed into a showplace of constantly changing display that prompted the *Harrisburg Telegraph* to remark, "There are new wonders on the famous battlefield every day, and it is worth going to see once a year."[21]

"A Community of Beggars Living off the Pilgrims of Patriotism"

Reflecting on the popularity of Gettysburg in 1896, a *Baltimore Sun* editorial termed Gettysburg not simply a Civil War battlefield, but "a memorial of

FIGURE 11. Spring Grove Cemetery in Cincinnati, about 1890 (Cincinnati Historical Society)

the whole struggle." In the spirit of a commercial culture, the author considered this a practical measure. "We could hardly afford to make a Gettysburg of every town where an important engagement was fought during the Civil War," he wrote, "nor would there be, without so much competition, a sufficient supply of tourists to keep all the towns running." Indeed, by 1896 Gettysburg heralded America's new leisure industries, perched between the older genteel and the new mass culture. Even though railroads and the federal government had in effect seized control of the battlefield before the turn of the century, townspeople seemed more than willing to join in the partnership. Although no statistics were kept on the number of tourists until after the turn of the century, a locally produced guidebook estimated that 150,000 had visited the park the first two years of the railroad's operation. By 1894 the *Philadelphia Times* speculated that "every tourist from abroad" made an effort to see the battlefield.[22]

As tourism became Gettysburg's leading industry, townspeople not only effectively responded to increased numbers, but also to the needs of tourists who were different from their earlier genteel counterparts. To the traditional services required by tourists, such as food, lodging, and guides, Gettysburg enhanced the modern pilgrimage experience with packaged touring, tourist photographs, souvenirs, and commercial entertainment of interest to working-class visitors. The town, in fact, became a national joke as a tourist trap, and no gear in the tourism machine was more responsible for turning Gettysburg into a current event than Gettysburg itself. In the process of creating the shrine, however, many townspeople anguished over changes the modern pilgrimage had wrought to their town.[23]

"The goose that lays the golden egg for Gettysburg," as a local paper termed tourism, enticed locals who otherwise would have been tradesmen or farmers into a seasonal industry. Town leaders viewed hospitality as a community responsibility. "Anything that tends to the financial benefit of our people collectively cannot but be of advantage to them individually," the Gettysburg Star and Sentinel commented. When excursions and veterans' groups arrived, the town saluted them with a band resplendent in navy uniforms fringed by gold braids, brass-spiked Prussian helmets, and white belts. Citizens were urged to appropriately decorate their residences with patriotic bunting during GAR encampments, reunions, "state days," anniversaries of the battle, and conventions. On these frequent occasions, the town sported gala arches, American flags, and red, white, and blue banners along the streets. Taking a cue from the success of department store display, the town hired professional decorators to trim the streets for the fiftieth and seventy-fifth anniversaries of the battle.[24]

Linchpins of the town's chief industry were hotels that catered to the growing middle class. With increasing demand from tourists interested in brief sojourns as opposed to the summer resort, hotels in town flourished while the Gettysburg Springs Hotel a mile away declined and finally closed. From three crossroads taverns at the time of the battle, Gettysburg by 1885 increased its number of hotels to six and then eight twenty years later. The most visible link in the chain of tourist enterprises, hotels packaged Gettysburg for tourists in sometimes imaginative ways. Hackmen waited at the town's two train depots to snare incoming travelers for their particular hotel. From the hotel lobby, which sold relics and souvenirs, tourists were provided with touring options by guides affiliated with the hotel. Tourists might, for example, buy a package that included lodging, dinner, a tour, and field glasses. Hotels also printed their own complimentary guidebooks or maps that marketed other town enterprises. A pamphlet from the Pitzer House, for example, included not only battlefield sights but advertisements for souvenirs and the message "Your Gettysburg Souvenir will have an extra Historical Value if bought at the JENNIE WADE HOUSE."[25]

Along with hotels, guiding grew as the railroads brought more visitors to town. By the last decade of the century, perhaps fifty townsmen—one hundred by World War I—engaged in the seasonal occupation, and most had no firsthand memory of the battle at all. Many began as construction workers on avenues and monuments, and then slid into a less-strenuous part of Gettysburg tourism. A few guides, such as William D. Holzworth, William

FIGURE 12. Tourists with guides and hacks on Little Round Top, ca. 1912 (Edwin Root Collection, U.S. Army Military History Institute)

T. Ziegler, and James T. Long possessed excellent reputations and went on to become hotel owners. Yet many visitors found the guides offensive and even aggressive in their pursuit of tourist dollars. Some cornered incoming tourists at the depots, and in their competitive frenzy flew into one another, fists flying, over potential customers. One experienced traveler termed Gettysburg guides "most grasping," and added, "If a visitor escapes with his watch, chain, and clothing he is lucky." Informed tourists often saw the guide as a raconteur of spurious stories and outrageous drivel "that compels his very mules to fold down their ears in pious mortification with their enforced part in the iniquity," according to one visitor. When large excursions arrived, guides sometimes whisked excursionists around the park in a race to arrive back at the depot in time to pick up a second group. In response to complaints, government stepped in to regulate these free-ranging entrepreneurs. The War Department assumed control of guide pricing and presentations in 1915 following a series of impotent town ordinances.[26]

Yet guides were essential to the Gettysburg experience. With the addition of each new monument, guides spiced their tours with anecdotes told to them by veterans. Guides well understood that tourists wanted human interest stories linked to observable features at the park instead of tedious lectures about national salvation or tactics. Whether the stories were true or not was irrelevant as long as they entertained and dripped with sentimentality. Every part of the landscape possessed a tale packed with metaphorical meaning. John Burns and Jennie Wade, for example, harked back to republican virtue, while yarns about Confederate and Union soldiers sharing water at Spangler's Spring and Barlow's Knoll underscored reconciliation. Ironically, while the stories soothed visitors with assurances of a simpler and more selfless time, they themselves were products of modern tourism. Although they emerged from commercial motives, the tales of gallantry found their way into guidebooks and, in the mid-twentieth century, onto roadside exhibits placed on the battlefield by the National Park Service.[27]

Similarly, souvenirs and relics also reduced the great battle to easily understood terms. Any business in town that trafficked in tourism sold relics, which grew scarcer over time. Rumors circulated throughout the country that Gettysburg's flimflam artists churned out bullets at a relic factory, also producing "finer and more costly" relics such as "skulls, with big leaden balls lodged neatly in the eyesockets or the jaw." Townspeople appeared to have had few reservations about selling any tangible memories of the battle, however grisly. In 1907, a guide tore down the barn he owned, which had been used as a field hospital, with the intent of fashioning souvenirs from the blood-stained timbers.[28]

Not only the growing scarcity of relics, but also increases in the number and types of tourists encouraged local manufacturing of souvenirs. Producers of canes, stereographs, and dried flower arrangements of the genteel era gave way to manufacturers of kitsch that lost its association with nature and possessed broad appeal. A variety of cottage producers as well as peddlers of Gettysburg bric-a-brac came and went between 1884 and the 1920s. John Good, who at the turn of the century produced wooden pistols, jewelry boxes, and statues, made batches for large excursions in advance after determining what type of souvenirs the excursionists might purchase. Like vials of water from the Jordan River or letter openers made from Mount of Olives wood, many Gettysburg souvenirs bore direct association with the sacred ground itself. Tiny glass viewers containing different park scenes were placed inside minié balls; small cannon were fashioned from battlefield metals and wood; battlefield clay furnished raw material for miniature monuments, cannon, or canteens.[29]

The view that such kitsch profanes sacred places fails to consider the social and psychological function of such goods. GAR posts prominently displayed Gettysburg relics and used gavels, inkstands, and podiums crafted in Gettysburg for conducting rituals. Souvenirs widened Gettysburg's access as much as improved transportation did. In an era enjoying an effusion of consumer goods, souvenirs seemed all the more precious because they were special commodities connected with a sacred place. With ever-increasing numbers of Americans able to enjoy a holiday, souvenirs allowed more people to link their own memories of a pleasant break from routine to a national memory. Like monuments, souvenirs substantiated the battle's story and Gettysburg's stature as a tourist site. In short, Gettysburg souvenirs democratized the shrine by enabling all pilgrims to possess part of it.

Personal photographs also spread the Gettysburg image. As at Niagara Falls, photographers stationed themselves at Devil's Den, Little Round Top, and East Cemetery Hill, the most popular tourist spots. There, before the widespread availability of inexpensive portable cameras, the photographers' shutters continually clicked for tourists who queued up for personalized souvenirs. Bearing a Gettysburg backdrop and label, these photos graced thousands of parlors and underscored Gettysburg's cultural significance. Mass-produced photos also brought a brisk business. In one week in 1904, 100,000 Gettysburg post cards were sold in town, and 75,000 mailed.[30]

Beginning in the 1890s, the opening of the first historic structures, reflecting tourism's shift over time from uplift to nostalgia, proved to be powerful vehicles for souvenir sales. Tourists paid twice, once for the time they paid guides to stop at a building, and again when they were persuaded to purchase souvenirs inside. Guides halted their teams at Meade's headquarters, where visitors were shown a few bullet holes and an old pump. Then, as a tourist in 1896 remembered, "your attention is called to a well-selected assortment of canes, paper weights, and souvenirs of the field." He added, "the system of sub-contracting among Gettysburg guides is wonderfully developed." Despite the insignificance of Jennie Wade's death to the battle's outcome, guides added the house to their tours when it opened in the early 1900s. The stop included a lecture by owner Robert Miller about the maid's sacrifice. "When he illustrates how and where she was shot tears run down the cheeks," a visitor reported, "and when he solemnly buries her in the yard, all gospel truth, even the hard-hearted visitor buys an extra dose of relics and souvenirs and tip toes out." At the house, visitors could ogle the purported dough tray Jennie Wade used at the time of her death and then purchase a miniature wooden dough tray.[31]

Despite symbiotic relations between commercial interests and the custodians of Gettysburg's memory, conflict did occur. In the early 1890s, an enterprising outsider proposed constructing a trolley across the battlefield as a service to the increasing numbers of tourists. The entrepreneur's ingenuity lay in applying the electric trolley, a popular transportation innovation in cities, to tourists. William H. Tipton, who labeled himself "The Battlefield Photographer" and earned the monicker "Boss" Tipton for his political clout in Gettysburg, helped secure approval for the venture from his post in town council. Already operating a seasonal studio at the southern end of the park, Tipton bought additional acreage near Devil's Den in anticipation of the new tourist traffic.[32]

The trolley opened the battlefield to the many who could not afford a hack, but it drew fire from some veterans' groups and the GBMA, which had planned to place memorials on the track path. In one instance, a veteran kicked Tipton's tripod down during a monument dedication because of the photographer's collusion with the trolley. The trolley also incensed the guides, as it combined touring with the excitement of a trolley ride for a fraction of the cost of a hack tour. Ensuing litigation against the trolley company reached the U.S. Supreme Court, which affirmed in 1896 that the government could protect the shrine's primary function of civic instruction over other uses. The trolley company simply moved its tracks, and until displaced by the automobile, the trolley continued circulating crowds in cars appropriately named after Union generals. As for Tipton, he constructed an amusement site typical for the turn of the century, including a refreshment stand, amusement area, dancing pavilion, and photographic gallery on his thirteen acres near the trolley tracks at Devil's Den. Until bought out by the War Department in 1901, Tipton Park, according to his wife, proved "very successful" and "quite a resort for excursionists," where thousands of souvenir photos were taken.[33]

On the bottom end of the souvenir business were the street vendors, or "fakirs," who also sometimes found themselves in the cross fire between other merchants and guardians of the sacred. Often these were the same youths who scoured plowed ground for relics that they sold for pennies to any purveyor of tourist services. At every important civic holiday, encampment, or celebration they hawked their goods. As early as 1878, they and refreshment vendors clustered so thickly along Baltimore Street during a GAR encampment a visitor commented, "[E]ven the monkey and fat woman show was on hand." At the battle's twenty-fifth anniversary reunion in 1888, the GAR *National Tribune* noted the "lemonade venders, side-show operators, and badge fiends . . . have occupied every available spot along Baltimore street and are in first-class condition to break the ears of visitors with their eternal clatter." The Gettysburg Battlefield Commission (GBC) moved to control faking by issuing permits, and then banning Sunday sales in 1898. The measure appears to have accomplished little, as on Memorial Day in 1911 the *Gettysburg Star and Sentinel* reported that "[t]he usual number of venders of souvenirs, relics, whips, canes, balloons, etc., were on hand with their jokes and wares." But as the town's Retail Merchants Association resented competition from fakirs, commerce as well as government attempted to assert control. The association argued that tourists often complained of faking as an annoyance, but more pernicious, fakirs sold souvenirs at lower prices than stores. Town council, just as it had moved to regulate guides, responded by requiring nothing more than a twenty-five-dollar faking license.[34]

Faking along with guiding were only the crassest forms of salesmanship employed by Gettysburg citizens. Other methods were more sophisticated. In the off-season polished guides such as James Long, William Holzworth, and William Ziegler traveled throughout the Northeast and Midwest lecturing about Gettysburg and its tourist attractions. Like veterans and railroads, these guides borrowed on sacred capital to clinch the sale, such as reciting the Gettysburg Address. In hopes of spreading the burden for publicizing Gettysburg, the veteran-guides encouraged merchants to form a Business Men's League in 1900 pledged to "the advertising of Gettysburg and the procuring of as many visitors as possible." The League and its successor organizations tried different approaches to improve the tourist business. Representatives were sent to conventions, urging members to hold their next meeting in Gettysburg. Committees worked with the railroads to offer round-trip single fares for special celebrations, or to have Gettysburg designated a "stopover" destination for western travel. Gimmicks intended to drum up business included offering groups free trolley tickets, souvenir booklets, and badges with minié balls attached. The new marketing techniques were aggressive, but actually reflected anxiety that plagued townspeople about potential decreases in tourism. After all, they reasoned, Gettysburg competed with many newer tourist locations, and commemoration of the Civil War might die off with its veterans. When the town mounted a festive celebration of the battle's fortieth anniversary in 1903, advertising widely to attract tourists, an unsatisfactory turnout generated worries.[35]

Yet many in Gettysburg cursed the day war came to their town and jolted them into the wider world. Some townspeople simply did not like the national limelight. Many felt choked by the federal government, believing it unfair for the government to condemn land that not only shrunk the tax base but could never be developed. Although the local papers boosted tourism, they often regretted its stultifying effect on industry. "It has prevented the location of factories here and has retarded the growth of the few we have," the Gettysburg Star and Sentinel lamented in 1900. About the time the Business Men's League formed to promote tourism, another organization, the Gettysburg Development Company, emerged to encourage industrial development. Although in the early 1900s the company tried to attract an automobile plant and a rolling mill, it secured only a few small-scale enterprises, such as a brick factory.[36]

More balanced economic development, however, represented only one part of the problem. An equally pressing concern was perceived moral decline resulting from a reliance on tourism. The papers praised the discipline industry entailed, dreaming of "steady employment" for citizens. They were aware that metropolitan newspapers habitually ridiculed Gettysburg townspeople as idle country sharpers fleecing pilgrims to a national shrine. "Nowhere else in the wide world is the art of squeezing so thoroughly understood and so highly practiced as at Gettysburg," a New York Times correspondent reported, while another newspaper called the town "a community of beggars living off the pilgrims of patriotism who make it their Mecca." In a rare moment of self-castigation, the Gettysburg Star and Sentinel admitted in 1903 that "something is radically wrong with our community." The editorial lashed out at the battle as ultimately "a source of injury to our town," which had "generally demoralized" citizens for industrial work. "Boys are brought up peddling in the streets who ought to be in school or in shops learning a useful trade; men who ought to be at work spend whole days waiting around in carriages and annoying visitors."[37]

Complaints about tourism focused on impropriety by the new excursionists as much as on the indolence tourism bred. Tourism had turned Gettysburg into a "Sunday resort," where "the noisy loud-mouthed excursionist is often in evidence." A variety of local temperance and sabbatarian groups issued a flurry of petitions in the 1890s and early 1900s demanding a halt to Sunday excursions, serving alcohol to tourists, and other threats to moral order. One group termed the observation towers erected by the War Department "especially objectionable," as they intruded into "that privacy of family life which is, or ought to be secured, by the U.S. Constitution to every citizen against the prying curiosity of stranger-tourists." In response to the agitation, a town council member argued at a meeting in 1895 that "the few dollars left here by such excursions was nothing as compared with the injurious effect upon the morals of the community." Town council did nothing, and when members of the State Sabbatarian Association petitioned council again in 1902 to end "all such traffic as violates moral order," the petition "was laughed at, joked at, and tabled," according to the *Philadelphia Public Ledger*. These critiques of the profanation of Gettysburg had little influence when it came to business and profit.[38]

Because the park had been developed as a shrine for civic and moral improvement, it was ironic that so many Gettysburg people found it profaning and a moral outrage. Tourism, the town's new means of producing wealth, affronted genteel standards and the dignity and stability of an older producer ethic. A Declaration of Principles drafted by the Citizens' League of Gettysburg in 1895 complained that "Gettysburg and vicinity are suffering from evils kindred to those which elsewhere have encroached upon the valued institutions of the people." Tourism brought the commercial revolution, most visible at the time in urban areas, full force on a small town. Dr. P. M. Bikel, president of Gettysburg College, defended sabbatarianism by arguing that Sunday rests from the tourist business could help avoid nervous prostration and collapse. Yet that was precisely the reason tourists came to Gettysburg on their free time. Whether as "day-tripper" excursionists out for a good time or as genteel tourists searching for edification, visitors patronized Gettysburg as an antidote to industrial society. Like it or not, Gettysburg citizens found themselves on the flip side of industrial production. Against this, the traditional moralist had no chance.[39]

Railroads and Urban Spectacles

Gettysburg depended on the railroads to feed it the raw materials of tourism. Using the most advanced business techniques and technology, railroads transformed Americans into travelers. Passenger departments marketed to all classes and slashed fares in the competitive environment. As a result of the railroad's targeting leisure as well as business travelers, between 1885 and 1900 rail passengers increased by 70 percent. While before the Civil War railroads emphasized aesthetic experiences, by the 1880s they peddled pleasure as well. By promoting existing tourist sites and constructing others, railroads created destinations appealing to everyone, including those too poor and too time strapped for all but day excursions. Inevitably, Gettysburg became part of this process. Trumpeting the GBMA's plans to create a park with avenues and monuments in 1881, the *Gettysburg Compiler* noted that "it is no more than natural that railroad people should turn an eye in this direction."[40]

When the long-awaited Gettysburg and Harrisburg Railroad eased access to Gettysburg in 1884, competition for passengers ensued with the established Western Maryland Railroad. Until the decline of trains in the twentieth century, railroad companies battled each other through advertising, ticket fares, and attractions. They plastered broadsides advertising special excursions to Gettysburg in nearby towns and cities. For the fortieth anniversary celebration, for example, the Western Maryland's broadside offered half fare to see a "Lavish Display of Fireworks, including a reproduction of Pickett's Charge," and announced "EVERYBODY IS GOING—DON'T MISS IT." Railroads offered veterans reduced or half fares for monument dedications, reunions, and anniversary celebrations. To churches, civic, and fraternal groups the railroads offered not only reduced fares but rebates as inducements to travel.[41]

Railroads mined the sacred treasure that cultural leaders hoped would infuse the lower classes with patriotism. Before the new tracks into Gettysburg were finished, a Gettysburg and Harrisburg official said the new railroad "means that the ground so historic in the great events of our nation shall be made readily accessible to the people" so that "thousands may have it in their power to stand on the sacred ground, hallowed by the blood of heroes." The railroad also seemed to realize that to hook their new market of leisure consumers, something more than edifying landscapes would be necessary. Indeed, railroads stood in the vanguard of marketing leisure to the working class and to the young middle-class members who strained against older genteel strictures. With portions of the Gettysburg battlefield taking shape as a contemplative, cemetery-like park, the Gettysburg and Harrisburg Railroad immediately constructed a line called the Round Top Branch that bypassed it. Two-and-a-half miles south of Gettysburg, the spur terminated at the shady groves of Little Round Top and Devil's Den, scenes of fierce struggles on July 2. There, with "the purpose being to make the grounds attractive and inviting," as the *Gettysburg Star and Sentinel* noted, the railroad blasted through masses of granite to construct pavilions for crowd entertainment. Round Top Park, as it was called, provided the primary destination for excursion trains that sped over the battlefield, offering a passing view. Both railroads hauled dozens of groups of tourists and "day trippers" to the park during the season, some numbering in the thousands. "It must be borne in mind that Round Top has attractions outside of historical prominence," the *Compiler* boasted.[42]

With the railroad's initiative providing an anchor, Gettysburg's tourist industry gravitated southward. At various times the area featured refreshment, souvenir and photography stands, pavilions for dancing, a shooting gallery, a casino, and flying horses. Occasionally amusement included daredevil stunts such as the performance of Professor Stookey, who walked a tightrope stretched between trees during an ox roast in 1886. More typically, excursion groups engaged in merrymaking such as dancing, target shooting, bag races, and wheelbarrow races. Some recognized that the railroads and their amusement area opened Gettysburg to new types of pilgrims by relieving the memorial park's seriousness. "Important points [of the battlefield] are in private control that keeps them for public advantage," noted the *Lancaster Intelligencer* in 1886. "New railroad facilities and corporate liberality and enterprise have contributed . . . to make the Gettysburg battlefield accessible and to enhance the interest of a visit."[43]

In many ways, the arrangement echoed the elegant rural cemeteries that featured beer gardens and amusement outside the gates. In fact, patrons of Round Top Park could cheaply and entertainingly access the adjacent memorial park after the trolley arrived in 1893. It was the success of the railroad's venture that lured the trolley company to run a circuit from town to Round Top Park, at one point on the loop sharing the railroad's tracks. Railroad and trolley worked hand in hand in a demonstration of technology serving democratic leisure. The amusement business fused patriotism, edification, and fun, as witnessed in the trolley's convenient tour "over the most historic points of the battlefield" with expert explanations at seven stops.[44]

Guidebooks issued by railroad companies also helped expand Gettysburg's appeal to a wider range of pilgrims. Breaking with the older practice of simply describing the aesthetic value of a place, the Gettysburg railroad guidebooks depicted the rails as a magic carpet ride to insouciance. Gettysburg offered "ample and convenient arrangements for recreation and enjoyment," zccording to the Western Maryland Railroad's guidebook, while the competing Gettysburg and Harrisburg's stated "all is young and laughing." Including anecdotes, battle accounts, and curious sights, the booklets shifted attention away from abstractions to Gettysburg as a novel escape from the ordinary.[45]

Guidebooks informed visitors in advance about attractions to consume visually on arrival, building anticipation and ensconcing common place-names such as "the Wheatfield" or "the Peach Orchard" in the American historical vocabulary. All "points of interest" deserved a visit, so that the Springs Hotel and the cannonball embedded in Sherfy's cherry tree re-

FIGURE 13. Trolley near Devil's Den and Little Round Top, 1890s (21P-2238, Gettysburg National Military Park)

ceived recommendation no less than the Soldiers' National Cemetery and Cemetery Hill. Guidebooks intended to increase passenger traffic and ensure customer satisfaction, and to do so they guaranteed the extraordinary from scenery, memorials, and rail travel itself. E. L. Godkin found them full of "balderdash, cheap sentiment, and attempts at lurid description" in an 1888 *Nation* article. "One of them seriously maintains that God Almighty created Little Round Top expressly to furnish a position in which Meade's army might save the Union."[46]

The railroads grew ever more sophisticated in their approaches to packaging and marketing Gettysburg. In 1884, its first year of operation, the Gettysburg and Harrisburg offered round-trips from Harrisburg to Gettysburg for groups of five or more at three dollars per person, which included a guided tour of the battlefield. As an example of the industrial efficiency of modern pilgrimage, the same railroad that year packaged Gettysburg for the time-conscious traveler with an accordion-fold brochure titled "Gettysburg, How to See It Quickly." The Pennsylvania Railroad offered eight different classes of excursion tickets to Gettysburg, and in 1887 the Pennsylvania Railroad opened a tourist bureau that packaged lodging, food, and chaperons with an itinerary linking Gettysburg, Luray Caverns, Washington, D.C., and other sights.[47]

Cutting-edge marketing strategies made the historic site attractive to heterogenous groups of leisure consumers. A trip to Gettysburg meant not so much a pilgrimage to venerate the past as an encounter with the modern. Nowhere can this be better illustrated than through the proliferation of Gettysburg images. Duplicated en masse by railroad guidebooks, postcards, stereoscopic views, engravings, a plethora of guidebooks published by Gettysburg entrepreneurs, and media articles, the images served to brand Gettysburg in the public imagination. Railroads understood the importance of images for business. When the Gettysburg and Harrisburg first opened its line into Gettysburg in 1884, it hired a landscape photographer to produce views that could be used as engravings for its tourist guidebook.[48]

Railroads were only one part of the communication improvements that homogenized America and disseminated the Gettysburg image. Evidence points to the breadth of Gettysburg's popularity for both the middle and working classes. In Milwaukee, a Captain C. W. Hyde opened a Gettysburg museum around the turn of the century in which he displayed, among other relics, "a button from the dress of Jennie Wade." Maine veteran John F. Chase built a career around the hideous wounds he received at Gettysburg. Taken for dead, Chase inspired poetry and sheet music for purportedly muttering, "Did we win the battle?" as a burial detail spirited his mangled body to the grave. But Chase exploited this patriotic story to market his patented wringer and water still, patriotic and temperance lectures, and the Gettysburg cyclorama, which he accompanied on tour. Chase's promotional pamphlets, featuring an illustration of his naked, shattered torso grasping a flag, suggest a carnivalesque attraction. In 1886, General St. Clair Mulholland, a veteran of the battle, formed the Gettysburg Exposition Company and contracted with artist Frank Briscoe to paint a series of ten paintings of the battle, each fourteen by twenty-four feet. Mulholland wrote to an acquaintance as the scenes neared completion: "The paintings are magnificent and I think and hope will pay well." Mulholland took the paintings on tour beginning at Williamsport, Pennsylvania, using veterans' organizations as a network to arrange exhibitions offering matinees for children and half-price admission for GAR members.[49]

Beyond the railroads, the Gettysburg cyclorama, painted by the French artist Paul Philippoteaux, served as the most influential medium for disseminating Gettysburg and emphasizing the battle narrative. The cyclorama performed the same function as the railroad by commingling working-class and genteel audiences in a form of mass commercial leisure. Partially art but mostly spectacle, cycloramas were panoramas that enveloped urban audiences in massive circular canvases depicting natural, biblical, or historic scenes. Such potentially uplifting themes attracted middle-class viewers to the sensationalistic illusions engineered by platforms, lighting, and three-dimensional realia. Earlier in the century, the great canvases depicting scenery had often been wound on a reel and unraveled for spectators while a narrator explained the scene. Yet by the second half of the century, railroads had brought to reality what the unfolding panoramas offered in illusion. Cycloramas by that time focused on historical themes that honored America's past and became part of the era's civic celebration. They provided the nineteenth century a transition between still-life graphics and motion pictures, while presaging illusions conjured by Disney "imagineers."[50]

Philippoteaux and his crew painted four identical canvases of the climactic moment of the battle, Pickett's Charge, which were displayed in Chicago, Boston, New York, and Philadelphia beginning in 1883. Depicting martial glory and sanitized combat, the paintings amused and instructed thousands of urban dwellers over the years they remained on exhibit. Impresarios sold guidebooks that included the battle's history along with an orienting map for the scene, and sometimes hired veterans to explain the action depicted. The *Boston Transcript* termed the painting's benefits to civil religion and moral order a "healthy contribution to popular recreations, as it decidedly inspires patriotism and enlarged views." By placing viewers in the center of the story, it took the audience back to July 1863 in a way that monuments could only dimly achieve. Other artists copied Philippoteaux's interpretation of the battle, and the canvases traveled as far as Paris and Sydney, Australia. Although the cyclorama did not find a permanent home in Gettysburg until 1913—copies had appeared under tent in 1894 at the Bloody Angle—profits from its exhibition elsewhere encouraged efforts to house it in Gettysburg at the turn of the century. A corporation calling itself the Gettysburg Cyclorama Amusement Company solicited stock subscriptions for permanent display of the "large earner and a sure dividend payer." Gettysburg newspapers consistently pushed the initiative as a way to encourage repeat tourist business as veterans died off. Appropriately, the cyclorama that did find a home in Gettysburg, supposedly one of the originals painted by Philippoteaux, had hung in sections in a Newark, New Jersey, department store display prior to its arrival.[51]

The Gettysburg cyclorama sometimes appeared on the midway entertainment strip of the great fairs that characterized the period, showing up as late as the 1933 Century of Progress Exhibition in Chicago. Although the fairs celebrated American progress, they used symbols of the past as psychological anchors. Gettysburg exhibits went on display in the formal exhibition areas of many fairs, beginning with the 1876 Philadelphia Centennial Exposition and ending with the 1939–40 World's Fair in New York. For the St. Louis World's Fair (1904), the War Department prepared a large relief map, nine by twelve, as well as dozens of printed maps and photos illustrating tourist improvements on the battlefield. One entrepreneur tried to sell stock for a proposed exhibit at the 1893 Columbian Exposition that he estimated would raise $1.5 million. His scheme consisted of a series of dioramas showing the three days' fight, accompanied by artillery and musketry fire, presenting "a realistic representation of actual war." This quest to add texture to the cyclorama's illusion never came to fruition, but Gettysburg exhibits at all the great fairs oriented the public to the shrine's story and tangibility.[52]

But Gettysburg also was a spectacle in its own right, a permanent seasonal display mounted in a collaborative effort by railroads, Gettysburg townspeople, and state and federal governments. From 1878 to 1938, approximately the same period as the great fairs, Gettysburg hosted not only tourists, but GAR reunions, Blue-Gray reunions, Pennsylvania National Guard encampments, and other military displays that offered grand theater and drew thousands of spectators. From mock battles, fireworks, and parades in 1878 through army maneuvers and simulated air attacks by "flying fortresses" in 1938, Gettysburg threw parties celebrating the status quo and national might.[53]

A broadside issued by the Western Maryland Railroad Company offering "low-rate tickets" to the 1913 fiftieth anniversary celebration assured that "aside from the sentiment of the occasion, it will prove most attractive from a spectacular point of view." On celebratory occasions, Gettysburg, like the great fair midways, became a colorful marketplace of festive fun that harked back to premodern market fairs. In addition to local vendors and fakirs selling lemonade, souvenirs, peanuts, and relics, catchpenny operators sometimes included traveling showmen, such as "Dr." Ryell T. Miller, who brought a Custer automaton and relics of the Custer massacre to the 1888 twenty-fifth anniversary festivities. Pawnee Bill's Wild West Show promised Memorial Day crowds a thousand performers and "the only one in the wide, wide world that depicts truthfully . . . the habits and customs of wild west frontier life."[54]

Both Gettysburg and the great fairs were considered unifying national experiences, significant arenas for civic and moral instruction. Like the great fairs, Gettysburg offered a whiteway of inspiring monuments and scenery, but also a midway in town and at Round Top Park. Presenting both edification and entertainment, Gettysburg justified insouciance for the genteel through its patina of moral uplift, but it also extended higher ideals to the working class. In this way it hurried along the demise of leisure as strictly moral improvement and blended it with pleasure in aiding the formation of mass culture. Even monuments, the quintessence of the genteel landscape, were part of the era's "overillustration" with their animated statuary. For all the power invested in monuments to contain memory, their competitive display contributed toward "image thinking" that focused on representation of the battlefield. Moreover, unlike the symbolism of classical designs, heroic action depicted on monuments emphasized the narrative of combat rather than abstraction of historical meaning.

The sabbatarian who reasonably argued in 1900 for a state law forbidding "picnicking, sightseeing, or other worldly pleasures" at Gettysburg on Sundays would have seemed mad a few years later. The edifying side of Get-

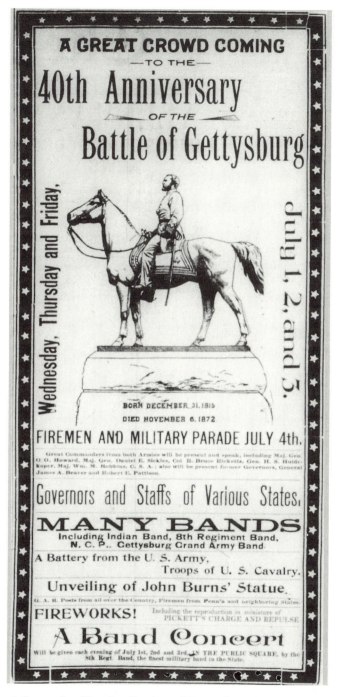

FIGURE 14. A Spectacle of Parades, Bands, and Fireworks: Advertisement for the Fortieth Anniversary Celebration (*Gettysburg Star and Sentinel*, June 17, 1903)

tysburg had to adjust to the tinkering of commercial culture just as the fairs functioned to homogenize the public. Fed by the railroad, Gettysburg became a crossroads of America, exposing visitors to the same transportation technologies, commercial leisure, and national symbols. Additionally, the market must be given its due for aiding reconciliation of North and South by encouraging the idea of a common heritage of valor. After all, like Batchelder and McConaughy before them, the railroads, hostelers, souvenir dealers, guides, and others wanted to appeal to all regardless of their sectional sympathies. Typical of the promotion for Gettysburg is this statement from an 1885 railroad guidebook: "It is not intended that the narrative shall suggest the passion of the conflict, nor rouse in the least the bitter feelings which separated the men on Cemetery Hill from those on Seminary Ridge during the sad days of July, 1863." Yet at the same time, the market contributed to national amnesia of the war's lingering racial issues.[55]

Finally, Gettysburg and the great fairs are linked to America's Victorian commercial culture perhaps best expressed in the middle-class parlor display. Both Gettysburg and the fairs rose as the parlor, the essence of Victorian culture, reached its peak. The typical parlor's kitsch, books, artwork, and natural specimens collapsed the world into objects and reflected the moral elevation and cosmopolitan character of their owners. Parlors were, then, "memory palaces" stuffed with totems of the world's attainments, while the act of adornment itself was equated with progress. Like lookouts, panoramas, and scenic photography, parlors provided a "view" on the world. They miniaturized, like other "memory palaces" of the period: the great fairs, which collapsed human achievement into a fairground, and the battlefield of Gettysburg, which some argued reduced the entire Civil War to a large collection of monuments.[56]

Both Gettysburg and the great fairs produced souvenirs that enhanced the "memory" function of many parlors. Souvenirs, prints, stereographs, and Bachelder's panoramic map all reduced Gettysburg for home use. When Henry and Charles Speece began producing miniatures of the monuments— that is, parlor kitsch—it was just as reasonable that the monuments on the field were giant replicas of the miniatures. In 1890 a tourist wrote to Bachelder (who in describing his panoramic map wrote, "Imagine yourself in a balloon two miles east of the town of Gettysburg") suggesting that important points on the battlefield should be color coded just like his map.[57]

All three memory palaces changed, however. At Gettysburg, the pleasure seeker increasingly replaced the genteel tourist, fairs featured more "midway" entertainment, and parlors and their kitsch faded in favor of less sentiment and greater function. Even parlor stereographs of edifying natural views devolved more and more into scenes showing people in comic situations. This change in parlor entertainment coincided precisely with the advent of Round Top Park at the nation's memory palace.[58]

The shrine at Gettysburg grew along with America's commercial culture,

as much a product of that world as the great exhibitions, railroads, department stores, and public amusements. Competition for display by veterans,
the town's development of tourism, the corporate drive for rail passengers,
and homogenizing urban spectacles pushed Gettysburg to the forefront of
American culture. Together, they had transformed Gettysburg into what
Daniel J. Boorstin labeled a "pseudo-event," significant because the media
and merchandisers made it so. Of course, there were limits to the courtship
of the sacred and secular. The 1896 Supreme Court case restricting the
rights of the trolley seemed to affirm that the park had a special meaning
beyond the market. Yet even this meaning had changed from the years
immediately after the Civil War. No longer narrowly interpreted as the
death knell of treason or site of sublime contemplation, Gettysburg became
part of the story of America's abundance, unification, and national might.
Far from being forgotten in the hoopla, the story of the battle found a
staunch ally in the marketplace. The trouble was, as a product of the market that hummed by masking its unpleasant inner workings, Gettysburg was
another illusion that eclipsed the fundamental issues of race and freedom
that propelled the war and continued to linger.[59]

Chapter Four

☆ ☆ ☆ ☆ ☆ ☆ ☆ ☆ ☆ ☆

A Place for Tourists and the Oppressed

IN 1886 A NEW HISTORY of Adams County, Pennsylvania, described the county seat of Gettysburg as a "National Mecca" whose renown had "spread all over the civilized world." The author cited features appealing to both refined and popular tastes, including the battlefield park's "broad avenues" and "imposing landscapes" as well as "the park on Little Round Top." This combination made Gettysburg "one of the most inviting places to the tourist and the oppressed in the great cities, and pleasure seekers in the world." Published as the development of two distinct parks progressed, one by the railroad for amusement, and the other by the GBMA for edification, the text presciently described the types of pilgrims the shrine would host for the next three decades. Because Gettysburg offered something for everybody, it served as "a favorite resort to all."[1]

The new types of pilgrims—middle-class tourists, wage-earning excursionists, and veterans—brought vitality to Gettysburg lacking in their genteel predecessors. The new middle class clung to edification and self-improvement while expressing exuberance through leisure. Just as earlier tourists had embraced tools to improve their scenic gaze, the new middle class welcomed devices such as trolleys, avenues, bicycles, or cameras, which transformed tourism into recreation. Below them the lower classes used Gettysburg to escape industrial routine, ironically often bringing premodern forms of celebration to this modern resort. For veterans, Gettysburg sanitized personal as well as collective memories. Whether visitors experienced Gettysburg by rail or through other commercial venues, its reproduction transformed the battle into both glorious memory and amusement.

The new visitors were drawn by more than simply the spreading Gettysburg image. The other key variable that transformed Gettysburg was the increased leisure made possible by American industry. While the nation's remarkable advances in manufacturing reduced production jobs to specialized tasks, as compensation it reoriented Americans from producerism toward a new ethic of consuming goods and experiences. Enjoying decreased working hours and increased income, working-class Americans flocked to ball parks, amusement parks, playhouses, movie theaters, and excursion destinations like Round Top Park. The new commercial venues offering instant gratification presented alternatives to institutions such as libraries, art galleries, museums, cemeteries, and parks like the embellished battlefield. Increasingly, the genteel order that had dominated most of the nineteenth century failed to satisfy a burgeoning industrial populace with newfound money and time. Gettysburg's park for merrymaking alongside a park designed to impart moral lessons accounted for the shrine's broad-based appeal.[2]

While a sharp boundary separated Gettysburg's arenas for contemplation and fun, the behavior of middle- and working-class visitors sometimes overlapped. New white-collar workers as well as youths straining to escape the constraints of gentility sought vigorous activity as an antidote to increasing pace and routine. Some elders shook their heads over the new exuberance, considering it a sign of moral decline. Comparing the world of the 1860s with America in 1900, one veteran despaired that people appeared "restless and uneasy unless they are being continually saturated with abnormal and unwholesome pleasures, luxuries and unnatural excitement." Violent spectator sports and literature, strenuous outdoor activity, exotic dances, and parks designed for amusement instead of uplift moved toward center stage of American life.[3]

In some respects, distinctions among the three primary types of pilgrims during the railroad era—middle-class tourists, excursionists, and veterans— are arbitrary. Most arrived in clusters as members of organizations rather than in private family groups. Many of the working class of the time absorbed or at least affected middle-class mores. As for the third type of visitor, veterans represented a discrete group, though they hailed from a range of social classes just as they had during the war. Yet clues help identify the class status of visitors. Most working-class people could not afford an extended holiday, but might enjoy a day's outing by taking advantage of reduced railroad fares. The middle class could afford lodging and new recreational equipment such as bicycles and cameras. And while middle-class travelers might occasionally write about a trip to Gettysburg, working-class excursionists left few reminiscences of their visit. Finally, working-class visitors often brought with them premodern forms of celebration that contrasted with middle-class activities.[4]

Middle-Class Tourists

In 1888 a writer in *Grand Army Review* termed the visitors to "Glorious" Gettysburg "reverent pilgrims who imbibe patriotism with the mountain air and superb scenery." Genteel touring clearly continued into the era of rail, monuments, and amusements. But the economics of tourism reflected not an ascent of the genteel resort but decline. Gettysburg's representative attraction for genteel respose, the Gettysburg Springs Hotel, suspended business in the 1890s as middle-class travelers sought more vigorous vacations, railroads improved access to restful seaside resorts, and brief excursions to the battlefield skyrocketed.[5]

Improved transportation may have changed the composition of travelers to Gettysburg, but some visitors continued to find the sublime in the landscape. A visitor in 1899 wrote of his sense of being overwhelmed at Gettysburg was much like the ocean's sublime effect on a genteel observer. Admitting he had visited Gettysburg six times, the tourist noted, "[I]t always seems like going inland to the sea; so great is it, so boundless in the reach of its blessed influences that, like ocean waves, roll out to break upon the most distant shores." He found the divine presence at Gettysburg an emotional experience that dwarfed human enterprise, writing "Ah! Let us close up our little books, fold up our little papers—our little voices be stilled in this mighty presence."[6]

Such genteel commentary grew increasingly rare, although the pursuit of uplift lingered. Aspirants to middle-class status—the new white-collar workers of industrialization—were expected to exhibit interest in edifying sights. Middle-class tourists perceived the battlefield through a variety of props that masked entertainment with a patina of uplift, starting with the railroad. As railroad executives were well aware, passengers purchased experience as well as efficient transportation. Railroad cars presented the moving sweep of scenery prized in parlors, tourism, and panoramic and landscape art. Responding with aesthetic sensitivity characteristic of earlier tourists, a passenger crossing South Mountain into Gettysburg in 1894 noted the "grand and beautiful scenery," with "mountains from either side clothed in the colors of the fairies, a pretty dark green." The railroad's continuous panorama might also improve historical appreciation of the landscape. "Could we have a better pictorial view of history than the Gettysburg breakfast-table on the railroad train?" asked Major General O. O. Howard in 1890.[7]

Middle-class travelers took advantage of railroad package tours that combined efficiency with value by including Gettysburg among other edifying sights such as Luray Caverns and Washington, D.C. For many parsimonious souls, the promise of an uplifting experience justified the expense of luxuries such as Pullman and refreshment cars. Middle-class members who formerly had stayed home began traveling because of the railroad's marketing to special groups. Single women, ordinarily proscribed from travel by moral strictures, were encouraged to ride the rails to Gettysburg on the Pennsylvania Railroad's chaperoned tours. The first of these, a winter excursion chaperoned by a Mr. Van Pelt and Miss Beatty, arrived just after Christmas in

FIGURE 15. Passengers on an 1891 Pennsylvania Railroad package tour that included Gettysburg, Luray Caverns, and Natural Bridge (AR 133.a, "1891 Pennsylvania Tour," William L. Clements Library, University of Michigan)

1894 at the Eagle Hotel. In the flying snow next morning, the women toured the battlefield in sleighs, bundled in blankets, and "looking like a tribe of Indians," according to the *Gettysburg Star and Sentinel*, and "as merry as a lot of schoolchildren."[8]

The railroad stimulated travelers' imagination: "The approach to town by rail is made picturesque by the sudden appearance of equestrian and other statuary," a writer in *Harper's Weekly* observed in 1901, "producing an effect rather startling." Once on the field, the collection of sculptures interested many tourists, who found them a fantasia of monstrous shapes. By the time most monuments had been added, the rural cemetery's value to public uplift had declined and the battlefield's monuments tended to entertain. Even the 1899 annual report of the park commissioners admitted, "This is already the best marked field in the world, and all who come to see it are *surprised and delighted*" (italics added) by the fairy land of Brobdingnagian soldiers, horses, canteens, bullets, and other sculptures. The sheer tonnage of monuments in a variety of styles was termed by one visitor "stupefying." Heightened interest in real-life adventure and action transferred into realism in art, which, when commissioned by veterans to commemorate their participation in the battle, animated the field. Comparing the staid formality of Père Lachaise in Paris to the "living monuments" of Gettysburg, a tourist commented, "Everywhere upon that great, great battlefield one sees the soldier in action," and the effect "brought the blood tingling to our faces."[9]

Under the guise of improvement, middle-class tourists also discovered titillation in mechanical additions to the landscape. Like the railroad, the towers, avenues, and trolley could stimulate and amuse while aiding appreciation of scenery. Though latter-day preservationists viewed the trolley as a heinous intrusion on sacred ground, for Victorian visitors it improved access and perspective on the landscape. For some, it updated the quest for scenery by enlisting modern transportation technology. After all, the juxtaposition of nature and technology proved popular at tourist attractions such as Niagara Falls or Mount Washington. In 1899, a group of Pennsylvania teachers holding a meeting in Gettysburg took the trolley ride six times, and one thought the trolley ride made the battlefield reveal its divine purpose. As he sped along, he saw "the radiant and perfect rainbow of promise flung upon the black storm cloud of war [and] the memorials that crowd the wondrous field coming one by one within that glorious arc of light."[10]

While the trolley may have aroused the aesthetic sensibility of middle-class tourists, it also placed the park within reach of working-class excursionists. Before the trolley's construction in 1893, all arriving by rail were at the mercy of hackmen who often raised their rates when crowds swelled. While a hack and guide cost visitors six dollars, a twenty-five-cent guided-trolley tour provided a rapid and entertaining orientation to the landscape. Not for nothing did Gettysburg hackmen, guides, and livery businessmen unite in opposition to the trolley. When in 1896 the U.S. Supreme Court forced the trolley only to move its tracks, the New York Sun cheered that "[t]o the innumerable pilgrims who visit Gettysburg the decision will insure the continued opportunity which they could not otherwise enjoy of seeing the battlefield."[11]

Like the railroad, the trolley gave all visitors a chance to momentarily invert the industrial order of modern life. Visitors could transform a machine into fun as at an amusement park. Moreover, while the trolley's cooling breeze in transit provided refreshment on muggy days, its touring platform also allowed visitors freedom not available with a guide. "One can get off at any point, and walk about, and wait for the next car," a veteran remarked. As for the trolley's desecrating effects, that appears to be a late-twentieth-century invention. Instead of finding railroad and trolley a visual offense, visitors viewed the technology as complete mastery of the shrine. An editorial in the Baltimore Sun in 1896 found the memorialization work of the GBMA more pernicious to the battlefield than the trolley. "The great, wide avenues, laid out for the purpose of making different battle points accessible, change the scene from its original appearance a thousand-fold more than the little electric railroad." Signs of progress, important to a nation destined for greatness, enhanced the scene of a national shrine where past flowed through present and into the future.[12]

Middle-class visitors found stimulus not only in trolley and train. Five dominating steel towers, erected by the War Department in the 1890s, provided strenuous activity along with a commanding view of the landscape relished by the middle class. Scrambling to the top of the towers became part of the Gettysburg tourist itinerary. "No visit is complete without going to the summit of Big Round Top and then climbing to the top of the 100-foot tower, from whence he has a complete view of the entire battlefield and lines," a visitor commented in 1908. One of the battlefield commissioners, William Robbins, scaled to the top of Big Round Top tower with a judge, his wife, and his daughter, where father and daughter busied themselves by snapping scenic photos with their new camera. Gaining in affordability and popularity through the 1890s, the portable camera permitted tourists to "freeze" memories of a break from routine but doomed battlefield photographers who had set up shop at popular spots.[13]

By the early 1890s, the middle-class urge to escape gentility's smothering folds added to improved bicycle design produced a national cycling mania. Part of this middle-class vogue resulted from the bicycle's freedom of travel, unconfined by railroad schedules and jostling fellow passengers. Cyclists escaped to the countryside en masse, spurred on by advice columns in outdoor magazines and newspapers. The craze arrived in the 1890s, when the number of cycling tourists prompted the Gettysburg Star and Sentinel to predict, "It is clearly apparent that the day of the horse is about to end. . . . Bicycle parties are the popular feature everywhere."[14]

Like Central Park, the avenues constructed at Gettysburg were well known for recreational trotting—"a paradise for driving," as a newspaper stated—but wheelmen also found the smooth roads an oasis for cycling. The headline of a short-lived Gettysburg newspaper, The *Battlefield*, blared in 1896, "The Bicycle Circuits of Gettysburg: The Finest Boulevards in the World—Better than those of London, Paris, and New York." Combining sport with edification could succeed as a leisure pursuit for middle-class cyclists, at least enough to justify a day of riding at Gettysburg. But Gettysburg also attracted amateur daredevils and stuntmen who careened down the sleek slope of Little Round Top—sometimes unsuccessfully.[15]

Most wheelmen simply wanted to peddle, and on the day riders enjoyed respite from work, Sunday, hundreds could be seen whirling down the park's avenues. Often groups pressed for time would ride the train into Gettysburg, spend the day awheel, and then depart by rail. Presaging problems brought by the automobile in the next century, cyclists caused accidents by frightening horses or crashing into pedestrians, sometimes injuring themselves in the process. In 1897, the same year the town installed bike racks in response to the new touring market, the park commissioners posted special "Bicycle Rules" requiring bells, lights, and dismounting near restive horses. The rules also forbade stunts such as swerving, not using the handlebars, and, with remarkable understatement, "playing musical instruments" while riding. Bicycles posed the extreme challenge by middle-class tourists to the genteel park. The flexibility of cycling foreshadowed other recreational activities, such as hiking, horseback riding, and cross-country skiing, in the next century that blended the quest for landscape with physical activity.[16]

Gettysburg offered more than simply scenery where an important battle occurred. For the middle-class tourist, it combined many elements—scenery, amusing rides, recreation, fantastic landscape, and thrilling stories—that made it interesting. With life growing ever more fragmented in the workaday world, Gettysburg offered an integrating experience of release tempered by an ambience of uplift. The image of Gettysburg, seen in a million postcards as a landscape full of heroism and myth, offered perfect cover for fun under the guise of elevation.[17]

"Day-Trippers"

If the new middle-class visitors mixed remembrance with play, working-class excursionists generally played without remembrance. Cultural control by the genteel elite affected most of these people only dimly, and many continued traditional cultural practices. In some ways, plebeian excursionists brought to Gettysburg by rail recalled the gawkers who descended on the smoking battlefield in 1863. Whether rural or urban, they nurtured no pretenses about self-improvement through leisure, instead seeking immediate release from humdrum lives. In the years immediately after the battle, excursionists arrived for picnics on Culp's Hill or Little Round Top by the existing Hanover and Gettysburg line. But when the new railroad arrived in 1884, the size of excursions, their frequency, and the type of excursionists changed. Once Round Top Park opened that summer, the local newspapers reported five or more excursions a week instead of one, sometimes bringing black as well as white visitors.

In building the new Gettysburg line, along with a park to attract excursionists, railroad officials realized that invigorating plebeian interest in Gettysburg required more than a park for pensive sauntering. For decades, the urban working class had chosen as leisure haunts "pleasure gardens" with dancing, fireworks, and other entertainments over rural cemeteries designed to elevate public taste. Like the new middle class, working-class day-trippers—called the "shoe box" crowd by the people of Gettysburg because they brought their own food—used Gettysburg to mask play through pilgrimage. The excursionist presence was evident in notices forbidding "indulging in pic-nics, or merry making of a nature inconsistent with the solemn and sacred associations of this field forever consecrated to patriotism."[18]

Although railroads regularly promoted Gettysburg excursions, the era's ubiquitous fraternal or religious organizations also mounted them to raise revenue. Sponsoring groups with Byzantine monikers such as the Improved Order of Heptasophs or Knights of the Golden Eagle generally did not require of excursionists membership in the organization. Until outlawed in 1914, organizations could obtain special rates from the railroad, sell excursion tickets at a higher fee, then pocket the difference. Sometimes, as in the case of excursions from Philadelphia or black excursions from Baltimore, day-trippers numbered upwards of five to seven thousand.[19]

Paralleling the nation's postwar industrialization as the century progressed, excursions to Gettysburg grew more efficient. With railroads requiring ever greater numbers and drawing new types of passengers, excursions lost the ritualistic flourishes that signaled their presence on sacred ground. Few anymore bothered to commemorate their visit with a band-led march through town to the Soldiers' National Cemetery. Instead, as excursion trains steamed in to Gettysburg, they wound onto the spur that crossed the battlefield and terminated at Round Top Park. Commemorative activity varied depending on the group. Religious organizations might enjoy a picnic, scramble around the rocks on Little Round Top and Devil's Den, and then sightsee in the afternoon. Open excursion groups were more mechanistic. Following promotion in Philadelphia papers, the railroads brought 7,094 excursionists one Sunday in 1897. As advertised, the reputable guide James T. Long delivered a lecture to "a dense mass of humanity" at the High Water Mark while other throngs jammed the trolley cars.[20]

Many day-trippers seemed to care little about the significance of the ground, however. "Not have enough time here?" responded a Newark, New Jersey, excursionist when asked if the six hours sandwiched between train travel were sufficient to see the battlefield. "Why it's nothing but a grave-yard anyway. I could see it all in ten minutes." A group sponsored by the United Brewers' Association disembarked in Gettysburg and immediately made a beeline to the nearby Firemen's Festival without exploring the bat-tlefield until later. When the Gettysburg cyclorama and then a moving picture theater came to town, they served as additional attractions for the attention of day-trippers. In 1915, over three thousand excursionists, "most of them young men and women, out for a day's pleasure," according to the *Adams County News*, enjoyed themselves by writing postcards and flitting between the battlefield, cyclorama, and movie theater. While Gettysburg businessmen appreciated day-tripper dollars, some townspeople expressed dismay at other mementos left behind by excursionists, such as litter, van-dalized monuments, alcohol-related incidents, or tobacco juice (sometimes splattering women's dresses).[21]

Because most excursions no longer connected individuals to the sacred ground through group rituals, day-trippers had greater personal flexibility. Round Top Park, three miles south of town and beyond authoritarian con-trol, served as a key attraction for excursionists, as it provided them an opportunity to avoid the battlefield completely. Many exclusively patron-ized the refreshment stands, dancing pavilion, and other attractions that occasionally appeared, such as a shooting gallery or flying horses. Some-times, groups found the park a convenient place for lubricating fun with alcohol, exploring carnivalesque behavior over the edge of respectability. When the King David Masonic Lodge arrived from Baltimore with 1,014 passengers, members "brought a large quantity of beer for their own use, but it was practically free and the bad effect of such an arrangement was appar-ent, particularly among the boys." Clever excursion groups found ways to circumvent alcohol regulations. A group arriving in 1895 parked its refresh-ment car in town so as not to violate Sunday liquor laws at Round Top Park. Nevertheless, "beer was openly dispensed on Sunday" in the park because the excursionists had thoughtfully sent ahead twelve kegs of beer the previous day.[22]

The possibilities of Gettysburg, where one might slide from a pleasure park to a memorial park and back again, attracted Baltimore black excur-sionists. The absence of African Americans in park documentation gener-ated by administrators or veterans' organizations does not mean blacks did not visit Gettysburg. It is true that in the twentieth century's age of auto-mobile tourism, blacks have comprised a small percentage of the total num-ber of tourists. But a close examination of black and white newspaper arti-cles, squibs, and advertisements during the age of rail reveals a rich story of black visitation. Their experience permits an examination of how this "in-visible" minority used a commercially shaped national shrine for its own

FIGURE 16. African American visitors pose at Devil's Den ca. 1890s (Pennsylvania African-American Photographs, no. 11426, Albert and Shirley Small Special Collections Library, University of Virginia Library)

ends, and how the shrine in turn used blacks to unify whites. At the same time, the story of black excursionists permits a glimpse of how blacks celebrated in the new arena of commercial leisure, and how this traditional celebration clashed with expectations both of whites and of the black leadership.[23]

From 1880, when the first excursion of "colored waiters" disembarked, and especially after Round Top Park's construction until the advent of World War I, black excursionists from Baltimore arrived at Gettysburg frequently during the season. As the nineteenth-century's "black capital," with eighty thousand African Americans by 1900, Baltimore featured a plethora of black benevolent organizations, secret societies, and church groups. With black leadership urging middle-class virtues as a path to progress, these organizations sponsored a variety of charitable programs as well as lyceums and schools for purposeful self-improvement. At the same time, the one-time coexistence of slaves and free blacks in Baltimore had spawned a number of traditional plebeian black-owned leisure establishments such as grog shops and gambling dens. As did white organizations, black groups supported their benevolent activities by sponsoring both "moonlight" and day excursions to resorts such as Havre de Grace, Brown's Grove, and Round Bay, Maryland. Further afield, black organizations such as Galilean Fishermen, the Primrose Social and Delmonico Circle, or Brilliant Star Pasture of the United Order of Nazarenes journeyed to excursion points at York, in Pennsylvania, Pen-Mar, in Maryland, and Round Top Park. For these groups, Gettysburg served as a novel destination to escape the miasma of Baltimore.[24]

But Gettysburg possessed special significance for the largest and most sustained Baltimore black excursion to Round Top Park. Although the date of celebrating slave emancipation varied widely according to region, Baltimore's black GAR posts sponsored an annual Gettysburg excursion in September commemorating the 1862 preliminary Emancipation Proclamation. Like the GAR nationwide, Baltimore's black Lincoln, Guy, and Logan posts had grown remarkably in the late 1880s. For two decades beginning in the 1890s, the outing that sometimes attracted more than seven thousand blacks into Gettysburg raised funds for the posts' benevolent aid to veterans' widows and orphans. The railroad opened Round Top Park on a September "off day" of Monday for the celebration to avoid racial commingling.[25]

Recognized as the war's turning point and subject of President Lincoln's famed "new birth of freedom" address, Gettysburg might at least have been acknowledged as an important symbol of emancipation. Although the British *Northern Whig* commented in 1885 that "the tablets at Gettysburg commemorate one of the most significant events of the present century—the death of slavery and the dawn of civil liberty," such recognition was absent in American addresses about the battle's significance. To the contrary, Gettysburg became a special place to reunite white Northerners and Southerners under the banner of common Anglo-Saxon valor. Gettysburg's symbols of shared heroism in stone, rituals, and festivities contributed to national amnesia of the war's lingering racial issues. Moreover, Gettysburg presented a bad layout for black visitation, and the sacred ground itself reinforced white superiority. The town's Democratic paper continually stirred racial animosity, and townspeople showed little sympathy for black equality. Every black excursion that included dissipation or violence received detailed coverage and censure by the local press. Amusement at the park sometimes painfully reinforced racial caricatures and stereotypes. Fun at the expense of blacks resembled the "coon dunks" and "free watermelon days" at the era's great fairs or amusement parks. White tourists, for example, enjoyed chuckling over black jittering, drunkenness, and cakewalks at Round Top Park, or gawking at black excursionists. In 1899, two Philadelphians hosted a watermelon-eating contest for blacks near Devil's Den, where a crowd gathered to watch the eight contestants. According to the *Gettysburg Star and Sentinel*, "Some of the spectators laughed at the funny spectacle until they cried."[26]

Mindful of demonstrating black worthiness, dignity, and morality, black leaders expressed ambivalence about celebrations and excursions in Baltimore's sober *Afro-American* and *Ledger* (merged as the *African-American Ledger* in 1900). On the one hand, they realized that annual celebrations of black emancipation could perpetuate its memory. And with their embrace of refinement as a means to progress, black leaders believed excursions to natural areas might elevate the race. Baltimore's black community, in fact, funded a Free Excursion Society that subsidized excursions for poor women and children. But on the other hand, excursions and celebrations contradicted middle-class virtues of industry, thrift, and sobriety. Black Baltimore featured a number of strong reform organizations dedicated to elevating blacks to a middle-class standard. Again and again the black papers condemned excursions as a waste of valuable resources and celebrations as excuses for license. Estimating in 1899 that blacks had squandered millions on excursions, The *Ledger* stated that "added to this enormous amount is the cost for string bands and regalia, to say nothing of the many fights, police court scrapes, broken limbs, and the character of girls who have been ruined on these excursions, together with the demoralizing effect in general." By the lights of black progressives, excursions in reality chained blacks under the guise of freedom and hindered their advancement. Baltimore's African Methodist Episcopal ministers in 1905 resolved that "excursions heretofore given for and by our people have not been conducive to their moral improvement" and urged abstention.[27]

While incidents related to the Gettysburg excursions bore witness to black concerns, the success of the annual emancipation-day outing ensured their continuation. The parties ranked as the largest ever to arrive in Gettysburg and were alleged by the *Baltimore Sun* to be the largest ever run out of Baltimore. For example, the 1903 excursion brought seventy-four coaches arriving over a four-hour period. "There was a continuous mass of colored humanity from the Western Maryland Station to the Public Square," according to the *Gettysburg Star and Sentinel*. Every conveyance in town was pressed into service, the trolley used every inch of standing room, and several well-lathered horses died under the burden of work. Estimating that the excursion cost ten thousand dollars, the *Afro-American Ledger* pointed to the foolishness of the GAR charity that returned perhaps 10 percent to the black community. "Can we afford such extravagance as to spend ten thousand dollars for one day's pleasure? We think not," the *Ledger* declared.[28]

The outings proved popular because the excursionists enjoyed a good time at Gettysburg. Whether the GAR featured commemorative activity honoring emancipation during the excursion cannot be determined from existing sources, but some black excursionists did engage in sightseeing among the monuments. Most, however, spent the day at Round Top Park and many filtered through town to patronize bars. While occasionally the Gettysburg press labeled the excursionists a "jolly bunch" or "a happy, reveling crowd," more often than not accounts reported "a scene of general debauch" or "Gettysburg Witnesses Annual Orgy." As long as the revelers confined themselves to Round Top Park, they escaped harsh censure, but when their merrymaking edged into town, it shocked the stolid burghers. Between 1909 and 1915, the papers reported such affronts to propriety as drunkenness, razor fights, brawls, vile language, pickpocketing, public urination, shootouts, gambling, and alcohol-related accidents. Particularly repulsive to white sensibilities were the "disgraceful scenes" acted out by black women, who got drunk, engaged in hatpin fights, and provided liquor to children. "It is a pitiful and humiliating scene," lamented the *Adams County News*, "to see a drunken man giving an exhibition of what is more becoming to a four-legged animal, but to see a drunken woman planted in the middle of Center Square half clad and wallering in the mud, is not pitiful, but about the most disgusting exhibition that any person would care look upon." Just before the Gettysburg emancipation celebrations came to an end during World War I, alarmed Gettysburg townspeople began preparing for excursion day by summoning state troopers and securing a court order to close all bars.[29]

Not only Gettysburg whites prone to racism displayed concern over excursionist antics. Baltimore's black press repeatedly abhorred the "rowdyism" and "very shameful and mortifying nature" of excursionist conduct, fully aware of its harmful effect on the race as well as race relations. "Allowing something for the usual exaggerating account of what takes place on a colored excursion, when the account is written up for the white press," the *Afro-American Ledger* commented in 1916, "it is quite true that many excursionists feel that an outing is a signal for all kinds of mischief, and it is not an enjoyable occasion unless they 'let themselves go.'" To be sure, only a tiny percentage of the black thousands who descended on Gettysburg were responsible for the excess. Still, excursionists focused the celebration on revelry and imbibing. Following years of experience with the holiday, a Gettysburg paper commented after town bars were closed to excursionists in 1916, "A celebration of Emancipation Day without some good spirits is no celebration at all, in the minds of not a few of the celebrators."[30]

Yet it was precisely the opportunity to celebrate that made Gettysburg attractive as an excursion destination. The battlefield's significance to the war made it an appropriate spot for black veterans to commemorate emancipation. Beyond its symbolic value, Gettysburg's distance from Baltimore, and the further isolation of Round Top Park, offered a unique arena for blacks to celebrate black freedom. Emancipation celebrations across the South originated in slave Christmas festivities that had followed harvest and featured libation, exuberance, and carnality, a legacy of premodern Europe that permitted a topsy-turvy world of frolic and license to temporarily prevail. Although violence among slaves often resulted, slave owners encouraged the annual release from drudgery as a safety valve for the slave system. Because owners furnished alcohol and suspended daily routine for the holiday, to slaves they appeared benevolent and deserving of continuing loyalty. Moreover, as Frederick Douglass realized, this temporary inversion tricked blacks into confusing "a dose of vicious dissipation" with freedom. After this faux liberty sunk them to the depths of degradation, Douglass argued, they happily returned to subservient status, thankful for their master's paternalism. The *Afro-American Ledger* reintroduced Douglass's theme for free blacks living in industrial society. The paper observed that while the consumer spree—for leisure or display goods—offered temporary release, it robbed blacks of money, time, and dignity, and in the end only served to reaffirm the racial hierarchy.[31]

As a holiday celebration familiar to most blacks, Christmas offered the traditions on which to mold their own emancipation festivities. Although this form of roistering grew increasingly archaic with the tame and the orderly celebrating of the industrial era, it persisted in the rural postwar South. But in urban Baltimore, with its progressive black leadership eager to erase the marks of slavery and adopt elevating middle-class habits, such traditions came under increasing censure. Paradoxically, an excursion to Gettysburg allowed the continued practice of familiar holiday forms within the structure of commercial leisure, away from the reproachful gaze of elders. For excursionists, the Gettysburg battlefield's importance rested not in its symbolic significance as a struggle that ensured emancipation, but in a literal freedom from authoritarian pressure urging self-denial, restraint, and self-discipline. At Gettysburg, blacks could not only escape the city, but break boundaries just as white excursionists and middle-class tourists broke boundaries. Following embarrassing incidents in 1916, the *Afro-American Ledger* lamented about excursionists, "The fact that they are in a strange town, where they do not meet the reproving glances of friends they respect, seems to relieve them of all responsibilities to be self-respecting and decent."[32]

Black leaders not only objected that excursion celebrations were a legacy of slavery that perpetuated dependency and racial subordination. When representatives of the black community "cut up all kinds of shines" among whites, as the *Afro-American Ledger* put it, they stigmatized the entire black race. "Good behavior will gain for us what voting never can secure," the paper remarked. Separated by their revelry, eyed by tourists and townspeople as a curiosity, and labeled as brutes, degenerates, and simpletons, black excursionists reinforced white racial attitudes. Their archaic form of celebrating did not measure up to the modern standard of commercial culture, which helped push them outside Gettysburg's commemorative purview and aided the white monopoly of the memorial. As a place where whites might mingle as a privileged group sharing pride of white accomplishment and propriety (excepting the occasional tippling trippers), Gettysburg served as a unifying force. Yet this status of "Americanness" rested on the contrast with the alien "other" unable to observe behavioral codes.[33]

Although affiliated with the latest transportation technology and marketing, the black emancipation celebrations represent one of the few examples of persisting noncommercial leisure at Gettysburg. The excursions provide an intriguing example of folk celebration surviving because of its alliance with commercial culture. While Gettysburg provides an example of how the market helped transform the war's lingering racial issues into a safe preoccupation with white valor, the market also worked in the other direction. Both the black GAR posts and Gettysburg merchants were reluctant to end the excursions because of their profitability. And when as early as 1894 Gettysburg church congregations asked the railroad to stop black excursions, the general manager of the railroad refused, explaining that "it would be difficult under the provisions of the Interstate Commerce Law to discriminate against this particular class." Again with some irony, it was not the sacred, but the secular, aspects of Gettysburg that worked to counter racial discrimination. "Their quarter or dime is as good as anybody else['s]" a black wrote to the *Afro-American*, and when propriety discouraged excursionists, the market welcomed their dollars. Their archaic form of celebrating, however, had a parallel among the group of visitors one might least likely expect: veterans.[34]

Veterans: Memory and Play

The surge of Union veterans to Gettysburg beginning around 1880 mirrored a national revival of interest in the Civil War. Until death slowed the flow of aging veterans to a trickle after World War I, thousands of veterans came to Gettysburg annually during the season. They arrived on a wide variety of missions and represented a range of backgrounds and social classes. Although almost all were organized in groups, many brought family members with them. Some came with regimental survivors' organizations to dedicate monuments or revisit established monuments. Many returned to participate in reunions of corps, brigades, and regiments or in anniversary reunions of the battle, which also hosted Confederate veterans. A number of Union veteran groups made annual pilgrimages to Gettysburg. The GAR's Department of Pennsylvania, for example, held annual encampments on the battlefield from the late 1870s until 1894, and intermittently thereafter. All helped develop Gettysburg as a therapeutic place to readjust wartime memories, reconnect with bygone youth, or temporarily invert the status quo.

Gettysburg's expanding image in the late-nineteenth century heightened veterans' sense of the park as sacred ground. The press consistently referred to returning veterans as "pilgrims," and many were as devout. One called the trip a "holy journey." Another visiting with the 15th Massachusetts Regiment Association in 1900 remembered that "a deep hush" fell over the group during its first stop at East Cemetery Hill. "We felt the presence of that spirit host whose blood had moistened and hallowed the ground on

FIGURE 17. Dedication of the monument of the 124th New York. In the late-nineteenth century, scenes like this were repeated hundreds of times, and veterans frequently returned afterward to visit their monument. Note band on the left, heroic pose of statue, the abundance of cut canes, and the "fakir" on the right selling relics (no. 31, William Tipton Album, William L. Clements Library, University of Michigan)

which we stood." Like the medieval shrine whose association with the saintly could generate miracles, Gettysburg might serve as the veterans' holy font. If the shrine could guarantee immortality, it could surely restore the body as well as the spirit. A past departmental commander of the GAR called Gettysburg an "elixir" for aging veterans, and another veteran wrote to the *National Tribune* that "being like the average old soldier, somewhat in need of repairs," his physician advised "to try his never failing cure—a trip to Gettysburg."[35]

Yet for all their reverence, veterans coveted the illumination Gettysburg's sacred aura cast on them. "When other battles, notable as many were, lose their significance, the memory of Gettysburg will never die," the *Grand Army Review* asserted in 1886. GAR members were convinced that the Civil War sealed the United States' destiny as the millennial republic. The combination of civil religion extolling Gettysburg as the Armageddon of civilization and market-generated promotion magnified the role of those who fought there. Gettysburg's cachet rose to such heights that the father of a boy slain at Perryville insisted by the 1880s that his son had died at Gettysburg. "No matter where he rendered help or how he performed his service," Pennsylvania Governor and veteran James A. Beaver said in a 1905 speech, "it is enough for any survivor of the battle to say, 'I was at Gettysburg.'"[36]

Gettysburg boosted veterans' self-importance in proportion to the battle's distended image. Veterans arriving for monument dedications, reunions, or encampments were bombarded with encomiums. Parades, rituals, and in particular GAR uniforms enabled veterans inured to the monotony of workshop or farm to temporarily wield an authoritarian role. "A sufficient number of captains and majors are running around loose to make a corps, and the colonel and general straps are plentiful enough to fill the necessary quota of a brigade," a New York Herald correspondent wryly noted at the 1888 reunion. "In fact the private soldier is like the accommodations—hard to find." Like the regiments who erected monuments but saw no action, or squabbled over more visible display space for their monuments, veterans scrambled for position in the hierarchy of glory. A satiric account of two veterans meeting during the twenty-fifth reunion in 1888 suggests how they strained to fall under Gettysburg's halo:

> "Now, then Jim, where were you?"
> "Well, our sutler wagon was way off here, say about twelve miles."
> "Where were you?"
> "I was with the wagon train off this way, about seven miles."
> "Say, we've got this thing down to a dot and we ought to write a letter to some newspaper."
> "Z'actly, Jim, and we can't do it too soon. It's left to us to straighten out this tangle, and we are the men to do it."[37]

As change in the late-nineteenth century grew more bewildering, veterans selectively reshuffled wartime memories. Amazed at the discontinuity with the past, Major General Daniel E. Sickles commented, "The transition from 1863 to 1890, little more than a quarter of a century, almost confounds the imagination, and makes the reality seem like a dream." Memories suppressed immediately after the war were now cleansed of pain and recycled. "The old 28th presents a large hold on my recollections," a New Yorker wrote in 1912, recounting marches and campaigns as "never to be forgotten events treasured away in the archives of memory." Reunions enabled veterans to readjust memories for present circumstances while reveling in their special status. At "Campfires" held by many reunion groups in the courthouse, participants indulged in reverie around bean soup, music, dancing, speeches, and sentimental anecdotes about campaigning. "With them it is war all the time," commented the *National Tribune* about veterans at the 1888 reunion. Gone altogether was the fear, discouragement, and war-weariness expressed in letters written during the war.[38]

Veterans had shaped the battlefield into a grand national parlor, or "memory palace," full of objects designed to recall the fighting. "From Culp's Hill to Round Top, the tragic story of those fateful days is told in enduring bronze and granite," a veteran wrote. "My mind went back to July 2, 1863," a veteran of the 95th Pennsylvania remembered as he paused at the base of his regiment's monument in 1899. "What a change right here! Peace and quietness reign supreme, but yonder monuments tell a sad, sad story." Devices such as cannon, avenues, towers, and trolley aided the softening of memories. Competitive monumental displays nestled within nature along with the latest advances in transportation and steel structure technology transformed past carnage into present valor. A veteran who climbed Big Round Top tower remembered, "We gazed down upon the rocks and trees, and could almost imagine we could see the gallant Farnsworth with his cavalry dashing into the Confederate lines to meet death."[39]

But monuments and other battlefield additions alone did not satisfy veterans trying to confirm identity and create congenial memories. Thanks to the GBMA and its successor, the Gettysburg Battlefield Commission (GBC), so much of the battlefield had been preserved that it created transition space for memories. Trenches and lunettes improved by the GBMA as well as bullet, shell marks, and deformed trees were promoted by veterans' organizations as a reason to return for reunions. "So well preserved are the features of the battlefield that any man engaged in the battle can readily pick out the spot where his command fought," the *Grand Army Scout and Soldiers' Mail* remarked. "Gettysburg can be visited with far more interest than any other battlefield." The landscape's power to shake loose memories of youth startled veterans. "I went over the ground in 1882 with Wilson and . . . my memory was as fresh and sure as when we fought there," Major General John R. Brooke crowed. Sometimes the jolt melted intervening decades, transporting veterans back to the scene of action. "I imagined that I heard again the order, 'Forward into action! Unlimber! Commence firing!'" recalled a former Confederate upon visiting the spot where his battery, the Georgia Troup Artillery, had served. "I imagined that shell and shrapnel were exploding in the trees around us, killing and wounding men and horses." The scenes appeared so vivid he "saw again the particular shell that exploded above me; I felt again the shock as it struck me."[40]

Memories that failed to dovetail with fresh perceptions produced uneasiness, as when in 1885 Major General Winfield Scott Hancock felt he had wrongly marked the spot of his wounding during a visit twenty years earlier. Veterans circumvented the problem of memory slippage by reaching group consensus. Accompanied by famed *Boston Transcript* correspondent Charles Carleton Coffin, about two hundred Massachusetts veterans returning in

1885 traversed every spot where they remembered fighting. As they "retold the pathetic incidents of deadly combat," the Bay Staters reenacted their battle formations, then visited barns and houses where some of them had lain when wounded. If a group could not reach agreement on memory, outside help might be solicited. Searching for a well at which all remembered drawing water, exasperated veterans of the 10th New York Battalion finally inquired at a nearby residence. When the owner informed them the well had been filled and showed them the spot, the veterans expressed appreciation for "much in the way of verification for which we were very grateful."[41]

Veterans sought out tangible reminders of the battle other than landscape. Relic hunting became a significant part of reunions that observers noticed from the first 1878 encampment to the great reunion in 1913. At the 1888 reunion, a *New York Times* correspondent commented that hundreds of veterans, "in couples or larger parties, walk the fields with heads bent as if hunting a trail." During the fiftieth reunion, National Guardsmen protected parts of the battlefield against digging and cutting, but according to an observer, every veteran took home one to a dozen relics nevertheless. Reminiscent of vandalism at rural cemeteries, not only remnants of war but chips of monuments and branches cut into canes proved popular. Nor was that all. Some old soldiers dug up small trees and bushes to plant at home, and at the 1913 reunion a veteran literally shoveled sacred ground into two suitcases he then shipped back to Iowa.[42]

Unlike other visitors, veterans did not acquire souvenirs only to possess part of the Gettysburg image or ease the transition back to everyday life after a pleasurable hiatus. Possession of a relic thought to be associated with a personal combat experience could authenticate that experience and reduce the battle's magnitude or horror. Defying park regulations, veterans believed exploiting the shrine for souvenirs demonstrated their ownership—which justified sacking it. "I don't care," one aged veteran replied to a reproach after he had removed part of a rock from Devil's Den. "I helped put that bundle of rocks into American history, and I guess I can now have a piece of 'em." Relics were capable of rescripting the past. Owning a relic meant that now the past could be controlled, evoked in a nonthreatening manner similar to the way in which the battlefield managed memories.[43]

Veterans most enthusiastic about relics were those who hunted them near their wartime posts. A Wisconsin veteran in 1888 dug near the boulder where he had been wounded, determined to find the bullet that maimed his wrist. When he failed, he vowed to return and continue the search the following day. During their 1885 visit a group of Connecticut veterans offered five dollars for the shell that had burrowed instead of bursting and killing them near their Culp's Hill position. Much to their delight, searchers moved a rock and found a shell the veterans pegged as "theirs." Against regulations, one of the battlefield commissioners, William M. Robbins, gave a fellow Tarheel a boost to cut off part of a tree under which the former Confederate remembered sheltering himself during July 3's bombardment.[44]

Like bones of saints, relics need not possess a pedigree if the bearer believes its authenticity. As the above examples suggest, the most generic specimens might be embraced by veterans as objects associated with their personal experience. One veteran approached in town by a boy selling relics was overjoyed at the self-assurance of finding among the treasures the knife he had lost on Little Round Top July 2. Rusty objects once intended to tear flesh and shatter bone could reduce a near-deadly experience to youthful adventure. Canes or other natural objects could be placed as just one of innumerable items competing in the parlor "memory palace." Major General Abner Doubleday, for example, had a piece of shell that tore through his hat and lodged in his collar turned into a paperweight. Used as a curiosity or bric-a-brac, a relic or souvenir became parlor clutter that could help relieve the burden of the past. Harmless and interesting tangible reminders of Gettysburg could accompany pleasant memories of glory days.[45]

Along with relics, souvenirs, and the battlefield, re-creations of combat served as another way veterans exercised control over their memories. The "elephant," as new Civil War recruits had referred to combat, could be tamed, enjoyed, and transformed into a playful mountain pony. Survivors' groups sometimes reenacted their combat role, as did the 20th Connecticut after dedicating its regimental monument in 1885. "The charge was executed with vigor and the cheering was first-class," the *Gettysburg Star and Sentinel* remarked, "but it was easier work than the one they were celebrating." Veterans also performed symbolic reenactments such as the recurring ritualistic march of Pickett's veterans to the High Water Mark, where they shook hands with former foes.

Pyrotechnical war could restore days of youth lost to dread, terror, and foreboding. Beginning in 1881, the Department of Pennsylvania GAR staged volcanic sham battles as a regular feature at its annual Gettysburg encampment. Often conducted in conjunction with other Gettysburg reunions and dedications, the battles attracted thousands of spectators. Although sometimes the veterans staged an additional battle in the town square (which in 1882 "aroused vivid memories of '63 in the minds of inhabitants"), usually the combatants squared off at twilight on East Cemetery and McKnight's Hill. Reintroducing the Civil War as entertaining pyrotechnics, opposing "Union" and "Confederate" forces engaged to the tune of martial music in dusk flared by hundreds of Roman candles, rockets, small cannon, and firecrackers. Veterans cheered as the battle lines swayed back and forth, both sides capturing prisoners, who were marched to the rear. Combat cleansed of horror evoked wartime memories. According to the veterans' *Grand Army Scout and Soldier's Mail*, at the 1884 battle "[t]he old soldiers among the spectators all agreed that the skirmish seemed very natural and like old times." This time, however, the action delivered what many initially had enlisted for: glory, adventure, and fun. As late as 1922, two 12th New Jersey veterans watching a National Guard reenactment of Pickett's Charge rushed to the wall, grabbed the rifles of two "fallen" guardsmen, and opened fire into the oncoming "Confederate" lines "with the cheers of onlookers."[46]

Almost every gathering of veterans included formal rituals such as parades, panoply, and speeches, but the old soldiers also engaged in play reminiscent of wartime camp activities. In a society growing increasingly atomized, play enabled veterans to reengage the youthful camaraderie of war without the tension. Their special status legitimized reversion to boyish behavior and enabled them to push the limits of propriety. "Here they enjoy themselves as they cannot any other place," the *Gettysburg Compiler* commented in 1886. At the first GAR encampment in 1878, organizers billed "camp sports" as part of the agenda to veterans still in the prime of life, but the term did not necessarily imply athletic events. In addition to a kind of football, veterans enjoyed hayrides, sack races, band concerts, balloon ascensions, picnics, and dances as well as less-reserved activities.[47]

Although veterans abandoned strenuous play as the years progressed, drinking, fireworks, and burlesque parades were perennial favorites. The Columbia Club, for example representing veterans from the Philadelphia Corn Exchange Regiment, annually set off tens of thousands of firecrackers in town, to the dismay of burgesses. In what may have been the first veterans' beer party at Gettysburg, four hundred veterans from a GAR post showed up in 1877, performed the usual rituals and sightseeing, then while quaffing ample amounts of "Lancaster beer" at the Springs Hotel, the "fiddle and bow were applied industriously." One hotel owner recalled employing a bartender day and night just to keep veterans supplied with beer during reunion weeks; a GAR member claimed the veterans brought enough booze with them to supply the people in Gettysburg as well as themselves. Yet for all the drinking, recorded incidents of intoxication were few in relation to the number of veterans, due perhaps in part to the GAR emphasis on self-control. Some playfulness that resulted in injury suggests festivities included alcohol, however. At the twenty-fifth anniversary of the battle, in a spirit of "misdirected fun," according to the *New York Times*, a prankster set fire to a straw bed on which several veterans slept and severely burned one. When Ohio dedicated its monuments in 1887, one veteran went home early after being injured in a spree of tossing display cannonballs back and forth. One of a group engaged in folderol at the 1894 Pennsylvania GAR encampment "became excited" and began "slashing about with a knife," slicing the limbs of surrounding comrades until tranquilized with a tent pole.[48]

But the use of alcohol usually served the ends of conviviality and frolic. Veterans returned again and again to Gettysburg because it combined a site of shared memories with a place where they could find release. Chill Hazzard, department commander of the Pennsylvania GAR, might have been speaking for all veterans when he said in 1898, "We want to go to Get-

FIGURE 18. Vendors and amusements on Cemetery Hill along the Baltimore Pike during the 1878 Department of Pennsylvania Grand Army of the Republic Encampment, 1878 (David Meskers collection)

tysburg . . . where every man can be amused from the time he steps from the train until he leaves the town." This insouciant spirit aided reconciliation between former foes. Beginning with McConaughy's 1869 reunion at the Springs Hotel, and then more successfully in the 1880s and culminating with the fiftieth reunion in 1913, a variety of Blue-Gray reunions invited Confederate veterans to Gettysburg. Southern attendance improved from two in 1869 to several hundred in 1888 to thousands in 1913. Yet festivities that welcomed former traitors with "a blaze of various colored lights, rockets and Roman candles" seemed in bad taste for some whose memory of a nation torn apart remained fresh. During the gala twenty-fifth reunion, the *New York Times* asked whether such reunions "do not tend to dull the keen sense of the righteousness involved in the war."[49]

Indeed, as apostles of order always have despaired, festivals erode rationality and, in this case, sectional self-righteousness. In the opinion of the *London Times*, the Gettysburg celebrations might be considered improper but nevertheless broke down old animosities. "If to some minds a spot on which 50,000 human lives were sacrificed may seem an equivocal scene for a festival," the paper commented in 1888, "they who have been holding it, at all events, have redeemed its grizzly horrors for a generous burial in its soil of old quarrels and old spites." Those who attended the reunions left with happy thoughts and fraternal feelings. "I spent four days with the boys in blue," a Virginia veteran wrote following the 1888 reunion. "I never enjoyed anything so well in my life." The festive atmosphere added levity missing in rituals and speeches. In 1913, a group of Virginia veterans armed with broomsticks, newspapers, and powder loaded two display cannon and set them off after midnight while wailing "Dixie." When the ensuing blasts brought many a somnambulant Yankee veteran staggering to the scene, the old Rebels marched around with torches singing other wartime Southern airs.[50]

These symbolic acts of reconciliation were grounded in deeper changes. From postwar America's rapid transformation emerged shared feeling among veterans that all who had proved their manhood during the war were worthy comrades in arms. As "alien strains" of eastern Europeans, certified as inferior by science of the day, poured into the country, veterans could share pride in the myth that Anglo-Saxon heroism forged a powerful new America. At the same time, relentless industrialization bred nostalgia for the passing of agrarian life that helped Northerners lament the Old South's demise. And from the psychological perspective of aging, the green and salad days of robust youth, however unpleasant when lived, increase in happiness proportionately with advancing years. Thus individual and collective memory shifted with time, and by the 1880s veterans North and South could celebrate martial valor without any discussion of the knotty issues that caused the war or their outcome.[51]

Tactics, courage, and gallantry could be played out nationally in the flood of books, serials, newspaper articles, veterans' organizations, and monuments. But Gettysburg was part of this management of memory. In its report of the fiftieth anniversary reunion, the state of Indiana termed the celebration "just one glad season of forgetfulness of the trials and hardships of the past." Trials and hardships disappeared among former enemies in banter about glory days; the war was reduced to an achievement in which only the exclusive club of Northern and Southern heroes could share. One former Confederate who found himself surrounded by Union veterans wrote, "It seemed to be a treat to these old vets to get a live Reb in a corner, and with him fight the great battle over again." At the 1887 reunion, a reporter noticed Union and Confederate veterans "wending their way across the former bloody battlefield, and were heard recalling thrilling memories of the desperate contest waged about the Clump of Trees, Cemetery Hill, Round Top and other points." Indeed, reconciliation required such a festival of cameraderie and fun. When an entrepreneur opened Richmond's grim Libby Prison as a Chicago tourist attraction, the *Boston Journal* shuddered that while veterans could never meet amicably at such a "dark and ghastly" place, "the veteran from the North and the veteran from the South can meet on fraternal terms at Gettysburg."[52]

The festive atmosphere also provided a stage for releasing social tension. The Department of Pennsylvania GAR included several posts around Philadelphia that had formed cliques they labeled "Lambs," "Razors," "Hawks," and "Goats" in deference to the monikers of Philadelphia clubs that mounted antimilitia parades in the antebellum era. By the 1880s, these cliques adopted simple but distinctive uniforms—specially colored shirts, pants, belts, and ties—they wore at Gettysburg. Their unofficial entertainment enlivened the GAR encampment for spectators and provided "a source of endless fun" for other veterans, according to the *Gettysburg Compiler*. The cliques took charge of hosting picnics, dances, and sack races, and played countless pranks. But they most delighted thousands of spectators packing Gettysburg's streets and East Cemetery Hill through antics that mocked military authority, regimentation, and ritual.[53]

At every Gettysburg encampment from 1878 to 1894, the groups staged burlesque parades and plays based on tradition, which they brought from Philadelphia. The common peoples' ridicule of authority during Philadelphia street festivals had emigrated with English colonists. In Philadelphia and other industrializing cities, working-class people blended elements of customary street burlesque with commercial theater to mock the powerful, a creaking militia system, or blacks. Often militia protesters adapted Christmas celebrations that involved carousing, caterwauling, and cacophony. Costumed, sometimes transvestite, revelers known as "fantasticals" and "callithumpians" pounded away on pots or blew horns, demanding "treats" door to door that, if denied, might result in violent ransacking of property.[54]

Ceremonies at Gettysburg intended to solemnify were typically undermined by the Lambs, Razors, and similar Pennsylvania GAR groups. Appearing "grotesquely dressed . . . rigged out in all the colors of the rainbow, surmounted by every conceivable species of headgear," their most characteristic antic involved comic imitation of a formal GAR parade or mincing behind one. Occasionally they added props such as a "Jumbo" elephant float, a pet lamb to head their procession, or goats pulling miniature cannon. "Just recall our old Christmas eves, when, equipped with tin horns, parties of men, paraded Chestnut and Eighth Streets, creating an almost infernal din with their instruments of torture to weak nerves, and you have a correct idea of what we realized for almost an hour," an observing veteran noted after an 1884 Gettysburg revelry. In time, the veterans added a kazoo band to parody the military brass bands accompanying GAR parades.[55]

Staged performances mixed burlesque of the military with parody of memorial activities. Almost every summer the veterans staged a mock court-martial and execution for an absurd infraction, after which a "burial detail" carried away the "body." At one performance, the Lambs erected a "monument" to a leader "immortally wounded by a malt shot" while a veteran in drag played the deceased's widow. Crowds delighted in speeches filled with double talk ridiculing the pompous, bombastic oratory that characterized familiar memorial rituals.[56]

These traditional forms of protest at a modern shrine could affirm as well as subvert the status quo. For example, in 1880 before a large crowd, state officials, and national GAR commanders, the "fantasticals" executed "an old African woman" in a staged performance. Condemned in a mock court-martial for selling water as whiskey, the prisoner's execution mimicked the way Sepoys were dispatched by the British in India. *Proceedings* of the annual encampment reported that "[t]he boys went through this performance with undisturbed gravity, while the spectators were constantly convulsed with laughter." Perhaps for observers at the time the skit possessed multiple meanings, among them possibly reference to an incident that occurred during the war. But on other occasions during Gettysburg encampments, the veterans used derogatory racial disguises such as performing "darkey musicians" or officers depicted in blackface. In Philadelphia, young men from working-class neighborhoods used transvestitism and blackface to mock blacks, women, and immigrants. Masking aided the youths' aggressive attempts to maintain racial, ethnic, and gender order in their neighborhoods. Ironically, premodern play brought by both blacks and whites to a modern shrine symbolizing "a new birth of freedom" perpetuated racist sentiment and inequality.[57]

Like the Baltimore blacks celebrating emancipation, veterans realized that Gettysburg provided an annual opportunity to temporarily invert the social order. At Gettysburg they could evoke the upside-down world of carnival by dressing in female attire and mocking or affirming the status quo. There is no evidence that anyone in town or in the GAR hierarchy objected to the ridicule; on the contrary, Gettysburg papers indicated that townspeople eagerly anticipated the burlesque antics, and GAR officers even participated in them. Possibly, like gentry or slave masters, GAR leadership found in such revelry harmless release that ensured stability the rest of the year. By emphasizing the humorous, vulgar, and grotesque, burlesque reduced the sacred and its oppressive burden. Perhaps the enthusiasm of performers and audiences indicate exhaustion with the era's pace of change as well as its intense memorialization. Burlesque represented not just another way to control memory of the original event, but an effort on the part of pilgrims to maintain Gettysburg as a true shrine characterized by extremes of memory and play.

Experiencing Gettysburg beyond Gettysburg

Tourists, excursionists, and veterans visited not simply a place, or even a shrine, but an image created by the marketplace. Gettysburg exemplified the critics' claim that "over-illustration" threatened the nation. Images positioned Gettysburg as a Mecca for pilgrimage, creating anticipation for a trip to the sacred ground. A Gettysburg visitor's diary from 1889 illustrates this point. The young man and his colleagues arrived in Gettysburg on July 12 after a five-hour train ride. "I can't hardly immagin [*sic*] I am nearly in Gettysburg," the youth wrote. Climbing the wooden observatory on Cemetery Hill, he observed, "The things looked very much like the pictures, and almost as if I had seen them before." A decade later, a former Confederate colonel recalled that as his train approached Gettysburg, "there loomed up Big Round Top. I had not seen it for thirty-five years, but it was very familiar. Then Little Round Top, Cemetery Ridge, Cemetery Hill, all places that were world renowned." The larger-than-life image of Gettysburg even obsessed a crippled Michigan veteran who admitted in 1889 that "the war made a wreck of me." Paralyzed from the waist down on Little Round Top, Orvey S. Barrett nevertheless expressed that "it is the paramount desire of my life to visit Gettysburg—but in my present condition it is impossible."[58]

Images aided the Victorian compulsion to transcend spatial and temporal confinement. New towers and railroads conquered space, while monuments, stereopticon and stereograph views, sham battles, and the Gettysburg cyclorama provided the public improved ways to incarnate the original event. The massive cyclorama canvas not only eliminated distance so that people everywhere could visit Gettysburg; it conquered time by enabling the public to recover a cleansed version of the battle, and in some cases replaced the original event. In larger metropolitan areas such as Boston, Chicago, or Philadelphia, the cycloramas went on display in specially constructed round buildings illuminated by skylights. Patrons entered through darkened corridors, climbed stairs to a platform, and were suddenly surrounded by the panoramic sweep of Pickett's Charge, including plunging horses, exploding caissons, and the clash of infantry. To draw patrons into the scene, impresarios created a simulated no-man's land in front of the canvas, filled with broken carriage wheels, fences, knapsacks, muskets, and straw-filled dummies. "Every effort is made . . . to dispel the idea that it is a fiction and to place the spectator amid the dread actualities of a real battle," a *New York Times* correspondent wrote. Another termed it a "living story" presented "with a vividness that is almost ghastly in its reality." So convinced were a few patrons of the scene's authenticity that they climbed over the railings to enter the action.[59]

Not only simpletons and rubes found the cyclorama convincing. The veterans' *Grand Army Review* featured the cyclorama on the front page of its November 1886 issue, commenting, "It is a wonderful production, something that the first visit will beget a longing to see again and again as the very best means of studying the actual features of the ground and action at the very crisis of that grand attack." Soldiers present at the original event agreed. John Gibbon, Union commander of the 2nd Corps, which had repelled the assault, visited the Chicago cyclorama three times in 1884 and hoped to return. Gibbon, who even penciled a rough sketch of the cyclorama's layout, described the "startling" effect of the great canvas after he emerged from the gloomy passageway and ascended the platform. "The perspective and representation of the landscape is simply perfect and I say nothing more than the truth when I tell you it was difficult to disabuse my mind of the impression that I was *actually on the ground.*" To prove he had not been duped, Gibbon then analyzed the techniques used to create the illusion. Although he agreed with the flattering way the artist depicted him ("I am represented on a prancing sorrel [I rode a grey] with drawn sword waving forward some approaching infantry."), he found the historical accuracy "not very true to fact." Nevertheless, he implored another veteran to visit the cyclorama, "and rest assured you have got a sight to see before you die."[60]

Some veterans were not only persuaded by the cyclorama's re-creation of history, but even chose it over the original. Although promoters who toured the South with a copy of the cyclorama in 1895 reported low attendance in some states, a Confederate veteran who saw it at the Tennessee Centennial Exposition in 1897 called it "one of the most realistic pictures ever painted." *Confederate Veteran* responded with an endorsement of the cyclorama's redemption of Southern honor. Neither loss nor shame was present on the canvas, only glory that immortalized the South's finest hour. The painting corrected memory, depicting "the brave Pickett and the gray-coated heroes" met by "an outnumbering enemy," that "tells a tale of heroism unequaled in history." To a Union veteran, however, the cyclorama seemed "a monument" useful "to show what it cost to preserve this Union and put down treason and rebellion." When a copy was exhibited in Gettysburg at the 1913 reunion, an observer in the cyclorama building recalled "men of both sides gathered, finding it easier to locate their positions in the vivid reproduction of the scenes than on the widespreading landscape." The *Grand Army Review* noted, "In fact the veterans pretty universally feel as one distinguished General expressed himself that 'he'd like to have it in his backyard and spend all his leisure time there.'" Not all veterans agreed with the overall approbation of illusion over substance. "There is a heap of military and moral difference between a battle in Gettysburg and a cyclorama in Philadelphia or Chicago," groused Frank Moran, a veteran who claimed he lost "my eye, my liberty, and my watch at Gettysburg" and had managed a cyclorama. Disgusted with the cyclorama's popular perversion of history, Moran continued, "I cannot honestly help feeling that so far as a correct understanding of what really happened at Gettysburg is concerned, the living as well as the dead have been badly 'stuffed in cycloramas.'"[61]

Yet few complained about a medium that both entertained and replaced history with a preferred memory. A masterful blend of sensationalism and uplift, the cyclorama appealed to everyone, and not simply veterans. The cyclorama met the litmus test of improving leisure for the ostensibly historic and patriotic lessons it taught. Indeed, cycloramas presaged the movies as a medium for breaking down the distinction between working- and middle-class entertainment. While the middle class might advocate the Gettysburg cyclorama as a way to inculcate patriotism in the immigrant masses, it also offered them the kind of intense experience they sought.[62]

The critics' charge of "over-illustration" by the turn of the century was symptomatic of a larger reaction against the decline of genteel culture. By the time he wrote his autobiography in 1895, E. L. Godkin lamented the ascendance of a "pseudo culture," stoked by magazines, newspapers, and new money, which threatened "mental and moral chaos." By the turn of the century even middle-class visitors used Gettysburg to escape suffocation from gentility. The contemplative landscape of the earlier period had been replaced by entertaining action monuments, a rattling trolley, a whistling train, and a pleasure park, as well as a cyclorama meeting the needs of new types of pleasure seekers who wanted to break boundaries of ordinary social roles and rationalized life. Veterans transformed the battlefield into entertainment and spectacle with their heroic monuments, fireworks, parades, and encampments. For working-class excursionists with newly acquired money and leisure, Gettysburg offered opportunities for play removed from authoritarian scrutiny. In 1918, toward the end of the railroad era at Gettysburg, a government inspector at Round Top Park was shocked to find prostitutes exiting from excursion trains packing whiskey and beer. The inspector reported, "On a single evening over 50-couples were detected and driven from hiding places behind the tablets, monuments, rocks and trees of the reservation."[63]

Yet rather than being threatened, the sacred had shifted. By the turn of the century, an enjoyable visit to Gettysburg included reviving the battle's memory through trolley tours, monuments, sham battles, museums, and by 1913, the cyclorama. Many visitors as well were simply unschooled in the genteel aesthetic, which made them appear irreverent. Black excursionists, for example, celebrated in traditional ways that shocked middle-class sensibility and encouraged condemnation. And if some visitors were ignorant of the battle's great sacrifice, they displayed a keen awareness of Gettysburg's image. In general, when visitors traveled to Gettysburg, they were prepared for the extraordinary but they also hoped to escape the city and relieve the humdrum of routine. It was between these two poles characteristic of shrines that middle-class tourists, veterans, and excursionists moved in varying degrees during a visit.

PHASE THREE

☆ ☆ ☆ ☆ ☆ ☆ ☆ ☆ ☆ ☆ ☆

1920-1970

TV, Hot Bath, Cold War

As a result of the Civil War, it is our inescapable position to be committed to freedom broad enough to encompass all men, of all races and creeds and backgrounds.

—BRUCE CATTON, *Gettysburg College*, 1961

Chapter Five

☆ ☆ ☆ ☆ ☆ ☆ ☆ ☆ ☆ ☆ ☆

"These Are Touring Days": Mass Culture
Transforms Gettysburg

A STACCATO but rompish "aj-ooo-ga!" and "blee-eep" of automobile horns pierced an October eve in Gettysburg a half-century after the battle. Reminiscent of the gala celebration that welcomed a new railroad to Gettysburg three decades earlier, a parade of over fifty autos festooned in red, white, and blue snaked through streets and battlefield avenues. The festivities that night marked Gettysburg's part in local dedications all along the three-thousand-mile path of the new Lincoln Highway connecting Boston and San Francisco. Appropriately named for the figure whose mythological stature rested in part on his connection to Gettysburg, the memorial road initiated by the automobile's growing popularity ran straight through the center of town. Soon the automobile would dominate Gettysburg tourism by changing both the landscape and the way tourists experienced it. In its rise to preeminence in American transportation, the car ended communal train touring and privatized travel. By the 1950s, a post–World War II wave of automobiling families had transformed battlefield, lodging, restaurants, and commercial attractions.[1]

Along with film, radio, mass-circulation magazines, advertising, and finally television, the car linked the nation in cultural uniformity. The sharp edges of distinct genteel and working-class cultures blunted and melded into a homogenous mix. Ironically, the new culture heightened the need for reassurance about the American past. Rapid change created demand for space free of commercial clutter, and inevitably motorists began to expect this from Gettysburg. In addition, the shock of two world wars, a depression, and a prolonged Cold War punctuated Gettysburg's preciousness. Jolted by American leadership on the world stage, the meaning of the shrine shifted along with its facelift. By the 1960s, Gettysburg had outgrown the symbolism of reconciliation and assumed new stature as a shrine of international freedom.

The twentieth century brought Gettysburg another change: government and local commercial interests, instead of railroads and veterans, assumed lead roles in sponsoring Gettysburg tourism. Together, the U.S. Department of the Interior's National Park Service along with new entrepreneurs vastly enlarged the tourist enterprise. Both constructed contrived attractions for Americans on the road, recapturing the battle's narrative using technologies familiar to mass culture. Where once local ad hoc organizations coordinated marketing and hospitality, now media professionals promoted Gettysburg. And continuing the nineteenth century's circulation of Gettysburg engravings, stereographs, posters, and printed matter, the new mass culture disseminated the Gettysburg image through film, radio, mass-circulation periodicals, books, and product advertising.

Government and the National Park Service

As the federal government expanded in the twentieth century, it played a greater role in the development of Gettysburg. Government had impressed the state's imprimatur on the battlefield since 1863. In addition to passing incorporation bills, state and federal governments had purchased land and funded monuments, reunions, and dedications. The 1895 Sickles Act established the battlefield as a national possession under control of the War Department. In the interest of intersectional unity, the War Department's Gettysburg National Military Park Commission muffled the "vast cemetery" of Union monuments by encouraging monumentation from Southern states and adding descriptive tablets that aimed to create a national memorial. What was new about government intervention in the twentieth century involved not only encouraging and supporting tourism, but designing a tourist attraction for automobile travelers, who were part of a developing mass culture.

The automobile's increasing popularity as a recreational tool stirred demands for suitable roads and places to see. At the turn of the century, Americans owned 8,000 vehicles. A decade later, they registered over 450,000, and in 1920, 8 million. By 1960, the decade visitation at Gettysburg peaked with over 2.5 million visitors, and the number of cars registered increased to 61 million, or one for every 2.3 individuals. During this half-century of phenomenal growth, automobiles spread from the upper to the working class. But early roads traveled by increasing numbers of motorists, unlike railroad tracks owned by corporations, often were wretched farm lanes maintained by local governments. In 1914, the *Adams County News* reported that "bad roads resulted in the loss of much automobile traffic" to Gettysburg.[2]

Governmental response did not dally long behind the demand for roads, working such wonders that the *Adams County News*'s complaint could be transformed into a marketing pitch by 1920. A guidebook published that year touted "First class State and Federal roads," which "supplement admirably the highway system which centers at Gettysburg" and "make about every point of interest quickly and easily accessible." As early as 1911, Gettysburg profited from the Sproul Act for eight thousand miles of state road, which soon rebuilt the Gettysburg-Harrisburg Road. The federal government's acknowledgment of responsibility for interstate roads after World War I resulted in still grander projects.[3]

"These are touring days," the *Gettysburg Compiler* commented in the summer of 1916, remarking on the parade of cars bearing out-of-state licenses. "This great movement of intercommunication and travel . . . makes one of its greatest appeals in a popular sense through the vast and even distribution of money for which it is responsible." Federal highway acts in 1921, 1934, and 1956 created coast-to-coast networks of numbered, interconnected roads and limited-access freeways. Along with Pennsylvania's and other federally financed turnpikes, the system in effect subsidized both automotive and travel industries. While the car ended railroad passenger service to Gettysburg by the 1940s, it more than compensated for the loss. Except for dips during the depression and war years, tourist numbers increased from 727,395 in 1929 to a record 1,554,238 in 1939 and over 2 million in 1963, thanks to the world's best highway system.[4]

This intercontinental network proved a nationalizing force in several ways. Opening the exchange of goods and people, highways smoothed regional differences and helped bring uniformity to American life. In the process of altering time and space, roads produced a double irony. On the one hand, highways joined other earmarks of modernization in generating wistfulness for an earlier day. On the other hand, as part of the world's most democratic travel system, roads enabled Americans to escape the present. Many cultural pundits realized that highways held unfolding didactic potential for the masses. The nineteenth-century's genteel program for uplift through nature and edifying attractions flowed into a quest for scenic parkways, vistas, and sites significant to the nation's past. "The roads are to be our most hopeful educators," antiquarian Wallace Nutting wrote in his autobiography.[5]

Some government roads were proposed as memorials to inspire nationalistic sentiment by linking historic places with personages. Lincoln, Lee, and Gettysburg figured in these schemes, with the idea of a Lee Highway coursing into Gettysburg proposed but abandoned in 1919. For a time, the Lincoln proposal held greater promise. As the centennial of Lincoln's birth approached, for example, Congress in 1908 considered constructing a seventy-two-mile boulevard from Washington to Gettysburg as a memorial to the martyred hero. Plans called for a landscaped parkway 150 feet wide with a trolley lane on one side for the hoi polloi. The *Washington Post* enthused that the highway "by its very nature shares in the life of the people," and "would lead men for centuries to a field that must become more and more holy ground." However noble the sentiment, highway, tourist, and realty interests pushed the concept. The chair of the National Good Roads Board remarked that the highway would "prove more effective than any other means in cementing this nation into a solidified whole" and thus most fittingly memorialize the Union's savior. Although advocates of a Gettysburg-Washington boulevard sporadically introduced legislation into the 1930s, Congress in the end favored the unpedestrian, classical temple at Potomac Flats.[6]

Even if not memorial highways, roads aided memory and its manifestations in the marketplace. By erecting wayside markers and comfort facilities, government supported patriotism, public education, and the travel industry. Pennsylvania, for example, tried to first restore the sylvan wood for motorists in 1921 by planting hardwoods along major roads, and four years later completed plans for historical markers along the Lincoln Highway running through Gettysburg. Among the seven hundred state historical markers erected before the 1940s, two dozen on the approach roads to Gettysburg competed with billboard advertising that followed automobilists into the area. "From any direction, those approaching Gettysburg will be reminded—miles in advance—that they are nearing historic country," the *Gettysburg Times* remarked.[7]

In addition to orienting tourists, the state encouraged motorists to spend their travel dollars in the historic Keystone State. In 1941, months before the United States entered World War II, the Pennsylvania Department of Commerce published colored guidebooks available free to those who read its illustrated travel advertisements placed in metropolitan newspapers. "Your vacation dreams come true in Pennsylvania," the ads promised, and urged, "See Pennsylvania—Birth State of the Nation." Motorists were assured, "You'll enjoy every mile you drive in Pennsylvania" because of "40,000 miles of modern highways." Scenes of people enjoying themselves at historical sites, including Gettysburg, were juxtaposed with similar illustrations of leisurely swimming, camping, golf, and fishing. The ads not only placed historic shrines in the service of commerce, but also conflated historical touring with recreation.[8]

The public sector did not stop with highways and tourism promotion. Federal and state governments provided for a wide array of tourist needs. Campgrounds, parks, marine facilities, golf courses, and historic sites offered government-sponsored pleasure opened to any car owner. Beginning in the late 1920s, government worked with the private sector to democratize history for an automobiling nation. Restoration and re-creation of earlier America accelerated with the number of cars on the road. As opposed to the nineteenth-century memory palace of display cases full of relics and memorabilia, period rooms such as the Jennie Wade house in Gettysburg provided, beginning around 1910, both a new way to display objects and a visage of past reality. Within two decades, whole villages were reconstructed as entertainment and popular education.

Those organizations that had done so much to radically change America—government and automotive-related corporations—now attempted to reincarnate the America they had shattered. Industrialists such as Henry Ford, who made cars affordable, and J. D. Rockefeller, Jr., began work on Colonial Williamsburg and Greenfield Village in the late 1920s with far-reaching consequences. Both saw the restoration of past historical environments as responsibilities of their class, just as the previous generation of industrialists had underwritten institutions of high culture. Ford sought a way of understanding history through objects rather than texts, a history easily grasped by the people who drove his products. Williamsburg offered tangible details of colonial life, but also costume scenes that could entertain a popular audience. The approach paid off in stunning attendance figures at the former colonial capital.[9]

At the same time private initiative launched Williamsburg, Greenfield, and other similar projects, the U.S. Department of the Interior's National Park Service assumed a similar joint role of didacticism and entertainment. Founded in 1916 for natural and historic conservation, by the 1920s the Park Service aimed to enhance tourism to national parks through maps, guidebooks, recreational facilities, lodging, and alliances with entrepreneurial tourist services. Staging the American past for motorists accelerated when the Park Service quadrupled its historic holdings in 1933. That year it assumed control of both the Agriculture Department's and War Department's historic sites, cemeteries, and battlefields, which included Gettysburg. Grappling with the Depression's enervating effects, the New Deal attempted to shore up flagging patriotic sentiment through cultural projects. Along with federally sponsored history, travelogues, theater, and music suitable for popular taste, the Park Service functioned as a tool for instilling pride in American achievement. The Park Service summarized its aims with a 1934 poster captioned, "The Adventures of Today Are the Memories of Tomorrow."[10]

Like Henry Ford, Park Service officials realized that the stimulating effects of historical scenes could provide a powerful antidote to the shortcomings of conventional history. The first director of the Park Service's historical division declared in 1935 that "the task is to breathe the breath of life into American history for those to whom it has been a dull recitation of meaningless facts—to re-create for the average citizen something of the color, pageantry, and dignity of our national past." Achieving such results, however, required the Park Service to tinker with the landscapes they had inherited. Earthworks were re-dug, outbuildings replaced, or modern appurtenances on houses removed to produce a "show-and-tell" scene. Historic landscapes might induce memory, but only if a semblance of their original appearance were interpreted for a public accustomed to staged attractions. While modernity made the past seem remote, a culture growing ever more awash in images made it possible to reduce the past to visual stimuli.[11]

When the Park Service assumed control of Gettysburg National Military Park (GNMP), it faced a double dilemma. Not only was it saddled with a park that reflected the leisure practices of an earlier day, but it also had to reconstruct memory of the battle for a new public of auto travelers. As genteel culture faded and blended into mass culture, the "text" of the Gettysburg necropolis became merely a collection of old-fashioned memorials. Whereas in 1908 a writer in *Review of Reviews* lauded Gettysburg as "a magnificent park," by 1932 a Park Service official condemned the battle landscape as "literally monumented almost to the cemetery—or graveyard—condition." No longer did monuments attract the leisurely carriage driver; rather, motorists sped by the collection of meaningless stones. Nearly gone by that time too were the pilgrim-veterans who quickened memory of the battle with rituals and personal tales of fighting. As veterans, railroads, and genteel culture vanished, so too did the memories of Gettysburg conjured by them. Reinvocation of the battle's memory required carving out a new shrine through landscaping and interpretation appropriate for a growing mass culture. It appeared to alarm bureaucrats that, as a Park Service historian pointed out, most tourists "drive at leisure and without direction through the park."[12]

How to convert this "vast cemetery" into a park meaningful to the motoring public? Aided by historical specialists, the Park Service responded immediately upon taking charge of the site. "Our task is to see that it meets the requirements of an exacting public," superintendent James R. McConaughie asserted in his first annual report in 1934. "There can be no better way to do this than to exert every effort toward restoring it to the condition as found during the world famous battle fought over its grounds." The monuments had to remain, but as a solution the Park Service should "carefully plant [trees and shrubs] so that numerous monuments will appear to fit and be screened so as to not to unduly affect the landscape."[13]

As outlined in a 1937 master plan and echoed in subsequent park plans, McConaughie charted a long-term course for revamping the park. With manpower initially supplied by the Public Works Administration, Civil Works Administration, and Civilian Conservation Corps, the Park Service muted the presence of monuments by emphasizing a period landscape. Beginning in the 1870s, the GBMA had rebuilt disintegrating lunettes as a way to provide objects for the tourist gaze, and later the War Department reconstructed walls and reforested. But attempting to create period scenes out of a genteel park was a dramatic departure. Crews planted here and cut there, restored dwellings and barns, replaced concrete fence posts with split-rail fences, and rebuilt or constructed stone walls. In the initial stages of the restoration, some who retained vivid memories of the battle's sacrifices found the work profanatory. Howls of indignation ensued, for example, when the Civilian Conservation Corps rebuilt the sinking, sagging wall at the scene of Pickett's Charge in 1933. Southerners in particular condemned dismemberment of the wall "washed in the blood of their forefathers," and "aroused protests which were heard even in Washington."[14]

In the early days the Park Service tried to clear away anachronisms and achieve the appearance of age rather than an exact correspondence to the 1863 landscape. Fifty years after McConaughie began the process, one of his successors as park superintendent echoed, "We're trying to create a historyscape," and "we can restore the battlefield areas as much as possible to the way it appeared one minute before the battle opened on July 1, 1863." During the 1950s and 1960s, the Park Service cleared trees and brush sprouting since the battle and restored more buildings. Farm fields once outside the formal avenues and lines of monuments now were part of the historic landscape and integral to staging the scene. Features attractive to the railroad era were swept away as if they were an embarrassment. Spectral remnants of bygone pilgrimages, including buildings at Round Top Park, trolley tracks, copper wires, and railroad tracks crossing the battlefield all vanished between World Wars I and II. When in 1945 the Park Service finally acquired the stretch of Round Top branch railroad crossing the battlefield, the superintendent immediately moved to restore "the entire scene . . . to the appearance it had when the armies of the North and South locked here in battle in 1863." By 1971 officials employed the phrase "scenic easement" in discussing construction of camouflaged walkways as well as removal of observation towers, utility poles along highways, and even the Park Service's own visitor center.[15]

The new sensibility of trying to make the park appear antiquated meant not only conquest of the old but ongoing struggle with the new. Monuments desiccate memory within an object; switching the burden of memory from artifice to landscape, however, requires space and swells the scope of memory as far as the horizon. When it launched battlefield restoration in the 1930s, the Park Service began to combat "eyesores," such as garbage dumps and junkyards, that jarred the scene. The demands of visual purity also prompted their continuing efforts to preempt intrusive development by purchasing additional land for the park. No longer would a policy of acquiring strips of land for memorialization suffice. Ultimately, the Park Service's drive to sanctify by guaranteeing perpetual visual purity doubled the park's size from 2,530 acres in 1933 to 5,733 by the end of the century. This imperious policy might be contrasted with a 1904 assertion by the GNMPC that "monuments occupying but a comparatively small space" adequately commemorated events and that "the acquisition of any further extensive tracts of land here by the United States would be a waste of public funds."[16]

Cleansing the landscape involved human as well as matériel resources.

Along with other services catering to automobile travelers, the number of guides mushroomed with the growth of automobile touring. But these interpreters, many of them townspeople, did not always fit the Park Service vision. Although abuses had driven the War Department to require licensing by examination in 1915, guides continued to pose problems for the Park Service when it assumed control. The examination may have reduced the number of lies, anecdotes, and legends "at variance with history," as the GNMPC had stated. But the advent of the automobile nourished shabby guide activities such as hustling along the roadside, truncating tours, and doubling as hotel bagmen. These were hardly new tricks, but guides could more easily perform them with increasing numbers of visitors dispersed along highways instead of concentrating at rail stations. The automobile increased the tempo of a pokey trade rooted in oral tradition, encouraging behavior "suggestive of the street carnival or of the shoddy shop keeper who buttonholes his prospects and tries to drag them into his store," as the *Gettysburg Times* complained in 1946. Sometimes guides flagged down motorists or jumped in front of cars, with their policelike uniforms and badges adding to tourists' alarm. The Park Service tried a number of approaches to correct the problems, including opening fixed guide stations, conducting seminars for guides, reexaminations, selective monitoring, and even a failed attempt to bring the guides under civil service. Eventually flagrant abuses subsided with self-monitoring among the guides themselves as well as improved control by the Park Service, although in 1953, a tourist complained in 1953 that her guide, a nonagenarian born four days after Lincoln delivered the Gettysburg Address, fell asleep four times during a tour (though luckily not behind the wheel).[17]

But the Park Service clash with guides represented more than obliterating commercial irritations from the battlefield. After all, the Park Service aimed its restoration at educating in an entertaining way, part and parcel of orienting automobile tourists to the battle. When the Park Service took charge, guides offered the only interpretation available outside of the War Department's lifeless iron tablets. But the guides' often folksy presentations seemed at odds with technology and downright noxious considering the imperative of popular education. (At one point they were admonished on elementary hygiene such as clean fingernails and a washed and shaved face.) Improving guide service was simply part of increasing professionalization of American society, continuing the progressive dream of "experts" managing every part of life. Further, guides waged a struggle for years against the Park Service's attempts to orient tourists now arriving from twenty-eight different access points. Guides objected to the Park Service's directional signs, printed information, and display maps as a threat to business. Aware, however, of the urgency of patriotic didacticism, the guides in 1936 adopted a resolution stating that "the *only* [italics added] way to understand" the battle was through a guide using "words that will instill in the visitor a greater love of country and a greater appreciation of the sacrifices these men have made."[18]

The guides, however, fought a losing battle. Guides essentially carried on the veterans' oral tradition of telling stories, which the Park Service hoped to overcome with technology. Moreover, only one-quarter of visitors driving through the park enlisted a guide. To the Park Service, the site itself served as "source material" providing instruction to tourists, as an official stated in 1943. Yet while a restored battlefield might engage visitors, on its own it could not inform a public that had not only lost personal touch with the Civil War but was atomized in terms of transportation. As Superintendent McConaughie observed in 1936, restoration was a hook to "promote an ease of education," but "an educational program is definitely needed to replace the personal knowledge of yesterday." Devising innovative ways to interpret the battlefield for mass culture would be an ongoing project of the Park Service as it assumed greater control of the tourist experience.[19]

Even before the Park Service took charge of the battlefield, the War Department grappled with ways to help motorists understand it. In 1929, after President Herbert Hoover toured the field and found the clutter of monuments and tablets confusing, an examining War Department board recommended a novel solution. In an example of progressive problem solving, it proposed erecting three-inch wire ribbons spanning concrete posts fifty feet apart, where each unit was positioned. One post would feature a description of the unit stationed at that location, "using large letters and few words, making the marker readable from a moving car." If adopted, this method would have confounded the restoration ethic. Instead, the Park Service started with much less obtrusive methods of interpretation, gradually relying on images and sound reproduction appropriate for the age.[20]

With the automobile the logistics of circulating tourists around the park had passed from hackmen, railroads, and trolley companies to the federal government. To orient motorists, the Park Service initially used directional signs and fliers but gradually expanded its tourist and interpretive services. Beginning in 1949 it licensed tours by private bus companies, which added canned narration for passengers by the 1960s. It also designed an automobile route that followed the battle's development chronologically, but this posed difficulties that never were satisfactorily resolved. The goal for busy motoring tourists, as a superintendent remarked in 1942, aimed to help them "visit the principal features of the park in a normal sequence and in the shortest possible time." Even if the sequential car tour failed, the Park Service met the needs of time and convenience by 1947 with seven roadside exhibits that explained key sites with maps and illustrations. Essentially the exhibits fixed in print and graphics what the guides transmitted orally, and focused visitor attention on the story of the battle. Expanded to ten a decade later, some stops by the 1970s featured "push button" canned narration and enabled motorists to tour without leaving their cars. Yet the modernization process failed to completely obliterate the anecdotal oral tradition. Some turnout exhibits featured apocryphal human-interest stories told by guides during the railroad era.[21]

Ironically, while the Park Service struggled to bring Gettysburg within the scope of modern touring, it reached back to the nineteenth century for its key attraction. In 1941 the Park Service purchased a copy of the Gettysburg cyclorama that had been a commercial attraction in Gettysburg since the 1913 reunion. Despite the huckersterism associated with this entertainment rendered archaic by movies, the cyclorama's bloodless valor and hoariness prompted the Park Service to describe it as "a national historic object to be permanently preserved for the benefit and inspiration of the people of the United States."[22]

The Park Service acquired the painting to display in a new visitors' center. Just as the cyclorama depicted the climax of the battle, so too would it serve as the climax of the tourist experience. Earlier, the Park Service had tried to "hold the visitors' interest and aid visualization" through orientation talks at its museum in the town's post office, using the battlefield relief model shown at the St. Louis Exposition. Tourists, however, seemed more interested in the cyclorama, and as a result officials viewed it as the park's premier exhibit. "It is the most important exhibit we shall ever have in the park," wrote a Park Service historian in 1946, "and everything else we do should be built around it."[23]

The need for a new visitors' center grew ever more apparent to the Park Service as visitation exploded in the postwar period. Visitation had dipped during the Depression's worst years and again during the rationing days of World War II, but then steadily rose from 659,000 in 1950 to 1.3 million in 1960 and 2.6 million by 1970. The Park Service's Mission 66 program, launched in 1956, aimed to upgrade its national parks for the flood of tourists over the next ten-year period. At Gettysburg, Mission 66 included significant improvements for motorists, including resurfaced park avenues, additional roadside exhibits and turnouts, and, in 1962, the long-planned visitors' center that opened in time for the battle's centennial. To offset vestiges of the original Union memorial, the Park Service also considered constructing a "Johnny Reb" museum on Seminary Ridge for the Civil War Centennial, but the concept never came to fruition.[24]

Situated on a ridge near the sacred ground's apex, the paramount High Water Mark, the center had been designed by renowned architects of the International Style, Richard Neutra and Robert Alexander. Its stripped, functional lines accommodating the cyclorama prompted the *Washington Star Sunday Magazine* to lament that it "looks like a gas tank." Yet the paper added that the structure "will provide unprecedented facilities for the 1.5 million visitors," featuring "all the needs for tourist creature comforts and guidance, and exhibits that will thoroughly acquaint visitors with details of the battle that was fought there." Easy access, ample parking, comfort stations, a stream-fed reflecting pool, and air conditioning encouraged visitation, while ramps and exits facilitated crowd flow. An architectural historian stated that the architects "carefully choreographed" the procession from parking lot through the building onto the battlefield to create "a dynamic relationship" between interpretation and the park. As Park Service officials intended, once there tourists could "obtain a summarized interpretation of the battle," and conveniently walk to the battlefield's significant spots. Within the building, media technology turned the story of the battle into entertainment. Dioramas, a film, a sampling of artifacts, and the cyclorama reintroduced with light show and canned narration provided quick stimulation for tourists on the go. In a word coined by Disney staffers, the center served as the "wienie" of the park, transforming its core into something much like the malls that were rapidly spreading over the American landscape.[25]

The building stood as a focal point for the battlefield, but the cyclorama became the pivot point for the building. Neutra placed an observation platform outside, so that visitors might see the real battlefield from approximately the same position as the landscape depicted in the cyclorama. The juxtaposition was a sleight of hand for a culture that thrived on illusions, for reality conformed to the image: the Park Service attempted to shape the battlefield to look like the period portrayed on canvas. With the battlefield's split rail fences, rebuilt stone walls, and restored farm buildings, visitors could see that the battlefield looked much like the painting. The irony was that a cyclorama, a fossilized commercial entertainment that in the park's genteel phase had been driven to sideshows and midways, now occupied center stage of the shrine. An entertainment form that had glorified the nation for commercial ends at innumerable cities and towns now glorified the nation as an intrinsic part of that nation's sacred ground.

Neutra's design and the building's location must be viewed within the context of the Cold War. Although displays inside and on park roads focused on the battle's narrative, the building itself connected past glory with present challenges. The avant-garde framework of steel and glass (later nicknamed "Starship Enterprise" by some Park Service personnel) abruptly linked past and present with its space-age design. Perched on Cemetery Ridge where a nation was reborn, the building pointed to future American triumph abroad and beyond to the stars. It exuded an aura of rapidly advancing technology enabled by the supremacy of Western capitalism. Within, the structure included even the sort of gadgets that graced the postwar suburban home—louvers that served as blinds, sliding glass walls that created an outdoor forum, and a hidden podium. The whole dovetailed with American culture's ubiquitous push-button products and futuristic design in an age of unlimited technological optimism. All this framed the cyclorama's Brobdingnagian canvas and lent credibility to an archaic entertainment.

For all the cyclorama's sanitized and romanticized imagery, it may have

been the most impressive and graphic way to inspire tourists immersed in a
visual mass culture. However distorted the image, its juxtaposition with the
real battlefield brought to life a memory that monuments no longer could
evoke. The painting still offered both sensationalism and edification, but
now for those who hoped the American past might provide fun and togetherness during an annual family vacation. It also connected families to the
national family's struggle against global tyranny, and left the impression
that war is a glorious affair when waged for American ideals. According to
Neutra, a prewar Jewish immigrant, the building's central location near the
site of the Gettysburg Address and the High Water Mark suggested that it
served "as a shrine for many nations and the free world." Dedicated ninety-
nine years to the day that President Lincoln delivered his famous speech,
the visitors' center heralded "the new era of human freedom which began
with President Lincoln's restatement of America's principles," according to
the Park Service. With its sensual enticements for the millions who hit the
road every summer, the visitors' center revealed the federal government's
pains to inculcate patriotism through stunning obeisance to American tourism. "Let's really have concern for the visitor," a Park Service official wrote
in 1964, "and let's really give him 'the time of his life.'" Just as the federal
government underwrote the lives of those who traveled to Gettysburg through
Federal Housing and Veterans' Housing Administration loans, the National
Highway Act, and myriad other ways, so too would it channel their leisure
to patriotic ends. In America-on-wheels, drive-in patriotism joined other
new pleasures such as drive-in restaurants, movies, and shopping. Of course,
the larger goal of civic inspiration could be easily discarded in the pursuit of
fun.[26]

During its first four decades as custodian of Gettysburg, the Park Service
registered remarkable accomplishments. It had initiated a process of transforming a genteel park into a simulation of the original battlefield, which
effaced older attractions and required a continuing quest for more space.
From guides and monuments, it transferred the burden of memory to devices appropriate for mass culture that once and for all focused attention on
the battle. By the early 1970s, the Park Service's expansive policy governed
not only private enterprises like guide services and mass-transit touring, but
also engulfed a pastiche of formerly commercial attractions such as the cyclorama, the Gettysburg National Museum, and the "Electric Map" of the
battlefield. In developing a vortex for automobile touring, it contributed
significantly to the local economy. And it transformed the park into a con-
sumer-friendly enterprise that controlled the visitor experience from inviting school groups to hosting ranger-led campfire talks. As early as 1941,
then-Superintendent J. Walter Coleman said, "We are in the tourist business, and we are interested in attracting as great a number of visitors here as
possible."[27]

The Park Service's transformation of Gettysburg was not without ironies.

To jolt visitors into the past, the Park Service employed modern business methods such as master planning and public relations. Restored houses masked plumbing, heating, and electrical systems, and so too did the battle-field, with its hidden sewage and electrical systems, wells, and water lines installed for tourist convenience. And as the overhauled park drew more tourists, it struck up against the interests of private enterprise spawned from that success. Much as the railroad's Round Top Park had attracted photo-graphers and impresarios eighty years earlier, the visitors' center dangled a lure for impresarios, restaurateurs, and other entrepreneurs to set up shop on private land nearby. Only now they clustered near the center of the battle-field instead of the southern end, creating a garish strip on land demanding more visual purity than ever before. To legitimize their enterprises, some borrowed the imprimatur of the federal government, such as "National Civil War Wax Museum" or "National Riding Stables." And as an enter-prise labeled the "National Tower" planned to rise over three hundred feet above the nearby visitors' center in the early 1970s, it kicked off a firestorm of controversy created in part by the Park Service's accomplishments.[28]

New Promoters, New Meanings

While the state retailored Gettysburg for mass culture in the twentieth century, mass culture itself used Gettysburg as grist in its homogenizing mill. The automotive industry and its auxiliaries promoted Gettysburg for motor-ists, while other agents of mass culture such as film, radio, televison, and mass circulation magazines featured Gettysburg as a theme. By the 1960s Gettysburg reflected a national mass culture of automobile travel and family entertainment.[29]

Automobile clubs, highway organizations, and manufacturers of autos, tires, and other accessories used Gettysburg for publicity. In 1913, a year after the attempt for a federally financed Lincoln Memorial Highway from Washington, D.C., to Gettysburg failed, auto-related industrialists formed the Lincoln Highway Association to develop a transcontinental highway. Ostensibly honoring Abraham Lincoln, a pathway "teaching patriotism," as one promoter stated, the project in reality served the interests of the road-building and auto industries. Linking Boston with San Francisco, the 3,389 mile Lincoln Highway (later designated U.S. Route 30) that billed itself as "the Main Street of the Nation" ran through the town where Lincoln had delivered his most famous speech.

Not only progress but publicity concerned the Lincoln Highway Associa-tion, which launched a public relations campaign before improving an inch of road. By 1915, the association had published a guidebook for the entire route. After World War I both the middle-class American Automobile As-sociation (AAA) and the elite Automobile Club of America (ACA) published guidebooks specifically for Gettysburg. Gradually this early motoring literature displaced earlier railroad guidebooks, yet differed because of its support from local advertisers that dictated worthwhile sights. Thus as automobiles and highways shrunk the nation, the motoring industry turned Gettysburg into an important pause in the accelerating present. By 1925, the *Gettysburg Times* chimed that "Gettysburg is favored as one of the main attractions and stop-over points on that wonderful white ribbon of road that connects the Atlantic with the Pacific."[30]

But the automobile was only one agent of mass culture that assimilated Gettysburg early on. Film, at the turn of the century a working-class novelty, also used Gettysburg while struggling to broaden its niche in public entertainment. In 1913, when one-reel silent films dominated the movie business, producer-director Thomas Ince created a five-reel film titled *The Battle of Gettysburg*. Shot near Ince's studio in Malibu, California, the battle scenery hardly resembled south-central Pennsylvania. Yet perhaps because of its epical proportions for the time—studio publicity claimed the movie used twenty-five hundred extras—*Moving Picture World* called it "the most stupendous effort ever put forth in motion pictures," which included "spectacular scenes of awe–inspiring sensationalism." Even though war dramatization may have thrilled pre-World War I audiences, the film ended on a hallowed note with an actor playing Abraham Lincoln delivering the Gettysburg Address. A broadside for the film claimed its purpose was "to teach adequately the significance and true value of a conflict whose broader meaning is often lost in the recollections of sensational skirmishes, heroic charges."[31]

Civil War veterans and others thronged theaters as far away as San Francisco to view the film during fiftieth anniversary week in July 1913. But the film's greatest significance was not that Gettysburg could be brought to life for millions simultaneously. It also aimed to broaden the market for film beyond the typical working-class audience by attaching itself to Gettysburg's cultural prominence. Many films by 1913 had used the Civil War as a context for short sentimental drama or comedy. But *Gettysburg* attempted to address the challenge posed by movie moguls like Adolph Zukor, who envisioned expanding the film market to middle- and upper-class audiences through feature films using genteel themes. At the same time, working-class audiences who already patronized film might be elevated and patriotically inspired. Although several decades passed before film helped produce a truly mass culture, one of its keys to success created mass audiences by grafting middle- and working-class interests.[32]

Gettysburg figured also in the advertising capabilities of film, evident in the medium's power to bestow legitimacy and fame to anything thrown on the screen. Again appealing to the genteel, the advisor to Gettysburg's first promotional film, shot in 1914, counseled that the advertisement be filmed "primarily as an educational feature." Gettysburg was also used to capitalize on the illusion that film captured reality. When the Lincoln Highway Association filmed a lengthy publicity movie for the coast-to-coast road in 1915, producers featured Gettysburg along with cowboys, homesteaders, and happy campers farther west. Towns were not only asked to decorate their streets, but to launch road improvements for the filming so viewers would think work was underway. The film industry's additions of sound, color, and more sophisticated cameras in subsequent decades permitted greater opportunity to manipulate the shrine. When MGM filmed *The Battle of Gettysburg* in the 1950s, it substituted statues on monuments for actors. Using shadow, color, light, sound, and camera angles, the film brought to life the heroic action figures that were in their day both an attraction and an intentional distortion of the historic event. Thus film improved on the original illusion, animating monuments for a public no longer capable of interpreting them, and resuscitating their sensationalism through a familiar medium.[33]

Responding to the public need for reassurance during the trauma of depression, the entertainment industry produced a vast array of films, recordings, literature, and graphic arts that celebrated the nation's past. Along with its partial restoration of the battlefield, the National Park Service's 1935 film *The Blue and the Gray* featured Gettysburg as the movie's highlight. The film materialized President Lincoln through an actor who, shown in outline profile against scenes of the park, narrated the Gettysburg Address supplemented by patriotic choral music. Popularity of the homespun Lincoln reached dizzying heights with Carl Sandburg's multivolume biography and Hollywood productions centered on Lincoln or Lincolnesque characters. The New Deal's Federal Theater Project produced a play about Lincoln, *Prologue to Glory*, that moved on to Broadway and then the 1939 New York World's Fair. Similarly but less successfully, the Federal Music Project in 1938 staged *Gettysburg*, an opera about the battle's aftermath and Lincoln's speech. Following a live performance, NBC broadcast the opera nationally on the Fourth of July 1938. The federal government's sponsorship of the seventy-fifth reunion that same week combined advertising agency publicity and national coverage in the press, radio, and newsreels to cast a Hollywood halo of celebrity on the shrine. One crabbed veteran was so pestered by autograph seekers he charged a dime for the service, reporting to his attendant, "By cracky, I made eighty cents."[34]

Even print fiction, which enjoyed smaller audiences than radio or film, helped promote the Gettysburg image. In 1945, the Gettysburg National Military Park superintendent noted that the Civil War "is a popular subject in our literature and our drama" and "[I]ts heroes are becoming legendary." Over five hundred novels about the Civil War had been published by 1948, some of the twentieth century's most popular appearing as Gettysburg-related fiction. These included Stephen Vincent Benet's *John Brown's Body* (1928), MacKinlay Kantor's *Long Remember* (1934), Joseph Pennell's *The History of Rome Hanks and Kindred Matters* (1944), and Ben Ames Williams's *House Divided* (1947). In the 1950s, children's books such as Alida Sims Malkus's *We Were There at the Battle of Gettysburg* (1955) and Mac-Kinlay Kantor's *Gettysburg* (1952) brought the battle narrative to life for postwar baby boomers. Although print never popularized history like film, historian Bernard DeVoto found Civil War novels prevalent enough to write, "Probably less than a hundred thousand Americans have read an adult history of the Civil War and Reconstruction, but three million have had some of its data and forces visualized for them by fiction."[35]

By the post–World War II era television, films, magazines, and advertising in its various mediums washed the nation in a flood of colorful images. A popular if distorted past honed out of Westerns, Disney films and Disney Land, neocolonial housing and furniture, and historic sites helped fight a Cold War enemy that had repudiated its own history. In a nation reinvigorated by abundance, what better way to celebrate America than visually consume the past? Americans were urged to "See the U.S.A. in Your Chevrolet" on television. Too, in older favorites and two hundred new mass-circulation magazines that appeared after World War II—one was even titled *Look*—they received similar colorful commercial messages. A two-page *Saturday Evening Post* advertisement, for example, featured a family driving through a dreamy historical landscape that included Gettysburg in a station wagon labeled "America's Schoolhouse on Wheels." General Motors sponsored scenes of motoring families snapping photographs at Old Nantucket or Custer Park titled "There's nothing like a car to enrich your family life." Kodak itself ran a "Make History Come Alive" advertisement, which depicted a family gathered in a darkened living room with Dad showing a slide of junior straddling a cannon.[36]

Not surprisingly, family-centered advertisements appeared alongside travelogues about historic sites in the same Cold War–era magazines. *Better Homes and Gardens*, *Good Housekeeping*, the *Saturday Evening Post*, *Holiday*, *Travel*, the *New Yorker*, *Time*, *American Heritage*, the *New York Times Magazine*, travel sections of metropolitan newspapers, and others urged family pilgrimages to Gettysburg. Most offered suburbanites touring advice and prescribed attractions that turned the battle into family entertainment. Commercial museums, the electrified cyclorama, bus tours with canned narration, and the battlefield landscape were equally endorsed as paths for escaping the present.[37]

Gettysburg Merchants, Minimoguls, and Media Manipulators

The Gettysburg tourist industry dramatically readjusted to meet the needs of mass culture. Thanks to the automobile, by midcentury Gettysburg boasted more restaurants, hotels, and souvenir stands than any town of comparable size in North America. While immediately after the battle town boosters

America's
schoolhouse on wheels

Our country is big and so [...] its history. To see even a pa[...] of it in comfort requires a fa[...] sized American car.

FORD MOTOR COMPANY THE AMERICAN ROAD, DEARBORN, MICHIGAN

The Ford Family of Fine Cars

FORD • THUNDERBIRD • EDSEL • MERCURY • LINCOLN • CONTINENTAL MARK IV

FIGURE 19. "The roads will be our best educators": Cold War–era ad suggesting that by touring America's historic sites, "America's schoolhouse on wheels" could promote both family togetherness and civic education. Gettysburg is on the right of this history dreamscape (*Saturday Evening Post*, June 27, 1959)

took the lead in shaping a genteel tourist destination, and during the railroad era veterans' groups and railroad corporations developed the shrine, the new wave of automobile tourists prompted townspeople to again seize the initiative. Unlike their predecessors, these twentieth-century Gettysburg entrepreneurs were generally not scions of families present during the battle but outsiders who sniffed a travel revolution aborning. Dramatically different from the attractions for railroad excursionists, the tourist empire they built complemented the federally sponsored central attraction for vacationing families.

Near the turn of the century, a succession of local initiatives including the Business Men's League, Retail Merchants' Association, Gettysburg Booster Club, and after World War I, the Chamber of Commerce addressed concerns over declining tourist numbers and regulating the flow of tourists. Covering their business sensibility with a mantle of patriotism, these groups attempted to secure a permanent army installation, National Guard of Pennsylvania camps, and a training camp for World War I recruits. They also campaigned for tourist amenities such as improved highways and town streets. Members attended political party conventions and annual meetings of fraternal organizations to pitch for Gettysburg as a meeting site. The importance of publicity was underscored by the 1913 reunion, when townspeople experienced a burst in tourism and a noticeable rise in Southern tourists. Businessmen attributed the stream of Southern license plates to "the favorable impression taken home by the Confederate veterans who participated in the big battle anniversary." One businessman advised the tourist industry to coddle the burgeoning Southern market by refraining from using the term "Rebel" and acknowledging "Confederates and their valor" in advertising.[38]

With more automobile tourism, townspeople recognized a stark difference in travel patterns. Instead of scheduled trains disgorging hundreds and sometimes thousands of passengers all at once in town, the automobile dispersed tourists over time and space. "Many are convinced," the *Gettysburg Times* remarked, "that the growth of the town will be in proportion to the increase in number and development of automobile-powered vehicles." Yet the business community realized automobile tourism placed visitors out of their control. Many were travelers on their way elsewhere and diverted their travel route for a brief spin around the battlefield. Automobile tourists also could arrive on any of the town's eleven different roads and motor around the battlefield without stopping in town. One estimate before World War I pegged the proportion of tourists who entered town at one-third of the total. As a result, the *Canonsburg Daily Notes* reported in 1915, "[T]ourists since the automobile came into general use do not yield so much revenue as in the days when all visitors traveled by train." The solution involved not only the simple business practice of taking attractions and services to the customers, but also improved promotion.[39]

Beginning in the 1920s the Chamber of Commerce brought system to publicity, an initiative made all the more credible with the emergence of modern advertising floated by mass-market journalism. New highways so lubricated the flow of traffic that a promotional nudge might entice the weekend recreation seeker, cross-country motorist on the Lincoln Highway, or seasonal nomad heading to or from Florida. As early as 1922, when over five thousand encamped U.S. Marines staged Pickett's Charge and exploded a blimp, the Chamber took advantage of the free spectacle by commissioning an Atlantic City ad agency to advertise the event in the Sunday sections of seven metropolitan newspapers. With faith in advertising's magic, the Chamber by 1924 had hired a full-time secretary and opened an office in the courthouse where visitors could obtain tourist information. Manager of the Hotel Gettysburg Henry Schaarf, a convert to advertising, pressed for more publicity by urging "a united Gettysburg, to further enhance the attractions of the battlefield." Believing "[e]verybody should be a salesman for Gettysburg," Schaarf launched a "Battlefield News Bureau" out of the hotel that for several years mailed out its own press releases and photos.[40]

The Chamber used modern advertising to enhance tourism and create a new image. C. E. Sloane, the Chamber's first executive secretary, charted this course in a 1925 speech. "Publicity and advertising are the two main factors in keeping Gettysburg on the traveler's map," he said. Only promotion in the modern marketplace could fan flames from the dying embers of a long-ago event. But keeping Gettysburg a current rather than a past event required sculpting an appealing contemporary image. "We cannot let the glories of '63 and the *attractions staged then* [italics added], suffice at this time to maintain the spirit of attractiveness," Sloane added. As if it were a primitive deity demanding sacrifice, advertising was so associated with maintenance of the industry that when the Depression eviscerated tourism, townspeople thought additional advertising expenditure would restore its health.[41]

Realizing, for example, that every automobile could serve as a mobile commercial, the Chamber in 1931 began attaching Gettysburg bumper stickers on visitors' cars. And year after year beginning in the 1920s, the Chamber cultivated the public school market by mailing hundreds of invitations for high school classes to visit the sacred ground. By the post–World War II period, five hundred busloads arrived annually, to which the Chamber extended guide and hotel reservation services. The Chamber also introduced guidebooks for the motoring public in 1925 with Rand McNally's *Gettysburg: The Heart of the New America*, referring to Gettysburg's easy accessibility through intercontinental highway connections. Distributed nationally, the booklet eliminated the florid, romantic descriptions of the railroad era. Instead, illustrations predominated with text limited to paragraph descriptions, "thus eliminating all solid tiresome reading matter," as the *Gettysburg Times* commented. Now, in accord with photojournalism, advertising, and movies, illustrations alone built recognition and anticipation with no need for the time or abstract reasoning required by text.[42]

Promotional literature assembled a new set of attractions around the battlefield appealing to the motoring public's leisure pursuits. One conflated "the Shrine of all Nationalities" with the nearby Caledonia Golf Course, Michaux State Forest, "excellent" trout fishing, and deer hunting. Gettysburg was both a memorial and a sanctuary from urban life—"A perfect week-end outing"—now only a leisurely drive away. After the Gettysburg Travel Council assumed tourist promotion responsibilities in 1954, the "sights to see" booklets grew much more family oriented as wholesome commercial amusements and services proliferated. Bachelder's guidebook had used the genteel Springs Hotel, and railroad guidebooks later used Round Top Park to enhance Gettysburg's appeal. By the 1960s, folding the expanding number of tourist enterprises within the shrine's canopy created a mega–tourist site.[43]

The Chamber also attempted to revive the lucrative nineteenth-century rituals of monument building and reunions. Hoping to nurture the Southern trade, the Chamber encouraged governors of Southern states to erect monuments to their fallen heroes. Appreciating the power of wizened veterans to draw media attention, the Chamber invited the GAR for "one glorious encampment once more" in 1926 and the United Confederate Veterans for a seventieth reunion of the battle in 1933. The onset of depression appears to have dampened these initiatives along with tourism, but in casting for ways to revive the sunken industry, the Chamber tried again in the late 1930s as tourism resurged. With Americans clinging to their past for reassurance during the economic crisis, the Chamber launched the enormously successful seventy-fifth anniversary celebration in 1938. A mix of patriotism and spectacle featuring doddering veterans and what the *Philadelphia Inquirer* called a "monster military parade" of whippet tanks, bombers, and other military hardware, "The Last Reunion of the Blue and Gray" flooded half a million visitors into the town lavishly adorned by a decorator who had festooned every presidential inauguration since Woodrow Wilson's. More important, as a national festival illuminating a dreary decade, the spectacle that featured the upbeat President Franklin Roosevelt thrilled the media. Over one hundred print and broadcast journalists set up camp and required thirty-five miles of wiring to churn out radio, newspaper, magazine, and newsreel features.[44]

Spinning Gettysburg into national consciousness, the festival was the brainchild of Chamber Executive Secretary Paul Roy. A Wisconsin journalist who had wandered from several different newspapers, Roy landed at the *Gettysburg Times* in 1924 as news editor. Described as "a dynamo of original and practical ideas," Roy worked his way to the Chamber's top spot in part by launching civic events he then skillfully publicized. Roy also produced *Human Interest Stories of Gettysburg,* a collection of some fanciful, some truthful tales of the battle that nevertheless became the best-seller among tourist guidebooks. "As a salesman, he has no peer," the *Gettysburg Times* saluted after Roy successfully steered the state commission administering the anniversary celebration. "He has resold Gettysburg to the world as a national shrine of America at a time when something of just this nature had to be done to keep Gettysburg from slipping into oblivion," the paper went on. By stating that Roy "has resold Gettysburg," the *Times* meant that Roy had managed to feed Gettysburg into the national media mill. Roy of course benefited from the growth of radio, newsreels, mass-circulation magazines, and highways that were increasingly homogenizing the nation. But both helped project Gettysburg onto the national stage as a shrine accessible to all Americans that combined patriotism, progress, national togetherness, and fun.[45]

Communication improvements disseminated the Gettysburg image faster and farther than ever before, but also shifted the use of space at the shrine. Tourist businesses previously confined to railroad junctions in town and the Round Top Park area began fanning out onto the roads surrounding Gettysburg. To serve lodging needs of automobile tourists, for example, camp-

FIGURE 20. Swope's tourist cabins on West Confederate Avenue, 1940s, part of a complex that included a refreshment stand, dance pavilion, picnic grounds, and, as the chief attraction, a shed spuriously labeled "Gen. Longstreet's HQ, July, 1863." Other motoring tourist plazas featured gas pumps and small museums (111-0056, Gettysburg National Military Park)

grounds followed by tourist cabins, then motels, and finally chain motels forced the last Gettysburg hotel to close in the 1970s. Roadway enterprises became fixed parts of the landscape surrounding Gettysburg, but also shaped visitors' experience. In 1925, Zink and Hartzeil's Campground on the Lincoln Highway advertised not only souvenirs, but a Battlefield Museum, an "unusually interesting collection of relics of the Gettysburg Battlefield." About five years later, S. W. Swope dragged an outbuilding from a nearby farm to his land on Seminary Ridge and labeled it Longstreet's Headquarters. Although no documentation connected the shed with Confederate General James Longstreet, Swope used it to anchor a tourist plaza that included a dance hall, tourist cabins, picnic tables, and a refreshment stand. Some entrepreneurs, following the trend that combined education and entertainment, likewise opened structures of dubious historical significance but legitimated them with period furniture. Whether tourist cabins or refreshment stands, other new tourist concerns invariably included "museums"—a few curiosities, cold drinks, and souvenirs.[46]

Entrepreneurs also employed new technology to package the battle narrative in a visually stimulating manner familiar to visitors. In 1939 George Rosensteel, owner of the National Museum built in 1921 for the new auto trade, opened The Electric Map. This huge relief map, which Rosensteel's son Joseph spent six years designing and wiring, employed hundreds of colored light bulbs and switches to explain the battle in half-hour presentations. In time, the Rosensteels added canned instead of live narration, and expanded the theater as the combined show-museum-souvenir shop grew into Gettysburg's largest tourist attraction. Despite the distortion of presenting the battle as twinkling entertainment, the Electric Map received praise from Park Service historian Frederick Tilberg, who termed it "an interpretive method of broad popular appeal as well as a means of relating a true story of battle action." Not far away from the National Museum, another impresario improved on this sensationalism with a diorama staged on a model of the Gettysburg landscape. Opened in the early 1950s, the Gettysburg Diorama presented the struggle as canned drama starring over three thousand toy soldiers animated by lighting effects and artificial smoke.[47]

Along with technologies, a perceptive but bold approach to the leisure business helped create the shrine of mass culture between 1950 and 1970, when tourist numbers quadrupled. LeRoy E. (L. E.) Smith, whose Mercedes' license plate justifiably read "Le Roi," served as the linchpin behind the transformation of Gettysburg. Smith, like Roy, hailed from the Midwest and cut his teeth in the media. As a youth he won an award as the nation's top salesman for *Pictorial Review* magazine, and then attained a major's rank flying bombers in World War II. After the war, Smith launched a magazine distribution business in Gettysburg that he expanded into souvenir wholesaling. But he knew his souvenirs needed outlets. With an eye toward the Park Service's new visitors' center, Smith bought commercialized historic buildings and cheesy amusements such as the Lincoln Train Museum and Hall of Presidents Wax Museum, then built a "period" mall he named Old Gettysburg Village. And because tourists require services, he invested in a Holiday Inn high-rise, a second large motor hotel, and a cafeteria, and secured the concession for battlefield bus tours from the Park Service. By 1970, few of the 2.5 million visitors arriving avoided a market relationship with L. E. Smith. Looking back, after finishing his empire a few years before his death, Smith said, "The thing that made me successful here is that I could see opportunity where no one else could see it." But many catchpenny operations followed Smith's success, so that by the time the Park Service opened its new visitor's center in 1962, Gettysburg resembled Niagara Falls or Gatlinburg. The town had no zoning ordinances, which made it "open to every huckster," as the *Harrisburg Evening News* stated in 1970.[48]

No one did more than Smith to complete the changes begun by the automobile revolution a half-century before. Smith knew that the more attractions Gettysburg claimed, the longer tourists would stay and the more dollars they would spend. He had a keen sense of who most automobile tourists were—families on annual vacation—and what they wanted to see: entertainment with a patina of patriotic uplift. After all, families arrived to bond around the stability of an American past that provided some comfort from the dislocation of suburban life and Cold War doom. Most important, Smith grasped the importance of images in a culture where television permeated nearly every American home by the mid-1960s. With surface impressions growing ever more important for success, Smith helped found the Gettysburg Travel Council and embraced Dale Carnegie training to cultivate "winning" images.[49]

In its rapid ascendance to the apex of mass culture, television had further sensitized Americans to images that were, paradoxically, universal yet ingested privately among family members. Furthermore, television drama from *Davy Crockett* to *Robin Hood* accelerated a trend toward history-as-entertainment. Smith's Jennie Wade House and Wills House where Lincoln stayed, for example, were fitted out with wax dummies and audio recordings. The National Civil War Wax Museum, opened in 1963, boasted that "[t]hrough the most modern sound and lighting effects, combined with the newest theatrical techniques, and of course, life-size action packed figures, visitors are thrilled by the unfolding of Pickett's Charge and the re-creation of Lincoln's immortal Gettysburg Address." Bus tours over the battlefield, with passengers listening to narration by television actors or newscasters, reflected familiarity with TV "stars." Attractions such as Fort Defiance and Fantasyland, which opened in the late 1950s, evoked Walt Disney's familiar television images of American toughness and family togetherness—images that particularly appealed to Cold War suburbanites huddled against danger on the "crabgrass frontier." And when Gettysburg celebrated the Civil War Centennial, the battle's anniversary featured not only solemn rituals; although the Pennsylvania Centennial Commission desired "a dignified and meaningful observance," the festive commemoration featured a reenactment using canned sound effects along with "living vignettes" of the battle. Even though the Park superintendent admitted the *tableaux vivants* "were not what they should have been, historically speaking," the *Gettysburg Times* claimed tourists rated them among the best centennial events. It is hardly surprising that cameramen from CBS and local television stations filmed the reenactment spectacle, even encouraging reenactors to stage a special hand-to-hand fight scene near the High Water Mark.[50]

Television did more than precondition the public for staged techniques at Gettysburg. Celebrities created by the new medium also were employed in a way that boosted both star and shrine. This technique was hardly new. In 1941, Mrs. Helen Longstreet and the group that planned to erect a

monument to her husband, Confederate General James Longstreet, enlisted
Mary Pickford as part of their publicity campaign. At the end of World War
II, George Rosensteel, owner of the Gettysburg National Museum, planned
to augment his Civil War displays with rooms devoted to sports and entertainment figures. Although the plan never came to fruition, Rosensteel
claimed he had received hearty cooperation for the project (which was to
include a Betty Grable exhibit) from motion picture executives.[51]

Television enlarged the Hollywood halo because it possessed a larger lens
than the movies did. For the Centennial extravaganza in 1963, the Gettysburg Centennial Commission's public relations mill borrowed from the
instant recognition the medium provided by hiring television personalities
to work the event. The Commission chose NBC Television commentator
Ben Grauer, "who will provide a vivid word-picture of events" for the opening day program, according to a press release. "A veteran screen and television actor" who appeared in *The Defenders* narrated the spectacle of Pickett's Charge. Though at the time principals connected with the Centennial
considered "living history" battles questionable and even profaning commemorative activities, celebrities tended to legitimate reenactments for the
public.[52]

Celebrity use of television to pull Gettysburg into the "boob tube"
reached its apogee with television "personality" Cliff Arquette. A bit actor
who performed in theater, radio, and movies, Arquette found his niche on
television when he developed the rustic comic character "Charlie Weaver"
in 1948. Appearing on quiz shows, variety programs, and on the *Jack Paar
Show* as Paar's foil, Charlie Weaver was, according to a publicity announcement, "the beloved hick of millions of fireside TV sets." In private life
Arquette combined skill as a graphic artist and woodcarver with his interest
in the Civil War. Along with L. E. Smith and another partner, he founded
"Gettysburg Tours, Inc.," which shuttled tourists around the battlefield in
Mercedes buses. Through Arquette's television connections, the company
enlisted actor Raymond Massey and Hugh Downs, of 20–20 fame, to nar-
rate the recorded tour.

Nor was that Arquette's only Gettysburg venture updating an old tourist
service for new audiences. In the mid-1950s he purchased part of a former
orphan's home near the National Cemetery and stuffed it with his creations
and collectibles. Essentially the museum mirrored an old Barnumesque curiosity cabinet suitable for family leisure. But Arquette's marketing genius lay
in repackaging yesterday's tourist trap for the television age. He publicized
ordinary displays with humbug such as "exciting techniques of 'Light and
Sound' recently developed in Europe." Arquette also unleashed his television connections. Originally labeling the enterprise Cliff Arquette's Soldiers
Museum, in a few years he billed the place as Charlie Weaver's American
Museum of the Civil War—identified by a large electric sign out front. But
he also capitalized on the "as seen on TV" phenomenon by featuring "full

FIGURE 21. Opening Day of Cliff Arquette's Soldiers Museum on Baltimore Street, March 2, 1959. The museum was filled with guns, hand-carved soldiers, and dioramas. By the 1960s Arquette had renamed the business Charley Weaver's American Museum of the Civil War (Walter Lane Collection, no. 24864-3, Adams County Historical Society, Gettysburg, Pennsylvania)

size vignettes" of television stars Tennessee Ernie Ford and Jonathan Winters. Like L. E. Smith, Arquette sensed postwar Gettysburg's tourism potential if it could be adapted to mass culture.[53]

The Cents of Historic Preservation

At the same time both Arquette and Smith operated tourist circus wagons, they jumped on the bandwagon of historic preservation. By the mid-1950s, tourism to historic sites functioned as an important part of a widening leisure industry. But historic touring means that tourists are consumers of sights distinguishable from the present. When the Park Service took control of the battlefield, it followed the twentieth-century trend of reserving precommercial space to set it apart as historical. In effect this policy equated Gettysburg's sacred ground with appearance. Gettysburg entrepreneurs thus walked a tightrope when they created new products that endangered the historical vista.

Smith and Arquette seemed to realize that their success as impresarios rested in part on their personas as crusaders for landscape purity. Smith's properties developed land previously undisturbed near the High Water Mark and East Cemetery Hill, yet Smith helped found Historic Gettysburg— Adams County and National Heritage Associates, the latter with a corporate purpose "to acquire and preserve historical sites in and about Gettysburg." In its first maneuver, National Heritage Associates purchased the Jennie Wade house, moved it to make way for Smith's Holiday Inn, and tacked on a gift shop and "museum." Although Smith bought only two historic buildings, which he bastardized with "talking walls" and wax dummies, the national weekly paper *Grit* stated in 1974 that Smith "wanted Americans to know their past and take pride in it" and "furthermore, he has made it pay."[54]

Arquette made the shrine pay too, but again by using his television persona as leverage. In 1959, Arquette agreed to chair the emergency committee of the Gettysburg Battlefield Preservation Association (GBPA), which pledged to buy privately owned land whose development could potentially "destroy the original farm character of the battlefield." Just three months after the GBPA formally organized, Charlie Weaver asked viewers for "a buck to save Gettysburg" on the Jack Paar show, for which contributors would receive an ersatz deed. Within a week so many responses to the request poured into Gettysburg—many asking for "deeds" as Christmas gifts—that the GBPA rented an office and hired help to process them. The response illustrated not only the mass appeal of television, but its power when combining Charlie Weaver and Gettysburg. With his suspenders, cornball humor, and avuncular, folksy appearance, Charlie Weaver evoked memories of small-town security to suburban viewers undergoing relocation and threats of nuclear annihilation. And because he resembled the Civil War veteran of a generation earlier (by 1960 they were all gone), Charlie Weaver was a perfect match for the town that promised tourists the American past.[55]

Charlie Weaver's appearance months later on CBS's *Person to Person*, in which he discussed preservation while guiding viewers through his museum, seemed more transparent salesmanship. But Arquette's summons on national television represented the opening salvo of a struggle continued through the 1960s by others in the media. Mass-circulation serials featured articles about "the Second Battle of Gettysburg" illustrated by photos of a Stuckey's gas station–restaurant near a monument or Steinwehr Avenue crammed with tourist enterprises. The media's "Second Battle" launched by Arquette ended with its own Pickett's Charge. In the early 1970s, a devel-

oper proposed building a 307-foot observation tower near the new visitors'
center with its mall-like parking lot. By that time attractions as dissociated
from the Civil War as Land of Little Horses, Jungleland, or International
Village formed part of a family-oriented touring vortex netting $15 to $21
million per year. As might be expected, booster organizations that had been
developing ever more sophisticated methods of attracting tourists favored
the tower. So did local government, which viewed it as a way of replenish-
ing tax dollars lost to federal land ownership. The press, Civil War organizations, historical associations, environmentalists, and, initially, the Park
Service decried it as an intrusion and desecration. But the Park Service
suddenly changed course in mid-1971, granting the developer right-of-way
over federal land when he agreed to move the site. A last-ditch stand by
Pennsylvania Governor Milton Shapp, who delivered an injunction in person to stop construction, failed in a series of court appeals. By the time it
opened for business in 1974, the National Gettysburg Battlefield Tower
symbolized the evil of commercial intrusion on sacred ground, even though
it offered edification and entertainment just like the enterprises of many of
its detractors.[56]

In and of itself the tower represented nothing more than the latest manifestation of the oldest Gettysburg tourist service. From the beginning,
guides had ushered tourists to the battlefield's promontories so they could
obtain a better view and, hence, a better understanding of the original
event. A variety of devices followed that improved the view or else miniaturized the battlefield as a novelty in parlors, theaters, and great fairs.
Bachelder's 1863 "isometric map," which he described as "[I]magine yourself
in a balloon," was followed by George Arnold's battlefield tower, War Department steel towers, Hershberger's panorama, stereographs, the cycloramas, and Briscoe's panoramas. In the twentieth century, the three-dimensional War Department relief map shown at world's fairs, the Electric Map,
the Gettysburg Diorama, and the recycled cyclorama likewise offered novelty while enhancing viewer perspective of the battlefield. As part of this
continuing legacy, the tower's developer planned to employ contemporary
audiovisuals so that tourists "will feel they are part of the scene itself." He
termed his project "a classroom in the sky" that would "heighten the
viewer's understanding of the battle" and produce "better citizens." Too, as
Gettysburg appeared at all the great fairs and often seemed like one with its
midway and whiteway, the tower's design replicated the latest world's fair
attraction, the "space needle." Constructed while the Cold War and Vietnam continued, the tower with its steel girders, gun-metal color, and space-
age design seemed to update Gettysburg as a symbolic victory of industrial
capitalism over opponents of progress. As a latter-twentieth-century addition to the landscape, the tower harmonized with Neutra's nearby modern-
istic visitors' center erected a decade before. And as for the tower's desecrating influence—a "honky tonk intrusion," as Governor Shapp labeled

it—a few observers pointed out the obvious, that such concern was belated. The tower "can't be any more of a mockery to those men who died in battle than all the rest of the money-making schemes around," a Gettysburg resident pointed out in the *Gettysburg Times*. But she added that Gettysburg's image, and not commercial intrusion on the landscape, posed the real threat to memory anyway. "The major battle fought in Gettysburg is so commercialized and glamorized," she said, "that all true sense of the horror of that war has long been forgotten."[57]

But that was precisely the point. The Park Service, entrepreneurs, and tourist organizations had combined to shape a shrine where visitors could lose themselves in pleasant family activity. There was no need to challenge tourists with messy issues such as the meaning of the Civil War, its causes, or how Civil War firearms could shred flesh and spill blood. But because of its inescapable, dominating reminder of the present from which Americans sought escape, the tower became a cause célèbre in the 1970s and catalyst for generating public concern over a deteriorating *visual* environment. The tower and all the other tourist services and attractions whose glare re-minded visitors of contemporary life simply were not what they were paying to see. With this realization emerging from the tower controversy, the Get-tysburg tourist industry grew much more sensitive to creating the historical ambience tourists expected. Arquette and Smith were ahead of their time, prophets who realized that the *appearance* of preserving the historical envi-ronment could bring both financial and public relations rewards. Smith, in fact, planned but never brought to fruition a Living History Area that would reenact Civil War camps and battles, much like Disney's America planned in the 1990s. L. E. Smith, like Dale Carnegie with his guidebooks to personal success, intended to present a surface appearance of stability and substance, put people at ease, and create the illusion that there are places safe from markets.

The Image of a Cold War Shrine

Gettysburg's salience during the Cold War era owed something to a media event beyond manipulation of memory. During the 1950s, Gettysburg shone in the media spotlight as the home of the nation's chief executive. Dwight D. Eisenhower, hero of World War II and president from 1953 to 1961, bought a Gettysburg farm in 1954 with hopes of retiring there. The first home "Ike" and his wife Mamie ever owned, the 496-acre farm, consum-mated the couple's pleasant memories of Gettysburg framed decades earlier when Ike served as commander of a tank school at Gettysburg. Ike's retire-ment plans accelerated, however, when he opted to recuperate in Gettys-burg from a 1955 heart attack. As a result, Gettysburg continuously ap-peared in the news.[58]

After Ike set up a presidential office in the Gettysburg post office, *U.S. News and World Report* called Gettysburg "the unofficial capital of the nation." Cabinet members came to visit, news conferences were held in the Hotel Gettysburg, and crowds gathered when Ike arrived in town. Cameras snapped and whirred when Ike brought famous people to Gettysburg such as Bernard Montgomery, Winston Churchill, Nikita Khruschev, or Charles de Gaulle. It may have been an exaggeration that the battlefield "now ranks second to Mr. Eisenhower as a tourist attraction," as *U.S. News* concluded, but the Eisenhowers encouraged construction of several motels, restaurants, and the sale of "Ike and Mamie" souvenirs. Ike, however, represented more than a television celebrity like Cliff Arquette. After all, the Cincinnatus of Western civilization opted to settle at the pastoral site of the Civil War's greatest battle. As chief executive of a nation characterized by both unparalleled affluence and tension, his avuncular visage provided comfort from Cold War hostility and domestic change. Reported to be small-town "everyday folks" by the people of Gettysburg, the Eisenhowers on their little farm offered a model for lackadaisical withdrawal from the world's problems. Ike easily folded into Gettysburg's image not only as a quintessential American tourist site but a place of retreat. In effect, the couple functioned as the *Good Housekeeping* seal of approval for Gettysburg.[59]

Neither Ike nor Gettysburg were fossilized relics fissured from the present, as each strengthened the other to forge contemporary meaning for the shrine. Ike, now commander in chief, had been helmsman of victory in Europe and could handily manage national challenges; Gettysburg, site of national tragedy and renewal, also provided confidence for confronting the future. The match dovetailed easily into the era's anachronistic dissonance: colonial furniture and space age design, religious faith and faith in technology, Disney's Tomorrow Land and Frontier Land, Davy Crockett and Elvis, Grandma Moses and Jackson Pollack, Westerns and outer space.[60]

Ike invigorated the shrine about the same time mass culture began to split the past from the present. Tourism had changed, and so had Gettysburg's sacred significance for a nation confronted with freedom at home and abroad. The Cold War revived Gettysburg's symbolic place in American exceptionalism, expressed as the rebirth of a nation divinely ordained for global leadership. Perhaps the first to hint at Gettysburg's broadened role was the first Cold War chief executive. When President Harry S Truman toured the battlefield in 1946, characteristically driving with wife, Bess, as a passenger, he suggested that the phrase on the Eternal Light Peace Memorial should be changed from "Peace Eternal in a Nation United" to "Peace Eternal in a World United." The following year, Congressman Wat Arnold of Missouri felt a surge of nationalistic pride after visiting Gettysburg, and in a subsequent radio address urged all Americans to visit Gettysburg during such "troubling times." For a nation that served as "a leading exponent of world peace and human rights," Gettysburg inspired "the same hope for a brighter future that it meant for Abraham Lincoln." Gettysburg girded Americans in the armor of a heroic past that would galvanize the nation for postwar challenges. Similarly, the era's greatest popularizer of the Civil War, Bruce Catton, wrote in 1955 that Gettysburg was "a beginning and not an ending . . . the meeting of a test, the paying by all the people of a price beyond calculation for an opportunity that is not yet fully realized." By 1961 Catton had expanded the theme in a speech at Gettysburg College. "As a result of the Civil War," Catton concluded, "it is our inescapable position to be committed to freedom broad enough to encompass all men, of all races and creeds and backgrounds." The legacy of Gettysburg, then, echoed a newly inaugurated president's "new frontier" of missionary obligation on a global scale.[61]

Catton grounded his grandiose rhetoric in the physical landscape of Gettysburg. "To visit Gettysburg is to step back into the American past," he wrote, and promised that "you may have trouble remembering just what century you are living in." This was exactly the image the scions of mass culture, including the Park Service, the Chamber of Commerce and the Travel Council, the automobile marketers, state tourist bureaus, and even forward-looking impresarios tried to build. All had helped translate Gettysburg into easily comprehensible, graphic terms for a mass audience that paid for the illusion of stepping into the past. Besides, encouraging spending on cars and family vacations to see America firsthand was part of the Cold War struggle. As for the accompanying sacred meaning during the Cold War, the commitment to freedom Catton saw in Gettysburg produced an overseas venture in Vietnam that ended illusions about global missions. It turned another page in the Gettysburg story to one illustrating that Gettysburg could thrive on sacred meanings no bigger than the battle itself.[62]

Chapter Six

☆ ☆ ☆ ☆ ☆ ☆ ☆ ☆ ☆ ☆ ☆

"Dad Got Us There in a Day": Automobiles
and Family Touring

JAMES MURPHY and his family packed the car in early summer 1964 and left on a vacation that included visits to historic sites administered by the National Park Service. The Murphys began the trip by visiting Civil War battlefields in Tennessee such as Lookout Mountain and Chickamauga. Then they drove into Virginia, stopping at the colonial ruins of Jamestown and exploring the Revolutionary War's victory battlefield, Yorktown. After touring Fredericksburg, another Civil War battlefield, the family drove north to Gettysburg. When the Murphys returned home, James felt so elated by the sojourn he wrote a letter commending the Park Service for its excellent personnel and services. "Above all," Murphy wrote, family members were impressed by "the beauty and wonder of all our historic sights that have been faithfully preserved in their original form." Unaware that the Park Service tinkered with many of these sites to "preserve" their "original form," Murphy and his family evidently felt the visual effects met their expectations. Like millions of other families who hit the road every summer, the Murphys validated their "American-ness"—and enjoyed family entertainment—by visiting historical places with a visible past.[1]

By 1964 Gettysburg had earned anew its earlier Mecca sobriquet. Only this time, Gettysburg served automobile pilgrims instead of veterans and excursionists. Now numerous attractions and throngs of auto tourists exaggerated the sacred ground just as excessive monumentation and crowds of disgorging day-trippers had generations earlier. Gettysburg's tourist numbers doubled from 639,894 in 1950 to 1.3 million in 1960 and doubled again a decade later to over 2.6 million. But the agents of mass culture discussed in the last chapter did not transform Gettysburg alone. Gettysburg changed because American society changed. In 1970 the chief park ranger maintained the tourist boom occurred simply because "more families are taking advantage of the park as a recreation area."[2]

Mid-twentieth-century automobiling pilgrims differed from those of the railroad era not only in their primarily family groupings, but also because they reflected less racial, economic, and behavioral diversity. And in contrast to their predecessors, the new visitors freely expressed concerns about the shrine to those in authority. Unlike James Murphy, many felt Gettysburg failed to meet their expectations precisely because anticipation built by travel literature, magazines, and broadcast media conditioned the public to imagine Gettysburg as a sanctuary from change. When post–World War II development belied the image of an innocent, precommercial past, Americans were quick to express outrage even as this development responded to their needs as tourists.

The car's triumph affected American life more than any other technological innovation, perhaps most of all in terms of leisure. It aided national homogenization by bringing city to country and country to city, allowing the development of suburbs and suburban life. As the automobile transformed the nation, so too it changed Gettysburg and the experience of touring it. Like film and then television, the automobile extended the nineteenth-century quest of lifting people beyond the confines of neighborhood. By 1960, automobiles and highways had opened Gettysburg to unprecedented numbers, even if the new tourists reflected uniformity of the expanding American "middle."[3]

From the early 1900s the car offered freedom, a chance for spontaneous and self-controlled touring not restricted by railroad tracks nor schedules. Indeed, in its early days the car served as an instrument of escape from the dictatorship of railroads and the heavy hand of systematic mechanization. The first auto tourists, braving substandard roads not matched by strength of equipment, often were fleeing the stifling confines of gentility through adventuresome "real-life" experience. Auto travel on rutted dirt roads with few services placed tourists in a more direct relationship with the environment than either earlier rail or later auto travelers. Gettysburg, in other words, was but one part of an ongoing activity. The machine, with its limitations and capabilities, became the centerpiece of the trip. And although auto tourists no longer mingled with strangers on passenger cars and in train stations, early touring presented more opportunities for sociability than later auto touring. The Gettysburg tourist of James Murphy's day enjoyed a more insulated, routine, and private experience, usually in family groups. As cars proliferated, highways improved, and vacations became standard fare after World War II, the family and the dynamics of family controlled touring.[4]

Before improved production and higher wages democratized automobiles, only the elite could afford motoring. To critics, automobiles initially represented silk-stocking leisure akin to polo or fox hunting. President Woodrow

Wilson, for example, thought the motoring set displayed an "arrogance of wealth" potentially disruptive to social order. When plans developed early in the century for a boulevard between Gettysburg and Washington, D.C.—introduced in Congress as ultimately unsuccessful legislation for the Lincoln Memorial Highway—Gettysburg Commissioner John P. Nicholson advised against the highway's exclusiveness. "It would be largely used by tourists who desire to indulge in the luxury of traveling in a manner that is beyond the means of the general public—such as by automobiles and tally-hos," he wrote.[5]

Yet automobilists did not need the seventy-mile stretch of smooth road to find motoring happiness at Gettysburg. Once the War Department's Gettysburg National Park Commission assumed control of the battlefield in 1895, it transformed all the battlefield's roads into over twenty miles of avenues. Considered the state of the art in road building at the time, the avenues supported the park's genteel design for contemplative promenading or carriage drives. Before widespread highway improvement following World War I, however, automobilists viewed the smooth stretches as an oasis for sport in a desert of rutted roads.[6]

But autos did not conform to an ambiance intended for repose, especially the way sports drove the new vehicles. As early as 1905, the National Park Commission reported to the Secretary of War that "[t]he fine avenues seem to be a special inducement to large and numerous automobile parties who persistently disregard the rules and regulations governing the park." Automobilists jarred the park's tranquillity with noisy, malodorous machinery and boisterous behavior. The car provided the toy some needed to flout strictures they ached to abandon. "The auto has taken much pleasure from those who drive the avenues behind horses," the *Gettysburg Compiler* lamented in 1907. Accidents resulted, such as one in 1904 in which a horse frightened by an auto jolted its carriage and dragged a passenger, who soon died from her injuries. (Years later, an auto caught fire scaling Little Round Top, scattering tourists, and another smashed into a cannon, which the *Gettysburg Times* reported as "[a] twentieth-century machine lost out to a Civil War cannon.")[7]

Park authorities found themselves losing the control they enjoyed with touring buggies or crowds systematically arriving by train. Before World War I, for example, trucks hauling booze parties furtively stole on the battlefield "with no desire of hearing the story of the battle." In response to the problems, the Gettysburg National Park Commission updated its regulations governing visitor behavior to include restrictions on motorists. Auto speeding forced the park commission, and after 1933 the National Park Service, into hiring guards and motorcycle police to run down offenders. Mischief makers eluded the constabulary by stealing onto the battlefield for "rapid moonlight spins" after hours, turning some avenues into "veritable speedways," according to the *Gettysburg Times*. Given a choice between contemplating monuments and accelerating on avenues, the avenues won out for many visitors. Recreational speeding on the battlefield appears to have ceased as a significant problem in the park with the advent of better roads outside the park, particularly four-lane limited-access highways.[8]

Gettysburg combined with auto touring offered new pleasures other than speeding. Before automobiling became an insulated, private activity it produced cameraderie similar to travel on trains or trolleys. Like the bicycle clubs of the late-nineteenth century, groups of auto owners would gather for "runs" to Gettysburg from nearby cities such as Baltimore or Harrisburg. Some of these meets, which continued until world War I, were endurance contests among advocates of the "strenuous life"; others were called "sociability runs" that participants held annually, arriving in Gettysburg with horns tooting and pennants waving. For many, the trip offered a contest with mud, ruts, rain, and speed in open vehicles of uncertain reliability. Such contacts with nature appealed to middle- and upper-class motorists who yearned to feel elemental human struggle. To the uncertainty of driving many tourists added "roughing it" by rejecting hotel lodgings typical of rail touring. Mirroring a national fad, Gettysburg too experienced a camping craze in the 1920s. The *Gettysburg Times* reported in 1921 that camping by visitors had depressed the town's hotel business. Some of these "tin-can tourists," as they were known, simply wanted to avoid hotel costs, but as the *Times* noted, "wealthy people, especially those with children, have found it great sport to spend several nights camping under the stars."[9]

Most campers were like a Macon, Georgia, physician who drove all the way to Gettysburg "for health and recreation," packing tents, air mattresses, a portable stove, and ice chest. tin-can touring quickly became less primitive, noncommercial, and free spirited. With a characteristic nose for the tourist dollar, farmers along the Lincoln Highway began charging for space in their fields, creating gaggles of campers. In 1922, in the interest of public hygiene and a clean environment, the Pennsylvania Forestry Department established public campgrounds, including a popular one at nearby Caledonia. By the mid-1920s, Gettysburg landowners had set up several private campgrounds with limited services. Like auto runs, campgrounds facilitated sociability with fellow travelers of different regions and social classes. But the advent of commercial campgrounds signaled a trend toward greater exclusivity, privacy, and comfort that omitted the lower classes. Economic barriers, beginning with the automobile and gradual decline of rail service, prevented blacks and other urban poor from continuing the custom of Gettysburg excursions.[10]

Into the 1930s, the drive to Gettysburg by auto served as the main event in a self-managed journey that provided release from routine. Because the car allowed tourists to control machines for a change instead of being controlled by machines, speed fascinated drivers. Gettysburg became a brief respite for the real objective of covering distance, which seemed the only

FIGURE 22. "Tin-can tourists": Motorists camping west of Gettysburg along the Lincoln Highway, 1920s (Photograph Albums no. 10399, Albert and Shirley Small Special Collections Library, University of Virginia Library)

topic worth discussing in postcards sent home. "We reached McConnellsburg last night," a tourist wrote from Gettysburg in 1916. "We reached here at 10:30. After dinner we are going over the battlefields. We leave here and will make York tonight, then on to Trenton and Delaware Water Gap and on home." Gradually as the novelty wore off and as highways improved, automobile touring became as mechanistic as the railroad travel from which early motorists hoped to escape.[11]

Aside from motorists' ability to control the journey, the unexpected provided part of the freedom from routine. Drivers venturing to Gettysburg along unfamiliar roads could usually count on a sudden and unanticipated turn of events as the trip unfolded. When Pierce Furber, his wife, and baby daughter left Philadelphia on the Lincoln Highway for Gettysburg, a seven-mile detour of concrete pavement suddenly veered them north. On the next detour, a zigzag path routed them considerably out of the way and sometimes east instead of west. They then hit a "bumpy old macadam road" that to Pierce Furber's relief did not wake the baby. After crossing the Susquehanna at Harrisburg, the Furbers puzzled over two different signs to Carlisle, one pointing right and the other left. Afterward they learned that both roads led to Carlisle, but Furber admitted "the incident caused us a little loss of patience."[12]

For those adventuresome enough to undertake a cross-country or north-south journey, Gettysburg served as a convenient and familiar layover. Immediately after the 1913 reunion, townspeople noticed an influx of Southern motorists, and three years later an amazed *Gettysburg Compiler* reported, "Automobiles of all descriptions, bearing strange state license tags and loaded with more or less luggage, are the objects of much local curiosity at each stop." By 1936, an observer recorded license tags from every state except New Mexico during one September weekend. Many of these travelers were sucked into Gettysburg not by choice, but because major arteries ran through town. In addition to the east-west Lincoln Highway, New Englanders used Gettysburg as "a gateway to the South," leading to "winter playgrounds below the Mason-Dixon Line," according to the *Gettysburg Times*.[13]

Yet most automobiling motorists targeted Gettysburg chiefly for a weekend recreational retreat on their day off, Sunday. In 1916, a park employee conducting a survey in August discovered that Pennsylvania licenses accounted for 65 percent of the 591 vehicles tallied in a week. "The weekend automobile tour to the battlefield is coming to be more and more recognized as one of the nicest outings that can be arranged by people from Pennsylvania, Maryland, and Washington," the *Adams County News* noted. By 1921, the *Compiler* estimated that five thousand to seven thousand autos entered Gettysburg on a balmy September Sunday. It is impossible to determine how many arrived to see the battlefield as opposed to those who simply intended to use park roads for a spin. Either way, motoring offered not only the escape of recreation but escape into nostalgia, reassuring motorists with a sense of stability evoked by agrarian America.[14]

Ironically, the authentic experiences motorists sought were often romantic notions conditioned by the latest advertising and publicity of automobile industries and organizations. Not only did newspapers and magazines fire up the public with travel columns, news, and advertising about auto travel, but Lincoln Highway and automobile association publicity encouraged Americans to hit the road of fun and escape. National Touring Week, a 1916 scheme launched by auto manufacturers, encouraged all motorists to "take a vacation all at once and turn the week into a great holiday." In 1921 the Pennsylvania Hotelman's Association publicized a Triangle Tour, consisting of a round-trip drive from Harrisburg through Gettysburg, Chambersburg, and return. Drives across the continent particularly fascinated the public, and many of those who completed the journey cashed in by publishing explorer-like accounts of the details, sometimes sponsored by auto manufacturers. George Stevens' and James Larmer's 1915 *Transcontinental Trip in a Ford*, a travelogue and guidebook, recorded the drive through Gettysburg on a seventy-one day, eighty-four-hundred-mile journey.[15]

Like those who found the trolley, avenues, railroad, monuments, and pavilions a boon to touring, some Civil War veterans apparently found the
automobile a welcomed instrument of memory. It suddenly expanded the
range of touring and permitted a quick grasp of a big story. Confederate
veteran David Gregg McIntosh, who had commanded an artillery battalion
during the battle, enlisted a guide and two automobiles for his party of
seven in 1910. At first McIntosh felt disquieted by the machine, as the
driver proceeded "at the most rapid speed, turning some of the sharp curves
in a way which made me feel the dangers of the battlefield were being
repeated." The mental image of a septuagenarian veteran whisked along
while holding his hat, then positioning himself like a gunner while his
daughter-in-law snapped a picture, brings into relief the technological distance traveled in the half-century since the battle. By the end of the tour,
though, McIntosh admired the methodical efficiency of auto touring over
the reposeful plodding of horse and carriage. "With the frequent stops made
by us," he wrote, "I am satisfied we could not have covered half the distance in the same time with horses, and we returned to the hotel well
satisfied with our day's work."[16]

Automobile touring opened a fissure between the motoring public and
the monumented park's aesthetic. Veterans had invested millions in realizing the dream of erecting "monuments of art and taste," which were losing
their power to evoke the past. Before the turn of the century many thought
the park looked like a "vast cemetery"; by the 1920s some tourists thought
the battlefield *was* a cemetery. In an America transforming with telephone
lines and electricity, advertising and automobiles, the temporal distance
from the battle increased. With the decline of veterans who constructed
and visited them, monuments no longer carried as much symbolic weight,
and the sentiment invested in them vaporized along with the sentimental
age that produced them. Moreover, a more mobile America brought fewer
regionally oriented tourists focusing on a particular state or hometown
monument and more visitors oriented to the total scene.

But monuments also failed in part because automobile speed destroyed
their pensive effect. Self-controlled auto touring simply demanded more
rapid response from the landscape than monuments designed for contemplative touring could deliver. Equally significant, the automobile's victory
for individual freedom, along with other tools of mass culture, had reduced
the genteel grip on culture. Not only had older forms of authority been
challenged, but the images of mass culture accustomed the public to graphic
rather than symbolic representation. Motoring tourists who expected a visible past when they escaped to the countryside viewed monuments simply as
objects that muddied the battle's memory. Speeders, runners, campers, and
weekend recreationists all were trying to find "real life" in a park full of
artifice. One tourist who in 1916 drove on to Antietam battlefield after
visiting Gettysburg reported, "We secured at Antietam what we missed at

Gettysburg: the vision of a battle. It did not come from government roads, nor acres of land turned into a park. . . . It came from the fields of grain serving as they had served in war time, fulfilling their mission as the soldier fulfilled his." Because monuments impeded a view of the original landscape, they became objects more for forgetting than remembering. A War Department official in the 1920s understood that monuments failed to aid the "casual observer" touring the battlefield, the "ninety-five percent of tourists who drive through the park without stopping, acquiring such knowledge as they can by hasty glances at monuments and markers."[17]

Thus auto tourists expected a less formal, symbolic, and particularistic approach to touring, with more emphasis on the battle narrative. Again, this was only a partial break with the past. Like many earlier visitors, the auto tourists enjoyed the curious, the gruesome, the unusual. While speeding past monuments, auto tourists found, for example, commercial museums with easily understood realia and sensational attractions interesting. An observer in 1915 noted that "all tourists" visited the Jennie Wade house, a commercial pioneering effort in restoring a Civil War interior. Here they could pay homage to the secular saint popularized in guidebooks and postcards by viewing a few relics, bullet holes, and the bread tray Jennie Wade purportedly used when martyred. By the 1920s, auto tourists patronized conglomerate ma-and-pa enterprises along the Lincoln Highway that sold campsites, groceries, gas, food, soda, souvenirs, and usually included a makeshift museum. These clusters of services appealed to motorists who with one stop could refuel, refresh, find entertainment in the past, and be on their way. A Confederate veteran visiting one of these in the 1920s described it as "crowded with babbling, chattering, heedless sightseers, buying postcards, souvenirs, and milk." He recalled that the "museum" included "a few pistols, a saber or two, some old prints and—a saucer filled with human teeth picked up on the battlefield!" The cyclorama also held its appeal into the auto age. A National Park Service historian thought the cyclorama's popularity made it the most important Gettysburg exhibit, noting in 1941 that tourists who viewed it "were very much impressed and loathe to leave the building."[18]

Aside from the Electric Map and the National Park Service battlefield restoration in the 1930s, Gettysburg added few further attractions until the efflorescence that occurred in the 1950s and 1960s. Yet it would be incorrect to suggest that the station-wagon-driving, luggage-toting family abruptly replaced the sociable, recreational weekend tourist in the 1950s. Changes in Gettysburg touring after the 1920s indicate the later boom represented pent-up demand experienced in other parts of the economy. In other words, had no depression nor war intervened, Gettysburg would have been transformed a decade or more earlier. As it was, 721,395 tourists were recorded in 1929, but the Depression cut the number to 204,380 by 1933. Gettysburg experienced a steady rise to the 1.5 million mark of 1939—a record not matched again until 1960—followed by another dip to 66,761 in 1943 because of wartime tire and gas rationing. Already, by the late 1920s mass family touring had replaced the motoring culture of nomads and the sporting crowd.[19]

More discretionary income and time beginning in the 1920s developed a mass culture of leisure consumers that produced a post–World War II flood of tourists. Real wages grew significantly along with leisure time, while falling prices of goods due to production efficiency enhanced the purchasing power of wages 50 percent. America's older producer ethic of work-and-save gave way to a consumer ethic of work-and-spend, lubricated by installment buying and an advertising industry that preached pleasure *now*. Although the poor and minorities were excluded, factory workers along with the upper classes fed at the cornucopia of cars, appliances, and other consumer goods produced by modern manufacturing. The new consumers provided a vast market for radio, movies, newspapers, magazines, and advertising that not only bombarded the culture with uniform images but generated icons recognizable everywhere. The introduction of sight and sound from radio and movies produced a new self-awareness and powerful universal experiences for all Americans. A swirl of genteel and working-class culture blended into an apparent classless society of leisure consumers that swelled and solidified after midcentury with the triumph of television. The irony lay in the fact that the inexorable sweep of this universalizing, commercial culture coerced Americans into enjoying it all privately in cars, in theaters, and at home.[20]

Cheaper cars and installment buying enabled the new army of consumers to demonstrate their enthusiasm for automobiles as leisure machines. By 1926 the number of cars registered had quadrupled from a decade earlier, and just before the Depression Americans boasted one for every five people. Some pundits, including the industrialist most responsible for democratizing the car, Henry Ford, imagined the automobile a tool for enhancing family life through shared travel experiences. With extensive road improvements by 1930, many who previously had expected nothing more than an occasional trolley or railroad excursion now could drive themselves to a destination far from home. The automobile represented the quintessential agent of mass culture, mixing people of different classes, breaking down regional differences, and enabling a blend of working-class pleasure and genteel self-improvement. While on the one hand, the car offered spontaneity and insouciance, on the other it could be an instrument for family didacticism and privacy. For example, William Sergeant, an industrial employee from Dayton, Ohio, who had not graduated from high school, viewed the automobile as an educational tool for his family. As participants in a trend that grew after World War II, Sergeant drove his family to a different site of Americana every summer. In 1940, the Sergeants visited Gettysburg, and in other years they drove to Niagara Falls, Philadelphia, Lexington, and Con-

cord. By that time Americans spent 5 percent of their incomes on vacations, greater than the total of any other recreation, with 80 percent of
those outings using automobiles. Tourist grouping by families inspired new
advertising appeals, such as one for the 1938 seventy-fifth reunion extending an invitation "to come, bring your family, be Gettysburg's guest for this
never-to-be forgotten spectacle."[21]

The new tourists demanded and received different stimulation from motor travel than had their earlier elite counterparts, who sought the sublime
in landscapes. Under the new aesthetic, motorists expected not only sensual pleasure from driving but also an encounter with "old-time" America,
free of modern reminders. The interwar decades' rapid change followed
by economic crisis induced nostalgia that the automobile could remedy
through visual reassurance. A public more visually oriented than ever before expected to encounter precommercial America when they took to the
road, an image they imbibed from movies, newspapers, magazines, and
travel bureaus. Historical destinations contrived by the media, government,
and private agencies became a major preoccupation of tourists. While the
National Park Service began restoring Gettysburg and other historical sites
to their period look, attractions such as Williamsburg, Greenfield Village,
Sturbridge, and others emerged as sanctuaries from the present. The past
became a pseudoevent created by a vast array of government and commercial media appealing to longings for escape and entertainment. For example, in the wake of hoopla government agencies generated for the seventy-
fifth reunion in 1938, *Reader's Digest* published an article about Gettysburg
that stated, "There is an aura of history over the quiet landscape; the air is
heavy with heartbreak, and ghosts speak to you." Such assurances created
expectations of "authentic" sites of memory that would be set off from the
present. The paradox of searching for the authentic in the contrived, and
the precommercial in the commercial, seemed to disturb no one.[22]

As "authentic" attractions grew more fabricated, so did touring. Auto
touring lost its cachet as "real life" adventure when tourists encountered
mechanical breakdowns, bumpy roads, and commingling with strangers.
While early tourists came from the middle and upper classes, new motorists
emerged from the working class in the 1920s and 1930s. To these travelers
who "roughed it" aplenty in real life, a holiday of camping and mud holes
made little sense. At the same time, motoring tourists tried to avoid the
traffic congestion and expense of downtown hotels. In response to the demand for home comfort on the road, cabins and lunch counters replaced
campsites and cookouts. In the 1930s, campground owners and others constructed tourist cabins and cottages. Some cabins were little more than
primitive summer shelters where guests shared an outdoor latrine. Others
like Curnal Butt's 1938 complex featured cottages with private modern
baths, a luncheonette, and gas station within walking distance to the new
Electric Map and High Water Mark. By the post–World War II period,
motels—in effect, connected cottages—had begun to appear in Gettysburg.[23]

The new facilities built outside of town shared little with Gettysburg's half-dozen hotels clustered near the railroad stations. Cottages obliged motorists with convenient access, but also demonstrated a growing tourist preference for middle-class comfort on the road. Increasingly, this meant privacy for families. The public spaces that characterized rail tourism became private space in the automotive age. Tourists no longer rubbed elbows with strangers on trains, nor did they experience communal situations in hotel lobbies, restaurants, or campgrounds, for that matter. Improved roads and autos further sealed travelers so that touring from start to return could be experienced privately and comfortably, shared with only family members.[24]

In just a few decades, automobiles had irrevocably changed the Gettysburg tourist experience. The car's popularity registered a complete triumph when it finally drove out the option of railroad travel to Gettysburg by the end of World War II. In its meteoric rise it had changed itself from an upper-class sport to recreation for the masses. The vagabondism and adventure that early on distinguished auto from rail travel disappeared. Driving by car became a means to an end rather than an end in itself. Four-lane highways and improved cars insulated tourists from the environment, especially so with automobile air conditioning. It threw the nuclear family back against itself as an autonomous touring group sharing vacation experience. By the end of World War II, all the elements of the new touring stood in place to be carried to new extremes by the floodtide of baby-boom families.

The Cold War Family Tourist Invasion

Gettysburg's post–World War II tourist boom that doubled and then quadrupled tourist numbers from 1950 to 1970 paralleled the growth of suburbs and suburban families. Two decades of uncertainty and deprivation following prosperity of the 1920s had created hopes for realizing an American Dream of tranquility, home ownership, and comfortable living. The soaring postwar population added 29 million new Americans in the 1950s alone, a record proportional to fecund India. Along with Cold War defense spending, pent-up demand unleashed a flood of consumer spending that expanded the economy far beyond pre-Depression Levels. A 1959 *Life* magazine double issue titled "The Good Life" explored a full-bore, mass-production economy's benefits to average workers, observing, "What used to be the small leisured classes became the big leisured masses." Enabled by the car's ever-increasing popularity, suburbs growing by one million units a year beginning in 1950 anchored this consumer society and accounted for 85 percent of the nation's growth twenty years later.[25]

This brave new world of housing developments, transplanted urbanites, shopping, television, tailfins, and the threat of nuclear annihilation broke with the past, but Americans still anxiously looked backward. Mass culture provided plenty of opportunities for finding pioneer origins even if the new homesteaders raised lawns instead of crops, fought crabgrass instead of drought, and cooked over a fire only occasionally in summer. The suburban interior with its knotty pine and colonial furniture connected culturally to a vogue for television and movie Westerns, ranch houses, Norman Rockwell covers, Grandma Moses prints, Disney films, and a "New Frontier" of challenges. But suburban life also harked back to the genteel agenda of improving leisure and domesticity. Crabgrass frontiersmen of the suburbs pursued hobbies, church activities, and home improvement as important leisure activities. Consumerism may have echoed self-indulgence rather than self-restraint, but spending could be justified as a way to enhance family life. McCall's magazine idealized the domestic "nest of goods" with a 1954 issue on "togetherness" of the companionate family. The editor observed that "men, women, and children . . . are creating this new and warmer way of life not as women alone, or men alone, isolated from one another, but as a family sharing common experience." This sharing of leisure in the suburbs, a mix of electronic entertainment and purposeful nurturing, conditioned tourist experiences at Gettysburg.[26]

The car and the family vacation was one of the best expressions of family "togetherness." By 1963, 43 percent of all American families reported averaging six hundred miles on extended annual vacations. For a week or two families could exercise complete control of their lives as they entered the vast system of American highways. Considering the break with the past Americans faced, it was no coincidence that historic sites predominated as destinations. Vacations to historic sites not only allowed parents to control family leisure for didactic purposes, but also served the purpose of raising patriotic future citizens. At the same time, historic restorations at Disneyland, Sturbridge, Williamsburg, Mystic Seaport, or Gettysburg entertained members of a visual culture on the road just as on television and in the movies. Few, perhaps, realized that family-centered consumption of goods or travel to historic sites supported American values and aided Cold War supremacy. On the road, as in the ranch house, supermarket, or church, Americans acted out their nation's freedom and abundance as a counterpoint to godless communism.[27]

American families received plenty of encouragement to travel from both public and private sources. The federal government supported family "togetherness" in the suburbs and on the road. Postwar legislation offering Federal Housing and Veterans' Administration loans ensured suburban development fueled by bloated defense contracts. Family touring was encouraged through the Interstate Highway Act of 1956, which linked the nation with forty-one thousand miles of four-lane highways. To complete the circuit, the National Park Service provided places to see, arguing that its treasures replaced spiritual energy lost in modern living. Cultural nationalism provided a popular theme for television and movies, while corporate America exploited colorful print advertising that featured American historical themes. Major mass-circulation magazines and Sunday newspaper supplements endorsed family trips to Gettysburg as a way of escaping the present.[28]

The car offered families choices in customizing trips centered around children. Interstates and turnpikes enabled families to include a wider range of educational attractions than their counterparts had a generation earlier. Typical of tourists traveling from the west or south, the Lawrences of Kansas City visited Washington, D.C., first before turning north to Gettysburg in the early 1960s. Others with younger children might include a stop exclusively devoted to children's entertainment. Heading south from Vestal, New York, the Purdys paid for a few hours of mechanical amusements at Hershey Park before continuing. Recalling the impressions of a childhood trip to Gettysburg in 1959, Judith Green wrote, "All we saw was how pretty Gettysburg was: rolling green meadows, a little apple orchard, low stone walls, bronze sculpture gently cradled in the landscape." The car also produced a novel environment where "togetherness" meant family singing, word games, or games involving passing sights to keep children entertained, even if close proximity, especially on a hot day, also produced conflict.[29]

Once in Gettysburg, families jaded by travel, heat, and sometimes too much "togetherness" needed a place to stay. The postwar wave of family tourists spawned a new lodging industry in Gettysburg. Although some cottages and tourist homes hung on, motels decisively wrecked the Gettysburg hotel business by the 1970s, when the last hotel closed. Commercial campgrounds reappeared in Gettysburg, updated with hot showers and flush toilets. Tourists loaded with specialized camping equipment no longer considered camping "roughing it," but wholesome family recreation and an additional bonding opportunity. Of the Lawrence family trip in the 1960s, Robert Lawrence remembered "camping the most because my Dad had us all laughing until we cried, as we lay in the dark tent and he talked about lost Confederates dropping by asking which way the battle was." For families like the Lawrences, camping also served as a way to extend the length of the trip by saving money.[30]

Most postwar tourists, however, demanded consumer comforts provided by the motel with its privacy, easy access, ample parking, modern baths, television, and sometimes pools. As in the rest of the country, Gettysburg's motels started as small, family-owned businesses after World War II, and by 1971 the Gettysburg Travel Council listed thirty-seven. The largest, evidence of mass culture in the lodging business, were motor inn chains such as Howard Johnson's and Holiday Inn. Referral chains such as Best Western or Quality Inns accounted for many other Gettysburg motels that also exploited national recognition for a coast-to-coast clientele. Like the car, restaurant, or television program, motels extended suburban life while allowing escape from it. Indeed, motels with their familiar entertainment and mediocre hamburger-fries-Coke restaurants often served as the capstone of a day's driving. If touring soured, the kids would perk up with HoJo cola and hot dogs, and everybody could enjoy television and a dip in the pool. Sylvia Miller, who toured the battlefield with her husband and two children in 1968, recalled, "The kids were not impressed, whining about the heat in the open territory, longing for a cool dip in the exquisite pool we left behind."[31]

Touring Gettysburg provided families a uniform family bonding experience. Following a tour of Gettysburg with his family, a congressman wrote to Secretary of the Interior Stewart Udall, "My family and I had one of the most interesting, rewarding, delightful and educational experiences that we have known together in many, many years." What made Gettysburg special was its ability to reconnect atomized suburban families to each other and the national memory. In a country threatened within and without, responsible parents took their children to Gettysburg for a straightforward lesson in being American. "It is indeed fine that such an historical area is maintained," a parent wrote in 1960, "and that the children of our country can gain an intimate knowledge of our heritage, something that is apparently considered unfashionable in the public schools today."[32]

Reminiscent of the genteel "memory palace" for self-improving leisure, the car provided touring families with Ford's envisioned "history lesson on wheels." Piling out of the car to explore museums or highlighted sites became a ritual and a family game. Families could share their country's past in a way that engendered "togetherness." Children might be allowed the privilege of reading roadside displays while tracking the Park Service's prescribed touring route. One tourist reported that when she and her husband rented a cassette-tape battlefield tour in 1971, "We put our five-year old in charge of flicking the stop play switch, and turning the volume control knob." Like the bygone parlor, the car connected the family to larger memories through images, objects, and activities. Photography, the most popular tourist activity, captured family "togetherness" within the national memory, as urged by Kodak advertising. Family poses alongside cannon became a cliché of tourism, guaranteeing an indelible image in a world of instability. Yet even without a visual record, the out-of-ordinary nature of touring produced enduring memories whose recounting reunited families long afterward. In 1965, for example, Jim Warren's family, visiting Gettysburg on their way to the New York World's Fair, stopped at Gettysburg's National Civil War Wax Museum. In a corner they observed an armed and uniformed figure whose head swayed back and forth in a slow arc. "Feel his head," Jim's brother suggested. "It feels real." With advice typical of a domineering big brother, Jim warned, "Don't touch it, Bill." Suddenly the figure sprang to life. "Aren't you going to take my picture?" Everybody jumped, and Jim recalled, "I remember Dad blanched white." Such private memories originating in the family search for national memory remained vivid long after photographs yellowed and lost their vibrancy.[33]

The quest to infuse a memorable national moment into family memory may not have excited children, but it did persuade parents. In 1964, for example, "as a reward for having taken the family to Disneyland the year before," John Dynia's father insisted on a more sobering family vacation to Gettysburg. Sometimes the tour provided parents a rare opportunity to reaffirm parental authority or show off. In 1959, Marine Corps officer Frederic Green packed his wife and five children in their white 1957 Plymouth with tailfins and push-button transmission. A serious tourist, Captain Green would not consider patronizing tourist attractions that might entertain his children, ages eight, six, four, three, and eighteen months. Instead, according to his daughter Judith, he shuttled them around in the Plymouth and "not only narrated but also acted out all the troop movements and commanding officers' roles in Pickett's Charge, Little Round Top, Cemetery Ridge. . . . For a finale, he recited the Gettysburg Address." Sometimes parents provided the knowledgeable Boy Scout or exemplary student carte blanche to lead the family tour. When Joan Berghey's son received an "A plus" on a term paper about Gettysburg, his parents rewarded him with a trip to Gettysburg and the honor of leading a family tour over the field. Whether parents or children took charge of touring, parents felt that dipping at the well of the national past edified children and strengthened the family.[34]

But most parents realized that children could be pushed only so far on vacation, and felt compelled to compromise as they did at home. Besides, with leisure centered around children, play was to be expected as long as some time could be devoted to learning. For a child, touring the battlefield could be boring and confusing. Captain Green's daughter Melanie, for example, felt puzzled at "lots and lots of open space, which made no sense at all in the context of what Daddy was talking about." Not only the battle, but its significance escaped children. John Dynia's brother asked his father why no water appeared at the High Water Mark.[35]

Boys seemed to have no trouble amusing themselves when touring grew dull, however. The battlefield, with its observation towers, boulder outcroppings, and cannon, could serve as a playground. John Dynia and his brother raced up and down towers, for example, while Jack Lawrence spent his time peering into cannon barrels to find a loaded one. But even if the national memory escaped them, most boys could create an imaginative past of their own. Playing war represented a step toward adolescence by advancing beyond early childhood play and mimicking adult behavior. Carol Ann Theuer remembered of her family's 1971 trip that her three sons "had a ball playing soldier." To many boys raised in the afterglow of World War II, the battlefield's stone walls, cannon, and split-rail fencing appeared to be a giant version of the early 1960s Civil War playset sold by Sears and other retailers along with a miniature Fort Apache. Aiding boys' entry to play was the town's souvenir business, whose merchandise had shifted from the expired market for parlor kitsch—miniature monuments, silver spoons, optical viewers—to toys for boys. Parents bought felt kepis, slouch hats, miniature cannon, Rebel flags, and toy guns. If a symbol of Gettysburg were chosen for the era of family automobiling, it would be the ubiquitous felt kepi. "Once I got my kepi," John Dynia recalled, "I never wore my mouse ears again." Souvenirs now ended up in toy boxes for children instead of in the parlor, as they had in past generations of touring. Parlors with their miniaturization of the world in bric-a-brac had given way to family rooms that focused on family leisure, metaphorically the same route Gettysburg followed.[36]

It might have been easy for boys like ten-year-old George Stafford, armed with a souvenir musket firing corks, to entertain himself at a shrine celebrating male valor. The gender socialization of girls, however, dictated that the space did not welcome girls' play. When Judith Green and her two younger sisters, five and three, were introduced to Gettysburg in 1958, their shepherding grandparents ushered them to the commercial area of town without entering the battlefield at all. And in the days before the 1990s Gettysburg Barbie doll, virtually none of the available souvenirs, including pincushions or ceramic plates, could be turned into girls' playthings. Adults thought the lessons of Gettysburg of greatest importance for future warriors, and besides, the trip might provide an opportunity for father-son or mother-daughter bonding. As the author experienced in 1958, Dad took the boys to inspect a gun collection while mom and sister visited the Hall of Presidents with its First Lady display. Girls who did contrive their own satisfying play on the battlefield could be censured for inappropriate behavior. In 1952, for example, the Whitmores' twelve-year-old twin boys walked Pickett's Charge with their father while mom and the girls, seven and four, dallied behind. Bored, the seven year old began picking daisies and buttercups, then proceeded to stuff bunches of them into nearby cannon mouths. When the males returned from their history walk, the boys bristled at the sight. "This is a battlefield—you don't do that!" one yelled. Although condoned within family-centered leisure, spontaneous play reinforced customary gender dominance, roles, and parental authority under the exaggerated conditions of touring.[37]

Parents might have hoped their children learned something during a trip to Gettysburg, but in reality touring often functioned less like a schoolroom and more like the family rec room with Walt Disney tuned in on TV. The need for leisure appealing to all family members during the 1950s and 1960s had prompted governmental and private impresarios to launch family-oriented amusements. Most turned the story of the battle or Lincoln's visit into simple entertainment, reflecting leisure familiar to Cold War families. In many cases, they used the P. T. Barnum technique of brushing the sensational with a veneer of uplift. One, a joint diorama and cafeteria, even issued diplomas of completion as an imprimatur of educational substance. Some dusted off or retooled nineteenth-century attractions and recloaked them with a modern mantle of electronic entertainment; others progressed no further than the dusting.

If historical themes alienated some family members, all could share familiar technologies that now served as mediums for old activities and attractions. Lights, sound, and space-age structure furbished the cyclorama, while battlefield touring on air-conditioned buses featured a popular media personality's narration punctuated with sound effects. Even better for family privacy were tape-recorded tours played in the car. If the tapes did not help children understand the battle, at least the sound effects did not bore them. In 1971 the Guzik family of four rented a cassette tape tour during a rainstorm, and, according to Mrs. Guzik, "listened as the magic of electronics brought into the car the sound of artillery, the neighing of horses, and the shouts of soldiers mingled with the bugle call to arms." She reported at the tour's end, "Rain or no rain, we had our fun," and added, "[W]e left a great deal smarter—and happier."[38]

Families could find entertainment masked as didacticism at flashing dioramas or the town's numerous wax museums, a popular form of twentieth-century amusement. The 1960s Lincoln Train Museum and National Civil War Wax Museum, for example, featured wax figures, sound and light effects, and motion illusions. In 1964 a tourist visiting the Lincoln Room at the Wills House, which included a wax figure of Lincoln surrounded by period furniture, found the show convincing. The orchestration of music, manipulated light, and mannequin reciting the Gettysburg Address produced "a strange effect" in the small room. "Sane men keep telling themselves hokum, hokum," he wrote, "but it is a losing fight, with the battlefield and cemetery a scant half-mile away." The popularity of such amusement over pedantry might be seen in the 1963 Civil War Centennial. On the one-hundredth anniversary of the battle, the anniversary committee planned a potpourri of rituals and pageants. While fewer than five thousand visitors attended somber ceremonies at the Peace Light, over thirty thousand turned out to watch a reenactment of Pickett's Charge, despite protestations by Civil War scholars and authorities. Terry Thomann, a boy looking on with his family, was disappointed that smoke generators and canned gunfire substituted for the real thing, but "[i]t was still cool." Among the most popular attractions of the three-day celebration were the *tableaux vivants*, or living vignettes of apocryphal battle tales, positioned at six spots around the battlefield.[39]

Families patronized other new attractions that had nothing to do with the Civil War but served suburban leisure as much as those that did. Some quickly disappeared, but others of longer durability deserve mention. Each symbolized American freedoms defended by Cold War families in suburbia.

The Prince of Peace Museum, a tableau of wax figures depicting the life of Christ, capitalized on the postwar era's high percentage of family attendance at mainstream Christian churches. Actually, theophanous waxworks were more central than peripheral to Cold War Gettysburg, the shrine of one nation under God. Many parents who understood their responsibility in the struggle against godless communism found the museum obligatory. Similarly, the nation's frontier foundation as manifested in television Westerns, Davy Crockett, coonskin caps, and Fort Apache playsets found expression in Fort Defiance. Proprietor Clyde Culver opened the business in 1961 with a gun collection housed in a reconstructed blockhouse outside of town. With a tinge of sensationalism, after the Kennedy assassination he featured a display of presidential assassination weapons. When Culver added a stockade and outbuildings he labeled Frontier Town, business improved dramatically. Attempting to link his operation with the battlefield, Culver hired reenactors to demonstrate Civil War equipment and weapon firing years before the Park Service initiated "living history."[40]

Postwar tourists' hunger for family fare is best demonstrated by the popularity of Fantasyland, which dwarfed the era's God-and-guns attractions. A storybook village sharing the name of a Disneyland park that had opened just a few years before, Fantasyland attracted young families with incarnations of Mother Goose, the Lollipop Tree, the House that Jack Built, Humpty Dumpty, Rapunzel's Castle, and activities such as boating and pony rides. When World War II veteran Kenneth Dick and his family opened the park in 1959, the *Gettysburg Times* reported that twenty-one thousand visitors passed through the gates in three weeks, "proving" the attraction "popular beyond the dreams of the owners." Crowds so strained the facilities that visitors used windows for exits, and Dick soon expanded with more buildings, landscaping, a carousel, and a train ride.[41]

Like the Prince of Peace Museum and Fort Defiance, Fantasyland possessed firmer links to Gettysburg's sacred ground than its fairy-tale theme suggested. A motor club newsletter termed Fantasyland "unusually beautiful" and "a fairy-like woodland, with tiny brooks that wind a crooked path. . . . Wild flowers, little animals, and song birds of all colors and descriptions are found everywhere." Another termed it "a restful haven of beauty, a spot to get away from all the tensions of life while spending a few hours among the trees." In other words, some observers viewed Fantasyland much like nineteenth-century genteel tourists described the battlefield—as a scenic park where one might find repose from modern life within the sublime possibilities of nature. Fantasyland even resuscitated train travel to Gettysburg with an 1863 replica that wound through scenic forest, tunnels, and bridges. Although the battlefield's aesthetic appeal as scenery faded with genteel culture, a commercial enterprise now revived that function for a new group of tourists. The difference lay in Fantasyland's total orientation toward children, who were the real focus of postwar families. Little wonder the *Gettysburg Times* called Fantasyland "the popular new Gettysburg tourist Mecca," a term of pilgrimage once reserved for the battlefield. "It's a wonderful change of pace to find such 'lands' as yours in this hurried world we live in," a visitor wrote to Dick. If Gettysburg functioned as a haven from the present where families could find rejuvenation from frenetic suburban life, they found it at Fantasyland.[42]

Like Fort Defiance, Fantasyland included allusions to the frontier mania that swept suburbia. Western media fare was replicated with the Wagon Train and Fort Apache amusements, where children could metaphorically participate in the struggle against frontier enemies of American civilization. On Fantasyland's Wagon Train, for example, children rode a train of small covered wagons that Indians attacked during the journey. Anticipating the National Park Service's "living history" activities years later, kids on board grabbed toy guns supplied with each wagon and shot it out with the Indian attackers. Similarly, costumed shootouts between cowboys and Indians at Fort Apache encouraged audience participation. A columnist for the *Reading Eagle* described a frontier "gunfight" in 1967 between cowboys and Indians staged before a large crowd:

> The Indians were tried by a jury of volunteers selected from the audience and were found guilty. The judge decided they should be burned at the stake. After the band of Indians were tied to the stake and the marshall and his men turned their backs, the Indians escaped. Holy canaries! That's when the gunfight started. Of course the marshall and his men were victorious. The Indians were shot down from lookouts and the wall surrounding the fort.[43]

The scene has charm in light of Cold War culture, in spite of its ethnically demeaning implications in the twenty-first century. In an unremarkable expression of candor, the mayor of Gettysburg stated, "These kinds of things are needed because children are brought by parents, and they get tired of going over the battlefield." Yet considering the numbers of yellow buses and cars that unloaded at Fantasyland, parents likely viewed the show as at least as instructive of the American heritage as Davy Crockett or perhaps Gettysburg, for that matter. The idea of the frontier had a powerful grip on suburban imaginations, and parents no doubt enjoyed what was in effect a three-dimensional cowboys-and-Indians movie suggesting America's continuing crusade against barbarism. Within a familiar context, the show also offered not only an alternative to canned electronic entertainment, but an occasion for commingling of families. Besides, except for the costumes, the drama differed little from the spectacle of the Pickett's Charge reenactment that celebrated America's military glory.[44]

In the postwar market dominated by family touring, Gettysburg required space for leisure centered around children. Responsible parents might have tried to make the national memory a family experience, but did so on a

FIGURE 23. Cowboys 'n' Indians drama at Fort Apache, Fantasyland, early 1960s
(Thelma Dick collection)

vacation designed for "togetherness." At Fantasyland, families could find
"togetherness" without packing in as much learning as possible, and thus
duplicating the stress they encountered in the suburbs. When enthusiasts
complained that Fantasyland profaned Gettysburg, Dick explained in a letter to the *New York Times* that he too was a patriotic veteran who had been
awarded the Purple Heart fighting as a Marine in the Pacific. Did Gettysburg have to be completely given over to the memory of the Civil War?
He appealed, "Here, my children (we have three darling little girls) and
yours, who are too young to understand the Civil War, will have something
to do and see." In this way, Fantasyland added to rather than detracted from
the sacred ground in terms of attracting pilgrims. If Fantasyland helped
Gettysburg's image as a shrine that welcomed children, no doubt that image
swelled when the First Family dropped by from nearby Camp David on
three occasions. On their third visit, in May 1963, Caroline Kennedy and
John, Jr., pulled the First Lady in opposite directions trying to show her
Mother Goose and Zippy the Chimp. Caroline promised, "I'll be back again,"
but not all stories at Fantasyland ended happily.[45]

Parents spent time and resources fostering families, and that meant fun as
well as edification. Exactly where Gettysburg's attractions belonged on the

continuum of these two poles often blurred. An imperceptible slope slid families from a sound-soaked cassette tour to a sound-and-light wax museum to Fantasyland. All were entertainment geared for the postwar suburbanite. And all provided escape from Cold War anxiety to a past untroubled by civil rights, nuclear war, or communist subversiveness and aggression. By the 1960s, Gettysburg seemed suspiciously like television, the master of suburban leisure. At the turn of the twentieth century, Gettysburg had been bifurcated into genteel and working-class parks; by the 1960s it reflected mass culture, segmented into channels for consumer choice. If children tired of the battlefield, parents could flip the dial, just as they did at home, to a wax museum. Once that grew tiring, another flip brought Fantasyland.

Tourist Expectations and Consumer Organizing

Only with the advent of automobiles and mass culture did visitors begin complaining about the present intruding on the shrine. The automobile's commercial impact brought gas stations, groceries, campgrounds, billboards, and homemade signs along roads to meet the motoring market. Automobilists intent on escaping the commercial clutter of cities were instead confronted with a landscape much like the one they had fled. Images of Gettysburg shaped by the Chamber of Commerce, automobile guides, and family magazine articles heightened the frustration by assuring tourists they could "step into the past" at Gettysburg.

Realizing the ill effects of unchecked commerce on the tourist industry, providers took steps to control visual dissonance. As early as 1940, the Pennsylvania Department of Commerce removed hundreds of signs along the Lincoln Highway. In 1946, a state planning-board executive advised Gettysburg businessmen to remove excessive signs because they repelled tourists with "the appearance of a midway at Coney Island rather than a historical center." In an open letter the same year, Park Superintendent J. Walter Coleman informed the people of Gettysburg that tourists complained about "the extent to which we deviate from the historic past." If "signs, building fronts, new structures, and general atmosphere" could conform "to the period of the Civil War," he advised, tourists would leave with a favorable impression. Even the guides, themselves the subject of many a tourist complaint about commercial blight, condemned the growth of tourist cabins and souvenir stands. "For business reasons the Battlefield must not be destroyed," they resolved in 1946. Thus important promoters of the tourist industry, including the savvy Cliff Arquette and LeRoy Smith, understood that tourists visiting Gettysburg expected "the past" set off from the present in a special preserve.[46]

But the tourist bonanza after World War II prompted more development that further jarred tourist expectations. Retreat from the present seemed even more urgent with the postwar spread of a standardized landscape consisting of suburbs, interstate highways, malls, and franchised motels and restaurants. A visitor in 1950 complained that he noticed a fence near the High Water Mark made of barbed wire and green steel posts. "Was there any barb wire and steel post during the Civil War?" he asked. Few among the floodtide of postwar travelers grasped the paradox of expecting both suburban comforts and a precommercial landscape. Williamsburg and other historic sites had solved the problem by contriving entire past environments that blocked the present from view by locating services on their fringes. Gettysburg, however, was different because it was a living community ringed by a patchwork of federally owned land. With no zoning until the 1970s, Gettysburg faced development of any battlefield land not owned by the Park Service.[47]

The tourist search for precommercial space was a commercial problem, however, because the area's appearance as a historic site attracted customers. By the late 1950s, popular magazines such as *Parade* and businessman-celebrity Charlie Weaver urged Americans to write their representatives or send money to "save" Gettysburg. *Parade* featured an interview with President Eisenhower by syndicated columnist Jack Anderson in which he said, "I think it is a pity this one piece of terrain is not kept so that youngsters can see it nearly like it was in 1863." Responding to a *Pittsburgh Press* article, a couple wrote to President Eisenhower, "Must it be sold down the river for exploit too[?] Enough of God's natural scenery is going fast enough in huge acreage for house development and Super Market space." Another wrote, "I know that we have to make way for progress but not this way." Schoolchildren too were mobilized against the forces of modernity, launching "Save Gettysburg" fund drives. A thirteen year old thought a Gettysburg "overrun by ranch houses and hot dog stands" threatened all tangible proof of American identity. "If Gettysburg is destroyed, why not take away Lincoln's log cabin. Destroy Old Ironsides, Put houses on Valley Forge?" Consumers were organized for a pristine Gettysburg through the Committee to Save Gettysburg, promoted by *Parade*, or the Gettysburg Battlefield Preservation Association (GBPA), which Charlie Weaver endorsed.[48]

Born out of revived interest in the Civil War, the GBPA represented a new and specialized group of consumers. With the increase in leisure time and pursuit of hobbies, Americans turned to study of the Civil War. Many found inspiration in the Civil War novels and histories of Douglas Southall Freeman, MacKinlay Kantor, Burke Davis, Clifford Dowdey, and Bruce Catton. For these enthusiasts, visiting battlefields like Gettysburg became an extension of reading or gun collecting. Park Service officials noted their growing presence as early as 1945, and realized the need for more sophisticated interpretation. In 1947 Robert Cheffey, motivated by *Lee's Lieutenants* and other works, packed up the books and his young bride for a tour of

Gettysburg. There, the couple enlisted a guide, "an elderly war-veteran type gentleman," and seated him in the backseat. After noticing the books and stumbling over Cheffey's questions, the guide grew agitated. "What are you trying to do? Is this some sort of trick? Are you trying to trip me up?" he asked, and told the Cheffeys to drive him back to the guide station.[49]

Civil War buffs brought enthusiasm to touring unmatched by other visitors. Focused on strategy, tactics, leadership, and weaponry, they were a serious-minded bunch. By the age of the atomic bomb, Civil War heroes were mythological; the war's tangible remains, holy relics. It was not at all unusual by the postwar period for buffs to drive a complete circuit of Civil War battlefields in Pennsylvania, Virginia, and Maryland. One enthusiast who had driven from California to visit Civil War battlefields in 1958 was "horrified" at the condition of the Gettysburg cyclorama, owned by the Park Service since 1941. "This painting is one of the most precious tangible objects in our country and vividly depicts the most sacred moment in our nation's history," he wrote to the Secretary of the Interior. "I rank the painting at Gettysburg alongside the Declaration of Independence and Bill of Rights as far as overall value to the nation goes." Now the former entertainment of midways had lost its commercial associations and possessed an aura of sacred inheritance. One hobbyist who had just visited Fredericksburg, Chancellorsville, and Manassas "felt disgust and national shame" on entering the "awful museum [Gettysburg National Museum] with its cheap and shoddy souvenir shop and Coney Island atmosphere." But then, Gettysburg had long become a shrine that raised expectations far above other relatively undeveloped Civil War sites.[50]

With revived interest in the Civil War, groups of afficianadoes organized Civil War Roundtables in many American cities to provide buffs with a forum. The concept spread swiftly to smaller cities and appealed to a broad range of occupational types. A Park Service official attributed the "change in visitor attitude" after World War II to an increase in "Civil War history clubs composed of 'fans' who manifest great enthusiasm." Thus buffs were accustomed to organizing and gathering for fellowship and didactic purposes. And so it happened that the second Civil War Study Group held in 1959 at Gettysburg College decided to form the GBPA. Through its solicitation efforts, which included selling ersatz deeds, enlisting Boy Scout and Girl Scout canvassers, and placing donation receptacles in the visitors' center, the GPBA eventually saved over two hundred acres of battlefield land from development.[51]

While this trend would reach its apex only later in the century, the emergence of the Civil War buff and the GBPA after midcentury signaled the beginning of a power shift from the Park Service and town entrepreneurs to an "expert" consumer. The conflict between historic and family tourist space continued through the tower controversy of the early 1970s. After that, the moral scales tipped in favor of the buffs, who pressed not just for preservation, but restoration of the battlefield to its original appearance. Enterprises such as Fantastyland and Fort Defiance were shut down and their remnants obliterated, a triumph of enlightenment over philistinism.

Or was it? A *Saturday Evening Post* article titled "Let's Not Surrender Our Battlefields" used a photograph of Fantasyland as an example of crass commercialism on sacred ground, a visual symbol of what was wrong with Gettysburg. But in a subsequent issue, a reader argued that "[s]ome, perhaps most, who fought in our great battles may have preferred seeing a merry-go-round, a line of laundry, or even a smoking factory, to seeing the land they fought and bled over preserved as a kind of sanctuary for unwilling ghosts and troops of old ladies who come annually in period costumes to lay a few wreaths." Could not Gettysburg continue as it had for generations, a park serving present leisure needs as well as venerating the past? Garry Wills, in a 1972 article about his family's visit to Gettysburg, described "the intrusive clatter of money and scramble of profiteering spiders," and noting that "no place is more defiled or exploited by commercialism." Yet he admitted his children needed to be entertained, and they enjoyed play at the "cheap and gaudy stuff," including a miniature golf course. Indeed, what could be more important at a national shrine than supporting the health of the American family? Both history and family togetherness were expected in postwar Gettysburg. As they sampled abundance at home and on the new interstate highways, Americans shivered at the thought of global communism and knew that Gettysburg had something to do with their freedom.[52]

The automobile brought personal control to touring and release from former restraints. At the beginning of the automobile era, visitors had used the battlefield for recreational speeding, a stopover during cross-country driving, or escape from the present on weekend outings. After World War II, families arrived seeking "togetherness" by sharing the American past. As scions of mass culture, they blended the genteel and the working class of the earlier era, which had segmented the battlefield into separate parks. Now old reminders of working-class excursions, pavilions and tracks, had been removed, replaced by family amusements fit for a family shrine. The monuments of gentility remained, but in the motoring age they seemed but tombstones in a forgotten cemetery. Now that class was out and mass was in, all could agree on the power of visual stimulation to convey the past. The *Baltimore Sun* columnist who in 1972 compared the Gettysburg National Military Park's periphery to "the outskirts of Las Vegas" got it wrong. In reality Gettysburg functioned more like Disneyland, whose spatial segmentation into discrete parts took its cues from television. By the 1970s it seemed as if a dutiful and spoiled child had seized control of the television dial and forbade his less sober siblings from watching Davy Crockett or Snow White. Yet as farsighted impresarios such as L. E. Smith knew, everything that entered the tourist gaze, just as everything on television, was entertainment. And it paid.[53]

PHASE FOUR

☆ ☆ ☆ ☆ ☆ ☆ ☆ ☆ ☆ ☆ ☆

1970-2000

Heritage Gettysburg

While the troops maneuvered into position, the onlookers settled
in with blankets, picnic lunches coolers and soft drinks. . . .
With the battle finally engaged, many of the adults shifted
about the hillside seeking a better view. The younger children
screamed with fright as the cannons fired. Amateur photographers,
cameras at the ready, clicked off shot after shot.

—*Phildadelphia Inquirer*, June 24, 1988

You've got to choose between happiness and what people
used to call high art. We've sacrificed the high art.

—ALDOUS HUXLEY, *Brave New World*

Chapter Seven

☆ ☆ ☆ ☆ ☆ ☆ ☆ ☆ ☆ ☆ ☆

A Future in the Past

SHELL BURSTS splotched a July sky as advancing butternut-clad lines stiff-ened and belched fire into the mass of blue figures ahead. Musketry tore gaps in the ranks, but the resolute pressed on. With Virginia and Confeder-ate flags swinging, the gray line dissolved in the smoke, plunging wildly into a curtain of flame. In a few clouded minutes of stabbing, clubbing, and shooting, the ferocity subsided. A red, white, and blue banner of Union rippled victoriously over the scene of carnage as gray survivors of Pickett's Charge limped back toward the Confederate lines. Only the absence of shredded flesh and a raised, panoramic perspective—revealing tens of thou-sands of spectators sporting sunglasses and shorts, scaffolding for technicians and camera crews, and surrounding fields turned to parking lots—belied the scene's authenticity. For obervers and participants, the battle's 125th anni-versary highlight had succeeded.

Professionally produced and choreographed, the bloodless Pickett's Charge trailed two days of battle scenarios that together drew 12,000 participating reenactors and an audience of 140,000. The producer, Napoleonic Tactics, Inc., not only opened an office in town to sell spectator tickets, but col-lected registration fees from reenactors, sold video rights, and charged for food concessions and product endorsement. Staged a week before the actual anniversary date on private land landscaped to look like the battlefield, the reenactments nevertheless embarrassingly upstaged more solemn commem-orative activities. At a ritual rededicating the Eternal Peace Light on the July 3 anniversary date, the press reported attendance "fell far short of expectations." Little of the ten-day anniversary involved such somber cere-monies anyway. Rather, the program was a bazaar of living history encamp-ments, Civil War arts and craft displays, military history lectures, a collec-tors' relic show, and a book fair as well as reenactments.[1]

Only a quarter-century before, during the Civil War Centennial, cultural leaders had decried commercial activity and especially reenacting as inappropriate and distasteful means of commemoration. Yet by 1988, the sale of Civil War entertainment and goods appeared to be the unchallenged medium of memory, costing visitors to the 125th anniversary $10 million. The celebration's festive atmosphere could hardly be attributed solely to the triumph of entrepreneurs, however. Cultural authorities encouraged what previously had been censured as carnival. The 125th Anniversary Commission's chair said the commission endorsed "an action-packed calendar of events both educational and fun for the public." The National Park Service, which only begrudgingly acquiesced to a restrained reenactment ceremony in 1963, now hand-picked over a thousand reenactors to camp on the sacred ground and demonstrate weaponry, tactics, and camp life for the public.[2]

While the *Gettysburg Times* praised the anniversary affair as "magnificent," some voices dissented. Disgusted by mobs of paying voyeurs and the advertising slogan "Come help celebrate Gettysburg," a *Lebanon Daily News* editorialist found nothing to "celebrate" about the carnage of 1863 and especially censured "theatrics staged as a celebration." More poignantly from a historical perspective, retired Gettysburg College Professor Robert Bloom, who participated in both the early Gettysburg Battlefield Preservation Association (GBPA) and Civil War Centennial planning, expressed his dismay over the festivities. He pointed to two levels of understanding the Civil War, one "adult" and the other "juvenile." The "adult" approached the Civil War intellectually, as a transformative event, Bloom wrote. The "juvenile," contrastingly, "manifests itself in obsession with military strategy and tactics, with collecting mementos and souvenirs and, for some in playing soldier, an impulse which for most of us passed in reaching puberty." Now mass culture had rendered cultural arbiters and critics impotent, with cultural authority vested in giant media conglomerates and opinion surveys. Isolated, muffled by the din of the hoopla, Bloom seemed atavistic, priggish, oddly out of touch. The fact was that the baby boomers, who resisted traditional markers of adulthood, were now in charge. Even the GBPA that Bloom had helped found accepted a check for over two thousand dollars from Napoleonic Tactics, Inc., for supporting the 125th anniversary's reenactments.[3]

What distressed Bloom was not the blossoming of insouciance typical of celebrations, but, as he saw it, permanently rooted weeds that threatened to choke the garden of memory. Gradually they matured into the fourth phase in Gettysburg's development. By 2000, the shrine differed as dramatically from its manifestation in 1960 as 1960 Gettysburg differed from its 1900 form. The universal family experience of midcentury, the "togetherness" that connected parents and children through a national memory, had faded. Vacationing families still arrived, to be sure. But by 2000, Gettysburg seemed more like themed entertainment dominated by the Civil War aficionados Bloom deplored.

No longer did Gettysburg serve the grand saga about a nation charged with providential mission. Rather than inspiring Americans to envision a national destiny, Gettysburg was frozen as an antiquarian delicacy contrasting to the swill of the present. Ironically, this change emerged not as a sellout to commercial interests but through a reinvigorated dedication to Gettysburg's sacredness. What traditionalists like Bloom had not measured was the rise of a new sensibility that collapsed the previously separate play of tourism into sacred memory. The quest for authenticity now defined the sacred, a new meaning that emerged from commercial culture.

The transformation rose out of equally profound social and cultural change. Vietnam, Watergate, bumbling leadership, civil strife, economic spasms, and resulting exhaustion deflated American confidence and ushered in an era of self-doubt about national purpose. A seemingly united America of the postwar years dissolved into bickering groups and a spirit of cynicism toward authority. When the "victory culture" that sanctioned America's frontier struggles against Native Americans, Nazis, and finally Communists collapsed after Vietnam, so too did the sustaining myth of providential mission. Questioning about American purpose infected the past as well as the present, and in the rising conflict along gender, racial, and ethnic lines, the national epic was challenged by historians stressing the venality of erstwhile heroes. Once the celebratory national narrative ended, Gettysburg ceased its role as a shrine offering inspiration and symbolic importance for national progress.[4]

A social upheaval in American morals, customs, and attitudes also undermined old assumptions. In the 1960s and 1970s, many baby boomers opted for self-fulfillment over the responsibilities borne by their depression-and-war-generation parents. Along with marriage itself, family "togetherness" that characterized suburban leisure or vacations went out of fashion as an obstacle to personal freedom. Churches, which enjoyed high membership in the postwar years, lost members as Americans rejected dogma for personal spiritual experiences. Increasingly, ethnic identity added to the cacophony of dissent. Even America's postwar consumer society, built around shared family goods, aided fragmentation by appealing more and more to individuals. In a few decades, Americans had devolved from a reasonably obedient, united people to "a thundering herd of individuals," as a pundit remarked.[5]

Accelerating the pace of change were new electronic media that exacerbated differences and isolated individuals. The increasing tempo and unfamiliarity of life generated feelings of instability and doubt. In spite of unprecedented abundance, leisure, and individual liberty, a majority of Americans viewed the last quarter-century as a national slide into decline. Titles of popular books such as *America: What Went Wrong?*; *The Disuniting of America*; *The Twilight of Common Dreams*; *The Next American Nation*; and *American Apartheid* pointed to concern over national degeneration and fragmentation.[6]

Academic jargon used to describe the present era, such as *postmodern* or *postindustrial*, points to a sense of society being cut loose from stable moorings and drifting into uncertainty. Little wonder that Americans look wistfully backward and find solace in selective use of the past. Contrasting to traditional flag-waving rituals or monuments, the "heritage" vogue employs a variety of means to evoke memory. As opposed to written history, "heritage" complements an increasingly visual culture with a visible, tactile, participatory past. Historian Christopher Lasch, in the 1979 best-seller *The Culture of Narcissism*, noted the post-Vietnam malaise: "Our sense of reality appears to rest, curiously enough, on our willingness to be taken in by the staged illusion of reality."[7]

Yet heritage is not the restoration of a pre-Vietnam victory culture where America, always in the right, always wins. For one thing, heritage is primarily market driven; for another, it fragments instead of unifying society. With heritage, commerce creates the past as part of a vast public appetite for nostalgia. Historic restorations, public architecture, reenactments, theme parks, heritage tourism, historic films, and war games cater to an ever-increasing market of heritage patrons. *Reminisce: The Magazine That Brings Back the Good Times* is published under the maxim "Nostalgia is like a grammar lesson . . . you find the present tense and the past perfect." To touch, to see, to buy and possess, to *experience* the past characterize the heritage approach. Unlike monuments or carnivalesque attractions of the past, heritage relies on authenticity to provide psychic reassurance for an age adrift. Tourists explore mills, coal mines, prisons, and concentration camps to sense suffering; Time-Life books promises that one can "relive the horrors of Gettysburg in the comfort of your own home." Heritage aids divisiveness by attempting to resuscitate "authentic" racial and ethnic legacies, and further fragments society through contemporary marketing methods that herd consumers into groups.[8]

In this milieu "Heritage Gettysburg," the fourth and current stage of Gettysburg's development, began emerging around 1970. During the 1950s and 1960s, enthusiasts bought additional land and fought commercial blight to preserve a sacred vista at Gettysburg. But in the current era, groups of enthusiasts have transformed Gettysburg into a site of participation. Reenactors, for example, "make history" for thousands of spectators at annual reenactments and living-history encampments. One affinity group undertakes costly restoration projects that return the landscape to its supposed 1863 appearance. Far more than in the past, visitors see themselves as much as producers as consumers of the Gettysburg experience.

Media, Advertising, and the Rise of Affinity Groups

During every phase of Gettysburg's development, communication technologies played an integral part in the transformation process. In phase four, however, media itself led the transformation. Not only did it produce an image of Gettysburg so vivid it overpowered the place, but it also segmented the market for Gettysburg into diverse groups of consumers.

A key feature of heritage over history is the substitution of image for reality that turns illusions into authenticity. The power of images lies in their evocation of feelings regardless of historical facts. Public interest in the battle's narrative had been met by vendors through a wide variety of mediums since the battle ended. But with Gettysburg's historical meanings largely gone, the quest to experience the original event became more urgent. Moreover, images could shore up the pitiful inadequacy of monuments, the electric map, the cyclorama, or birds-eye battlefield views. Beginning in the 1970s "living history" demonstrations, large reenactments, realistic art, and other mediums attempted to tear through the veil intervening between present and past for a clear view of 1863.[9]

New forms of graphic art, fiction, and popular history disseminated fresh and beguiling images of what the days of '63 *really* looked like. Realistic artists—two of whom eventually established studios in Gettysburg—painted seemingly endless interpretations of select battle scenes with careful attention to minute details but not, thankfully, real carnage. As pessimism deepened during the denouement of Vietnam, Michael Shaara's *The Killer Angels* championed the military through the lens of Gettysburg. Shaara, a career soldier, wound together the fates of select officers at Gettysburg in a fictional tribute to bravery, self-sacrifice, and American character while ignoring the Civil War's seminal issues. The book proved extremely popular and won the Pulitzer Prize. Its skillful character development generated new American heroes, the Confederate General James Longstreet and the Union's Colonel Joshua Chamberlain, for a society in need of heroes. Despite its romanticism, the novel's engaging style, detail, and cleverness in blending fact with fiction convinced many that it presented a historical account of the battle. College history classes adopted it to pique student interest. Like George Lucas's *Star Wars* trilogy, *The Killer Angels* included rebels, civil war, and freedom fighting, and both were far enough from Vietnam yet close enough in characterization to meet the public need for myth.[10]

Photographs could satisfy a quest for authenticity no less than clever historical fiction. In 1975 *Gettysburg: A Journey in Time* compared dozens of 1863 battlefield photographs with contemporary photos of the identical scenes. The effect was to efface the intervening years and provide a startling sense of "being there." Although photos in 1863 were no more transparent windows into the past than they are now, the illusion provided by the innovative use of visuals produced new Gettysburg enthusiasts. Converts converged on Gettysburg and hiked the battlefield instead of driving park avenues, trying to verify sites the books depicted. A new type of guidebook followed. While the old railroad guidebooks oriented tourists to all sights within their gaze including monuments, towers, scenic lookouts, picnic areas, and nearby attractions, the new guidebooks focused exclusively on 1863. Tourists were literally placed in the shoes of Civil War soldiers through walking tours highlighted with period photos and first-person accounts of fighting.[11]

Still, the popularity of film interpretations of Gettysburg eclipsed all other heritage media. Moving images always had delivered a vividness lacking in print, but grew even more powerful with technological innovations of surround sound, big screens, high-definition television, and multiple television channels. Along with the vogue for reenactments, simulated environments, and restorations, television "offers a safe space of almost unlimited access to other places and times, 'elsewheres' and 'elsewhens,'" as one scholar comments. In the waning decades of the century, film and television cashed in on the heritage boom by soaking the airwaves with a bevy of "elsewhens," including a twenty-four part Civil War miniseries titled *North and South* (1986). In 1990, Ken Burns's eleven-hour *The Civil War*, which included a segment on Gettysburg, reached 14 million viewers. By juxtaposing period photographs with vocalizations of prominent period figures and re-created period music, *The Civil War* translated the era for a generation craving the real thing. Both Burns and the 1993 Turner film *Gettysburg*, a faithful rendering of *The Killer Angels* onscreen, repackaged Gettysburg for much larger audiences than Shaara or *Gettysburg: A Journey in Time*.[12]

Gettysburg and *The Civil War* enjoyed film's authenticating power—not only the illusion that visual media present truth, but the power to prod emotions, an invocation pivotal to heritage. The films opened imagination to the soldiers' experience of 1863 and made a nuisance of anything added to the landscape since. Both films prompted visitors to Gettysburg to discover the original event. "Films about the war have a tremendous power in creating a visual world and dropping you into it," noted the editor of *Civil War Times* magazine in 1998. "They capture a feeling and a time and persuade people to want to go deeper." In 1991, the season following debut of *The Civil War*, visitation increased by 13 percent on the heels of a 7 percent dip in 1990. The year after *Gettysburg's* release, 1994, visitation rose by 263,078, an increase of 19 percent over the previous year. This romantic, bloodless costume drama portraying the battle as a golden age of valor separated Gettysburg from the present in a faraway time. With its moving narrative, *Gettysburg* appealed to "Lost Cause" and Civil War nostalgia buffs. Its heroes were seemingly ground under the wheel of history, sacrifices on the altar of duty for issues out of their control. As such, the film dovetailed with other heritage productions such as *Roots* (1977), *Glory* (1989), or *Dances with Wolves* (1991) that enhanced group identity. White Americans no less than minorities searched for a "tribal" legacy that might provide community in an alienating present.[13]

The heritage industry reflected changes in national media and advertising that, in turn, mirrored centrifugal trends in society. As society showed signs of fissuring in the 1970s, electronic and print media too began splintering. Mass-circulation periodicals declined in a flood of new special-interest magazines. Television atomized from three channels into a smorgasbord of cable and satellite channels, videocassettes, and video games, augmented in the 1990s with online interactive computer services, interactive television, and CD-ROM technology. Advertisers backed away from mass marketing and began "target marketing" that capitalized on differences among Americans. Most conspicuous were the habits of baby boomers, whose consumer patterns favored more personal gratification and less compromise among family members than found in earlier generations. Target advertising furthered social fracturing by herding consumers into "image tribes" of like-minded individuals who felt a sense of belonging to the commercially created group. This trend toward market segmentation transformed Gettysburg from the national shrine of 1960 into Heritage Gettysburg of 2000.[14]

The explosion of television outlets brought new opportunities for disseminating Gettysburg. Live broadcasting of battlefield tours and school programs delivered nationally grew into regular features, thanks to Pennsylvania Cable Network and satellite transmission. Small film producers continuously create new features about the Civil War and Gettysburg, including *Civil War Journal*, *The Complete Battle of Gettysburg*, *Heroes of Gettysburg*, *Ghosts of Gettysburg*, an *Unsolved Mysteries* Gettysburg episode, and numerous reruns of the movie *Gettysburg*. Viewers of this wide variety of Gettysburg and Civil War programming create a virtual community of dispersed, anonymous enthusiasts sharing a common interest.[15]

An outpouring of Gettysburg monographs delved into increasing minutiae about the battle, due in large measure to Gettysburg-based Thomas Publications, which had published nearly seventy-five Gettysburg titles between 1986 and 2000. From the 1970s, the number of Civil War periodicals mushroomed from one to over a dozen by the end of the century. These focused on such specialized subgroups as military history enthusiasts, preservationists, battlefield tourists, relic and toy soldier collectors, wargamers, reenactors, "lady" reenactors, and even on Gettysburg buffs with *Gettysburg*, a magazine devoted exclusively to the battle. Personal computers permitted improved communication among members of all these image tribes and created new ones. The growth of Internet in the 1990s furthered the herding process not only through Web sites offering virtual Gettysburg tours, museums, documents, and images, but by enabling rapid communication among members of Civil War Listservs, including one dedicated to Gettysburg.[16]

These trends reflect contemporary America's postvictory, postfamily culture. By 2000, the nuclear family that embodied Gettysburg tourists at mid-century comprised only 23.5 percent of all American households, as compared to 45 percent in 1960. With Americans more atomized than in the past, image tribes provide an outlet for sociability around a self-perceived elevating pastime. Tribes tend to be overwhelmingly white, middle class (albeit reflecting a range of occupations), and geographically dispersed. Although some members pursue their hobby as family activity—some reenactors and wargamers, for example—most follow an enthusiasm on their own and, in keeping with what defines heritage, do not associate their enthusiasm with patriotism. While some image tribes demand scholarly rigor—touring and military history, for example—many ignore or even disdain professional historians. Some pursuits, such as reenacting, are subjective and concerned with impressions; some value skill, such as wargaming hobbyists. Members of each tribe share a common knowledge and argot, so all are "experts." What matters is whether the medium meets the heritage requirement of authenticity for the tribe. For adherents to New Age faith, for example, "Ghosts of Gettysburg" provides a link to the original event; a reenactment accomplishes the same for reenactors, and a virtual museum, for collectors.[17]

The particular type of goods valued by each "tribe" identifies the group. Electronic and print media introduce new products judged by their capacity to deliver authentic experience—a weapon reproduction, a new 3-D war game, a tour to a "lost" part of the battlefield. Advertising can reinforce the quest for authenticity, generate new converts, and sometimes launch new enthusiasms. Using full-page color reproductions, the magazines publish images of "what it really looked like" in order to sell numbered prints. Within the past decade, sculptors entered this promising market with series of figures that in turn generated a new group of collectors. Yet despite consumer overtones, image tribes lay claim to transcendent purpose. Reenactors make history "come alive" for the public, collectors assemble culturally important groupings of objects, buffs contribute to Civil War heritage through continuous exploration of events.[18]

But self-declared virtue creates exclusivity. Purity of membe ship in image tribes depends on defining boundaries between "outsiders" and "insiders." This is not to suggest, of course, that members restrict themselves exclusively to their tribe; indeed, they may embrace a primary enthusiasm but overlap onto several others. Tribes rallied around Gettysburg as both a festival site for a gathering of the clans and a sacred cause to champion. They not only progressed from merely consumers to constituents, and constituents to stewards, but from stewards to manufacturers of Heritage Gettysburg. Along this path developed new forms of exchange that broke down old barriers between the sacred and secular. From the occasional reenactment of the 1970s, reenactors evolved into an entrenched tourist attraction, staging battle scenarios, encampments, and parades as regular Gettysburg features. Collectors of Civil War art and military equipment, battlefield touring enthusiasts, Civil War bibliophiles, and "living historians" brought annual collectors' shows and permanent shops dedicated to their enthusiasms. A "supratribe" that became a magnet for all enthusiasts,

Friends of the National Parks at Gettysburg became the most powerful generator of heritage at Gettysburg.[19]

Gettysburg's New Producers

Founded in 1989 to improve the National Park Service's museum, within a year the Friends expanded its mission to supporting historic preservation and education at Gettysburg National Military Park and Eisenhower National Historic Site. In contrast to the subdued approach of the Gettysburg Battlefield Preservation Association (GBPA), which concerned itself only with acquiring battlefield land, the Friends immediately employed marketing techniques to build a member base. Following the success of direct marketing popular in the 1980s and 1990s, Friends expanded its membership to more than twenty thousand within a decade. The approach mimicked "club" programs corporate advertisers launched via telephone and mail solicitation. Offering new members a variety of perks, Friends' "relationship marketing," as it was known in the advertising business, created devoted members through continual dialogue and new benefits. "Free" calendars and stationery mailed with solicitations, discounts on Gettysburg tourist services and souvenirs, and goods such as embossed credit cards, hats, T-shirts, tote bags, and mugs branded with the Friends' logo built loyalty. Surveys sent with membership forms gave members and potential members a feeling of empowerment and lofty purpose.[20]

The Friends aimed at building and retaining membership from different Civil War image tribes by hosting frequent tours, seminars, "marches," and raffles at biennial meetings that awarded valuable relics, antiques, and prints. Members were allowed to display their personal collections at meetings. These regularly scheduled events counterpoised the huge relic, book, and wargaming conventions held in Gettysburg, offering members an opportunity for sociability. In effect the Friends mixed tribal members into a stew, pouring them out again into new minitribes. Friends established a hierarchy of seven membership levels based on the amount contributed, by 1999 ranging from Regular Member ($25) to First Corps Commander's Staff ($1,000). Each level received a more-valuable gift than the previous level, progressing from T-shirts and lapel pins to numbered and signed battle-action art prints, and the upper levels were feted with exclusive events.[21]

Members challenged to "[w]alk across the fields of Pickett's Charge in the footsteps of Armistead and his valiant men!" were promised "a weekend of fun and relaxation, all with an historical emphasis." Among the Friends' first undertakings was what the then president termed "a highly visible project" to spur membership: restoring visual purity near the Pickett's Charge site by burying overhead utility lines. A decade later, Friends not only brought the $1.2 million project to completion, but also had secured 350 acres for the battlefield. In what turned out to be a controversial stand, Friends supported the National Park Service's proposed "restoration" of significant battlefield areas. The project aimed to restore the Cemetery Ridge landscape by demolishing the museum and cyclorama center and constructing a new facility elsewhere with aid from a developer. Publicity sent to members in 1999 announced that "we expect to be participatory partners in a restoration of the 1863 landscape" throughout the park, "so that today's historian and visitor can view the same vistas that soldiers saw in 1863."[22]

The Friends' emphasis on authentic landscape appeared to be driven by popular demand. A 1990 survey to whip up membership received four thousand responses indicating that historic appearance of the park overrode other considerations. In turn, Friends continually whetted members' imagination with battle-action artwork prized as raffle gifts, exhibited in special artists' receptions, and sold to raise funds. The film *Gettysburg* also answered the quest for the real thing. The Friends' "Quartermaster" made the movie *Gettysburg* available to members before its retail sale, and subsequently sold a behind-the-scenes documentary, *The Filmmakers' "Gettysburg."* Within a year of the movie's cable release, Friends purchased six acres of land near Little Round Top that marked the scene of prominent action in the film. In a statement some might consider a confusion of illusion, Friends officials termed the purchase "the most historically significant parcel within the park's boundary still in private ownership." At the same time the Friends searched for guidance in the popular will, it nurtured that imagination.[23]

To be sure, Friends undertook other activities such as funding scholarships, cannon repair, monument preservation, publicity, lobbying, and otherwise allying with the National Park Service. Yet all doubled back to heritage—a past valued for its pastness and as leisurely pastime. Ironically, in seizing the sacred banner of heritage, Friends employed contemporary marketing and advertising techniques that erased old boundaries between the sacred and the secular. When "event marketing"—corporate sponsorship of events that projected the "right image"—grew during the 1980s and 1990s, corporations such as Metropolitan Edison, Columbia Gas, Herco (Hershey Park Group), and TNT donated funds for preservation, restoration, and reenactments. Innumerable touring groups mounted by university-based continuing education operations used Gettysburg as both a sacred and a cash cow. Reenactors donated funding for battlefield preservation; even the solemn GBPA began selling camping space to reenactors on land it had preserved and allying with formerly considered abominations such as the National Civil War Wax Museum. Everyone entering the war for heritage could expect a victory in public relations.[24]

By 2000, Friends boasted a remarkable record for an organization only a decade old. Indeed, for many the organization became an event in itself that filtered the entire Gettysburg experience. Yet the Friends' commercial methods that successfully cobbled disparate enthusiasts into a group of in-

siders inevitably dragged the sacred along with it. In a sense Friends behaved much like the railroad in 1900. Both used the latest marketing and
communication advances to sell the past, and both delivered pilgrims to
Gettysburg. But in the nineteenth century both railroad and consumers
clearly distinguished between sacred ground and playground, holy day and
holiday. By the twentieth, Friends had blurred the difference, and in addition to packaging the battlefield for consumers, Friends packaged consumers
for the battlefield. Surveying members and turning the responses back to
them, Friends tailored gazes and activities to suit the preferences of these
"insiders." Friends, however, only helped sow ground that the National Park
Service and town brought to fruition as Heritage Gettysburg.

A Future in the Past: Gettysburg Borough and Heritage Gettysburg

In fall 1994 the Walt Disney Company retreated from a proposed American
history theme park west of Manassas, Virginia, site of the first major Civil
War battle. Just thirty-five miles from Washington, "Disney's America"
aimed to capitalize on the city's annual influx of 20 million tourists. Had
plans for the $650 million project survived, it would have been the nation's
greatest heritage attraction, spreading out over three thousand acres with
nearly 2 million square feet of retail space, and gathering diverse elements
of heritage—historic malls, "living" museums, reenactments, films, corpo-
rate-sponsored commemorations—into one grand location. As Disney's
CEO Michael Eisner explained, the project hoped "to bring historical
events alive and to make the story of America more vivid and three-dimensional." Like other Disney theme parks it would have presented in effect a
celebratory film, with each visitor playing a part in stage sets ranging from a
Native American village to a Civil War fort and Ellis Island. In an interesting example of the way heritage confuses the "authentic," state and local
tourist bureaus expected the Disney park to serve as both a magnet and
channel selector for heritage tourism, navigating visitors to nearby "real"
colonial and Civil War attractions, including Gettysburg.[25]

Not only the complaints of environmental groups and wealthy not-in-
my-backyard landowners forced Disney to back off. Despite shielding itself
by enlisting historical luminaries as consultants and emphasizing the project's educational mission, Disney appalled many historians with its proposal. Such public pronouncements by Disney "Imagineer" Bob Weis that
"[w]e want to make you a Civil War soldier" and "[w]e want to make you
feel what it was like to be a slave" may have appealed to the public desire
for authenticity, but struck the historical community as presumptuous if not
trivializing. Organizing as Protect Historic America, historians maintained
Disney's America would degrade the surrounding historic landscape with a
whitewashed version of American history that amused rather than engaged.

The group placed an ad in the *New York Times* calling CEO Eisner "The Man Who Would Destroy American History"; member David McCullough, best-selling author and narrator of *The Civil War*, called the project an "attempt to create synthetic history by destroying real history."[26]

McCullough did not explain what he meant by "synthetic history" and "real history," a distinction growing increasingly unclear. As a historian who had profited from the heritage vogue by narrating cable documentaries and writing popular histories, McCullough nonetheless may not have understood the irony of his position. Nor did he perhaps grasp the influence of Disney on the presentation of the American past at historical attractions around the country. At any rate, had he and his peers looked just one hundred miles north to Gettysburg, they may have felt less sure about "real" history and who was destroying it. Even if they did not see mouse ears everywhere, they would have at least detected similarities to the "imagineering" of Disney. The same fall Disney retreated from its heritage theme park, a townsperson wrote a dismaying letter to the *Gettysburg Times*. "My town is being converted into an historical amusement park," wrote Thomas Henninger, "and it breaks my heart." At Gettysburg no gargantuan entertainment corporation had tried to overpower the nation with its own version of history. Rather, as Henninger charged, Heritage Gettysburg arrived "with the blessing of local, state, and federal bureaucrats" and "special interest groups." He implored, "I want my town back."[27]

More and more, heritage had sucked the life out of the real town characterized by pharmacies, haberdasheries, neighborhood bars, and groceries, and replaced them with restored and fake storefronts housing antique shops, "authentic" restaurants, collector's boutiques, period clothing shops, and other enterprises catering to Civil War image tribes. Henninger was not likely to get his town back, as more virtual experience was on its way in response to the heritage consumption tourists expected. In 1982, an Associated Press writer complained that the fast-food franchises in town were "a shock to the visitor expecting the brick sidewalks, dirt roads, and gas lamps of the 1860s." Along with the park, the town molded itself to consumer expectations that grew increasingly sharper thanks to film, television, press, and the Internet. During the 1990s a variety of "virtual" Web sites featured tours of battlefield and town, museums, a "3-D tour" of imagined 1863 Gettysburg, and a "battlecam" that offered a live view of the battlefield.[28]

The town's path to Heritage Gettysburg began with the Gettysburg National Tower and the controversy it generated in the 1970s. Widespread publicity about commercial desecration of Gettysburg induced a moment of introspection. Where was the gain if tourists were "driven away" because "we have cheapened the countryside with inappropriate commercialism?" the leader of a local group opposing the tower asked in 1971. "Why not preserve and restore what we have rather than rely on modern gimmicks?" he argued. "Gettysburg could then become known as a delightful old-type town to which tourists would be attracted and spend their money." The marketing sensibility of such a position overpowered traditional borough sentiment about the adjacent federal park. Since the late-nineteenth century, townspeople viewed themselves as struggling to raise revenues through tourism while being choked by the non-taxpaying behemoth to which they were chained. "Aesthetics to me is a bunch of nonsense!" said the borough manager in 1973 when asked about the visual appeal of downtown Gettysburg. Yet within a few years the town increasingly cooperated with the Park Service to create visual harmony. The borough that claimed nary a zoning regulation in 1970 boasted by 1990 a signage ordinance, a comprehensive zoning code, a historic and architectural review board, and a designated historic district. In the nineteenth century, locals urged more monuments to attract tourists. By 1993, as one official acknowledged, "maintaining the landscape they come to visit" sustained the $60 million tourist industry. It mattered not whether the installation of facades, brick sidewalks, or conversion of old buildings into period restaurants actually reflected Gettysburg 1863 because, as one proponent applauded, "it will help the image of Gettysburg."[29]

Of course, the town's raised consciousness paralleled national nostalgia for an earlier day during an era of rapid change. "Looking backward has again become a major industry," the *New York Times* reported in 1975, a decade that launched the "staged authenticity" of restored storefronts, neocolonial shopping centers, and the opening of Disney World. In ensuing decades, Disney's combination of stage set, shopping, and festival influenced new malls, museums, historic sites, downtown revitalizations, and established historical attractions.[30]

Gettysburg went a step further than Disney by gathering fair, festival, and shrine into one event within its borders. In 1983, the Gettysburg Travel Council joined with the Park Service and other organizations to launch Civil War Heritage Days, a rally of Civil War image tribes. Originally a week long, the festival in time extended an extra week and hosted hundreds of thousands of visitors. As the director of the Travel Council quipped a decade after its inauguration, "Local businesses expect blue and gray to equal plenty of green" during Heritage Days. The event allows reenactors to stage battle scenarios as well as demonstrate tactics and weaponry in a "living history" camp on battlefield land. Relic collectors throng what has been billed as "the finest show of Civil War memorabilia in the nation." Civil War book collectors, art collectors, and wargamers are attracted to separate fairs. By the 1990s, however, Heritage Days had become the everyday at Heritage Gettysburg. On any weekend during the tourist season, reenactors conducted demonstrations and strutted brick sidewalks lined with shops selling period costumes, Civil War relics, books, and art. Of course, festivals had always been part of Gettysburg. But now instead of celebrating national pride, progress, or the American family, they celebrated consumption of the past in a subjective quest for authenticity. Rage for heritage has even spilled over into nostalgia for earlier eras of Gettysburg touring, evidenced in the return of the reconstructed tourist cabin, antique touring limousines, a trolley, and steam locomotive touring.[31]

Gettysburg's seamless landscape of reenactors in town and on battlefield, collections displayed at the park and by merchants, and the huge National Park Service museum shop tend to fog the old distinction between the sacred and secular. Yet if it seems increasingly unclear where the battlefield leaves off and town begins, this is in part due to the town's industrious effort to carve sacred space from commercial space. The same year the town and National Park Service inaugurated Heritage Days, it also initiated storefront renovation. Incorporated in 1989, Main Street Gettysburg revitalized through heritage or, as its publicity announced, "to develop historic Gettysburg for the economic benefit of our community and to preserve her rich heritage for the benefit of our nation." Its Historic Pathway Plan was designed to counteract downtown decline resulting from strip malls and suburban flight. Whereas railroads once funneled tourists into town, the National Park Service had detoured tourists from downtown with its visitors' center and mall-like parking on Cemetery Ridge. By the late 1980s only 2 percent of the park's 1.7 million visitors bothered to stop and spend in the district near the square. Through a heritage environment coordinated with the battlefield, however, the town could reap more revenues from increased traffic, longer visitor stays, and upgraded property values.[32]

With the Historic Pathway Plan, gone were Gettysburg's earlier dreams of encouraging industrialization to gain freedom from dependence on tourism. Now the future cashed in on the past as progress. The town could look on the National Park Service as a business partner instead of a cruel master. Gone too would be the parasitic image of the town as a snare and a desecrating influence; now the town too could claim sacred ground. Veering away from the family friendliness of the 1950s, the plan enticed visitors into town by the paradox of guaranteed authenticity through a period look. At the plan's core was a multimedia presentation where "visitors are immersed in the battle taking place in the streets and homes of Gettysburg, and share the fear and trauma of its residents." In addition, "authentic" attractions, including a rehabilitated Wills House and railroad station where President Lincoln arrived, served as anchors for a tourist entertainment and shopping complex.[33]

To draw visitors into town, Main Street constructed a series of forty-two strategically spaced sidewalk exhibits that presented the town's story of the battle. To improve the historical ambience along the pathway, Main Street erected gaslights and continued to provide interest-free loans to businesses for facade improvements, including one that transformed a vacant G. C. Murphy storefront into a simulation of nineteenth-century shops. Bland buildings tourists had whizzed by for decades on the way to the battlefield

FIGURE 24. Wayside on Baltimore Street, one of over forty designed to draw tourists into town by integrating the town's history with the battlefield (author's collection)

were marked with tablets identifying their historical significance. Main Street's self-contained story of the town's "golden moment" could succeed because the hallowed shrine of battlefield itself seemed to be collapsing into a heritage complex.[34]

What Friends was to GBPA, Main Street was to the Retail Merchants Association, Chamber of Commerce, or Gettysburg Travel Council. The latter organizations had promoted Gettysburg by bundling all attractions into a package; Main Street and Friends manufactured attractions and packaged them into Heritage Gettysburg. Both tantalized the tourist quest for authenticity with contrived images and simulations, and both generated pseudoevents that attracted traffic to Gettysburg. Main Street even organized celebrations such as a Civil War band festival and a Yuletide Festival to extend the touring season. Both employed the latest marketing methods to survey constituents and solicit restoration funds from corporations and individual donors. Like Friends, Main Street innovated in offering something for women, attracting wives—and shoppers—who "often do not find the Civil War battles as interesting as men do," into town with sidewalk tablets focusing on women's roles during the battle. Main Street's 1994 visitor survey not only examined demographics and visitation patterns, but also tried to discover the type of attractions tourists might patronize, what features they preferred, and how much they would pay to see them.[35]

Main Street understood that heritage images beyond Gettysburg influenced consumers and controlled the town's image. Washington's *Weekend Entertainment Guide* noted in 1994 that "The PBS 'Civil War' series, the movie 'Gettysburg,' and the historical novel 'The Killer Angels' have made this small town of 7,800 a red-hot tourist attraction." Main Street acknowledged the boost media provided and planned on increased numbers of visitors because films like *Gettysburg* or *Civil War Journal* had preconditioned the market. The director of the Gettysburg Travel Council said Gettysburg "reaped the benefits" of Ken Burns's *The Civil War* for at least two years.[36]

The public fails to distinguish between media fiction and history because the reproduction creates authenticity. Image vanquished reality, transforming historic sites into themed entertainment where visitors could experience the hyperreal Civil War. Even the designers of staged reality were fooled. Authors of the Historic Pathway Plan targeted a market of "stressed" urban workers who wanted "authentic, living, historic towns rather than the artificial 'Main Streets' of theme parks and shopping malls." Gettysburg at least could claim it was no back lot, that the new facades and images were intended as mediums designed to connect with an actual past. But the danger of fakes is that they overpower the thing they represent. As Disney knew, Main Street America or Frontier Land could go anywhere tickets could be sold. The confusion was already evident in the flood of movie souvenirs sold in Gettysburg's themed shops that blurred image and battlefield. Of the variety of bric-a-brac related to the movie's hero, one T-shirt labeled "Colonel Joshua L. Chamberlain" featured the likeness not of Chamberlain but of his film portrayer, Jeff Daniels. Joining other virtual Gettysburg Web sites, in 1999 Main Street obviated the need to stroll the heritage pathway by launching its own virtual tour complete with virtual souvenir shopping. And in 2000 a hypertown of shops, entertainment, and lodging opened adjacent to Gettysburg's major artery featuring "historic looking" storefronts, stone pavers, and gas lamps. Thus tourists could skip the real town altogether and enjoy the fake after visiting the battlefield, which was growing ever more hyperreal itself.[37]

The National Park Service's Heritage Battlefield

By 2000 the National Park Service (NPS) served as the linchpin of Heritage Gettysburg in spite of commercialization. The NPS invited reenactors to perform on the battlefield, welcomed partnerships with developers, media merchants, and tourist enterprises, and planned massive projects designed to restore the landscape's 1863 appearance. Yet in welcoming collaboration with heritage producers, NPS also encouraged heritage consumers to express their views on the battlefield's future. Like the town's tourist industry, the National Park Service pulled away from the family-friendly Gettysburg of the earlier era to create an authentic experience for enthusiasts.

During the first half of the century, the automobile, the growth of family touring, and the Cold War prompted NPS to add tourist services and visual stimuli to the landscape. While Vietnam severed America's victory culture, galloping social and political change produced nostalgia for the experience of a seemingly uncomplicated past. During the tumultuous decade of the 1970s that began with Kent State and ended with the fall of the Carter administration, the NPS departed sharply from its past interpretation of the battle. Through the remainder of the century, NPS built on those initial steps aimed to deliver a combination of education and entertainment through authenticity.[38]

In 1969 the NPS introduced "living history"—that is, costumed em-ployees enacting the role of historical actors—to its program of tourist ser-vices. Six years earlier during the Civil War centennial, historians censured costumed dramatization and battle reenactment as distasteful, if not odious. Bruce Catton reminded the public in 1962 that Civil War battles were "not waged in a spirit of fun," but were "desperately real and profoundly, unfor-gettably tragic." Similarly, the *Richmond News-Leader* noted that reenact-ments "threaten to make a farce of the greatest tragedy in American his-tory" and were nothing more than "amateur theatrics, carried on by overgrown boys who get a thrill out of hearing guns go off." At the 1963 Gettysburg centennial, NPS officials agreed to allow Confederate reenactors to walk the field of Pickett's Charge toward blue reenactors on Cemetery Ridge but barred any weapon firing. The spectacle ended not with a simu-lated struggle at the wall but with a patriotic ritual of anthems, bowed heads, and prayer. To see firing demonstrations visitors crossed the street to Fort Defiance, which hired reenactors as an alternative to its cowboys and Indians shows. As the large attendance at even the ritualized centennial reenactment demonstrated, the public found reenactment entertaining.[39]

Yet by 1974, seven NPS rangers costumed as Civil War soldiers or civil-ians put on eight shows a day for tourists during the season. The NPS went so far as to establish a "boot camp" for training living history rangers. The fifteen-to-twenty-five minute shows proved extremely popular, possessing an entertainment value and authenticity that contrasted both to the canned narration on tour buses and confusion over Vietnam, Watergate, and na-tional purpose. Rangers emphasized the reality of being "back there" through first-person monologue, authentic props, and urging audiences "to imagine it is 1863." Even NPS employees, however, had reservations about the value of such presentations at the time. In 1973, NPS interpretive spe-cialist Frank Barnes wondered if the "living history" approach he saw at Gettysburg maligned the past and, rather than educating or inspiring, sim-ply amused. Display of "authentic camplife and safe firings . . . seem fun," he wrote in a memo to Gettysburg's park superintendent. Barnes asked, "What do weapons demonstrations—too often visibly enjoyed as fun—do for national unity and meaningful forgetfulness at Gettysburg and other Civil War battlefields?"[40]

Barnes, like Catton or, later, Bloom, were drowned by a stream that grew into a flood. By 1978 a newspaper termed Gettysburg's "living history" program "a major interpretive tool" explaining "the hardships endured by the Civil War soldiers as well as their equipment and uniforms." No one by that time questioned emphasizing the experience of the grunt soldier or common civilian at Gettysburg. Besides, everyone enjoyed stepping out of reality and into another role. "I like it more than anything!" said one costumed ranger in 1978. "I cease being a park ranger and actually become the character; I use slang, chew tobacco, spit on the ground, and even scratch myself." This was a universe removed from the genteel pleasure ground of a century before, with its winding avenues and monuments designed for uplifting contemplation.[41]

Beginning in the 1970s, the NPS also organized ranger walks tracing the path of original military maneuvers using "authentically-dressed interpreters" to take tourists "back in time to 1863 where they share in the confusion, tragedy, and triumphs of those fateful three days in July." The Pickett's Charge walk lined tourists up in a company front near the Virginia Monument and marched them toward Cemetery Ridge. According to the ranger in charge, the march gave participants "the feeling they've done something the average visitor has not"—tasted the *real* Gettysburg. School groups, a feature of Gettysburg tourism since the early 1900s, also were not immune to the NPS emphasis on authentic experience. An NPS program launched in the 1980s allowed younger children to "enlist in the Union army and experience the daily life of Civil War soldiers," while fifth through twelfth graders formed a company to "march, then charge, across the open fields toward the Union lines and 'The Angle.'" Like Fantasyland's Wagon Train amusement ride decades before, NPS provided hats and toy guns to aid the mystical retrogression. At a "sleepover" program in the visitors' center, each child was provided the identity of a real Gettysburg soldier and at the end of the weekend learned whether "he" lives or dies. Publicity claimed these experiential activities helped visitors "understand the Civil War," but apparently without the burden of history.[42]

The NPS that had eyed reenactors with dismay in the 1960s embraced them by 2000. In those intervening decades, reenacting had grown until an army-sized group of upwards of fifty thousand enthusiasts pursued authenticity down to authentic Civil War toothbrushes, socks, and underwear. As Gettysburg had been termed "the Mecca of the Patriot" in the late 1800s, so it became "the Mecca of the Reenactor" in the late 1900s. Grand monuments, which had lost their power to evoke memory, were eclipsed by artillery crews, squads of cavalry, and infantry performing for tourists near the Pennsylvania or Virginia Memorial.

By the time the NPS permitted shooting on the battlefield in the mid-1990s, reenactors increasingly entertained tourists. Crowds were treated to not only military displays, but to medical demonstrations and band concerts featuring "[m]usical performances by authentic Civil War musicians . . . much of it played on original Civil War instruments." The NPS invited the public to join in the dancing to Victorian music at the Cyclorama Center. Indeed, NPS sponsored few significant public events out of costume. Even sacred activities such as rituals at the Soldiers' National Cemetery, which earlier would have featured active military personnel, now looked like 1860s film sets overflowing with extras. The latest educational technology, paradoxically, could provide a medium for nationwide dissemination of this fictionalized past. By 2000 an NPS satellite broadcast about the battle, supported by a Web site featuring real soldiers' "identities," offered over 300,000 school students a "time tunnel"—back to campfuls of reenactors and park-employee narrators in period dress.[43]

But plays need stages, and "living history" shows represented only part of the new NPS focus. In 1969 NPS drafted a new master plan for the battlefield, with a basic goal to "simulate the historic conditions, and thusly create a mood that will allow the visitor to be receptive to the interpretive story." The plan initially considered removing of the visitors' center from historically sensitive land—even though the Neutra building was only a decade old—and building a new visitors' center from which visitors would be bused to key battlefield areas. But the NPS went further by launching a variety of projects over the next decades aimed at thrusting visitors into 1863 and, in the process, further dismantling artifice of both the family-friendly and genteel parks of earlier touring eras.[44]

In contrast to the park commissioners' 1904 assessment that monuments "occupying comparatively little space" could commemorate the battle, the park's boundaries were expanded to 5,900 acres in 1990 from a ceiling of 3,874 set by Congress in 1976. Previously, battlefield land embellished with monuments spoke for itself; even the addition of split rail fencing and other cosmetics beginning in the 1930s were designed only to provide a period look here and there. Beginning in the 1970s, a land acquisition program removed motels, proprietary museums and amusements, gas stations, and other tourist services from key scenes, while other modern intrusions were screened from view with trees. Extraneous park avenues constructed during the genteel era were removed along with utility poles. Sometimes, however, the NPS's concentration on authenticity seemed mind-boggling. When, for example, the NPS tore down the termite-infested Bryan farmhouse near the Pickett's Charge area, it precisely duplicated the original, board by board, with lumber hewed by period hand tools. Similarly, when the NPS opened the Slyder Farm as a working nineteenth-century farmstead, it employed original farm machinery, agricultural methods, and the same crops that were growing there in 1863. The NPS not only preserved a shrine; it manufactured a heritage landscape.[45]

FIGURE 25. "You can almost see them coming": Spangler farm on Seminary Ridge in 2000, following restoration (author's collection)

Considering that NPS adopted methods of commercial entertainment to convey the past to tourists, its support of the movie *Gettysburg* was not surprising. The film, which used thousands of reenactors as extras, legitimized "living history" on the big screen through a romanticized image of war. Not only did NPS cooperate fully in TNT's 1992 filming on the battlefield; it also altered the battlefield to meet the expectations of many thousands of tourists prompted to validate the narrative presented in film and book. In 1961, a tourist who had read John Pullen's *The Twentieth Maine* wrote to the park superintendent complaining that bushes obscured the regiment's monument made famous by the book. In reply, the superintendent stated that removing brush or adding roadways to ease access would "destroy the historic scene." Yet following publication of *The Killer Angels* thirteen years later, NPS installed a walkway to the monument and a small parking lot. After the movie, which boosted tourism by 19 percent in 1994, NPS improved these additions. It also added an exhibit featuring a recent artistic rendition of the fighting at the site, accompanied by a biographical sketch of the movie's hero, Colonel Joshua L. Chamberlain. Like the illustrated sidewalk tablets in town, the painting provided the site with the animation tourists needed to overcome the deadening effects of the monument. With much irony, to meet the need for authenticity, an imagined scene defined a real historic site made famous by a fictional book and movie.[46]

But the film had a subtler yet deeper effect on transforming the shrine into Heritage Gettysburg. In the wake of the tourist boost from the movie, early in 1995 a local developer proposed a new visitors' center and museum complete with an Imax theater showing a $5 million "dramatic overview of the battle." As part of the deal the developer would raze Neutra's cyclorama center, which both inadequately preserved the archaic cyclorama and corrupted visual purity. Thus the 1970s vision to return the area to its "original" appearance would be realized, although no one knew precisely what that appearance was on the days of battle. A new museum seemed a necessity in response to criticism that the current visitors' center and museum inadequately displayed and maintained its innumerable relics. A New York Times correspondent called the 1930s Electric Map there "close to being quaint in this high-tech era." Because of the unlikelihood of the federal government funding the project, the new Gettysburg superintendent, John A. Latschar, intended to unveil the plan as a unique public-private partnership. Soon, however, both he and the Friends backed off in a fusillade of criticism from battlefield enthusiasts wary of commercialism, government secrecy, and defilements to undisturbed battlefield land.[47]

But Latschar was a fighter experienced at developing heritage attractions. He had formerly served as first superintendent of the NPS Steamtown site in Scranton, Pennsylvania, which had cobbled together reconstructed iron furnaces, a Vermont train collection, and other bricolage under the NPS imprimatur. By 1997 he secured a proposal for the Gettysburg project that included an IMAX theater, National Geographic store, gift shop, Civil War arts and craft shop, and restaurant in addition to a museum and cyclorama gallery. Then Latschar led the drafting of a new General Management Plan that included options for removal of the old cyclorama and visitors' center, for landscape restoration, and most controversially, for building the new museum–visitors' complex on undisturbed battlefield land. After weathering congressional oversight hearings, public criticism, and legislators threatening to derail the plan, in late 1999 he succeeded in obtaining federal permission to implement the $76 million package. Within a year work was underway on the landscape and the layout for the new visitors' center complex to be constructed in a low-profile area. The 1962 visitors' center's verandah near the Pickett's Charge site helped visitors verify the scene depicted in the old cyclorama; now the battlefield would conform to the movie set visitors expected to see.[48]

In truth the new NPS plan placed the capstone on Heritage Gettysburg. Civil War News called it "the most sweeping restoration of the battlefield ever undertaken." When finished in ten or fifteen years, the plan will remove 576 acres of "non-historic trees" but restore 115 "historic" acres of trees and 160 acres of orchards (using ornamental rather than fruit-bearing trees). In addition to the reconstruction of thirty-nine miles of fencing, the plan calls for maintenance of firewood lots and thickets as they appeared at the time of the battle. Along with completing the burial of power lines from "major battle action areas," "non-historic" buildings are slated for removal. Ironically, although any parallels with Disney are unintentional— even conscientiously avoided—there are similarities to Disney's simulated landscapes. What visitors will see is not the 1863 battlefield, but a hyperreal version of it that conforms to their image of the original. Like Disney's African village, 1930s boardwalk, or other engineered environments, the simulation will be an "airbrushed" improvement on the original without authentic blemishes or unpleasantries. Unlike Disney's work, however, the restoration is not intended as a front to sell merchandise, and a view of the sacred ground will continue to be free of charge.[49]

Yet as with the sublime landscape or monumented battlefield a century earlier, such a visual feast is bound to serve as the hub of a heritage tourist center that melds public and private tourist enterprises. Latschar has argued that investment in the combined visitors' center–battlefield restoration means a local economic boost. The battlefield always had served as an anchor for fringe attractions such as the Springs Hotel, Round Top Park, or Fantasyland in successive eras of touring. But now park authorities envisioned a uniformly themed heritage complex with the reconstructed battlefield radiating commercial success for miles around. To those tourist merchants nervous about moving the visitors' center, Latschar reassured them of financial success. A persuasive part of the General Management Plan included an estimate that tourist spending in the community would increase by 21 percent, or nearly $24 million. By 1999, another consultant hired by NPS had enhanced the estimated increase to $30 million.[50]

Since the 1970s, NPS has aided private tourist enterprises by publishing "what to see" newspapers, permitting tourist information booths on government property, and cosponsoring living history pageants and Heritage Days. Now, however, NPS plans to integrate other sites of the Gettysburg Campaign into the battlefield tourist vortex. Rehabilitating and managing the Lincoln Train Station and Wills House, creating in effect a tourist corridor from the center of town to the battlefield, are key projects. "These kinds of investments result in positive economic impacts for local areas, created by increased visitation and local stays," Latschar said. Officials in neighboring cities such as Hagerstown and Harrisburg agreed, hoping to feel the economic effects of Gettysburg. Hagerstown had ambitions to be its own "hub of Civil War tourism," and Harrisburg in 2001 opened a $2.5 million museum officials believed would siphon off 10 percent of Gettysburg's tourists. Heritage paid, as everyone connected with the tourist industry realized.[51]

Like the Friends and town enterprises, Latschar understood the importance of harnessing enthusiasts to his initiative especially because the plan relied heavily on private contributions. Relying on the Friends and NPS marketing techniques, Latschar promised benefits for the image tribes: a new museum for collectors and heritage buffs, a purified landscape for reenactors, military historians, battlefield touring aficionados, and wargamers. Yet Latschar's publicity campaign, which included surveys and thirty public meetings, had to overcome resistance against NPS authority. Since the tower controversy, some preservationists had been lambasting the NPS as undemocratic and an unfit custodian of the shrine. Authority of all institutions and elites had been questioned since the 1960s, and to some extent was replaced by opinion polls, surveys, and attendance figures. Latschar's surveys and meetings indicated a high preference for restoration and reduction in commercial activity at the new visitors' center, although only enthusiasts bothered to respond. As Latschar skillfully showed, success depended on mobilizing segmented markets of the twenty-first century rather than the mass markets of midcentury.[52]

Latschar affirmed that the project included "re-sanctifying" the ground by removing the old visitors' center-cyclorama buildings and restoring the area to its 1863 appearance. He thus disarmed critics of the public-private museum who called it a "desecration," "a mall on the battlefield," and, most typically, "Disneyfication." Unlike the battles against commercialism forty years before, few could see the difference between the sacred and secular anymore. Strange twists inconceivable in the past, such a bizarre alliance of preservationists and rubber-tomahawk merchants aligned against the NPS, offered evidence of the confusion. Oddly, no one seemed to notice that themed landscapes were Disney hallmarks. Inherent in the concept of theme parks are entertainment and retail sales combined around a central attraction, whose image is the focus for consumption. Like Disney's Main Street that led to the Magic Kingdom, Gettysburg had similarly themed itself with shops serving a variety of Civil War image tribes. Media productions such as *Gettysburg* created a "closed loop" of marketing much as Disney's films market Disney World. And while town tourism found it profitable to wear the battlefield's sacred mantle, the battlefield profited from the town's commercialism. By the turn of the twenty-first century, NPS retail sales had evolved from selling three pamphlets in 1951 to hosting one of the largest tourist stores in town. The store not only showed the movie *Gettysburg* endlessly on television monitors perched over the merchandise; NPS also sponsored special exhibits of the action scenes of Civil War commercial artists. It seemed as if the images were NPS aspirations, a hope that visitors would be plunged into the scene of action. Now Gettysburg could become a full member of the heritage clones competing in the commercial leisure market to deliver authentic experiences, including joining Martha Washington for tea or in effigy burning at Williamsburg; ducking from whistling shot and rumbling floors at Pamplin Park's Civil War museum; "dressing up like an Indian" at the annual Custer reenactment in Hardin, Montana; walking through "immersive, experiential exhibits" at Harrisburg's National Civil War Museum; crawling in a Civil War tent, hefting a rifled musket, or trying on a soldier's blouse at the Western Reserve Historical Society; or stepping into the Ice Age at the Mashantucket, Connecticut Pequot Museum.[53]

By 2000, the nation's public space more and more had melded into commercial space, so that commercial values infused civic and religious institutions, while theme parks and malls had assumed a sacred aura. But at Heritage Gettysburg the secular disguised itself as the sacred and slipped effortlessly into sacred space. The new aesthetic of the sacred that demanded a tangible authenticity elevated the commercial and blurred the distinction between the two. U.S. Secretary of the Interior Bruce Babbitt said Latschar's project would "help restore historical integrity to some of America's most hallowed ground." Babbitt's comment raises an issue at the heart of the current heritage-tourism era. If all agree that certain ground is hallowed, does it need to have its historical integrity restored? Moreover, is there not a difference between preserving land to remember an event and transforming the land to look like it did when the event occurred? More important, this appeal to the authentic obscures its difference from past methods of remembering at Gettysburg. Nature and monuments no longer evoke memory for a culture demanding visual certainty of the real thing. If, as Lincoln said, the living could not hallow fields made sacred by sacrifice, perhaps the living could transform it into a heritage attraction. Inevitably, the sacred at Gettysburg had always been influenced by commercial culture, but now the sacred lay in the illusion of authenticity that emerged from commercial culture. The collapse of cultural authority surely accelerated this trend. Instead of a genteel elite and their heirs arranging public space for uplift, the responsibility had devolved on surveys, polls, and focus groups of consumers who now ingested the media without cultural arbiters. Friends, NPS, and Main Street looked for guidance among the image tribes of hobbyists who rallied around Gettysburg and voted for authenticity with their wallets. Thus by 2000, Friends members, reenactors, collectors, battlefield tourists, and others had produced their own tangible Gettysburg fantasy.[54]

Chapter Eight

☆ ☆ ☆ ☆ ☆ ☆ ☆ ☆ ☆ ☆ ☆

"It's 1863 All Over Again":
Heritage Tourists

IN SEPTEMBER 1997 Ed Smothers wrote a letter about his recent visit to Gettysburg, describing how a costumed park ranger portrayed a nurse who had aided the wounded. The collapse of time conjured by the performance particularly struck Smothers. "You could have sworn you were listening to her talk about the battle and the day afterward," he wrote. The actor led the group toward the scene of Pickett's Charge and paused on Cemetery Ridge. Gesturing at the surrounding fields, she shook her head over the frightful carnage. She grieved that some of the wounded lay where they fell for days without so much as a drink of water, and recounted how the amputated limbs of those who received medical aid piled up outside makeshift hospitals. "It was very moving," Smothers wrote of the presentation, "and I would recommend when you visit the park to take this in."[1]

Smothers's infatuation with a staged illusion suggests a subtle change in tourist expectations at the turn of the twenty-first century. While the World War II generation wrapped family bonding experiences in a cloak of patriotism, postwar sons and daughters generally sought a personal experience with the original event shorn of associations to national purpose or cross-generational bonding. But perhaps the medium of Smothers's letter, more than its message, characterized the new tourists. Smothers used his personal computer to write the letter, not pen and paper, and sent it electronically via Internet technology, not through the postal service. Moreover, he mailed the letter not to friends or relatives, but to an electronic discussion forum of enthusiasts who chattered endlessly about Gettysburg. A virtual community Smothers knew only through cyberspace, the group existed at the electronic interstices of other websites featuring virtual Gettysburg tours, wargames, shopping, live views, and 3-D simulations. The

Gettysburg of Smothers's letter, both a real and virtual theme park available anytime, anyplace was the Gettysburg the new tourists increasingly expected. Contrasting to the family and mass tourism of the postwar period, the baby boom generation could experience Gettysburg privately, but also within image tribes of insiders whose activities defined Heritage Gettysburg.

The new crowd's developmental path diverged widely from the route of their elders. Born between 1946 and 1964, the "baby boomers," around whom family vacations centered, represented 40 percent of the population by the mid-1980s. Instead of enduring the deprivation of depression and war as had their parents, the boomers enjoyed more abundance and personal freedom than had any other cohort in history. Boomers arrived at adulthood repudiating many of the morals, conventions, and institutions their parents honored, replacing the celebratory national saga with cynicism. Critics despaired over the abandonment of self-restraint within this "me" generation that discarded collectivity for maximum personal fulfillment. For many this transition was expressed by President Jimmy Carter, who lambasted Americans for a "national malaise" of "self-indulgence and consumption."[2]

With the decline of cultural authority and increasing isolation of individuals, media industries grew more powerful and turned more of life into entertainment. The twentieth-century's trend toward entertainment experienced in private continued with the explosion of cable channels and later the Internet, all of which helped enhance differences among Americans. Beginning in the late 1970s, advertisers capitalized on the combination of increasing social divisiveness and media outlets by targeting self-conscious groups instead of appealing to mass markets. The result herded Americans into contemporary counterparts to old ethnic groupings, "image tribes" of insiders who shared the same taste in goods—as well as their differences from excluded outsiders.

Families, once the backbone of pilgrims to Gettysburg, deteriorated and further frayed from the effects of target marketing. In contrast to the television, car, and rec room that brought families of the older generation together, family members now occupied themselves with individually owned goods in personal spaces. The advent of personal computers and the World Wide Web furthered atomization at both home and office, promoting more privacy while paradoxically linking users to global culture. As advertising and entertainment increasingly merged, more space was reserved for entertainment instead of edification. Home itself, once considered a refuge from commercial intrusion, faced commercial invasion from advertising and entertainment that similarly penetrated other market-free zones, such as schools, churches, museums, and public parks. Conversely, commercial spaces such as malls, bookstores, and theme parks assumed more and more of a sacred aura as venues for extraordinary experiences. In an interesting inversion, the marketplace enabled private space to ingest the public sphere and public space to be enjoyed privately.[3]

In spite of unprecedented abundance, Americans felt isolated, harried, and bewildered in an alien new world. Not only had the pace of change seemed to accelerate, but the decline of patriotism, civic organizations, religious denominations, and marriage set people adrift. American culture, by replacing cultural differences or creating ersatz culture through consumer image tribes, had deprived individuals of secure moorings. This threw Americans back on the media that saturated their lives, and boomers longed to part the veil separating them from a real world and an integrated self. Feeling like orphans suspended in the present, boomers searched for the authentic by going back to their youth, when parents cultivated self-absorption by encouraging free expression of the "genuine self." Ironically, the marketplace provided solutions to a problem it had created by selling therapy for the most private space of all, the self. Yet authenticity need not be pursued only via the spiritual self, for genuine experience also could be hunted down in other places and times. By 2000, half of all vacationing adults had taken "adventure" vacations within the past five years. For many tourists, theme parks offered integrated experiences in fabricated environments that literally lifted, spun, and shook them out of the world.[4]

Some from the boomer generation chose to embrace "heritage," the personal quest for experiencing the past. It was no coincidence that heritage emerged with the drive for authenticity. Both held out hopes of holism through genuine subjective experience, both smoothly dovetailed commercial with sacred, and both provided entertainment, relying on the visual and tangible in an era soaked with images and an abundance of goods. Both were equally "spiritual." Heritage, in fact, included a faith that required only belief with no appeal to the reasoned arguments of history. And heritage also atomized believers, although into groups of image tribes such as collectors, heritage tourists, wargamers, preservationists, and reenactors. Heritage offered therapy for a cynical postvictory culture where America's long-running story of triumph had finally ended with Vietnam. It reflected New Age religion, but it differed in its use of the temporal over the eternal. Heritage attempted to slow change by manufacturing moments of the past. A heritage moment could restore wholeness or provide a sense of control in an alienating world. Despite society's loss of national pride and purpose, heritage enabled its practitioners to descend into a private world of triumph, aided by increasingly sophisticated media technology.[5]

As they had in other arenas of American life, heritage boomers reshaped Gettysburg to suit the needs of a new kind of memory. During the Vietnam war, a journalist who noted tourists flocking to American battlefields observed, "These battlefields, these shrines, are a link between the generations of men in their continuing search to be at home in their world." But the link binding generations snapped along with the national narrative, and heritage boomers built a home at Gettysburg quite different from that sculpted by the earlier generation.[6]

Although many boomers brought their families, read roadside markers, and visited the Land of Little Horses, just as their parents had, others broke from the past. For example, heritage tourists jettisoned the flag waving, speeches, and other gestures of patriotism—unless they took place in a reenactment scnene—that once defined the sacred meaning of the shrine. Neither did many care about Gettysburg's potential as a special venue for family bonding, camaraderie, or insouciance that had attracted past visitors such as their parents, Civil War veterans, or day-trippers. With the decline of the national narrative, Gettysburg's meaning now rested in its delivery of virtual reality that promised release from the present. Even travel literature, which earlier hawked monuments or tourist attractions, now urged a direct encounter with the Civil War. "To bring the story of the Civil War to life, nothing quite matches walking over the very ground where the great battles were fought." *AAA World* admonished, "How would you have fared in the brutal conflict that pitted brother against brother for four long years?" But even though Gettysburg lost the sacred associations of a unifying shrine, the sacred had not disappeared. Rather, despite belief among heritage enthusiasts that the sacred—by their definition, the authentic—had been rescued from the commercial, the shrine had been co-opted by commercial enterprise. Even more important, the sacred had migrated into the subjective experience of visitors seeking "real" spiritual encounters.[7]

In accord with 2000 census figures indicating that the number of nuclear families had halved since 1960, the new Gettysburg tourists contrasted with the mass family market of midcentury. Typical tourists of the 1950s and 1960s may have looked like "June and Ward Cleaver with Wally and Beaver," according to an Gettysburg National Military Park (GNMP) senior historian. But now Gettysburg surveys of the 1990s showed family touring played only a minor role, and market segments of image tribe members were dominant. One 1994 survey found a preponderance of males among those surveyed, and almost 70 percent of the total were not accompanied by children, although half ranged in age from 20 to 39. Unfortunately, GNMP does not gather statistics on race, but the park superintendent probably correctly concluded in 2000 that Gettysburg's 1.7 million visitors were "disproportionately white and male." As for families that still arrived by 2000, no longer did they uniformly act as a unit bonding around shared experiences or goods. Women, who had traditionally either tagged along with their husbands or acted as responsible mothers of future citizens, now in many cases found Gettysburg a meaningful pastime. Children were taught to "feel what it was like" to be a Civil War soldier. Gettysburg became, in other words, a kind of giant hobby set for middle-class white America.[8]

Transformation of Gettysburg's cultural environment between the mid-1970s and 2000 signaled the arrival of the new consumers. Like American families whose members no longer need compromise in the quest for self-satisfaction, there would be no negotiations at Gettysburg on an environment delivering authentic experience. If there were one issue all members of the fragmented market could agree on, it was visual purity—even if the themed environment masked commercial space catering to a variety of "tribes." In the post-Vietnam drive for authentic restoration, tourist services of the family-friendly era, such as Stuckey's, Carvel, Fort Defiance, and Fantasyland, as well as a few gas stations and motels, vaporized in the wrecking spree. But subtler changes occurred that demonstrated the shift away from family tourism and toward the consumer of authenticity.

The town of Gettysburg more and more seemed like a hyperreal version of itself conceding commercial space to upscale tourism. While family-owned motels constructed in the 1950s and 1960s faced condemnation, closed, or declined, bed and breakfasts appealing to yuppies and dinks (double income, no kids) flourished. By 1993, fourteen B&Bs surrounded Gettysburg, with five in the borough, offering "comfortable escapes from tackiness in this small town," according to a Lancaster paper. Antique and gift boutiques also opened for the new trade, while coffee shops, ethnic restaurants, and microbreweries presented fashionable alternatives to fast-food franchises. *New York* magazine in 1989 termed the bed and breakfasts, period restaurants, antiquing, auctions, and craft shops as "amenities that will make this jaunt pleasurable even for those who aren't Civil War devotees."[9]

Although since the 1860s the battlefield had accommodated successive trends in American recreational activity, by the 1990s heritage proponents condemned any leisure pursuits other than those focused on the 1863 narrative. The old patriotic saga had been repackaged by popular books and films, but in the surge of new pilgrims, struggles erupted between outdoor recreationists and Civil War enthusiasts. With growing interest in direct experience with nature during the 1970s, outdoor enthusiasts used the battlefield preserve for hiking, biking, rock climbing, and naturalist activities. By the next decade, recreational use of the battlefield had switched to sports matching the competitiveness of boomers. Marathons and ten-kilometer races took advantage of the park's expansive avenues. According to the *Washington Post*, heritage enthusiasts found these recreational activities "inappropriate, even offensive." By 1993, Civil War Roundtable Associates, the umbrella organization for the nation's Civil War roundtables, adopted a resolution petitioning the NPS to drop the word *parks* from nomenclature for its battlefields. "They are not parks," a president of the associates explained in 1993, the year of *Gettysburg*'s release. "Parks are playgrounds . . . battlefields are shrines, not playgrounds."[10]

Few complained, however, about enterprises contributing to the themed environment or anything related to the Civil War, for that matter. Reenactor recreation—camping, shooting, and marching on the battlefield—offended only elders who recalled a different meaning of the sacred. Even races, if properly themed or dedicated to aiding the park, were acceptable. One five-kilometer Spirit of Gettysburg race appointed an Abraham Lincoln impersonator to hold the victory tape. Others donated registration proceeds to battlefield preservation, and featured Civil War reenactors at the starting line, occasionally even as runners. Conflict might erupt, however, over activities of "questionable authenticity and motives." The National Riding Stables advertised the opportunity of "riding through woods and fields that are reminiscent of the way soldiers would have seen them in 1863." Civil War Roundtable Associates, who apparently had no qualms about troops of mounted cavalry reenactors on the battlefield, objected that equestrian groups of tourists "interfere with the historic landscape." The stable's owner replied that, as for visual purity, "There were thousands of horses here during the battle," and referring to the continual stream of concession buses on park avenues added, "I don't recall there were any buses."[11]

New attractions at Gettysburg demonstrated the spreading vogue for heritage among the new generation. Reenactor organizations, GNMP, and town-staged "living history" shows proliferated, along with restoration of the landscape, as the century progressed. In the late 1970s, an Abraham Lincoln impersonator opened a small theater and presented nightly Lincoln soliloquies during the season. Impersonators of other Civil War personalities followed, and one theater in 1985 opened an "interactive drama" that involved the audience in a play featuring two Confederate reenactors. The proprietor claimed the play "brings an element of authenticity" to Gettysburg. While disappointingly few attended the somber commemorative observances scheduled on the actual date of the 125th anniversary, over 100,000 tickets were sold for the reenactment spectacles of the preceding week. Spectators so clogged town that motels were booked months in advance, gas stations ran dry, and film vanished from store shelves. Although the NPS allowed "living history" shows but banned reenactments on the battlefield, a 1987 survey of Gettysburg tourism found that respondents felt reenactors "should be allowed to have their activities at the actual battlefield locations."[12]

Such sentiment expressed a longing among many battlefield tourists to "be there" and "see them coming." An Associated Press writer noted in 1982 that "visitors trying to imagine the bloody, rainy July battle are hard-pressed to overlook the 1,320 memorials, monuments, and markers strewn across the battlefield." The story of the battle gripped tourists, who strained to visualize the swirl of combat, the assault columns, smoke, and screams, often at locations popularized by the book and movie. After all, the males at least had played imaginary war here as children. Visitors did not seem to feel they were pygmies by comparison with the soldiers of '63 as much as they wanted to fill their shoes. "During my trip," a visitor wrote in 1991, "I was sitting on Little Round Top listening to the quiet, and I could almost hear the sounds of muskets and see the men charging up at me."[13]

The longing for the thrill of the real also induced interest in restoring the authentic landscape. Only on a battlefield matching expectations stimulated by the book and movie could the narrative be imagined. "The area looks much as it did at the time of the battle, and the historical events can be much better appreciated by visitors," an Ohio couple remarked in 1990 after brush had been removed from Little Round Top. "We think the longer grass in the meadows and on the field adds much to the historical authenticity." Modern intrusions broke the spell of envisioning the action. One visitor intimate with the details of the film *Gettysburg* found it "troublesome" to see a parking lot below the 20th Maine position "when one might be in the process of imagining the bayonet attack that swept over the spot." Still, doubts about just what was authentic remained. A volunteer who helped construct a period fence on the battlefield in 2000 admitted that "the change to the view of the field is remarkable." But because the map used to site the fence had been surveyed years after the battle, he worried. "How do we know that the farmers didn't change the lines and locations of the fences, or use different styles?"[14]

Obsession with authenticity and surface appearance blurred the distinction between history and heritage. One proponent of presenting "the conditions and appearance that existed at the time of the battle" concluded, "This is what history is all about." Authenticity turned restoration into holy work in a society that had replaced faith in progress with faith in therapy of the past. One buff regretted that Gettysburg's simulacra did not go as far as Williamsburg or Disney World. "I firmly believe that what should have been done," he wrote, "was turn the entire town and environs into a frozen moment in time: July 1863." Apparently few cared to notice that authentic and restored environments were the hallmarks of commercial space, especially theme parks. Indeed, the 1998 GNMP proposal to restore the battlefield and build a new visitors' center through partnership with a private developer outraged many as desecrating. They sniffed out commercial villainy in the new building while overlooking that commercial culture infused their own assumptions about authenticity. "We CANNOT, we MUST not—stand by, and allow these blood-stained grounds—our hallowed battlefields—to be made into sites of commercialized mockeries," a woman wrote in 1997. Another who had complained about modern-day intrusions breaking the spell of imagination wrote, "Those who will not go to Gettysburg unless enticed to do so by the kind of facility now being proposed should stay away and go to a theme park instead." Thus the sacred came to be associated with authentic appearances that pulled observers into the past. In turn, it gave the illusion of being the antithesis rather than the product of the marketplace.[15]

If the automobile represented the technology that transformed Gettysburg into a mass culture site for families, the microchip enabled the emergence of Heritage Gettysburg. The personal computer and other electronic devices not only encouraged individuals to search for coherence in heritage, but also raised expectations of greater illusions at heritage sites. Increasing

Figure 26. Friends of the National Parks at Gettysburg volunteers building authentic worm fencing near Pickett's Charge site, 2000 (Friends of the National Parks at Gettysburg)

sophistication of technology in the service of theater ended the good old days of Gettysburg fakery, making the town's midcentury tourist attractions seem laughable. Flashing lights, "talking walls," and wax dummies, even those motorized with rudimentary jerking motions, "border on outright corniness," according to one visitor. Of course, some tourists found them worthwhile for their moth-eaten appearance and outrageous camp. A reporter for the *Washington Post* in 1995 commended them for their "genuine, home-grown gimcrackery as opposed to Disney worldiness," their "small-time, shopworn air," and "an earnestness to the presentation along with a certain endearing ineptitude." Visitors found public attractions equally antiquated. A correspondent for the *Boston Globe* touring the visitors' center was shocked to find "dimly-lit exhibit halls [and] the 'electric map' of the battlefield that resembles a large, seventh-grade science project."[16]

Heritage consumers knew better than to patronize old fakery because they realized how convincing new fakery could be. Effective use of technology, as at Disney World, would allow control of the narrative but also intense personal experience. "I think we would be greatly remiss if we did not take advantage of all available technology to tell the stories," an enthusiast wrote in 2000. "Wouldn't you like to see a 3-D holographic display of your favorite engagement, with you right in the middle of it?" Some who hoped heritage would relieve the burden of contemporary life saw its unnerving technology as a way to restore authenticity. Technology served as handmaiden to heritage, a tool useful in creating sensuous texture that jolted the audience into other times and places. Having seen the Jorvik Viking Center in York, England, which goes so far as to simulate offensive medieval odors, an enthusiast commented about attractions at the new visitors' center. "Some of the messy side should be presented," he wrote. Better yet, technology could confront visitors with the terror of modern warfare faced by common soldiers. Commenting on the proposed visitors' center, a television producer thrilled at the technological potential of immersing tourists in a combat situation. He urged that "the latest multi-media technology" could "show the bullets digitally erupting off the screen coming at you and the 'Surround Sound' of the cannon ball and concussion as it almost takes your head off." Then, as at theme parks that prod screams from audiences, "[w]ork in real fog effects coming from the screen from rifle fire."[17]

Although the heritage era emphasized subjective experience in contrast to the family-friendly era's patriotic education, youth entered the technology discussion if only because its influence separated them from their elders. "Today's generation of kids expect different things," a member of the GNMP's advisory committee said. Like the adults who poked fun at antiquated tourist attractions, youths smirked too but failed to appreciate the old-fashioned charm of shopworn gimmicks. Some adults expressed concern that if the latest technology were not employed to "interpret" the battle, youth raised with digital entertainment would forget the sacred story. "Give them an act you can bring them under the tent with," a technology proponent said, perhaps not fully considering the sideshow metaphor's truth. One visitor who advised installing "experiences rather than artifacts" to "connect" with kids suggested such high-tech gadgets as an electronic shooting gallery, virtual reality battle games, and a virtual Lincoln in combination with "living history" dress-up opportunities. Even conservative columnist George F. Will believed "the imaginative presentation of military history in a new facility here is vital, lest rising generations have no sense of the sacrifices of which they are beneficiaries." The consensus about technology and young people illuminated the fact that the Gettysburg narrative centered not on history, but on the sensory experience of "being there," and brought into the open how solidly memory had been attached to entertainment. Gettysburg now seemed less like a classroom for cultivating future citizens and more like a theme park for hooking future heritage consumers.[18]

While the potential of technology for the new visitors' center excited enthusiasts, mass-media technology already had delivered a postvictory narrative for heritage consumers. Gettysburg placed the capstone on a flurry of heritage film and print productions that answered a craving for realistic war scenes. Enthusiasts demanded painstaking detail to ensure authenticity of the images. A researcher for one of the Civil War realists who opened shop in Gettysburg remarked, "I suspect that the art is a way for them [consumers] to visualize what actually happened during this battle or any Civil War battle without actual photography." Visual representations provided the most jarring punch in the heritage toolkit for titillating the senses. Heritage consumers, however, wanted more than envisioning the past; they longed to turn past into present. A Civil War hobbyist who purchased a new book of Civil War stereo photographs, which included a viewer, termed the collection "emotionally striking. . . . It is like a small peek through a time machine."[19]

But the movie topped all other mediums for providing a sense of participating in the battle, short of reenacting. It not only satisfied heritage consumers, it generated them. The film converted many viewers to lifelong Gettysburg enthusiasts as it created a new market of Gettysburg consumers. "I read the book then watched the movie and that was it. I was hooked!" a woman wrote. "I can barely get enough Gettysburg/Civil War now." Others used the term "hooked" to describe the conversion they experienced. Like the newly popular combat paintings, *Gettysburg* drew fiction from history. With its simple plot and ennobling characters, the movie stirred the imagination with a compelling tale of soldierly duty with no complex issues attached. The film reduced the battle from a national possession to a subjective experience, replacing abstraction with coherence useful to fragmented lives. The movie so powerfully affected some viewers that they itched to climb into the action. One who claimed he had "seen the movie more often than I can admit to my wife" said, "I want to touch the experience that those men felt. . . . One way, I believe, is to participate in at least one major reenactment." Another who consumed both the book and movie confessed, "These have turned my life around." As a result, "I'm trying with much joy to become a Gettysburg 'expert.' Maybe work with reenactors in teaching someday."[20]

As the movie transformed viewers into heritage consumers, it also inverted their view of reality and displaced the battle itself. "People want you to give them the movie tour," a guide explained in 1994. Perspiring tourists showed up at the Lutheran Theological Seminary inquiring about climbing to the cupola featured in the movie or asked to see the hill where Colonel Joshua Chamberlain "won the war." Tourists visited Gettysburg not only because they had seen the film, but to ensure that Gettysburg conformed to the movie's images. "The movie 'Gettysburg' piqued my interest followed at first opportunity by a visit," a viewer wrote. "The relatively unspoiled vistas made it easy to picture the events." The movie even gave the impression that the battlefield itself, with its monuments and avenues, was inauthentic. Tourists asked directions to the nearby stage set where the "Pickett's

Charge" scene had been filmed, rubbernecking in a slow drive past the site as if it were the High Water Mark. Historic events paled in comparison to the drama on screen, which reduced the battle to the set of a play one might enter.[21]

According to a survey conducted a year after the film's release, more tourists visited Little Round Top, focal point of the movie, than any other spot except the visitors' center. Tourists fingered the 20th Maine monument, trying to find the name of Buster Kilrain, a fictional character in the movie. To futher blur illusion and reality, shops in town sold souvenirs related to the movie that featured images of the costumed actors who portrayed historical figures. The film not only turned Little Round Top into a sacred power point, but visitors began leaving offerings such as flowers, coins, or cigars on monuments to personages or units depicted in the movie. "*Gettysburg* is more than just a movie," an enthusiast noted. "Do we not owe it to our ancestors and heritage to experience and feel for four hours what they went through in four years?"[22]

The new tourists required an authentic-looking battlefield to let them enter the imaginative world seen on the screen. Thanks to reenactors and GNMP costumed rangers, tourists had hyper–Civil War soldiers to perform on the empty stage. A park ranger responsible for staging "living history" claimed in 1997 that visitors planned their vacations around such programs. But what actually filled the vacuum were principles of entertainment inducing sensations that had little to do with historical understanding. "These reenactors give them the 3-D image that helps them know what went on here," the park ranger said, "and the smell of gunpowder and the sweat on their faces is exactly what someone watching the real battle would have experienced." Even for public intellectual Garry Wills the performances aided vicarious participation in the event. "You can almost imagine yourself back in that incredible three days of carnage," he wrote.[23]

The illusions proved so authentic that a *Harrisburg Patriot* reporter's comments about visitors "coming to see history being remade" where "artillery roar, men moan" but "nobody dies" were more than simply clever. Enveloping tourists in sounds and sights gave them a momentary thrill of participating. "It's time travel for me," a spectator said at the 1988 reenactment. In a culture where entertainment increasingly defined reality, history too had been upstaged by showmanship—yet not surprisingly, this sleight of hand had slipped by undetected. Heritage gave tourists the impression it had liberated history from the shackles of intellectual labor. Tourists accompanied clichés about "time travel" and a "time machine" with comments suggesting that heritage provided a revolutionary method of teaching history, ennui-free. "I didn't let myself learn about the Civil War in school, I thought it was so boring," a tourist explained after exploring a Gettysburg living history camp. "Now, I think it's so interesting."[24]

Like those who believed entertainment technologies would enliven Get-

FIGURE 27. Visitors "experiencing" the Civil War at Gettysburg, 1994 (Friends of the National Parks at Gettysburg)

tysburg for youth accustomed to electronic imagery, some thought children in particular benefited from costumed performances. When asked what she would remember most about her trip to Gettysburg, a parent answered, "the living history tours" because "[i]t's easier for the kids to relate to." A father reported that when he and his nine-year-old son toured the Peach Orchard, a group of reenactors "involved him on an artillery crew and [he] told me that this is fun. History can be fun for all." Gone were the days of family vacations when parents connected children to pride in an exceptional nation. The old theme of passing on the past to the next generation lingered, but now the past meant heritage. "Do you worry, as we do, that we aren't instilling a love of our country's heritage into its future guardians?" read promotion for a 1996 Friends Family Weekend. Activities had little to do with understanding the Civil War, however, consisting of musket firing, a scavenger hunt, a "ghost walk" at Devil's Den, and sewing "a family battle flag which they'll carry during their reenactment of Pickett's Charge the following day." As the Gettysburg Battlefield Preservation Association

(GBPA) demonstrated, "Helping Youths Understand the Civil War" meant dressing children like soldiers to fight make-believe Civil War. Adults now handed down to children the value of intense subjective experience they relished.[25]

The shift from a unifying, shared confidence in national destiny to a personal quest for experiencing July 1863 manifested itself in ways that would have been previously considered unthinkable. Visitors reported a "curious sense of unreality" and a mystical transcendence of time. "You feel it; you sense it," one visitor wrote. "It's in the rocks, the trees, the air." Such subjective metaphysical experiences slid from "seeing them coming" to imagining an encounter with "them." While pilgrims to shrines have always anticipated extraordinary if not supernatural experiences, at Gettysburg visitors historically never mentioned the paranormal, let alone expected it. In his 1963 book *Gettysburg: The Long Encampment*, Jack McLaughlin claimed that no one had ever seen a ghost at Gettysburg. But by the turn of the century, visitors regularly reported strange encounters with the supernatural. A psychologist wrote in 1997 that the spiritual energy at Gettysburg "is powerful, sad, and at times a little frightening. One keeps wanting to look over one's shoulders." A tourist on the battlefield one night recalled that "Bill said he felt something press by him, and go straight to me. Never had such an experience in my life, and didn't especially want to have another." Yet others found the spirits more benign than frightful. One woman walking alone in Reynold's Woods tripped over a vine but felt a ghostly hand settle her back on her feet. "I could swear to you that the presence was actually smiling," she wrote of the incident. "I stood there for a bit, and finally I managed two words in a little squeaky voice, 'Thank you.'" Some visitors swore they felt "cold spots" on the battlefield, while photographers noticed their cameras failed to operate at certain locations. On the other hand, sometimes developed film revealed unexplained shadows, and a group terming itself the Adams County Ghost Hunter's Society asserted it photographed orbs of light floating through haunted Gettysburg houses.[26]

One cannot doubt the sincerity of such testimony nor the efforts of visitors to salvage a spiritual meaning from Gettysburg. As leisure grew more private and commercial in the waning years of the twentieth century, so too did religious faith. New Age alternatives to organized religion stressed individual spiritual experience, like heritage relying on a cornucopia of props to aid passage into another world. Yet even this most desperate endeavor to find authenticity in the most private realms of the self could not escape the marketplace. Popular magazines featured sensational copy about ghosts, regression, and channeling from the spirit world. The supernatural craze also dipped into the horrific and demonic, as witnessed in the popularity of thriller films and Stephen King novels. The "ghost tour" phenomenon appeared to combine both as, according to the "ghost researchers," the most common type of ghosts are spirits of those who died violently. Entrepreneurs responded to public interest with "ghost tours" of haunted places in heavily touristed areas such as Philadelphia, New Orleans, Charleston, and Gettysburg—which in its potential for horrible deaths surpassed the others.[27]

For tourists, Gettysburg's first ghost tour became the quintessential heritage attraction. Established by Mark Nesbitt, former GNMP "living history" ranger and author of Gettysburg fiction, the tour emerged from his 1991 book, *Ghosts of Gettysburg*. Released just in time for Halloween, the book reached number fifteen on Waldenbooks' paperback best-seller list within a week. Even the GNMP museum shop stocked *Ghosts of Gettysburg*. Although Nesbitt termed *Ghosts* "folklore that has never been recorded" and "part of the Gettysburg story just as much as census records are," the book featured an exaggerated form of the heritage blend of fact and fancy. Soon Nesbitt published *More Ghosts of Gettysburg* (again, in time for Halloween 1992) and launched his ghost tours, which during the season numbered as many as a half dozen a night. According to promotional copy, the tour offered a titillating walk "through night-darkened streets where it's not as quiet as it should be; to sites on the old Pennsylvania College campus where the slain once lay in rows, and the wounded suffered horribly, waiting to become corpses themselves; to cemeteries where the dead lie, sometimes not so peacefully." By 2000, three enterprises offered ghost tours in Gettysburg, some heightening the experience with coffins and plastic bones.[28]

Ghosts had become the vogue attraction of Heritage Gettysburg, as the cyclorama center, monuments, and sublime landscape had been chief attractions of past eras. Travel writers found that ghosts made good copy. The American Automobile Association (AAA), which at one time commended Gettysburg's monuments to tourists, now whet the traveler's palate with "Gettysburg may very well be, acre for acre, the most haunted place in America." *Car and Travel* further pointed visitors to the macabre night-doings of "buried heroes" walking in the cemetery, invisible babies wailing, and poltergeists. But perhaps the biggest boost came from cable television. In 1995, *Unsolved Mysteries* featured a program about Gettysburg's "inexplicable occurrences" on the heels of an A&E *Civil War Journal* production that put Nesbitt's books to film. With a viewing audience of 4 million at the time, *Civil War Journal* convincingly packaged the production by juxtaposing Gettysburg ghost stories told by those who experienced them with re-created scenes. Main Street Gettysburg further added to the legitimacy by hosting a special premier of the video featuring autographed copies and T-shirts.[29]

As might be expected, Gettysburg enthusiasts who created Heritage Gettysburg in general deplored the ghost phenomenon. These insiders condemned ghost tours as "disrespectful," "a carnival," or "whoredom," apparently overlooking the rest of the environment that helped them evoke their own highly subjective and often spiritual experiences. Besides, according to a ghost-tour guide, "quite a number of people" who participated were sure "they saw something during their stay." What really could lay better claim to the sacred than encountering the supernatural at Gettysburg, even if the outsiders paid to do what insiders did for free? Ghost tours simply exploited the vogue for authentic subjective experience sought in a variety of ways. As a vital part of Heritage Gettysburg, ghost tours aided transition of the shrine from a national sacred power point to a psychic one. In the end, were ghosts any less real than the pixels on a computer monitor, a television set, or a movie screen that shaped everyone's reality? Gettysburg's greatest boosters, the enthusiasts who emerged in the postvictory era, used Gettysburg to fashion their own spiritual meaning through activities grounded in the marketplace.[30]

Enthusiasts: Image Tribes

Evidence of enthusiasts could be seen everywhere in Gettysburg by 2000. In addition to the themed landscape they helped finance, many new enterprises signaled their presence. Instead of the family-friendly attractions of the earlier era, now the themed environment smacked of anything connected to Civil War hobbies. Toy muskets, kepis, and cannon for Cold War baby boomers had evolved into play goods for grownup boomers. Although relics of the battle had been sold as souvenirs to tourists since 1863, new shops sprang up selling Civil War memorabilia to growing numbers of collectors. For other tribes, new businesses peddled toy soldiers, war games, reenactor uniforms and paraphernalia, and collectable Civil War art. One shop traded exclusively in reenactor clothing for "Victorian ladies." In addition to the permanent shops, seasonal fairs catered to almost every interest and helped cross-pollinate enthusiasms.

Lodging also reflected deference to the tribes. As opposed to the one-story motels with exterior entrances looking out on other travelers, new motor hotels that sprang up were four-story buildings with interior entrances to rooms that protected guests from the outside. As the hotel trade now depended in part on image tribes booking space for weekend get-togethers, motel guests only need socialize with fellow enthusiasts in the motel. A couple of bed and breakfasts narrowed their ambience to authentic Civil War settings. The Doubleday Inn boasted a Civil War library, relic collection, Victorian furniture, pump organ, and performances by impersonators of Civil War luminaries. With even greater skill at dovetailing the fake and real, the Farnsworth House advertised real bullet holes, "Civil War period food," "relics" from the movie *Gettysburg*, and even fellowship with imaginary Civil War people in the hostelry's "haunted rooms." Yet the ultimate expression of imaginative entry into the past could be purchased at the Battlefield B&B, a Civil War–era farm, where guests "visit another time and place" through the inn's "re-creation of life during the Civil War." Special events such as Joshua Chamberlain Weekend and Lincoln Weekend allow guests to interact with impersonators of historic figures. Not only do the proprietors dress in period costume, serve period food, and offer rides in a period carriage, but they also keep Civil War uniforms on hand for guests to join the daily living-history demonstrations. A pleased customer termed lodging at the inn "total immersion" in which "you are drawn into the history of the time and place."[31]

Image tribes were a manifestation of a sophisticated hobbyist culture emerging from increased income, leisure, and family decline. No matter what their particular passion, they could be distinguished from casual tourists by their zeal for authenticity. Many belonged to Friends or GBPA, sharing with these groups a zeal for preservation and restoration. Tribes included reenactors, collectors, wargamers, and battlefield tourists, although many tribe members pursued more than one enthusiasm. Members of each tribe had unique objectives, such as collecting Civil War firearms, that provided a shared identity. Yet all shared an approach that did not require patriotism nor discussion of controversial issues. "I'm basically a meat and potatoes kind of guy when it comes to Gettysburg," remarked a battlefield buff who enjoyed "the nitty gritty" of tactics and weapons. "My eyes start to glaze over when esoteric discussions arise as to causes and social issues." Groups built fellowship not around family and children but around purchased goods and experiences—tours, computers, equipment, collectibles— through which they found community, authenticity, and even spiritual fulfillment.[32]

Battlefield touring aficionados included both those who regularly participated in group tours of Civil War battlefields as well as those buffs who exclusively studied Gettysburg's strategy and tactics. Some were autodidacts who, armed with new guidebooks, period photographs, and accounts of the battle by participants, tried to find correspondence between the landscape and the primary record. The new tours rejected the comfortable and detached view from the bus, instead seeking the sensations of Civil War soldiers by hiking fields, climbing fences, and crossing streams. "Gettysburg: A Walk Through Time" read the banner of a 1980s university continuing-education-sponsored tour. No longer passive sightseers, participants increasingly expected more depth. "Our tour guide [was] a bore," a woman wrote in her notebook during one of the early versions of these tours in 1979. "Spoke as though we were a bunch of tourists."[33]

No level of minutiae was too small to please the diehard enthusiast. Tour organizers continually looked for new sites to meet the insatiable demand of the increasingly well-versed devotee. Touring buffs could experience the climb up Big Round Top just like Oates's men, retreat from the Wheatfield like Bigelow's battery, or position themselves across the exact length of the 20th Maine's front. "What a treat to be able to go places normal visitors don't get to see, dead pigeons and all," said a woman to enjoyed a backstairs tour of the Wills House. "Any other student [of the battle] would have been drooling like myself," wrote a buff returning from a tour of little-visited sites that figured in the Gettysburg Campaign.[34]

Socializing proved as important to enthusiasts as their sense of purpose. A Friends tour coordinator noted in 1995, "We frequently observe an indefinable affinity develop among the participants." Such tours for many replaced family bonding of the fifties and sixties. One woman who attended a *Civil War Times Illustrated* tour said "I felt when it was over I had an extended family." One enthusiast stated that Friends' tours and gatherings "are ways of like-minded people interested in the battle of Gettysburg and the future of Gettysburg National Military Park to get together and see old friends and have a splendid time." Preserving and restoring, of course, became a sacred mission for the touring enthusiast, whose hobby relied on "historyscapes."[35]

Collectors, wargamers, and reenactors also gathered around Gettysburg to share hobbies that were highly subjective and intense. One enthusiast who expressed thanks to his parents for a childhood family trip to Gettysburg claimed "Gettysburg changed my life," and he subsequently became "a relic collector, historian, and reenactor." Enthusiasts sometimes found almost mystical identification with the 1863 warrior through the act of touring, preservation, collecting relics, or refighting the battle. "To me, artifacts are history," said a Civil War gun enthusiast who collected infantry weapons. Explaining his racks of weapons, he said, "I look at these and think about them every day, so there's real communication, a connection, and appreciation for what they are."[36]

Collecting and other hobbies require often substantial knowledge and skills that boost the enthusiasts' self-worth. Those with mundane jobs or fragmented lives can find a sense of mastery and integration through collecting Civil War memorabilia. Although collectors may dream of one day completing a collection, it is often an endless project. "I'm always hunting," says one collector. "I'm by no means satisfied." To outsiders, this quest may seem to be indistinguishable from other materialist obsessions. To collectors, their memorabilia transcend ordinary consumption by their hallowed associations with Gettysburg. Possibilities for themes are endless, ranging from autographs of generals to Gettysburg souvenirs. The uniqueness of every collection, the individual choice involved in deciding what to collect and how to texture the collection, provide self-satisfaction. "I started out buying anything that interested me," a collector said, who soon found more economy and stimulation collecting memorabilia from a regiment in which an ancestor served. For all its isolating tendencies, collecting, like reenacting or touring, offers community among insiders. As part of their tribe, collectors establish networks with dealers and peers who assist in locating items. Recognition is achieved through events such as Gettysburg's annual collectors' show, which awards prizes to recognize outstanding collections. And seasoned collectors watch the value of their artifacts grow as interest in collecting increases, spurred by media events such as the Ken Burns's series, *Gettysburg*, and *Glory*. Most of all, collecting allows individuals to manage a great event like Gettysburg and bring it under control.[37]

Similarly, wargaming played as a board game, on a computer, or with toy soldiers permits personal connection with the past. Players control a mini-world like collectors, but, by assuming the role of army commanders, often change the battle's historic outcome. "No matter how much you read about Gettysburg," one wargamer says, "there's a whole lot you just never pick up on 'til YOU'RE the one deciding who goes where and tries to do what." At the 2000 North Coast Wargamers annual convention in Gettysburg, for example, the main attraction featured a replica of part of the first day's field titled "Afternoon along the Cashtown Road" that the Federals could win this time around. Wargaming requires thorough grasp of the battle's strategy but also voluminous game rules. Like battlefield touring and collecting, wargaming is absorbing because it draws enthusiasts into never-ending activity. This may make for a good game, but has little to do with the meaning of Gettysburg.[38]

The playlike character of Heritage Gettysburg is most evident among reenactors. Like wargamers and battlefield buffs, reenactors long to experience the authenticity of the real event. But unlike wargamers, reenactors participate in the battle from the perspective of the private soldier rather than the commander. More than any image tribe, reenactors typify the merger of the commercial and sacred at Gettysburg. Reenacting illustrates how heritage responds to the social and psychological needs of the present rather than the past. As we have seen, evaporation of the national myth along with the corresponding rise of competing minority cultures produced a vacuum of meaning for the white majority that reenacting fills. It provides an alternative to the pride in American triumphalism lost with Vietnam and, for whites, a counterpoise to new myths emerging from multiculturalism. Most of all, reenacting presents a male bonding opportunity for a generation of men who feel they lost their fathers' authority and outlets for sociability. Feminism brought women into the male world of work and men shared their once-defining role as breadwinner. And in an age of the commercial celebrity, reenactors could consider themselves "stars." "I've found that inside every reenactor is an actor," a documentary film producer remarked in 2000. Reenacting offers both a coherent identity and Andy Warhol's fifteen minutes of fame. "If you're in the reenacting hobby, you're a frustrated actor and historian," said a Gettysburg reenactor interviewed in 1992. "This lets me get away from the humdrum life of an accountant and escape into history."[39]

Like other image tribes, reenactors believe they carry a burden of educating the public about the Civil War. "Monuments and street names don't work anymore," a reenactor at the 130th anniversary pointed out. "We've got to help them [tourists] learn and we do that by reenacting." Frequently they label themselves "historians," referring to their often keen knowledge of details. Tourists are invited to their camps at Gettysburg to mingle and ask questions. A woman who talked to a Confederate reenactor in 1992 left with "a new respect for our country's history." At a Children's Day Camp during the 1995 reenactment, reenactors set off a mortar, shot and sabered dummies, and blew up a small building to squeals of "cool," and "awesome."[40]

Reenactors control the present by removing themselves from it, and control the past by counterpoising academic history with heritage. "The reason the southern man fought was because he was defending his land," said a Confederate reenactor at the 130th anniversary reenactment. "I had eighteen ancestors who fought, and not one owned slaves in 1860." Yet there was also a sense of control that came from the illusion of participating in a great event whose outcome, for believers, has been temporarily suspended. For some, the fantasy could prove so overwhelming they might try to change history by breaking free from the narrative. At the 125th anniversary reenactment, a Confederate reenactor referred to "diehards" he knew who would "do anything to make up for lost opportunities or just get a feeling of changing history." During the reenactment of Pickett's Charge, a group of Confederate reenactors planned to rush the Union position and change history, but firepower drove them back.[41]

It was exactly that sense of "being there," a flash of time travel, that reenactors found so compelling about the hobby. "My heart began thundering, more from excitement than exertion," wrote Tony Horowitz in *Confederates in the Attic* of his march with fellow Confederates toward Cemetery Ridge. "Were these the first stirrings of a 'period rush?'" Another wrote, "I've had a couple of spots where I've had to say, 'whoa,' get a grip, this isn't real." Reenactors do not want to resurrect the Civil War in all its ghastliness, but strive to feel the intense moment of combat experienced by historical actors assumed to have lived "real life" that is somehow missing in the present. A participant at the 130th anniversary reenactment remarked, "The high is the same as heroin to an addict." The lexicon of reenacting included a term, "wargasm," to describe the subjective state of ecstasy rising from a time-jolt.[42]

But tweaking the senses to fool the mind depends on intricate and elaborate staging. The "visual smorgasbord," as the operations manager termed the 135th anniversary's staged scene, required every reenactor's cooperation so that everyone could share the illusion. Reenactors choose an "impression" from the Civil War period to model—sometimes a real historical figure—and the cost of uniform, equipment, and weapons, as well as props such as period camp supplies, can easily run into the thousands of dollars. But heritage thinking is required as well as heritage costume. Tips on achieving authenticity are communicated through several reenactor publications, which recommend such hirsute flourishes as dribbling cornbread crumbs and tobacco juice into one's beard, or allowing one's hair to dry while wearing a hat to achieve Civil War–looking hair. Those who threaten the spell with anachronistic garb or equipment are contemptuously termed "farbs" (the most civil of the many meanings attributed to this acronym is "fails to achieve reasonable authenticity"). At the other extreme, "hardcores" meticulously replicate supposed Civil War gestures, speech, and behavior, including fasting to effect a "starved" appearance. While reenactments omit authentic maiming and killing, some reenactors compensate by "bloating" like a corpse, and "field hospitals" simulate wounds with raw roast beef or fleshlike plastic "wounds" placed on the actor's body.[43]

In a culture already straining its relationship with reality, a hobby that so intensely aims to create the hyperreal easily slides into fantasy. At the 125th anniversary reenactment, two reenactors near the High Water Mark suddenly started weeping when the intervening years dissolved and "we could see the battle for a few moments." Reenactors often form their "impressions" out of dairies and letters written by real people, whom they believe operate inside them, if only during the magic moments. A reenactor wrote of being approached in camp by a woman dressed in black, who had come to Gettysburg to claim the body of her husband. Whether she knew she was performing or not, or whether she imagined she was the person she portrayed, could not be determined. "We are the characters we're playing," one reenactor said at the 125th anniversary reenactment.[44]

Those for whom the veil between past and present had dropped completely could find reassurance in a phenomenon paralleling the "ghost tours" in town. At the 135th anniversary reenactment Barbara Lane, a "clinical hynotherapist" who believes Civil War spirits enter the bodies of contemporary people, offered a "regression" seminar to a large audience of reenactors. Like the "ghost researchers," Lane claimed scientific legitimacy for "regression," which she explained as "an incredibly personal trip back in time." Several reenactors dressed as Civil War officers came forward at the session to discuss their past identities, one of which included Confederate General Henry Heth. Regression offered a novel approach to the heritage focus on experiencing rather than understanding the past. It demonstrated the desperation of some to escape the fragmentation of the twenty-first century and step into the shoes of another assumed to have "really" lived. Inevitably, far more than being confronted with past reality, reenactors find what they look for in authenticity that compensates for their disappointment with the present.[45]

Personal Computers and the Triumph of Privatization

America's personal computer (PC) revolution greatly reinforced heritage trends. By 2000, PCs had created new enthusiasts and even new image tribes, as Gettysburg could be accessed anytime around then world. Now computers filled the old role of public libraries, touring, or Civil War Roundtables, increasing convenience and frequency of the Gettysburg experience but also isolating the "tourist." A father bought the PC wargame Sid Meier's Gettysburg for his teenage son, for example, and within six months both claimed Gettysburg as a hobby. Conversely, a *Killer Angels* reader galvanized by the novel went on a Civil War binge that included buying a PC "to have access to other Civil War enthusiasts."[46]

The Internet and the Web broadened users' capability of dropping in on other places and times beyond the reach of cable and satellite television. The Web offered new forms of marketing for Gettysburg's tourist business, including GNMP, which had enlisted a Webmaster by 1998 and boasted one of the most visited sites of its kind. On-line novelties sponsored by Gettysburg merchants included 3-D models of Gettysburg, a "battlecam" featuring live battlefield views, and virtual shopping for collectibles. A Virtual Gettysburg Web site advertised a "powerful, interactive simulation" of the battlefield that offered "the closest thing to being there." From this site, one could even send a virtual Gettysburg postcard from a place one has visited only virtually. At any rate, enthusiasts initiated their own Web sites to display a virtual Gettysburg archive, museum, and wargames. In 1995 two brothers inspired by *The Killer Angels* launched a Gettysburg Discussion Group (GDG), or electronic forum, that by 2000 counted over seven hundred members and over fifty posts a day. Reenactment groups put up Web sites to attract recruits as well as provide information.[47]

The new communications tool created enthusiasts, but more important assembled them from dispersed locations as far away as South Africa and Australia. It created virtual communities of strangers who had nothing in common except an interest in Gettysburg. They could quickly gather to argue the merits of the planned visitors' center, for example, or debate tactics. Sometimes comments might be uninformed, but typically postings followed this pattern: "I suggested that General Sykes should have sent Barnes to the left flank rather than moving to the Wheatfield and shifting elements of the Third Corps to the left flank." Virtual communities create opportunities for individuals to socialize electronically in a society growing more private, more mobile, and busier. In addition to arguing about the battle, suggestions on what Gettysburg books to read or sights to see can be shared impartially in nonthreatening cyberspace.[48]

PCs permitted enthusiasts even more control over Gettysburg than reenacting, battlefield touring, or collecting. Surfers can "go there" anytime. For websites and the GDG, use is heaviest during work hours and slacks off evenings and on weekends. An enthusiast busying himself at work by feeding Gettysburg expressions into an anagram program confided to the GDG, "Don't tell my boss, but I've done little since installing it." But because Gettysburg could be considered "serious leisure," such lapses could be rationalized and perhaps considered the most productive moments of an insipid

job. And all who showed off collections, posted information, or demonstrated their expertise could feel important by manipulating Gettysburg into
their personal world. With its capability of gathering enthusiasts, allowing
individual control and recognition, and providing escape, the PC represented the perfect tool for heritage.[49]

Communications technologies always had led the way in delivering the
past at Gettysburg, but in the heritage era computers became even more
central by aiding flight from the present. In cyberspace, where all opinions
and images are equally significant, no one need address the larger questions
of historical continuity or proportion. Serious engagement need not burden
anyone surfing sites for morsels of trivia or a visual smorgasbord of historical
pageantry such as those found at reenactments. The fake blends with the
real as in the rest of heritage tourism. Individuals surf into freedom from
reality, where they can play out personal fantasies anonymously. The appearance of Gettysburg "ghost tours" at the same time Internet began constructing a virtual Gettysburg is more than simply a coincidence. Both are
part of an entertainment industry offering alternatives to real life, where
fragmented and lonely people in the twenty-first century attempt to connect with disembodied souls across an alternative universe.

The PC might be seen as the latest toy boomers employed in transforming Gettysburg into a theme park for hobbyists. Along with other features
of heritage tourism, PCs aided the transformation of Gettysburg from a
national shrine to a private, subjective experience. As opposed to genteel
touring after the Civil War, communal touring during the railroad era, and
the family tour of the mid-twentieth century, Gettysburg in 2000 increasingly served as a personal fantasy for dispersed enthusiasts. But at the same
time PCs transformed Gettysburg into leisure enjoyed privately, they helped
further gather enthusiasts into image tribes. PCs enhanced the trend of
changing Gettysburg consumers from passive to active, cultivating a sense
of belonging built on the exclusion of nonmembers. A member of the GDG
observed in 1997, "But it is we few who have been entrusted with the
memory of what happened here [Gettysburg]. To us has devolved the sacred
memory of those men, their bravery, their accomplishments." The insiders
believed that they were charged with responsibilities by virtue of their specialized knowledge, "pure" as a result of excluding outsiders.[50]

Despite the contrasts, attitudes of heritage tourists had their roots in the
earlier family-friendly period. That era, while focusing on "togetherness" of
American families within the national family, celebrated children above all.
By the 1970s, these children were coming of age just as confidence in national purpose shattered. Some of them continued childhood play into adulthood, but without the now-discredited saga of patriotism their parents encouraged. Gettysburg's key features today that distinguish it from earlier
eras, including make-believe stage sets, hobbies, playing war, and Halloween spook stories, were all part of baby boom childhood that boomers are

loath to leave behind. After all, retaining youthfulness is a supreme boomer value, as evidenced in the millions spent on youth-oriented advertising, health foods, drugs to maintain youthful vigor, and herbs purchased in an attempt to beat the clock. Of course, the older pattern of family touring remained, as parents and kids, now in minivans rather than station wagons, file into Gettysburg every summer passing on the tradition of uplift and wholesome family play. But the shrine has become a special preserve for youthful enthusiasm far more than a site for intergenerational bonding. Once again Gettysburg has become a mirror reflecting the image of an ever-changing America that seeks to find itself there over and over.

Epilogue

☆ ☆ ☆ ☆ ☆ ☆ ☆ ☆ ☆ ☆ ☆

The Most American Place in America

FROM THE PERSPECTIVE of 2000, my family vacation to Gettysburg over forty years before may just as well have been the distance between 1863 and the Civil War Centennial. By this time some adored family members existed only in memory, along with the '53 Ford, and both families and Fords had gone out of fashion. Gone too were the tourist cabins, restaurants, diorama, cyclorama building, gas stations, and ma-and-pa museums we patronized. Ike had long since passed away. The Gettysburg National Military Park (GNMP) opened Ike's farm to tourists, but after an initial surge, not many people went there anymore. In Gettysburg, Ike's war seemed more distant than the Civil War, and the years of his administration appeared politically soporific and culturally silly. Visitors no longer climbed the battlefield tower overlooking his home for the pride of citizenship that linked past and future glory. Now Gettysburg was simply a great Civil War battlefield instead of a major island in the archipelago of American shrines. My fantasies of "seeing them coming" back in 1958 had been Gettysburg's future. When I walked south along Cemetery Ridge forty years later, a group of reenactors staged a camp to my left, and on my right a troop of Union cavalry rode in back of a rail fence. Perhaps they too had found enchantment during a childhood visit and were trying to recapture the wonder.

Gettysburg appeared invigorated at the start of the new millennium. The town progressed toward merging seamlessly with the battlefield as part of a vast heritage complex of Civil War restorations and museums. A new foundation aiding development of the Lutheran Theological Seminary, whose appearance in *Gettysburg* attracted tourists, won a state grant to help restore buildings to their wartime appearance and create Civil War exhibits. Plans were announced to open a museum and gift shop in the Ever Green Cemetery gatehouse, a landmark since the battle ended. Main Street Gettysburg (MSG) finally raised enough money to restore the deteriorating train station where Lincoln arrived. Nearby at the Wills House with its Lincoln dummy, plans for restoration and a new Lincoln museum brightened when Congress enabled GNMP and Gettysburg borough to proceed with a joint tourist enterprise. With the ageless tension between town and battlefield seemingly ended, a reporter noted that town leaders expected the new partnership "to play a leading role as the borough's commercial center continues to evolve from general retail to heritage tourism." As for the battlefield, more restoration called for in the GNMP's new general management plan began near the Pickett's Charge area. Assuring ongoing progress toward 1863 authenticity, Friends of the National Parks at Gettysburg announced a Gettysburg Remembrance Trust for continuous restoration funding necessary to "keep this battlefield sacred," as the Friends' president stated.[1]

Yet the most symbolic event in a big year for the vitality of heritage came during the festival celebrating the battle's 137th anniversary. Following the usual heritage reenactment of Pickett's Charge, the looming, spiderlike National Battlefield Tower shuddered and tumbled to the ground in the year's most spectacular demolition and Gettysburg's most applied pyrotechnics since the battle. Termed "grand TV" by a television correspondent, the demolition eclipsed the reenactments that had become routine at Gettysburg. CNN broadcast the event live while other networks featured the falling tower on evening news programs and, as enthusiasts celebrated into the night, on news shows the next morning. Fifteen thousand spectators lining roads and ridges for miles around clapped and cheered as the juggernaut disappeared below the treeline. Immediately before implosion, reenactors fired cannon toward the steel structure. The illusion they performed this time, prompted by an equally illusory command by Secretary of the Interior Bruce Babbit, shot five miles of steel railing out of the sky. According to a Department of the Interior spokesperson, "The modern battle of Gettysburg ended" with the tower's demise—meaning that the American people had finally won the field after years of campaigning against polluting forces.[2] But the reality is more complex, ironic, and troubling than the celebrating would suggest. At no point during Gettysburg's fourteen decades of development did commercial interests suddenly intrude. Not only has Gettysburg been commercially packaged since 1863, but the shrine owes its iconic status to the marketplace. Successive waves of commercial representations made Gettysburg more real than reality and liberated it from its geographic location. In a process of continual negotiation with consumers, entrepreneurs have sold Gettysburg as a product partially within and partially outside its boundaries. Just as advertising sells intangibles such as love, popularity, or status, so the market sold Gettysburg and defined the way individuals experienced it.

Both as an opportunity for reflection and a busy year for heritage, the milestone of 2000 encouraged consideration of Gettysburg's changing aes-

FIGURE 28. Demolition of Gettysburg National Battlefield Tower, July 3, 2000 (Gettysburg National Military Park)

thetics. The fluid frontier between sacred and secular can be measured over time in the struggle between national narrative versus battle narrative, and monuments versus visual purity. Commercialism always catered to the needs of visitors to experience the maelstrom of battle. Guided tours, museums stuffed with relics, the cyclorama, authentic simulations, electronic explanations of the battle, and reenactors doing "living history" all emerged from the marketplace and in time were embraced by the battlefield's custodians. The tower's demolition provides a useful example of the shifting flow of cultural authority and standards.

When the tower fell with assurances that Gettysburg finally had been redeemed, the spectacle merely exposed a new era of secular and sacred mixing. A half century before, for example, cultural mavens considered reenactors a vulgar intrusion on sacred ground; their ritual status as legitimate ushers to the tower's demise would have been unthinkable. Go back fifty more years, and the position of reenactors and the tower would have been reversed. Genteel elites in charge of the battlefield did not tolerate playtime on sacred time. Veterans played war at Gettysburg as fireworks folderol off-set the somber tone of their rituals. Getting a commanding view of the landscape, however, was endorsed by the genteel for its edifying potential. The first print of the battlefield offered just months after the battle presented an aerial view, whose visual effect producer John Bachelder promoted as "Imagine yourself in a balloon over Gettysburg." A variety of "panoramas" blended genteel and working-class entertainment through raised perspective of battle action on the landscape. One of the first man-made tourist attractions, an observatory on East Cemetery Hill, sprouted about the same time officials envisioned a tower for the Soldiers' National Cemetery. Some monuments included observation towers, and the Gettysburg exhibit appearing most often at the era's great fairs was a three-dimensional topographic map of the battlefield. One plan placed before the GAR's national convention in 1899 proposed a three-hundred-foot stone tower at the site of Pickett's Charge!

Yet the view endorsed by the park's custodians in the nineteenth century differed from that of the twenty-first. Through views and objects, cultural elites for over a century had hoped to link individuals to their country and instill reverence for the nation. Standards imposed by these elites attempted to guide visitors in the appropriate manner of remembering the great event. At first, memorial devices such as urns, allegorical figures, and other abstractions masked war's carnage with classical symbols of heroism and sacrifice. But underneath the symbolism simmered curiosity about the battle's panoply, horror, and macabre aftermath, a magnetism one religious historian calls "a primal attraction to scenes of destructive power." Not only plebeians who ignored the genteel program gaped. Gettysburg initially catered to aesthetically minded genteel tourists, the touring market of the day, but they too enjoyed furtive peeks at battle wreckage while trying to imagine the awful grandeur of battle. For all its affectation, for example, the Springs Hotel promised visitors glimpses at damaged walls and fences that turned war into titillating curiosity.

As touring broadened to the lower social strata, including veterans, genteel standards exerted less cultural dominance. The graphic revolution progressively enhanced through technological improvements steadily eroded the power of symbolic representations to evoke memory. By the late-nineteenth century, veterans erected monuments that featured heroic action figures charging, shooting, or swinging a clubbed musket. At the same time, the cyclorama and its many clones fed new leisure consumers' appetite for voyeurism by placing viewers in the swirl of battle. When genteel and plebe gradually merged into mass culture after the turn of the century, electrified instruments such as dioramas, films, tape recordings, or the Electric Map tried to imaginatively pull consumers into the fighting. Still, while such devices up until the 1960s were marginalized as a kind of side show, they served as subtexts to Gettysburg's place in the national narrative.[3]

In a sense, Gettysburg had devolved from national shrine to family shrine to individual shrine. As cultural authority changed, the meaning it imposed on the battlefield changed along with symbolic standards. The classical monument linked sacrifice with landscape; action-oriented monuments reflected democratization of the shrine and a nation cemented by glory; Neutra's 1962 visitors' center connected the past with America's global mission and postwar families. Late in the twentieth century, if cultural authority did not collapse completely, it grew less collective and much more solipsistic. Rather than floated by cultural elites on top, authority more and more bubbled from a bottom nurtured by entertainment conglomerates. Now the unfading quest for recapturing the battle narrative could triumph free of larger meaning, and each individual could find the sacred in a personal encounter with the past.

Marketing trends and communication technologies promoted the decline of both cultural authority and collective experience. Expanding national markets mirrored the growth of the national shrine, which soothed sectional differences and by the twentieth century enveloped Gettysburg in homogenized mass culture. Yet late in the twentieth century, when marketing techniques diced consumers into image tribes, Gettysburg transformed into a subjective experience for groups of enthusiasts. By the twenty-first century, opinion polls and consumer surveys that served as surrogates for cultural arbiters in other arenas of consumer culture guided Gettysburg's future as well. Technology also aided the narrowing of cultural authority into a private concern. Communal rail travel gave way to private touring by families and finally to the Internet, which made it possible to experience Gettysburg in isolation.

Images delivered by mass media helped pull Gettysburg into privately enjoyed entertainment. Since the nineteenth century, Gettysburg images in a variety of forms promoted the shrine's mythical age of valor over the notion of obligation owed the past. But as the national narrative shattered in the late-twentieth century, images picked up the slack with a self-contained Gettysburg narrative that aided the dream of "being there." Illustrations and films abruptly grew less representational in attempting to restore the original event, and the quest for realistic images went so far as to stimulate the imagination with a rehabilitated battlefield. While in earlier phases Gettysburg controlled its image, by the latest phase images controlled Gettysburg.

A new aesthetic of the sacred also emerged. While formerly the sacred flowed into the present, today it remains frozen in the past. Until the late 1900s the battlefield had been an organic shrine of an optimistic people confident of their nation's destiny. Congressman Daniel E. Sickles, who drafted the bill creating Gettysburg National Military Park, proposed establishing a military base at Gettysburg as part of the memorial. After World War I, another congressman advanced the idea of placing captured German cannon at strategic locations on the battlefield. No sane individual would dare propose such schemes today. In the heritage era, the sacred has migrated from the site itself to the image of the site, from collective inspiration to individual experience. A shift in the use of memorial space calls attention to sacred ground with expanses of visually pure vistas, dirt roads, and rail fences instead of monuments. Props are being added to the landscape and reminders of intervening decades stripped away for an unmediated face-off with 1863.

The quest for an authentic battlefield is the chimera of an illusive culture. Rather than a cleansed shrine to past deeds, Gettysburg is being transformed to meet present needs—the need for reassurance provided by direct sensual experience. That requires methods popular in contemporary commercial entertainment once considered an affront to cultural authority. Sacred power now entertains on the one hand and awes on the other by immersion in simulations of the past. Of course, restoration and reenactment are pursued under the rubric of education. Yet what serves as a better example of heritage tourism? If restoration and reenactment are considered educational, why was Disney's heritage park, which planned similar participatory pageantry, censured as a superficial and simplistic approach to history? Contrasting to the cursory tours by battlefield guides or high school teachers in the past, innumerable continuing education enterprises now cater to the market for Gettysburg as a leisurely pastime of military particulars. Heritage consumers pay for seeing, sensing, doing, and experiencing, along with narrative details. Gettysburg reflects changes in educational methods that more and more borrow stimulating techniques from the leisure industry. Lectures nowadays provide verbal support for dazzling Power Point visuals; encyclopedias, teaching films, and Web sites are billed as "educational and entertaining"; textbooks that featured just a few graphs a generation ago now devote more space to colorful images than to print.

The restored landscape combines play and memory for those who have opted to prolong games of youth into adulthood. Gettysburg's old extremes of shrine and fair, reverence and cutting loose have disappeared, allowing enthusiasts play transformed into serious activity by the penumbra of Gettysburg. As the tower festival demonstrated, grown men can engage in play while simultaneously leading the heroic work of removing impurities from the sacred soil. This transformation has been accomplished not by cultural elites as in the past, but by heritage consumers voting not only through focus groups and surveys but also through financial support. The elites now consist of enthusiasts whose zeal to purify emerged from both a sacred sensibility and a desire for self-fulfilling leisure. The sideshow has moved from the periphery into the shrine itself, only this time former spectators are building the stage and directing the performance. Just as Gettysburg has been transformed from a public to a private experience, so too has public space become private space.[4]

Celebratory cannonading, cheering, and tinkling of champagne glasses as the tower went down muffled less mellifluous sounds. A segment of the heritage market was remaking Gettysburg into an image valued for delivering authentic experience. But is what this select group wants what the nation needs? Merging play with the sacred has helped divorce Gettysburg from its collective meaning, context, and connection to contemporary social reality. Well-intentioned zeal for purification has blinded the new elites to their exclusivity on the stage, leaving everyone else in the audience looking on. The reduction of Gettysburg to consumer choice has separated buyers from those who cannot afford to buy or those who choose commercial leisure other than heritage. Perhaps at no time in Gettysburg's history has the market absorbed so much of the sacred upon which it depends.[5]

For all the hoopla, by 2000 Gettysburg was a less-democratic shrine than it had been a century earlier. For one thing, heritage ill-positioned Gettysburg to aid national comprehension of the tragedy and struggle that began on September 11, 2001. For another, with current pilgrims disproportionately white and male, questions surface about Gettysburg in a nation with a rapidly growing minority population. African American leaders, academics, and GNMP administrators have expressed concern about the narrow scope of Gettysburg's constituency. By 2000, the GNMP had taken steps to focus more on the "new birth of freedom" inherent in the Gettysburg Address through the Wills House downtown and at the planned visitors' center. Ironically, the town historically at odds with the cultural elite may reestablish Gettysburg's link to national ideals.

Perhaps these efforts, and new ones in the wake of September 11, will help restore Gettysburg's place in the national narrative. Perhaps Gettysburg can help awaken the nation to the unending challenges posed by historical forces and its capacity to meet these tests. Yet the market for heritage that separates Gettysburg from the flow of history is not likely to abate, and dogmatism about purity has prompted some enthusiasts to term displays about slavery and freedom "politically correct spin." Moreover, as the play of visiting blacks once affronted whites, the authenticity considered acceptable play today by whites seems inappropriate to minorities. After all, reenacting not only puts play above politics, but also intentionally reinvokes a reality devoid of racial progress that was, ironically, precipitated by the Civil War. And incarnating Lost Cause mythology through pageantry mocks ground sacralized as a "new birth of freedom." In 1999, for example, an African American history professor describing his walk over the battlefield in the *New York Times* wrote of his "emotional detachment." While he fully appreciated the significance of Gettysburg to African Americans, on Little Round Top he came upon two reenactors assuming their Confederate identities for tourists. They themselves were simply other tourists role playing those who long ago might have saved slavery from destruction had they seized the hill. "I wanted to scream at them," the black visitor wrote, but instead trekked back along Cemetery Ridge, wondering how it came to be that he "still felt like an unwanted guest on this spot."[6]

In his most famous speech, Lincoln said the living could not hallow the Gettysburg battlefield any more than the dead who fell there already had. Successive generations ignoring those words have met with frustration over a work that defies completion. What this book has suggested is that Gettysburg is an ongoing project with no final meaning, an American shrine in a continuous state of becoming. Gettysburg always has reflected the current needs of its consumers, and the heritage vision is simply the latest stage. Contrary to the convictions of its proponents, heritage is hardly the culmination of historical revelation. Indeed, heritage has helped encourage forgetfulness about Gettysburg's historical meaning, associated with creating a more egalitarian society. Although Gettysburg never dealt with racial issues effectively, a century ago thousands of African Americans visited Gettysburg for annual emancipation-day celebrations. But the focus on authenticity has discounted the importance of race more than ever, and made African Americans feel less welcomed. Neither is authenticity helpful when the nation faces new trials. The disjuction between historical meaning and authenticity has thrown an important segment of history out of joint. Gettysburg will realize its potential when it finds a place for this wider meaning in its unfolding creation.

Notes

☆ ☆ ☆ ☆ ☆ ☆ ☆ ☆ ☆ ☆ ☆

Introduction

1. See John M. Vanderslice, *Gettysburg: A History of the Gettysburg Battle-field Memorial Association With an Account of the Battle* (Philadelphia: The Association, 1897); John S. Patterson, "From Battle Ground to Pleasure Ground: Gettysburg as a Historic Site," in *History Museums in the United States*, ed. Warren Leon and Roy Rosenzweig (Urbana: University of Illinois Press, 1989), pp. 128–57; "Zapped at the Map: The Battlefield at Gettysburg," *Journal of Popular Culture* 7 (1974): 825–837; "A Patriotic Landscape: Gettysburg 1863–1913," *Prospects* 7 (1982): 315–33; Edward Linenthal, *Sacred Ground: Americans and Their Battlefields* (Urbana: University of Illinois Press, 1991), p. 118; Amy Kinsel, "'From These Honored Dead': Gettysburg in American Culture, 1863–1938" (Ph.D. diss., Cornell University, 1992).

2. *USA Today*, September 26, 1997; *Boston Globe*, February 23, 1999.

3. David Nasaw, *Going Out: The Rise and Fall of Public Amusements* (New York: Basic Books, 1993), 4–5; R. Laurence Moore, *Selling God: American Religion in the Marketplace of Culture* (New York: Oxford University Press, 1994), pp. 3–10; Dona Brown, *Inventing New England: Regional Tourism in the Nineteenth Century* (Washington, D.C.: Smithsonian Institution Press, 1995), p. 10.

Chapter One: A Grand and Holy Work

1. *Gettysburg Compiler*, December 14, 1863.

2. David R. Smith, August 8, 1863, no. 4189, Gilder-Lehrman Collection, Pierpont Morgan Library New York, New York; J. Cutler Andrews, *The North Reports the Civil War* (Pittsburgh: University of Pittsburgh Press, 1955), 434; John S. Patterson, "From Battle Ground to Pleasure Ground: Gettysburg as a Historic Site," in *History Museums in the United States*, ed. Warren Leon and Roy Rosenzweig (Urbana: University of Illinois Press, 1989), p. 128.

3. John Sears, *American Sacred Places: American Tourist Attractions in the Nineteenth Century* (New York: Oxford University Press, 1989), pp. 6–7; Colleen McDannell, *Material Christianity: Religion and Popular Culture in America* (New Haven: Yale University Press, 1995), pp. 1–4.

4. John W. Daniel, *The Campaign and Battle of Gettysburg: Address of Major John W.*

Daniel . . . Before the Virginia Division of the Army of Northern Virginia at Their Annual Meeting Held in the Capitol in Richmond, Virginia, October 28, 1875 (Lynchburg, Va.: Bell, Browne and Co., 1875), p. 42.

5. Richard Bushman, *The Refinement of America: Persons, Houses, Cities* (New York: Vintage Books, 1993): 398–399; Daniel Walker Howe, "American Victorianism as a Culture," *American Quarterly* 27 (October 1975): 526–28; Thomas J. Schlereth, *Victorian America: Transformations in Everyday Life, 1876–1915* (New York: HarperCollins, 1991), pp. 118–25; Dona Brown, *Inventing New England: Regional Tourism in the Nineteenth Century* (Washington, D.C.: Smithsonian Institution Press, 1995), pp. 5–6.

6. Colin Campbell, *The Romantic Ethic and the Spirit of Modern Consumerism* (Oxford: Basil Blackwell, 1987), pp. 69–76; Jackson Lears, *Fables of Abundance: A Cultural History of Advertising in America* (New York: Basic Books, 1994), pp. 46–48; R. Laurence Moore, *Selling God: American Religion in the Marketplace of Culture* (New York: Oxford University Press, 1994), pp. 5–11, 31–38, 268–69; David S. Reynolds, *Beneath the American Renaissance: The Subversive Imagination in the Age of Emerson and Melville* (Cambridge: Harvard University Press, 1989), pp. 169–81; Leigh Eric Schmidt, *Consumer Rites: The Buying and Selling of American Holidays* (Princeton: Princeton University Press, 1995), pp. 3–6, 32–37.

7. Brown, *Inventing New England*, pp. 31–34; Anne C. Rose, *Victorian America and the Civil War* (New York: Cambridge University Press, 1992), pp. 111–12; *Philadelphia Public Ledger*, March 26, 1874.

8. Judith A. Adams, *The American Amusement Park Industry: A History of Technology and Thrills* (Boston: Twayne Publishers, 1991), pp. 4–6; Blanche Linden-Ward, "Strange but Genteel Pleasure Grounds: Tourist and Leisure Uses of Nineteenth-Century Rural Cemeteries," in *Cemeteries and Gravemarkers: Voices of American Culture*, ed. Richard E. Meyer (Ann Arbor, Mich.: UMI Research Press, 1989), pp. 306–20; David Charles Sloane, *The Last Great Necessity: Cemeteries in American History* (Baltimore: Johns Hopkins University Press, 1991), pp. 44–64, 87–94.

9. McDannell, *Material Christianity*, 108–14; Ever Green Cemetery Association, *First Announcement of Ever Green Cemetery, Gettysburg, Pa. With an Address at the Opening Ceremonies by Rev. J. H. C. Dosh . . .* (Gettysburg: Published by Ever Green Cemetery Association, 1855), pp. 3–7.

10. Brown, *Inventing New England*, 6.

11. Sears, *Sacred Places*, pp. 87–89; Michael Kammen, *Mystic Chords of Memory: The Transformation of Tradition in American Culture* (New York: Alfred A. Knopf, 1991), pp. 44–45.

12. See Gary Cross, ed., *Worktowners at Blackpool: Mass-Observation and Popular Leisure in the 1930s* (New York: Routledge, 1980), pp. 180–201; Patrick McGreevy, "Niagara as Jerusalem," *Landscape* 28 (Spring 1985): 31; G. M. Davison, *The Fashionable Tour: An Excursion to the Springs, Niagara, Quebec, and through the New England States* (Saratoga Springs, N.Y.: G. M. Davison, 1828), p. 25.

13. William Bromwell, *Locomotive Sketches, With Pen and Pencil, or, Hints and Suggestions to the Tourist Over the Great Central Route From Philadelphia to Pittsburg* (Philadelphia: J. W. Moore, 1854), 9; Daniel J. Boorstin, *The Image: A Guide to Pseudo-Events in America* (New York: Vintage Books, 1992), pp. 122–27; Henry M. Sayre, "Surveying the Vast Profound: The Panoramic Landscape in American Consciousness," *Massachusetts Review* 24 (Winter 1983): 728–30.

14. Howe, "American Victorianism as a Culture," 529–30; Katherine Grier, "The

Decline of the Memory Palace: The Parlor after 1900," in *American Home Life: A Social History of Spaces and Services*, ed. Jessica Foy and Thomas Schlereth (Knoxville: University of Tennessee Press, 1992), pp. 50–51, 54–58.

15. Brown, *Inventing New England*, pp. 4–6, 546–59; Boorstin, *The Image*, pp. 122–27; John Urry, *Consuming Places* (New York: Routledge, 1995), p. 28.

16. George Gross, *The Battlefield of Gettysburg: From the Philadelphia Press of November 27, 1865* (Philadelphia: Collins Printer, 1866), 5; Patterson, "From Battle Ground to Pleasure Ground," p. 128. The report of the superintendent of burials is found in "Report of Samuel Weaver," in *Report of the Select Committee Relative to the Soldiers' National Cemetery . . . as Reported to the House of Representatives of the Commonwealth of Pennsylvania, March 31, 1864* (Harrisburg, Penn.: Singerly and Myers, 1864), pp. 39–41.

17. *Adams Sentinel*, October 10, 1863; on August 11, 1863, the paper advertised the Franklin Repository's *History of the Rebel Invasion* and a portrait of Major General George G. Meade, *Hero of the Battle of Gettysburg*. For images produced by the photographers who arrived after the battle, see William A. Frassanito, *Gettysburg: A Journey in Time* (New York: Charles Scribner's Sons, 1975); and Frassanito, *Early Photography at Gettysburg* (Gettysburg: Thomas Publications, 1995). As for sheet music, the author discovered at least five pieces published shortly after the battle. For relics displayed at the Baltimore Sanitary Fair, see the *Gettysburg Compiler*, February 22, 1864; for Philadelphia, see the *Adams Sentinel*, April 19, May 17, 1864; *Gettysburg Compiler*, May 30, 1864; J. Mathew Gallman, *Mastering Wartime: A Social History of Philadelphia during the Civil War* (New York: Cambridge University Press, 1990), 157; Margaretta Meade's correspondence to David McConaughy appears in the May 17, 1864, *Adams Sentinel*. For information on canes shipped to sell at the fairs, see David McConaughy to Henry Carey Baird, May 3, 1864, Edward Carey Gardiner Collection, Historical Society of Pennsylvania, Philadelphia.

18. Linden-Ward, "Strange but Genteel Pleasure Grounds," p. 302; *Report of the Select Committee Relative to the Soldiers' National Cemetery*, pp. 37–38. The term "pleasure" frequently used by those discussing genteel leisure, referred not to amusement but release through experiences offering self-improvement and aesthetic uplift.

19. Kathleen R. Georg, "'This Grand National Enterprise': The Origins of Gettysburg's Soldier's National Cemetery and Gettysburg Battlefield Memorial Association," 16, Gettysburg National Military Park Library (hereafter cited as GNMPL) vertical file. McConaughy's plan for the soldier's monument appears in the *Adams Sentinel*, June 24, 1862. According to Georg, Saunders may have adopted the concept from McConaughy following a visit with the attorney in mid-August.

20. McConaughy to Andrew Curtin, July 25, 1863, photocopy in GNMPL vertical file.

21. Georg, "'This Grand National Enterprise,'" pp. 20–35; Wills to Curtin, July 24, 1863; McConaughy to Curtin, August 5, 1863; T. W. Conrad and others to Curtin, August 12, 1863; D. H. Buehler and E. G. Fahnestock to Curtin, August 14, 1863; copies in GNMP vertical file.

22. C. C. Buehler to Edward McPherson, December 9, 1863, General Correspondence, Box 48, Edward McPherson Papers, Library of Congress Manuscript Division. The letter to Gettysburg citizens, written August 14, 1863, is in the McConaughy papers at Gettysburg College Special Collections, and appeared in the *Adams Sentinel* on September 15, 1863, along with the response from those to whom he had addressed the Gettysburg letter.

23. Articles about McConaughy's addresses before the Historical Society of Pennsylvania appear in the *Adams Sentinel*, October 6 and December 15, 1863. The reference to Ingersoll is found in McConaughy to Henry Carey Baird, May 3, 1864, Gardiner Collection; McConaughy to "Dear Sir," May 16, 1864, Society Collection, Historical Society of Pennsylvania. McConaughy's identical letter to both poets dated September 13, [1869?], McConaughy Papers, Special Collections, Gettysburg College Library.

24. Copies of both the 1864 act and the supplement enacted April 24, 1866, are found in Box 49, General Correspondence, McPherson Papers.

25. McConaughy to John Jordan, November 23, 24, 1863, Society Collection, Historical Society of Pennsylvania; *Pennsylvania School Journal 15* (September 1866): 61.

26. *Adams Sentinel*, May 17, 1864; letter from McConaughy addressed "Dear Sir" (no date), Society Collection, Historical Society of Pennsylvania; George Bergson, ed., *The Legislative Record, Containing the Debates and Proceedings of the Pennsylvania Legislature for the Session of 1866* (Harrisburg: Printed at the "Telegraph", 1866), pp. 650, 368, 444; *Legislative Record*, 1867, pp. 427–28, 473, 910 contains McConaughy's introduction and discussion of "An Act to Incorporate the Gettysburg Asylum for Invalid Soldiers . . ."

27. *Gettysburg Star and Sentinel*, October 17, December 12, 1872, March 2, 1876.

28. John M. Vanderslice, *Gettysburg: A History of the Gettysburg Battle-field Memorial Association* (Philadelphia: The Association, 1897), pp. 210–12; *Gettysburg Compiler*, July 31, 1879.

29. For a biography of Bachelder, see Richard A. Sauers, "John B. Bachelder: Government Historian of the Battle of Gettysburg," *Gettysburg* 3 (July 1990): 115–12.

30. Accounts of Bachelder's activity in Gettysburg immediately after the battle are found in Bachelder's *Gettysburg Publications* (Boston: The Author [1880?]), pp. 1–3; *Gettysburg Compiler*, May 20, 1880; the *Gettysburg Star and Sentinel*, June 25, 1873; and William M. Robbins Journal, 22 December 1894, photocopy of original at the Southern Historical Collection, University of North Carolina, in GNMPL vertical file, p. 8. The Gilder-Lehrman Collection reposits Bachelder's Gettysburg sketchbook (GL 2670.01), which contains eight pencil sketches and watercolors, as well as a separate file of two drawings and one watercolor of Pickett's Charge (GL 2670.03).

31. Bachelder, *Key to Bachelder's Isometrical Drawing*, p. 1; in his promotional pamphlet *Gettysburg Publications* (Boston: The Author, [1880?]) Bachelder states he sold "thousands of copies" of the map.

32. S. B. Daboll to Bachelder, April 21, 1891, in John Bachelder, *The Bachelder Papers: Gettysburg in Their Own Words*, 4 vols., ed. D. J. and A. J. Ladd (Dayton, Ohio: Morningside House, 1994), 1:1811; J. Volnay Pierce [147th New York] to Bachelder, November 1, 1882, *Bachelder Papers*, 2; 910; Basil Hughes (11th Alabama Regiment) to Bachelder, February 24, 1867, *Bachelder Paper*; 2:305; W. S. Toombs (18th Mississippi Regiment) to Bachelder, December 22, 1871, 2:424; A. C. Underwood [Colonel, 33rd Masschusetts] to Bachelder, July 25, 1870, 1: 395–96.

33. Bachelder, *Gettysburg Publications*, pp. 1–3; Bachelder, *Key to Bachelder's Isometrical Drawing*, p. 10.

34. A full-page advertisement for the projected *Illustrated History of the Battle of Gettysburg* appears in Bachelder's catalogue *Gettysburg Publications*, published around 1880. In 1876, Bachelder produced three maps for the U.S. War Department, showing troop positions for each day of the battle, and the maps generated interest in his notes. Congress in 1880 awarded Bachelder fifty thousand dollars to compile the data into a

history of the battle. But the four volumes he produced in 1886 were disappointing, both ponderous and tortured. (See Sauers, "John B. Bachelder," pp. 117–19.) John B. Bachelder, *Gettysburg: What to See, and How to See It* (Boston: John B. Bachelder; New York: Lee, Shepard, and Dillingham, 1873), pp. i, 2–3, 3–4.

35. Vanderslice, *Gettysburg*, pp. 213–21.

36. *Gettysburg Compiler*, October 12, 1886.

37. J. Matthew Gallman and Susan Baker, "Gettysburg's Gettysburg: What the Battle Did to the Borough," in *The Gettysburg Nobody Knows*, ed. Gabor Boritt (New York: Oxford University Press, 1997), p. 144; *Gettysburg Star and Sentinel*, September 29, 1934.

38. Sally Broadhead, *Diary of a Lady of Gettysburg* (n.p., privately printed, [1863?]), p. 27; Worthington C. Ford, ed., *A Cycle of Adams Letters, 1861–1865* (Boston: Houghton Mifflin, 1920), 2:45.

39. *New York Times*, July 16, 1888, July 10, 1865.

40. *Adams Sentinel*, August 22, 1865; December 19, 1865.

41. *Gettysburg Compiler*, November 16, 1863. For other committees, see *Adams Sentinel*, June 27, 1865; *Gettysburg Star and Sentinel*, May 28, 1869. The effort to improve visible reminders of the battlefield for tourists can be found in the *Gettysburg Star and Sentinel*, March 3, and January 27, 1876; "Battle-Field Prospect Tower, $10 Certificate Loan," collection of David Meskers.

42. *Gettysburg Star and Sentinel*, April 26, May 3, 1878, August 10, 1881; *Gettysburg Compiler*, December 25, 1868.

43. Marsena Patrick, *Inside Lincoln's Army: The Diary of Marsena Rudolph Patrick, Provost Marshall, Army of the Potomac* (New York: Thomas Yoseloff, 1964), p. 268; Gregory Coco, *A Strange and Blighted Land: Gettysburg, the Aftermath of a Battle* (Gettysburg: Thomas Publications, 1995), pp. 344–46, 351.

44. Robert Bloom, *A History of Adams County, Pennsylvania, 1700–1990* (Gettysburg: Adams County Historical Society, 1992), pp. 253, 226; J. T. Trowbridge, "The Field of Gettysburg," *Atlantic Monthly* 16 (November 1865): 616–17; *Washington Daily Morning Chronicle*, November 21, 1863; "Letter From Gettysburg," unidentified newspaper clipping dated June 14, 1865, "Gettysburg Scrapbook," Box 48, McPherson Papers; *Philadelphia Inquirer*, August 30, 1869.

45. Trowbridge, "The Field of Gettysburg," p. 622; *Adams Sentinel*, April 19, 1864; Coco, *A Strange and Blighted Land*, p. 349. An example of the Tipton advertisement can be found in the December 11, 1874, edition of the *Gettysburg Compiler*.

46. *Gettysburg Compiler*, November 13, 1865, May 28, 1866, August 13, 1866, December 29, 1863. The Battle-field Hotel ad appears in the May 28, 1866, *Gettysburg Compiler*, while the Rose Farm ad in the same paper's August 13, 1866 issue.

47. *The Gettysburg Katalysine Water, Reports of Physicians and the People of Its Wonderful Cures. History of the Spring* (New York: Gettysburg Spring Company, 1868), p. 4; *The Gettysburg Katalysine Water. Its Source. History of Its Discovery and Wonderful Cures* (Gettysburg: n.p., 1872), pp. 9–12; *Gettysburg Sentinel*, December 26, 1865; *Gettysburg Star* clipping included with January 22, 1866 letter to Edward McPherson from E. Harmon, Box 6, McPherson Papers; *Gettysburg Compiler*, November 27, 21, 1865; J. W. O'Neal, *Contribution to the History and Use of the Katalysine Spring Water, at Gettysburg, Pa., and a Comparison of Its Powers with Waters at Foreign Springs* (Gettysburg: H. J. Stahle, 1876), p. 4; *Adams Sentinel*, January 30, 1866.

48. McDannell, *Material Christianity*, pp. 135–36, 45–147; Catherine Albanese, *Na-*

ture *Religion in America: From the Algonquian Indians to the New Age*, Chicago History of American Religions Series (Chicago: University of Chicago Press, 1990), pp. 136–42.

49. *Adams Sentinel*, November 21, 1865.

50. E. Harmon to Edward McPherson, January 22, 1866, Box 6, McPherson Papers; J. Rutherford Worster to Edward McPherson, November 12, 1866, Container 6, McPherson Papers; *Gettysburg Star and Sentinel*, April 1, 1868; *Gettysburg Compiler*, July 1, 1876; Bergson, *The Legislative Record . . . for the Session of 1866*, pp. 369, 444, 662, 755; *Gettysburg Compiler*, April 30, 1866; *New York Times*, June 26, 1869; *Gettysburg Star and Sentinel*, August 25, 1871.

51. *Gettysburg Star and Sentinel*, June 10, 1868; *Gettysburg Compiler*, June 1, 1881. The National Library of Medicine's historical collection contains two promotional pamphlets: *The Gettysburg Katalysine Water. Its Source* (1872) and *The Gettysburg Katalysine Water. Reports of Physicians and the People* (1868), cited above; *New York Times*, January 2, 1868; *New York Herald*, October 22, 1867; *New York Times*, June 26, 1869.

52. Bergson, *The Legislative Record . . . for the Session of 1866*, pp. 369, 444, 662, 755; *Gettysburg Star and Sentinel*, June 3, 1868. The petition, "A National Appeal and Response," appears in the May 23, 1868, *New York Evening Post*. Curtin's quote is from *The Gettysburg Katalysine Water* (1872), p. 58.

53. *Gettysburg Star and Sentinel*, November 13, 1868; *Gettysburg Compiler*, May 14, 1869; *New York Times*, June 26, 1869.

54. An advertisement for the reunion appears in the *Gettysburg Star and Sentinel*, May 28, 1869. The letter McConaughy sent to officers, addressed to "Dear General," is in the David McConaughy Collection, Gettysburg College Special Collections; Lee to McConaughy, August 5, 1869, McConaughy Collection. Descriptions of the large number of correspondents may be found in *Harrisburg Telegraph*, August 24, 1869, and the *Gettysburg Compiler*, August 20, 1869.

55. *New York Herald*, August 24, 1869; *New York Tribune*, August 26, 27, 1869; Webb to [no addressee], August 25, 1869, *Bachelder Papers* 1:376.

56. The *Harrisburg Patriot* on August 28, 1869, commented sardonically, "The tone of Davy McConaughy's invitation was as conciliatory and wheedling as that of the benevolent Mrs. Brown to Rob the Grinder." Earlier, on August 13, the *Gettysburg Star and Sentinel* reacted with less humor and more contempt, stating unequivocally, "The battle-field of Gettysburg must in all time to come be a memorial to the discomfiture of Treason and Rebellion, and of the triumph of LOYALTY and Freedom, and the attempt to make anything else out of it will prove abortive."

57. Bloom, *History of Adams County*, pp. 265–66.

58. *Gettysburg Star and Sentinel*, August 25, 1871.

59. "The Gettysburg Springs Hotel," photocopy of advertisement dated 1881, Gettysburg Springs File, Adams County Historical Society.

60. Bachelder, *Gettysburg: What to See, and How to See It*, p. 4.

61. Ibid.

62. *New York Times*, August 16, 1869.

63. *New York Times* July 10, 1865; *Gettysburg Compiler*, February 24, 1871.

Chapter Two: A Stream of Pilgrims

1. Cornelia Taylor to George Wicks, April 28, 1864, photocopy of original, Early Visitation folder, Gettysburg National Military Park Archive (herafter referred to as GNMPA).

2. Sarah Josepha Hale, "The Romance of Traveling," in *Traits of American Life* (Philadelphia: Carey and Lea, 1835), pp. 189–91; Newspaper clipping, "Letter from Gettysburg," June 14, 1865, "Gettysburg Scrapbook," Box 98, Edward McPherson Papers, Library of Congress, Manuscript Division.

3. Francis Lieber to Edward McPherson, September 16, 1865, General Correspondence, Box 49, McPherson Papers; Theodore Culver, "The Battle-field of Gettysburg," *Pennsylvania School Journal* 15 (October 1866): 93; S. Wylie Crawford to David McConaughy, November 27, [1869?], David McConaughy Papers, Gettysburg College.

4. Pennsylvania, House of Representatives, *Report of the Select Committee Relative to the Soldiers' National Cemetery . . . March 31, 1864* (Harrisburg: Singerly and Myers, 1864), pp. 37–38; Eric J. Leed, *The Mind of the Traveler, From Gilgamesh to Global Tourism* (New York: Basic Books, 1991), pp. 142–48.

5. Michael Jacobs, "Later Rambles over the Field of Gettysburg," *United States Service Magazine* 1 (January–February 1864): 71; John Robarts to Thomas Mullins, July 7, 1863, printed in the *Gettysburg Compiler*, July 21, 1896; Oliver J. Blocher to David Bucher, December 7, 1863, Box 1, Folder 2, David Bucher Paper, College of William and Mary Special Collections; *Lebanon Advertiser*, July 15, 1863; Robert Bloom, *A History of Adams County, Pennsylvania, 1700–1990* (Gettysburg: Adams County Historical Society, 1992), pp. 225–26.

6. Jacobs, "Later Rambles," pp. 66–72; *Philadelphia Press*, November 16, 1887; *Gettysburg Compiler*, July 20, 1863; Sally Broadhead, *The Diary of a Lady of Gettysburg, Pennsylvania from June 15 to July 15, 1863* (n.p.: privately printed, [1863?]), p. 27; Cornelia Hancock, *South after Gettysburg: Letters of Cornelia Hancock from the Army of the Potomac, 1863–1865*, ed. Henrietta Jaquette (Philadelphia: University of Pennsylvania Press, 1937), p. 5; *Lebanon Advertiser*, July 15, 1863; *Philadelphia Public Ledger*, July 15, 1863.

7. Mrs. Edmund Souder, *Leaves From the Battle-field of Gettysburg* (Philadelphia: Caxton Press, 1864), pp. 63–64; Jacobs, "Later Rambles," pp. 66–67, 72.

8. Gary Laderman, *The Sacred Remains: American Attitudes toward Death, 1799–1883* (New Haven: Yale University Press, 1996), pp. 73–76; Richard M. Powell, "With Hood at Gettysburg," *Philadelphia Weekly Times*, December 13, 1884.

9. Charles S. Wainwright, *A Diary of Battle: The Personal Journals of Colonel Charles S. Wainwright, 1861–1865*, ed. Allan Nevins (New York: Harcourt, Brace, and World, 1962), p. 254; Marsena Patrick, *Inside Lincoln's Army: The Diary of Marsena Rudolph Patrick, Provost Marshall General, Army of the Potomac*, ed. David S. Sparks (New York: Thomas Yoseloff, 1964), pp. 268, 271; W. Willard Smith to Montgomery Meigs, 10 July 1863, Box 663, "Gettysburg 1863" Folder, RG 92, Records of the Office of Quartermaster General, U.S. National Archives and Records Administration, Washington, D.C.; W. Willard Smith to Montgomery Meigs, 29 July 1863, photocopy of original, Gettysburg National Military Park Library (hereafter referred to as GNMPL) vertical file.

10. *Berks and Schuylkill Journal*, July 18, 1863; Souder, *Leaves From the Battle-field of Gettysburg*, p. 29; *Adams Sentinel*, November 24, 1863.

11. *Gettysburg Star and Sentinel*, May 22, 1907; *Adams Sentinel*, November 24, 1863.

12. *Gettysburg Compiler*, January 19, 1872; *Philadelphia Inquirer*, August 30, 1864; *New York Times*, August 16, 1869; *Adams Sentinel*, March 1, 1864; *Gettysburg Compiler*, March 14, 1864.

13. Gary Gallagher, ed., *Two Witnesses at Gettysburg: The Personal Accounts of Whitelaw Reid and A.J.L. Fremantle* (St. James, N.Y.: Brandywine Press, 1994), p. 82; George Gross, *The Battle-field of Gettysburg, from the Philadelphia Press of November 27, 1865*

(Philadelphia: Collins, Printer, 1866), p. 12; Isaac Moorhead, "A Visit to Gettysburg by Isaac Moorhead," *American Magazine and Historical Chronicle 1* (Autumn–Winter 1985–86): 23; Gregory Coco, *A Strange and Blighted Land, Gettysburg: The Aftermath of a Battle* (Gettysburg: Thomas Publications, 1995), pp. 349–50; *Philadelphia Inquirer*, August 30, 1869.

14. Newspaper articles about tourists can be found in the *Gettysburg Compiler*, November 30, 1863, February 8, 1864, May 8, 1865, June 12, 1865, June 18, 1866, July 21, 1871, June 11, 1873; and *Adams Sentinel*, August 19, 1863, March 22, 1864, June 13, 1865; Jacobs, "Later Rambles," p. 72.

15. *Pennsylvania School Journal* 15 (September, 1866): 43, 51; Gary Cross, *A Social History of Leisure since 1600* (State College, Penn.: Venture Publishing, 1990), pp. 96, 126; Donna Braden, *Leisure and Entertainment in America* (Dearborn, Mich.: Henry Ford Museum and Greenfield Village, 1988), pp. 25–28.

16. *Adams Sentinel*, August 22, 1865; *Gettysburg Compiler*, November 15, 1866; September 2, 1875; August 19, 1875; September 9, 1875, September 23, 1875; *Gettysburg Star and Sentinel*, May 27, 1868, August 19, 1875, September 2, 1875, September 9, 1875, September 23, 1875, July 18, 1877, May 17, 1878, July 11, 1878, August 29, 1878, May 20, 1880.

17. Patriot Daughters of Lancaster, *Hospital Scenes After the Battle of Gettysburg, July, 1863* (Philadelphia: Henry B. Ashmead, 1863), p. 20; *Gettysburg Star and Sentinel*, June 10, 1875; *Gettysburg Compiler*, July 15, 1875; *Gettysburg Compiler*, August 28, 1879, reprint of a letter dated August 18, 1879, to the *Philadelphia Press* signed "P.F.J."; Lieutenant Colonel Oscar Mack to W. W. Belknap, Secretary of War, July 2, 1875, Gettysburg National Cemetery File, Box 663, Consolidated Correspondence, U.S. War Department, National Archives and Records Administration, Washington, D.C.; *Gettysburg Star and Sentinel*, May 24, 1877.

18. *Gettysburg Compiler*, August 12, 1880; *New York Times*, June 26, 1869; letter to *New York Independent*, by Schuyler Colfax, reprinted in *Gettysburg Star and Sentinel*, June 19, 1867; "G.A.T." writing for the *Boston Transcript*, reprinted in the *Gettysburg Star and Sentinel*, September 18, 1879; this letter to the *Baltimore Sun* was reprinted in the *Gettysburg Compiler*, June 25, 1873.

19. *Frank Leslie's Illustrated Weekly*, July 24, 1869; *Philadelphia Press*, August 21, 1879; *Gettysburg Star and Sentinel*, August 7, 1879, August 25, 1885.

20. "Letter from Gettysburg," June 30, [1864?] *Cincinnati Gazette* clipping, Gettysburg Scrapbook, Box 98, McPherson Papers; Jabobs, "Later Rambles," p. 167; S. Wylie Crawford to M. L. Stoever, May 14, 1867, Union Generals File, Historical Society of Pennsylvania.

21. Eric Breitbart, "The Painted Mirror: Historical Re-creation from the Panorama to the Docudrama," in *Presenting the Past: Essays on History and the Public*," ed. Susan P. Benson, Stephen Brier, and Roy Rosenzweig, pp. 105–17 (Philadelphia: Temple University Press, 1986); pp. 105–6; Stephen Oettermann, *The Panorama: History of a Mass Medium*, trans. Deborah L. Schneider (New York: Zone Books, 1997), pp. 6–7, 13–21.

22. Oettermann, *The Panorama*, pp. 5–6; John C. West, *A Texan in Search of a Fight* (Waco, Tex.: J. S. Hill, 1901), p. 91, cited in Coco, *A Strange and Blighted Land*, p. 2; untitled newspaper clipping dated July 4, 1865, Gettysburg Scrapbook, Box 98, McPherson Papers; letter signed "Dr. Prime" appearing in the *New York Observer*, reprinted in the *Gettysburg Compiler*, September 30, 1875. An advertisement for "Hershberger's Panorama" of the battle appeared in the January 22, 1869, *Gettysburg Star and Sentinel*.

23. *Gettysburg Star and Sentinel*, June 13, 1878; Gettysburg jeweler Penrose Myers's advertisement for field-glass rentals appears in the October 3, 1883, *Gettysburg Star and Sentinel*; articles about the Round Top observatory appear in the April 27 and July 20, 1881 *Gettysburg Compiler*; letter to *New York Independent* by Schuyler Colfax, reprinted in *Gettysburg Star and Sentinel*, June 19, 1867; Theodore Cuyler, "The Battle-field of Gettysburg," *Pennsylvania School Journal* 15 (October 1966): 93; "G.A.T." to *Boston Transcript*, reprinted in *Gettysburg Star and Sentinel*, September 18, 1879; *Philadelphia Times* article reprinted in the *Gettysburg Compiler*, June 7, 1878; *Gettysburg Star and Sentinel*, October 6, 1871, letter from "Dr. Eddy."

24. Unsigned seventeen-page journal, General Correspondence File, Box 48, McPherson Papers.

25. *Baltimore American*, September 5, 1867.

26. Ibid; *Frank Leslie's Illustrated Newspaper*, July 24, 1869; Joseph Foster, untitled article, *Portsmouth Journal of Literature and Politics* 73 (August 8, 1863): 2; J. T. Trowbridge, "The Field of Gettysburg," *Atlantic Monthly* 16 (November 1865), p. 619; *Berks and Schuylkill Journal*, July 18, 1863; "G.A.T." in the *Boston Transcript*, reprinted in the *Gettysburg Star and Sentinel*, September 18, 1879.

27. Photocopy of original unsigned manuscript dated October 14, 1866, Early Visitation folder, GNMPA.

28. Liberty Clutz, *Some Personal Recollections of the Battle of Gettysburg* (n.p.: n.p., [1925?]), p. 15; *Philadelphia Inquirer*, August 30, 1869.

29. F. M. Stoke to J. M. Stoke, October 26, 1863, J. M. Stoke File, Gettysburg College Special Collections; Laderman, *Sacred Remains*, pp. 72–76; Moorhead, "A Visit to Gettysburg," p. 26; *Pennsylvania School Journal* 15 (September 1866): 55; W.W.H. Davis in *Doylestown Democrat*, reprinted in *Gettysburg Compiler*, August 13, 1869; *Gettysburg Compiler*, September 30, 1875.

30. *Gettysburg Star and Sentinel*, September 2, 1875; *Gettysburg Compiler*, September 2, September 23, 1875.

31. *Gettysburg Compiler*, September 2, 1875, July 9, 1873; *Gettysburg Star and Sentinel*, April 26, 1878, June 7, 1872.

32. J. C. Hendrix to Will [Leonard?], August 11, 1871, Abiel Leonard Papers, Western Historical Manuscript Collection, University of Missouri-Columbia.

33. Alan Kendall, *Medieval Pilgrims* (New York: G. P. Putnam's Sons, 1970), pp. 12–17; Victor and Edith Turner, *Image and Pilgrimage in Christian Culture* (New York: Columbia University Press, 1978), p. 28.

34. *Appleton's Hand Book of American Travel*, 9th ed. (New York: D. Appleton and Company, 1867), p. 169; *Gettysburg Compiler*, July 2, 1873; Trowbridge, "The Field of Gettysburg," p. 618.

Chapter Three: A Memorial of the Whole Struggle

1. *Harrisburg Patriot*, February 27, 1884; *Gettysburg Star and Sentinel*, February 26, March 4, 1884.

2. Alan Trachtenberg, *The Incorporation of America: Culture and Society in the Gilded Age*, American Century Series (New York: Hill and Wang, 1982), pp. 3–9; Thomas Schlereth, *Victorian America: Transformations in Everyday Life*, Everyday Life in America Series (New York: HarperCollins, 1991), pp. xi–xvi.

3. *Philadelphia Public Ledger*, July 3, 1903; George M. Frederickson, *The Inner Civil War: Northern Intellectuals and the Crisis of the Union* (New York: Harper and Row, 1965), pp. 217–25; John F. Kasson, *Amusing the Million: Coney Island at the Turn of the Century*, American Century Series (New York: Hill and Wang, 1978), pp. 4–6; Stuart McConnell, *Glorious Contentment: The Grand Army of the Republic, 1865–1900* (Chapel Hill: University of North Carolina Press, 1992), pp. 105–9.

4. Michael Kammen, *Mystic Chords of Memory: The Transformation of Tradition in American Culture* (New York: Alfred A. Knopf, 1991), pp. 44–45, 115, 194–96, Lyman P. Powell, "The Renaissance of the Historical Pilgrimage," *Review of Reviews* 8 (October 1893): 412.

5. Robert W. Rydell, *All the World's a Fair: Visions of Empire at American International Expositions, 1876–1916* (Chicago: University of Chicago Press, 1916), p. 2; Leigh Eric Schmidt, *Consumer Rites: The Buying and Selling of American Holidays* (Princeton: Princeton University Press, 1995), pp. 30–37; Warren Susman, "Ritual Fairs," *Chicago History* 12 (Fall 1983): 6; Leigh Eric Schmidt, "The Commercialization of the Calendar: American Holidays and the Culture of Consumption, 1870–1930," *Journal of American History* 78 (December 1991): 897–98; William Leach, *Land of Desire: Merchants, Power, and the Rise of a New American Culture* (New York: Vintage Books, 1993), pp. 175–77, 887–916.

6. Kammen, *Mystic Chords of Memory*, pp. 105–6, 115; Gerald F. Linderman, *Embattled Courage: The Experience of Combat in the American Civil War* (New York: Free Press, 1987), pp. 271–77; Michael Panhorst, "Lest We Forget: Monuments and Memorial Sculpture in National Military Parks on Civil War Battlefields, 1861–1917" (Ph.D. diss., University of Delaware, 1988), pp. 133, 268–69.

7. Robert N. Bellah, "Civil Religion in America," *Daedalus* 96 (Winter 1967): 9–11; *Adams Sentinel*, May 17, 1864, December 19, 1865.

8. *Gettysburg Star and Sentinel*, February 21, 1888; John M. Vanderslice, *Gettysburg: A History of the Gettysburg Battle-field Memorial Association, With an Account of the Battle* (Philadelphia: The Association, 1897), pp. 210, 214–29; Gettysburg Battlefield Memorial Association, "Address of the Gettysburg Battle Field Memorial Association" (n.p.: n.p., [1880?]), p. 2, Gettysburg Pamphlet Collection, Historical Society of Pennsylvania.

9. Amy Kinsel, "'From These Honored Dead:' Gettysburg in American Culture, 1863–1938" (Ph.D. diss., Cornell University, 1992), pp. 186–87.

10. Vanderslice, *Gettysburg*, pp. 261–62; Panhorst, "Lest We Forget," pp. 48–49; *Gettysburg Star and Sentinel*, May 6, 1884; *National Tribune*, July 28, 1898; *Milwaukee Evening Wisconsin*, February 15, 1888; *Philadelphia Times*, December 4, 1897.

11. *Gettysburg Star and Sentinel*, October 6, 1885; Count of Paris et. al., "Gettysburg Thirty Years After," *North American Review* 152 (February 1891): 146; Panhorst, "Lest We Forget," p. 133; Gettysburg National Park Commission, "Annual Report of the Gettysburg National Military Park Commission to the Secretary of War, 1904," in *Annual Reports of the Gettysburg National Park Commission to the Secretary of War, 1893–1904* (Washington, D.C.: GPO, 1905), p. 99; "The Van Amringe Granite Company" (Boston: Van Amringe Co., n.d), Gettysburg National Military Park Archive (hereafter cited as GNMPA) clippings file, vol. 5, p. 17; Van Amringe Company, *Military Memorials and Statues at Gettysburg, Pa., Compliments of the Van Amringe Co.* (Boston: Van Amringe Co., n.d.), pamphlet collection, Civil War Library and Museum, Philadelphia.

12. Jacob Hoke, *The Great Invasion* (Dayton, Ohio: W. J. Shuey, 1887), p. xxix; Panhorst, "Lest We Forget," pp. 41–42; "Gettysburg Monument Committee, 121st New

York Vols.," January 14, 1888, four-page printed letter, GNMPA clipping file, vol. 3, p. 161; "17th Regiment Pennsylvania Volunteer Cavalry Association, Lebanon, October 20, 1887," one-page letter, GNMPA clipping file, vol. 3, p. 157.

13. *Philadelphia Times* article cited in *Gettysburg Compiler*, September 22, 1885; Grand Army of the Republic, Department of Pennsylvania, *Proceedings of the 40th and 41st Encampments of the Department of Pennsylvania, Grand Army of the Republic . . .* (Philadelphia: Town Printer, 1887), p. 158.

14. David A. Buehler to John B. Bachelder, December 13, 1886, in John Bachelder, *The Bachelder Papers: Gettysburg in Their Own Words*, ed. D. J. Ladd and A. J. Ladd, 4 vols. (Dayton, Ohio, Morningside House, 1994), 3:1460; *Gettysburg Compiler*, December 18, 1888; Harlan D. Unrau, *Gettysburg: An Administrative History* (Washington, D.C.: GPO, 1991), pp. 58–59; Vanderslice, *Gettysburg*, pp. 241–44; Gustave Wuguitsky [treasurer, 20th Massachusetts Volunteers Association] to Gettysburg Battlefield Memorial Association, January 20, 1896, p. 20, Letterbook of Gettysburg Battlefield Commission, RG 92.10.4, Records of Gettysburg National Park Commission, National Archives and Records Administration.

15. Panhorst, "Lest We Forget," p. 74. Unsigned memo regarding survivors of Pickett's Division erecting a monument at Gettysburg in 1887, on letterhead, "Richard L. Maury, Counselor-at-Law . . . Richmond, Virginia." Edward Payson Reeve Papers, Southern Historical Collection, University of North Carolina, microfilm; *Richmond Whig*, July 31, 1888; Unrau, *Gettysburg: An Administrative History*, pp. 61–62; Norman Camp to Bachelder, December 3, 1889, *Bachelder Papers* 3:1682.

16. *Nashville Banner*, August 23, 1898, see also *Atlanta Constitution* editorial, August 21, 1898; W. A. Hemphill in *Atlanta Constitution*, August 21, 1898; *Gettysburg Compiler*, January 28, 1903.

17. E. A. Garlington, *Inspection Report of Colonel E. A. Garlington, Gettysburg National Park* (Washington, D.C.: GPO, 1904), p. 5; *Gettysburg Star and Sentinel*, September 8, 1896; Sophie Keenan, "Père Lachaise and Gettysburg," *Pittsburg Dispatch*, reprinted in the *Gettysburg Compiler*, May 29, 1894; *Philadelphia Public Ledger*, July 3, 1903.

18. *Baltimore Sun*, June 7, 1896; *National Tribune*, November 11, 1891.

19. *Century* article cited in *Gettysburg Star and Sentinel*, September 10, 1895; N. K. Floyd, *National Tribune*, July 28, 1898; Townshend cited in *Gettysburg Star and Sentinel*, September 9, 1901; David Charles Sloane, *The Last Great Necessity: Cemeteries in American History* (Baltimore: Johns Hopkins University Press, 1991), pp. 116–17; *Grand Army Scout and Soldiers' Mail* 5 (July 24, 1886), p. 7; John Sears, *Sacred Places: American Tourist Attractions in the Nineteenth Century* (New York: Oxford University Press, 1989), pp. 99–102; Roy Rosenzweig and Elizabeth Blackmar, *The Park and the People: A History of Central Park* (New York: Henry Holt, 1992), pp. 103–8.

20. *Philadelphia Public Ledger*, October 1, 1897; Panhorst, "Lest We Forget," pp. 41–42; *New York Times*, October 20, 1897.

21. *Gettysburg Star and Sentinel*, August 30, 1887; Karl Baedeker, ed., *The United States With an Excursion Into Mexico: Handbook for Travelers* (New York: Charles Scribner's Sons, 1893), p. 236; Leach, *Land of Desire*, pp. 3–8; Neil Harris, "Museums, Merchandising, and Popular Taste: The Struggle for Influence," in *Material Culture and the Study of American Life*, ed. Ian M. G. Quimby (New York: W. W. Norton, 1978), pp. 65–66; *Harrisburg Telegraph*, September 5, 1900.

22. *Baltimore Sun*, June 7, 1896; J. Howard Wert, *A Complete Hand-Book of the Monuments and Indications and Guide to the Positions on the Gettysburg Battlefield* (Harrisburg,

Penn.: R. M. Sturgeon and Co., 1886), p. 5; *Philadelphia Times* cited in *Gettysburg Compiler*, December 11, 1894. The number 150,000 is plausible; the first official statistic of tourism, recorded by a park guard in 1899, recorded 9,000 vehicles carrying 36,000 tourists on Hancock Avenue during a one-month period. "Report of the Gettysburg National Park Commission," in *Annual Report of the War Department for Fiscal Year Ended June 30, 1899* (Washington, D.C.: GPO, 1899), p. 330.

23. Wert, *A Complete Hand-Book*, p. 5; "Old Soldier," *Gettysburg Compiler*, October 7, 1903.

24. *Gettysburg Star and Sentinel*, June 23, 1886, August 14, 1885, September 1, 1885; *Gettysburg Compiler*, August 26, 1906; *Gettysburg Times*, June 23, 1938.

25. Robert Bloom, *History of Adams County, Pennsylvania, 1700–1900* (Gettysburg: Adams County Historical Society, 1982), pp. 262–63; Frederick W. Hawthorne, *A Peculiar Institution: The History of the Gettysburg Licensed Battlefield Guides* (Gettysburg: Association of Licensed Battlefield Guides, 1991), pp. 2–3; "City Hotel, John E, Hughes, Proprietor" (pamphlet, 7 leaves, [1895?]), Wisconsin Historical Society Pamphlet Collection; "Pitzer House, J. E. Pitzer, Propietor" (pamphlet, 7 leaves, [1900?]), Wisconsin Historical Society Pamphlet Collection; "Pocket Map of the Battle of Gettysburg, Compliments of the Eagle Hotel, Gettysburg" (fold-out map, [1895], cited in the April 2, 1895, *Gettysburg Star and Sentinel* as "just issued"), University of Virginia Special Collections.

26. Hawthorne, *A Peculiar Institution*, pp. 3–7, 11–12; *Gettysburg Star and Sentinel*, October 18, 1905; Frank Moran in the *National Tribune*, November 12, 1891; *Gettysburg Star and Sentinel*, June 12, 1888, June 8, 1897, July 27, 1897, April 25, 1899, July 3, 1901, August 29, 1906, August 21, 1912.

27. *Gettysburg Compiler*, March 7, 1906; Hawthorne, *A Peculiar Institution*, pp. 4–6.

28. *Philadelphia Record*, November 9, 1899, discussed in *Gettysburg Star and Sentinel*, November 14, 1899; on December 19, 1899, the *Gettysburg Star and Sentinel* reported that the rumor was being circulated "in various papers throughout the country"; Dr. Henry Stewart, "Reminiscences," *Gettysburg Times*, May 22, 1946.

29. *Gettysburg Star and Sentinel*, May 24, 1947; Jeanette Lasansky, *Central Pennsylvania Redware Pottery, 1780–1904* (n.p.: Keystone Books, n.d.), p. 64; Charlotte Plank, Gettysburg, to Mr. Eldridge, February 24, 1893 [regarding her sons' manufacture of miniature cannon], accession no. 1994.93.1, Chicago Historical Society; *Gettysburg Star and Sentinel*, May 16, 1899; September 10, 1902; *Gettysburg Compiler*, March 7, 1906.

30. Celeste Olalquiaga, *The Artificial Kingdom: A Treasury of the Kitsch Experience* (New York: Pantheon Books, 1998), pp. 13–19, 67–79; Colleen McDannell, *Material Christianity: Religion and Popular Culture in America* (New Haven: Yale University Press), pp. 41–43; Susan Stewart, *On Longing: Narratives of the Miniature, the Gigantic, the Souvenir, the Collection* (Baltimore: Johns Hopkins University Press, 1984), pp. 134–35; *Gettysburg Star and Sentinel*, August 3, 1904.

31. *Baltimore Sun*, June 7, 1896; *Gettysburg Compiler*, March 7, 1906.

32. Bloom, *History of Adams County*, pp. 267–268; Gary Cross and Rick Szostak, *Technology and American Society: A History* (Englewood Cliffs, N.J.: Prentice-Hall, 1995), pp. 145, 153; *Gettysburg Compiler*, July 11, 1893; Edward T. Linenthal, *Sacred Ground: Americans and Their Battlefields* (Urbana: University of Illinois Press, 1991), pp. 111–14.

33. *Gettysburg Star and Sentinel*, May 15, 1901; Adele Tipton to Congressman Lewis, May 8, 1902, General Correspondence, 1898–1907, Box 1, 1898–1907, RG 92, Records of the Quartermaster General, National Archives and Records Administration.

34. *Gettysburg Compiler*, January 16, 1907; *Gettysburg Star and Sentinel*, July 25, 1878, June 7, 1898, June 4, 1913; *National Tribune*, July 5, 1888.

35. *Proceedings of the Thirty-Ninth Annual Encampment of the Department of Pennsylvania, Grand Army of the Republic, 1905*, pp. 268–69; *Gettysburg Compiler*, May 1, 1900, June 12, 1900, February 26, 1901, June 15, 1904, June 10, 1903, October 3, 1906, July 10, 1907, November 17, 1909, *Gettysburg Star and Sentinel*, June 15, 1904, September 24, 1895, May 22, 1901; June 9, 1909, November 17, 1909, June 22, 1910.

36. *Gettysburg Compiler*, May 8, 1894, May 21, 25, 1895, May 4, 1904; *Gettysburg Star and Sentinel*, January 1, 1900, September 26, 1899, July 31, 1901, March 19, 1902, November 4, 1903, April 19, 1904.

37. *New York Times*, July 16, 1888; *Chambersburg Public Opinion*, n.d., GNMPA clipping file, vol. 2, p. 62; *Gettysburg Compiler*, September 26, 1899; *Gettysburg Star and Sentinel*, April 19, 1905, July 15, 1903.

38. *Gettysburg Compiler*, August 28, 1894, June 4, 1895; *Gettysburg Star and Sentinel*, May 14, 1895, July 31, 1894, February 26, 1895; *Philadelphia Public Ledger*, Feburary 10, 1902.

39. *Gettysburg Star and Sentinel*, February 26, 1895, March 6, 1901.

40. Alfred Runte, "Promoting the Golden West: Advertising and the Railroad." *California History 70* (Spring 1991): 63–64; Susan Walther, "The Railroad in the Western Landscape, 1865–1900," in *The Railroad in the American Landscape, 1850–1950* (Wellesley, Mass.: Wellesley College Museum, 1981), pp. 39–40, 44; *Gettysburg Compiler*, December 24, 1881.

41. *Gettysburg Compiler*, June 16, 1885, April 8, 1884, April 15, 1884, June 24, 1884; *Gettysburg Star and Sentinel*, July 1, 1884, November 16, 1897, September 18, 1900. The broadside along with others is in the GNMPA clipping file, vol. 4, p. 139 (the reenactment of Pickett's Charge was canceled).

42. *Philadelphia Inquirer*, September 18, 1882; Edwin G. Burrowes and Mike Wallace, *Gotham: A History of New York City to 1898* (New York: Oxford University Press, 1998), pp. 793–94; Rosenzweig and Blackmar, *The Park and the People*, p. 111; *Gettysburg Star and Sentinel*, September 26, 1883, May 13, 1884, May 27, 1884, *Gettysburg Compiler*, June 17, 1884.

43. *Gettysburg Compiler*, July 30, 1886; the post office was called "Sedgwick" after the Union Fifth Corps commander, as Pennsylvania already had a post office named "Round Top"; *Gettysburg Compiler*, June 27, 1887, September 6, 1887; *Gettysburg Star and Sentinel*, September 4, 1886; June 7, 1887; James T. Hare, *The 50th Anniversary of the World Famous Battle of Gettysburg* (Gettysburg: Gettysburg Board of Trade, 1913), p. 57. Often groups used excursions to generate revenue by overcharging members for tickets and realizing the difference. The Round Top branch carried tourists until 1941, when the Reading Railroad, a successor to the Gettysburg and Harrisburg, turned over to the National Park Service the five acres comprising Round Top Park as well as the railroad right-of-way. The tracks were torn up in 1942.

44. *Philadelphia Times*, October 4, 1897; Gettysburg Electric Railway Company [handbill] GNMPA clipping file, vol. 2, p. 47; Bloom, *History of Adams County*, p. 263.

45. J. D. Pyott, "Gettysburg Meeting," *Pennsylvania School Journal 48* (August 1899): 93; William Ralston Balch, *The Battle of Gettysburg: An Historical Account* (Harrisburg: E. K. Myers, 1886), pp. 31–32, 122–23; Thomas E. Jenkins, *Gettysburg in War and Peace: A Brief Review of Interesting Historical Facts and Incidents Relative to the Famous Three-Days' Fight* (Baltimore: Press of J. Cox's Sons, 1890), pp. 3, 88, 92.

46. E. L. Godkin, "The Gettysburg Celebration," *Nation 47* (July 12, 1888): 27.

47. Dona Brown, *Inventing New England: Regional Tourism in the Nineteenth Century* (Washington, D.C.: Smithsonian Institution Press, 1995), pp. 28–32, 61; "Gettysburg, How to See It Quickly" in vertical file, Wisconsin State Historical Society; *Gettysburg Star and Sentinel*, September 20, 1887; *New York Commercial Advertiser* cited in *Gettysburg Compiler*, June 7, 1892; *Gettysburg Star and Sentinel*, November 16, 1897, September 18, 1900.

48. *Gettysburg Compiler*, April 29, 1884.

49. "Catalogue of Relics from Gettysburg Battlefield and Other Fields, Owned by Capt. C. W. Hyde," Civil War Veterans' File, Wisconsin Veterans' Museum, Madison, Wisconsin; "The Battle of Gettysburg, by J. F. Chase," pamphlet, Newberry Library; "Souvenir—Our Flag," Newberry Library; "J. F. Chase, Inventor and Temperance Lecturer," pamphlet, Civil War Veterans' Collection, Wisconsin Veterans' Museum; "What It Cost Me and My Comrades, J. F. Chase," pamphlet, 1899, GNMPA, vol. 2, p. 137; Mulholland to John Badger Bachelder, December 24, 1886, *Bachelder Papers* 3:1464; *Williamsport Sun and Banner*, February 11, 1887; A. G. McElroy to Captain E. P. Reeve, September 10, 1888, E. P. Reeve Papers [microfilm], University of North Carolina Southern Collection.

50. John L. Marsh, "Drama and Spectacle by the Yard: The Panorama in America," *Journal of Popular Culture* 10 (Winter 1976): 581–89; a Gettysburg cyclorama impresario told him he used a "pitch man" to whip up interest in the painting, exaggerate its size, and periodically advertise a different name for the same canvas to enhance attendance.

51. "Cyclorama of the Battle of Gettysburg, by Paul Philippoteaux" (Boston, 1885?), p. 8; *Gettysburg Compiler*, July 24, 1894; Alfred Mongin, "A Study of Cycloramas: Preliminary Report," February 24, 1949 (RG 79, E 411, F 620–46, National Archives and Records Administration, Philadelphia), p. 6; *Gettysburg Star and Sentinel*, August 23, 1905.

52. "Battle of Gettysburg. A Comprehensive Description of the Greatest Work of the Celebrated French Artist Paul Philippoteaux, Now Being Exhibited in Battle of Gettysburg, Cyclorama Building on the Midway: A Century of Progress International Exposition, 1933" (Chicago: n.p., [1933?]), Chicago Historical Society; Kammen, *Mystic Chords of Memory*, p. 132; Rydell, *All the World's a Fair*, pp. 2–7; *Gettysburg Star and Sentinel*, December 9, 1884, April 29, 1939; *Gettysburg Compiler*, March 25, 1903; "Time Saver and Catalogue of America's War Museum, Greater American Exposition, Omaha, Nebraska, 1899," Chicago Historical Society; *Gettysburg Star and Sentinel*, March 17, April 6, 1904; October 9, 1907, February 24, 1909; "A Rare Opportunity: Gettysburg Battlefield and Museum Company," GNMPA clipping file, vol. 3, p. 236.

53. *Gettysburg Compiler*, July 10, 1888; *Gettysburg Star and Sentinel*, July 25, 1878; July 8, 1903; *Gettysburg Times*, July 4, 1938.

54. "Fiftieth Anniversary of the Battle of Gettysburg, July 1st to 4th, 1913," broadside published by the Western Maryland Railroad, GNMPA clipping file, vol. 7, p. 88; *Gettysburg Compiler*, July 26, 1878, January 16, 1907; *Gettysburg Times*, June 23, 1938; Paul Greenhalgh, *Ephemeral Vistas: The Expositions Universelles, Great Exhibitions and World's Fairs, 1851–1939* (Manchester, England: Manchester University Press, 1988), p. 45; *Gettysburg Star and Sentinel*, July 25, 1878, July 3, 1888; "Pawnee Bill's Historic Wild West" [advertisement] *Gettysburg Star and Sentinel*, May 23, 1899.

55. David Nasaw, *Going Out: The Rise and Fall of Public Amusements* (New York: Basic Books, 1993), pp. 71–73; Balch, *The Battle of Gettysburg*, p. 3; *Gettysburg Star and Sentinel*, December 12, 1900.

56. Katherine Grier, "The Decline of the Memory Palace: the Parlor After 1890," in *American Home Life, 1880–1930, A Social History of Spaces and Services*, ed. Jessica H. Foy and Thomas J. Schlereth (Knoxville: University of Tennessee Press, 1992), pp. 50–51, 62.

57. Lasansky, *Central Pennsylvania Redware Pottery, 1780–1904*, pp. 16–17; Harris, "Museums, Merchandising, and Popular Taste," p. 70; Shirley Wajda, "A Room with a Viewer," in *Hard at Play: Leisure in America, 1840–1940*, ed. Kathryn Grover (Amherst: University of Masachusetts Press, 1992), pp. 118–34; John Blaschect to Bachelder, December 8, 1890, *Bachelder Papers* 3:1779.

58. Grier, "The Decline of the Memory Palace," pp. 50–59, 67–70.nt59. Boorstin, *The Image*, pp. 36–44. Because racial issues are considered here only insofar as race enters the discussion of market and memory, those seeking complete treatment of the way racial issues were ignored in postwar America should refer to David Blight, *Race and Reunion: The Civil War in American Memory* (Cambridge: Harvard University Press, 2001); and Nina Silber, *The Romance of Reunion: Northerners and the South, 1865–1900* (Chapel Hill: University of North Carolina Press, 1993).

Chapter Four: A Place for Tourists and the Oppressed

1. *History of Cumberland and Adams Counties, Pennsylvania, Containing a History of the Counties*, Pennsylvania County and Regional History Series (Chicago: Warren and Beers, 1886), p. 203.

2. John Kasson, *Amusing the Million: Coney Island at the Turn of the Century*, American Century Series (New York: Hill and Wang, 1978), pp. 4–7; David Nasaw, *Going Out: The Rise and Fall of Public Amusements* (New York: Basic Books, 1993), pp. 2–4.

3. Robert Goldwaithe Carter, *Four Brothers in Blue: Or Sunshine and Shadows of the Rebellion* (1913; reprint, University of Texas Press, 1978), pp. 2–3; John Higham, "The Reorientation of American Culture in the 1890s," in *Writing American History: Essays on Modern Scholarship*, ed. John Higham (Bloomington: Indiana University Press, 1970), pp. 81–82.

4. Thomas Schlereth, *Victorian America: Transformations in Everyday Life, 1876–1915*, Everyday Life in America Series (New York: HarperCollins Publishers, 1991), pp. 209, 214.

5. "Glorious Gettysburg," *Grand Army Review* 4 (August 1888): 874; Robert Bloom, *A History of Adams County, 1700–1990* (Gettysburg: Adams County Historical Society, 1992), p. 266.

6. "Gettysburg Meeting" *Pennsylvania School Journal* 48 (August 1899): 93.

7. *Gettysburg Star and Sentinel*, July 9, 1894; Count of Paris et al., "Gettysburg Thirty Years After," *North American Review* 152 (February 1891): 139.

8. Susan Walther, "The Railroad in the Western Landscape, 1865–1900," in *The Railroad in the American Landscape, 1850–1950*, ed. Susan Walther (Wellesley, Mass.: Wellesley College Museum, 1981), p. 44.

9. Louise Morgan Sill, "A Much-Monumented Battle-field," *Harper's Weekly* 45 (October 12, 1901): 27; Gettysburg National Military Park Commission, "Annual Report of the Gettysburg National Military Park Commission to the Secretary of War, 1899," in *Annual Reports of the Gettysburg National Military Park Commission to the Secretary of War, 1893–1904*, pp. 51–56 (Washington, D.C.: GPO, 1905), p. 54; Louise Hale, "We

Discover the Old Dominion," *Harper's Magazine* 33 (August 1916): 402; Sophie Keenan, "Père Lachaise and Gettysburg," *Pittsburgh Dispatch*, cited in *Gettysburg Compiler*, May 29, 1894.

10. John Sears, *Sacred Places: American Tourist Attractions in the Nineteenth Century* (New York: Oxford University Press, 1989), pp. 182–208; "Gettysburg Meeting," p. 93.

11. David E. Nye, *Electrifying America: Social Meanings of a New Technology, 1880–1940* (Cambridge: MIT Press, 1990), pp. 85–106; *Philadelphia Times*, August 8, 1893; *New York Sun*, January 27, 1896.

12. *National Tribune*, July 13, 1899; *Baltimore Sun*, June 7, 1896; Colleen McDannell, *Material Christianity: Religion and Popular Culture in America* (New Haven: Yale University Press, 1995), p. 116.

13. *Gettysburg Compiler*, November 18, 1908; William Robbins Journal, May 11, 1903, p. 71, photocopy of original, Gettysburg National Military Park Library (hereafter GNMPL); Donna Braden, *Leisure and Entertainment in America* (Dearborn, Mich.: Henry Ford Museum and Greenfield Village, 1988), p. 297.

14. Gary Tobin, "The Bicycle Boom of the 1890s: The Development of Private Transportation and the Birth of the Modern Tourist," *Journal of Popular Culture* 7 (Spring 1974): 838–45; *Gettysburg Star and Sentinel*, August 13, 1895.

15. *The Battlefield*, June 27, 1896; *Gettysburg Star and Sentinel*, September 12, 1900, June 21, 1898.

16. *Gettysburg Compiler*, May 12, 1896; *Gettysburg Star and Sentinel*, June 15, 1897, July 15, 1897, August 3, 1897, September 27, 1898, June 6, 1899, July 23, 1893, March 11, 1903. The "Bicycle Rules" were printed by the park commissioners on large broadsides, an example of which is filed in the GNMPA clipping file, vol. 2, p. 75.

17. Nasaw, *Going Out*, pp. 34, 40–42, 71–73; Harlan D. Unrau, *Gettysburg: Administrative History* (Washington, D.C.: GPO, 1991), pp. 87–89, 100–101; *Gettysburg Compiler*, April 22, 1890.

18. Judith A. Adams, *The American Amusement Park Industry: A History of Technology and Thrills* (Boston: Twayne Publishers, 1991), pp. 4–6; John Bodnar, *Remaking America: Public Memory, Commemoration, and Patriotism in the Twentieth Century* (Princeton: Princeton University Press, 1992), pp. 32–33; printed notice dated August 14, 1894, in GNMPA clipping file, vol. 1, p. 61.

19. *Adams County News*, June 20, 1914.

20. *Gettysburg Star and Sentinel*, September 23, 1884; *Gettysburg Compiler*, July 29, 1884.

21. *Adams County News*, October 15, 1910, October 23, 1915, September 28, 1912; *Gettysburg Star and Sentinel*, May 31, 1887, November 8, 1887.

22. *Gettysburg Compiler*, June 27, 1887, September 6, 1887; *Gettysburg Star and Sentinel*, June 4, 1895.

23. See Amy Kinsel, "'From These Honored Dead': Gettysburg in American Culture" (Ph.D. diss., Cornell University, 1992), pp. 550–56; David W. Blight, "Quarrel Forgotten or a Revolution Remembered? Reunion and Race in the Memory of the Civil War, 1875–1913," in *Union and Emancipation: Essays on Politics and Race in the Civil War Era*, ed. David W. Blight and Brooks D. Simpson (Kent, Ohio: Kent State University Press, 1997), 151–79.

24. *Gettysburg Star and Sentinel*, June 17, 1880; *The Ledger*, February 11, 1899; Patricia Click, *The Spirit of the Times: Amusements in Nineteenth-Century Baltimore, Norfolk, and Richmond* (Charlottesville: University Press of Virginia, 1989), pp. 82, 102; Leroy

Graham, *Baltimore: The Nineteenth Century Black Capital* (Lanham, Md.: University Press of America, 1982), pp. 280–84.

25. *The Ledger*, May 14, 1898; William Wiggins, *O Freedom! Afro-American Emancipation Celebrations* (Knoxville: University of Tennessee Press, 1987), pp. xi–xix; Grand Army of the Republic, Department of Maryland, *Fifteenth Annual Encampment of the Department of Maryland, Grand Army of the Republic, Baltimore, February 18 and 19, 1891* (Baltimore: Shane and Company, 1891), p. 23.

26. *Northern Whig* cited in *Gettysburg Star and Sentinel*, November 24, 1885; J. Matthew Gallman and Susan Baker, "Gettysburg's Gettysburg: What the Battle Did to the Borough," in *The Gettysburg Nobody Knows*, ed. Gabor S. Boritt (New York: Oxford University Press, 1997), p. 167; *Gettysburg Star and Sentinel* August 15, 1899, September 5, 1899, July 22, 1903; Nasaw, *Going Out*, pp. 74–78, 92–93.

27. *The Ledger*, April 23, 1898, July 22, 1899, July 15, 1899, August 20, 1898; *Afro-American*, August 10, 1895; *Afro-American Ledger*, July 20, 1912.

28. *Gettysburg Compiler*, September 16, 1902, quoting the *Baltimore Sun*; *Gettysburg Star and Sentinel.*, September 16, 1903; *Afro-American Ledger*, September 19, 1903, July 30, 1904.

29. *Adams County News*, September 18, 1909, July 11, 1914, September 17, 1910, September 18, 1915; *Gettysburg Star and Sentinel*, September 10, 1913, September 14, 1914.

30. *Adams County News*, September 12, 1914, September 16, 1916; *The Ledger*, September 17, 1898; *Afro-American Ledger*, September 2, 1916.

31. Wiggins, *O Freedom!* pp. 25–34; Stephen Nissenbaum, *The Battle for Christmas* (New York: Alfred A. Knopf, 1997), pp. 264–85; Frederick Douglass, *Narrative of the Life of Frederick Douglass, an American Slave: Written by Himself* (New York: Signet, 1968), p. 85.

32. *Afro-American Ledger*, September 2, 1916.

33. *The Ledger*, August 20, 1898, September 17, 1898; *Afro-American Ledger*, June 27, 1914; Nasaw, *Going Out*, pp. 54–56, 238.

34. J. M. Hood, General Manager, Western Maryland Railroad, to Hugh D. Scott, Superintendent of the Baltimore and Harrisbirg Division, July 17, 1894, published in full in the *Gettysburg Compiler*, July 31, 1894.

35. Edgar Allan to E. P. Reeve, June 27 [1888], Edward Payson Reeve Papers, 1852–1948, Southern Historical Collection, University of North Carolina, microfilm; George Washington Ward, *History of the Excursion of the Fifteenth Massachusetts Regiment and Its Friends to the Battlefields of Gettysburg, Antietam, Ball's Bluff, and the City of Washington, D.C., September 14–20, 1900* (Worcester, Mass.: Excursion Committee, 1901), p. 15; *National Tribune*, June 29, 1899; Grand Army of the Republic, Department of Pennsylvania, *Proceedings of the Thirty-Eighth Semi-Annual Encampment, Department of Pennsylvania, June 8 and 9, 1904* (n.p.: n.p., 1882), p. 57; Charles Reagan Wilson, *Baptized in Blood* (Athens: University of Georgia Press, 1980), p. 30.

36. DeWitt Spencer Certificate, RG 15, Cert. 359, 048, National Archives and Records Administration; *Grand Army Review* 2 (November, 1886): 301; Stuart MConnell, *Glorious Contentment: The Grand Army of the Republic, 1865–1900* (Chapel Hill: University of North Carolina Press, 1992), pp. 168–69; 208–9; *Gettysburg Star and Sentinel*, June 7, 1905.

37. *New York Herald*, July 3, 1888; John Tregaskis, *Souvenir of the Re-Union of the Blue and the Gray, on the Battlefield of Gettysburg, July 1, 2, 3 and 4, 1888* (New York: American Graphic Company, 1888), p. 48.

38. Count of Paris et al. "Gettysburg Thirty Years After," 258; John Waller to Ziba Roberts, May 30, 1912, Schoff Civil War Collection, William Clements Library, University of Michigan; Linderman, *Embattled Courage*, pp. 279–89; "The Old Camp-Ground," *Grand Army Review* 2 (August 1886): 241.

39. Thomas Bell, "Gettysburg, 1886," *Grand Army Review* 2 (August 1886): 240–41; *Gettysburg Star and Sentinel*, June 15, 1886; *National Tribune*, June 29, 1899; Robert Beecham, *As If It Were Glory: Robert Beecham's Civil War from the Iron Brigade to the Black Regiments*, ed. Michael E. Stevens (Madison, Wisc.: Madison House, 1998), p. 113.

40. Broadside of the Association of the First Army Corps, "Reunion of Northern and Southern Armies, July 1–3, 1888," Albert VanDeusen Papers, 1881–1900, Duke University Special Collections; *Grand Army Scout and Soldiers' Mail* 2 (August 18, 1883): 4; John R. Brooke to Francis A. Walker, March 18, 1886, Civil War Officers Collection, Civil War Library and Museum, Philadelphia; W. A. Hemphill in *Atlanta Constitution*, August 21, 1898.

41. Winfield S. Hancock to Francis A. Walker, December 12, 1885, Collection of ALS and DS Civil War Officers; *Gettysburg Star and Sentinel*, October 13, 1885; "On to Gettysburg," *Grand Army Review* 4 (October 1888): 939.

42. *New York Times*, July 2, 1888; Elsie Dorothea Tibbetts, *From Maine to Gettysburg, 1863–1913* (Bangor, Maine: Bangor Cooperative Printing Company, 1913), p. 103; *Gettysburg Star and Sentinel*, May 13, 1903; *New York Herald*, July 4, 1888.

43. Tibbets, *From Maine to Gettysburg*, p. 103; Susan Stewart, *On Longing: Narratives of the Miniature, the Gigantic, the Souvenir, the Collection* (Baltimore: Johns Hopkins University Press, 1984), p. 135.

44. *New York Times*, June 30, 1888; *Gettysburg Compiler*, July 14, 1885; William M. Robbins Journal, June 23, 1898, photocopy of original in Southern Historical Collection, University of North Carolina, in GNMPL.

45. *Gettysburg Star and Sentinel*, August 3, 1881; Abner Doubleday to John Bachelder, November 25, 1885, *Bachelder Papers*, 2:1151.

46. *Gettysburg Star and Sentinel*, July 26, 1882, August 2, 1882, July 7, 1885, August 18, 1885, July 10, 1888; *Gettysburg Compiler*, August 2, 1882, July 10, 1888; *Grand Army Scout and Soldier's Mail* 3 (August 23, 1884): 4; *Gettysburg Compiler*, July 8, 1922.

47. *Gettysburg Compiler*, June 29, 1886, August 16, 1877; *Gettysburg Star and Sentinel*, June 20, 1878, August 29, 1883, July 10, 1894.

48. *Gettysburg Compiler*, October 25, 1898; *Gettysburg Star and Sentinel*, October 10, 1899, October 10, 1900; *Gettysburg Times*, July 5, 1938; Grand Army of the Republic, Department of Pennsylvania, *Proceedings of the Thirty-Third Encampment*, p. 227.

49. Grand Army of the Republic, Department of Pennsylvania, *Proceedings of the Thirty-second Encampment*, p. 226; John W. Frazier, *Gettysburg, 1887 and 1906: Reunion of the Blue and Gray, Philadelphia Brigade and Pickett's Division . . .* (Philadelphia: Ware Brothers Printers, 1906), p. 86; *New York Times*, July 2, 1888.

50. *London Times* cited in *Gettysburg Compiler*, July 17, 1888; John Barnett Gardner to John Badger Bachelder, February 17, 1890, *Bachelder Papers* 3:1694–695; *Richmond Times-Dispatch*, July 2, 1913.

51. Linderman, *Embattled Courage*, pp. 278–79; Linenthal, *Sacred Ground*, p. 94; Blight, *Race and Reunion*, p. 189.

52. Indiana, Fiftieth Anniversary Commission Report, *Indiana at the Fiftieth Anniversary of the Battle of Gettysburg* (n.p.: n.p., 1913) p. 37; W. W. Goldsborough in *Gettysburg*

Compiler, October 2, 1900; *Gettysburg Compiler*, July 12, 1887; *Boston Journal*, June 14, 1889.

53. *Gettysburg Compiler*, June 20, 1893. While Stuart McConnell in *Glorious Contentment* terms these group names "a reference to the practice of foraging in Sherman's Army," it is more likely they imitated the antimilitia clubs of Philadelphia, considering their point of origin and the fact that only a few Pennsylvania regiments served in the western theatre (p. 48).

54. Gary Cross, *A Social History of Leisure since 1600* (State College, Penn.: Venture Publishing, 1990), pp. 20–24; Susan G. Davis, *Parades and Power: Street Theatre in Nineteenth-Century Philadelphia* (Philadelphia: Temple University Press, 1986), 36–38, 77–109; McConnell, *Glorious Contentment*, pp. 46–48; Bell Irvin Wiley, *The Life of Billy Yank: The Common Soldier of the Civil War* (New York: Charter Books, 1952), pp. 173–74.

55. Grand Army of the Republic, Department of Pennsylvania, *Proceedings of the Thirty-Fifth Encampment . . . 1884*, pp. 244, 239; *Gettysburg Star and Sentinel*, July 27, 1881, July 12, 1887, June 26, 1894; *Gettysburg Compiler*, July 12, 1887, July 5, 1892, June 20, 1893, July 18, 1893.

56. *Gettysburg Star and Sentinel*, August 1, 1878, August 2, 1882; Grand Army of the Republic, Department of Pennsylvania, *Proceedings of the Twenty-Eighth Encampment . . . 1880*, p. 160; *Gettysburg Star and Sentinel*, August 2, 1882; *Proceedings of the Thirty-Second Encampment . . . 1882*, p. 211; *Gettysburg Compiler*, August 2, 1882.

57. Grand Army of the Republic, Department of Pennsylvania, *Proceedings of the Twenty-Eighth Encampment . . . 1880*, p. 163; Grand Army of the Republic, Department of Pennsylvania, *Proceedings of the Thirty-Second Encampment . . . 1882*, p. 210; Davis, *Parades and Power*, pp. 106–9.

58. John Urry, *Consuming Places* (New York: Routledge, 1995), pp. 132–33; photocopy of anonymous handwritten fourteen-page travelogue of author's five-day visit to Gettysburg, beginning with the date July 12, 1889, GNMPA Early Visitation folder; W. A. Hemphill in the *Atlanta Constitution*, August 21, 1898; Orvey S. Barrett to John B. Bachelder, July 8, 1889, *Bachelder Papers* 3:1606–7.

59. *New York Times*, May 14, 1882; "War's Awful Din," newspaper clipping pasted inside cyclorama brochure from Philadelphia exhibition, n.d., pamphlet collection, Civil War Library and Museum, Philadelphia; *Grand Army Review* (November 1886): 2.

60. John Gibbon to Henry Hunt, Omaha, Nebraska, September 6, 1884, March 6, 1885, Henry Hunt Papers, Gilder-Lehrman Collection; Pierpont Morgan Library, New York, N.Y.

61. *Gettysburg Star and Sentinel*, April 2, 1895; *Confederate Veteran* 5 (June 1897): 307; A. K. Storrie in *Grand Army Scout and Soldier's Mail* 5 (March 6, 1886): 8; Helen Minshall Young, "Comrades at Gettysburg," *Gettysburg Star and Sentinel*, July 10, 1913; *Grand Army Review* 2 (May 1887): 459; Frank Moran, "About Gettysburg," *National Tribune*, November 12, 1891.

62. *Grand Army Scout and Soldier's Mail*, March 6, 1886; *Boston Daily Transcript*, December 30, 1884; *Boston Evening Telegraph*, March 14, 1901.

63. E. L. Godkin, *Reflections and Comments* (New York: Charles Scribner's Sons, 1895), pp. 201, 204; Charles T. Congdon, "Over-Illustration," *North American Review* 139 (November 1884): 480–91; "A Growl for the Unpicturesque," *Atlantic Monthly* 98 (July 1906): 140–43; "Over-Illustration," *Harper's Weekly* 55 (July 29, 1911): 6; "Report of Major Charles Reed on the Conditions at Camp Colt, July 13, 1918," in Letters to

the Surgeon General's Office 1917 to 1927, RG 112, Box 12, National Archives and Records Administration, Washington, D.C., cited in Gary Adelman and Timothy Smith, *Devil's Den: A History and Guide* (Gettysburg: Thomas Publications, 1997), p. 150.

Chapter Five: "These Are Touring Days": Mass Culture Transforms Gettysburg

1. *Gettysburg Compiler*, November 5, 1913.

2. John Jakle, *The Tourist: Travel in Twentieth-Century North America* (Lincoln: University of Nebraska Press, 1985), pp. 120–21, 125–27; *Adams County News*, April 16, 1914.

3. Robert Bruce, *Gettysburg* (New York: American Automobile Association, 1920), p. 25; *Gettysburg Compiler*, August 16, 1911, June 24, 1916.

4. Gary Cross and Rick Szostak, *Technology and American Society: A History* (Englewood Cliffs, N.J.: Prentice-Hall, 1995), pp. 233–36; James J. Flink, *The Car Culture* (Cambridge: MIT Press, 1975), pp. 7–8; Harlan D. Unrau, *Gettysburg: Administrative History* (Washington, D.C.: GPO, 1991), pp. 150, 278.

5. Wallace Nutting, *Wallace Nutting's Autobiography* (Framingham, Mass.: The Author, 1936) pp. 124–25; Michael Kammen, *Mystic Chords of Memory: The Transformation of Tradition in American Culture* (New York: Alfred A. Knopf, 1991), pp. 261–62, 300.

6. Kammen, *Mystic Chords of Memory*, pp. 338–39; *Gettysburg Times*, December 3, 1919; *Gettysburg Star and Sentinel*, July 8, 1908; *Washington Post*, July 7, 1908; Merrill D. Peterson, *Lincoln in American Memory* (New York: Oxford University Press, 1994), pp. 206–8; George C. Diehl, chair of the National Good Roads Board, in *Gettysburg Star and Sentinel*, September 13, 1911.

7. *Gettysburg Compiler*, September 11, 1921; *Gettysburg Times*, March 10, 1925, April 24, 1948.

8. *New York Herald Tribune*, April 3, 1941, April 20, 1941.

9. Richard Butsch, "Introduction: Leisure and Hegemony in America," in *For Fun and Profit: The Transformation of Leisure into Consumption*, ed. Richard Butsch (Philadelphia: Temple University Press, 1990) p. 15; Kammen, *Mystic Chords of Memory*, pp. 310–16, 342–46, 351–70.

10. Harlan Unrau and G. Frank Willis, "To Preserve the Nation's Past: The Growth of Historic Preservation in the National Park Service during the 1930s," *Public Historian* 9 (Spring 1987): 19–22; John Bodnar, *Remaking America: Public Memory, Commemoration, and Patriotism in the Twentieth Century* (Princeton: Princeton University Press, 1992), pp. 169–73; 175–79; Barry Mackintosh, "The National Park Service Moves into Historical Interpretation," *Public Historian* 9 (Spring 1987): 51–54.

11. Verne Chatelain [First NPS Chief Historian], "History and Our National Parks" [June 1935], cited in Unrau and Willis, "To Preserve the Nation's Past," p. 22; Mackintosh, "The National Park Service," pp. 51–52.

12. McCleary, "What Shall the Lincoln Memorial Be?" *Review of Reviews* 38 (September 1908): 339; "Memorandum of the Proposed Transfer of Military Parks and Monuments for the Use of the Director in Connection with the Superintendents' Conference as Required by His Memorandum of March 5, 1932," cited in Unrau, *Administrative*

History, p. 141; Frederick Tilberg, "Museum Prospectus," January 23, 1947, Gettysburg National Military Park Archive (hereafter cited as GNMPA), folder 18–27.

13. Department of the Interior, National Park Service, "Annual Report for the Gettysburg National Military Park, Year Ending September 30, 1934," RG 79, E 411, Box 2493, National Archives and Records Administration (hereafter cited as NARA), p. 32; Department of the Interior, National Park Service, Gettysburg National Military Park, "Superintendent's Annual Report for the Year 1935–1936," by James R. McConaughie, RG 79, E 411, Box 2493, NARA, p. 46.

14. Unrau, *Administrative History*, pp. 154–59, 187; *Gettysburg Star and Sentinel*, November 17, 1934, *Gettysburg Compiler*, November 17, 1934; June 29, 1935; *Gettysburg Times*, August 1933, Gettysburg National Military Park Archive (hereafter cited as GNMPA) clipping file, vol. 9, p. 15.

15. Unrau, *Administrative History*, pp. 245–46, 277–81; "Memorandum of Superintendent, January 3, 1941, to Director, National Park Service," RG 79, E 411, Box 39, General Correspondence File, NARA; Park Superintendent Jerry Schober in *Richmond News Leader*, September 13, 1971; J. Walter Coleman quoted in the *Gettysburg Times*, February 27, 1946.

16. Department of the Interior, National Park Service, Gettysburg National Military Park, *Draft General Management Plan and Environmental Impact Statement* (Gettysburg: Gettysburg National Military Park, 1998), pp. xxiv–xxvi; Gettysburg National Military Park Commission, "Annual Report of the Gettysburg National Military Park Commission to the Secretary of War, 1904," in *Annual Reports of the Gettysburg National Military Park Commission to the Secretary of War, 1893–1904* (Washington, D.C.: GPO, 1905), p. 99.

17. Unrau, *Administrative History*, pp. 113, 134–35, 193, 273; Frederick W. Hawthorne, *A Peculiar Institution: A History of the Gettysburg Licensed Battlefield Guides* (Gettysburg: Association of Licensed Battlefield Guides, 1991), pp. 27–48; *Adams County News*, August 22, 1914; *Gettysburg Times*, August 6, 1921; "Annual Report of the Gettysburg National Military Park Commission to the Secretary of War, 1914," quoted in *Gettysburg Times*, September 30, 1913; *Gettysburg Times*, April 27, 1946; *Gettysburg Star and Sentinel*, August 16, 1941, June 22, 1946.

18. Unrau, *Administrative History*, pp. 150, 193; *Gettysburg Compiler*, August 22, 1936.

19. "Statement for National Battlefield Parks," Memorandum of Acting Director Oliver G. Taylor, September 3, 1943, Gettysburg National Military Park Library (hereafter cited as GNMPL) vertical file; Unrau, *Administrative History*, p. 150.

20. Colonel W. R. Gibson to H. Gerow, September 26, 1929, cited in Unrau, *Administrative History*, p. 129.

21. *Gettysburg Compiler*, November 9, 1935; *Gettysburg Star and Sentinel*, August 8, 1936; Roy Appleman to Regional Director, November 4, 1946, RG 79, E 411, Box 47, Folder 620–46, NARA; Superintendent James Coleman to Regional Director Thomas Allen, October 16, 1942, GNMPL vertical file, Prospectus 1940–60; Unrau, *Administrative History*, pp. 223, 275–76; Memo from Superintendent, GNMP, to Director, National Park Service, February 6, 1957, GNMPA, Folder 18–39; *Gettysburg Times*, July 8, 1957.

22. *Gettysburg Times*, April 4, 1942; "Memorandum of Agreement," July 22, 1941, among the U.S. Department of the Interior, Jeremiah Hoover of Newark, New Jersey, and the Gettysburg Water Company, cited in Unrau, *Administrative History*, p. 211. The agreement could not be accepted by the federal government until 1942 due to legal

technicalities. Acting Secretary of the Interior Abe Fortas designated the Gettysburg cyclorama a "national historic object" in 1944 (pp. 246–47).

23. Memo to Acting Regional Director, Region I, from Hillory Tolson, Acting Director, National Park Service, November 4, 1942, RG 79, E 411, Box 39, General Correspondence file; Memo from NPS Regional Historian Roy Appleman, November 4, 1946, RG 79, E 411, Box 47, Folder 620–46.

24. Robert Bloom, *A History of Adams County, Pennsylvania, 1700–1990* (Gettysburg: Adams County Historical Society, 1992), p. 399; Kammen, *Mystic Chords of Memory*, pp. 609–11; Unrau, *Administrative History*, pp. 253–54; Memo from Acting Regional Director George Palmer to Superintendent, Gettysburg National Military Park, September 21, 1961, RG 79, E411, Box 7, Folder D-22, NARA.

25. Memo to Superintendent, GNMP, from Fred T. Johnson, Acting Regional Director, NPS, October 14, 1942, GNMPL vertical file, Visitor Prospectus Folder 11–45; John W. Stepp. "A New Look for Gettysburg," *Washington Star Sunday Magazine*, February 11, 1962; Sarah Allaback, *Bulletin* (*Cultural Resources Management Bulletin*, National Park Service) "The Mission 66 Visitor Center," CRM 22, 9 (1999): 21.

26. Neutra's quote is taken from a 1959 speech he made in Gettysburg as reported in the *Gettysburg Times*, December 18, 1959; "Gettysburg National Military Park Visitors' Center to Be Dedicated," Press Release, National Park Service, November 18, 1962, RG 79, E 411, Box 5, Folder A-8215, NARA; "Reinterpretation," Memorandum from NPS Regional Director, Northeast Region, to Superintendents, June 1, 1964, GNMPA, Frank Barnes Folder.

27. Coleman quoted in the *Gettysburg Times*, April 9, 1941.

28. Unrau, *Administrative History, 154–59*. The Park Service launched a public relations program in 1941 and by the late 1940s offered public relations workshops for employees (p. 238).

29. *Adams County News*, August 22, 1914.

30. Jakle, *The Tourist*, pp. 122–25; *Gettysburg Times*, January 29, 1925; Lincoln Highway Association, *The Complete Official Road Guide of the Lincoln Highway*, 3rd ed. (Detroit: The Association, 1917); American Automobile Association, *Official Automobile Blue Book*, vol. 3, *New York, Pennsylvania, New Jersey, Maryland, and the District of Columbia* (New York: Automobile Blue Book Publishing Company, 1918), p. 523; Robert Bruce, *Gettysburg for the Motorist* (New York: Automobile Club of America, 1919), p. 1; Robert Bruce, *Gettysburg* (New York: American Automobile Association, 1920).

31. Frank Thompson, "A Moving Picture: The Original Gettysburg Movie," *Civil War Times Illustrated* 35 (April 1996): 57–61; *Moving Picture World* cited in Thompson, p. 60; "The Battle of Gettysburg," broadside, GNMPA clipping file, vol. 7, p. 173.

32. Eileen Bowser, ed., *The Transformation of Cinema, 1907–1915* (New York: Charles Scribner's Sons, 1990), vol. 2, *History of American Cinema*, ed. Charles Harpole, pp. 177–78; *San Francisco Examiner*, July 2, 1913; Neal Gabler, *An Empire of Their Own: How the Jews Invented Hollywood* (New York: Crown Publishers, 1988), pp. 24–28, 48.

33. *Adams County News*, May 30, 1914, March 27, 1915, March 11, 1916, Neil Harris, *Cultural Excursions: Marketing Appetites and Cultural Tastes in Modern America* (Chicago: University of Chicago Press, 1990), p. 186; *Minneapolis Sunday Tribune*, June 23, 1957.

34. Kammen, *Mystic Chords of Memory*, pp. 460–62, 509; *Gettysburg Compiler*, May 11, 1935; Warren Susman, "The Thirties," in *The Development of an American Culture,*

2nd ed., ed. Stanley Coben and Lormar Ratner (New York: St. Martin's Press, 1983), pp. 226–27; Kenneth Bindas, "The Genesis of a New American Opera: Gettysburg, the Federal Music Project and Nationalism," *Mid-America: An Historical Review* 69 (Spring 1987): 71–85; *Richmond Times-Dispatch*, July 5, 1938.

35. Superintedent, GNMP, to Regional Director, NE Region, May 9, 1945, RG 79, Box 47, Folder 620–46, NARA; Catherine Clinton, "Gone with the Wind," in *Past Imperfect: History According to the Movies*, ed. Mark C. Carnes (New York: Henry Holt, 1995), p. 132; Bernard DeVoto, "Fiction and the Everlasting If," *Harper's* 177 (June 1938): 43; Robert Bloom, "The Battle of Gettysburg in Fiction," *Pennsylvania History* 43 (January 1976): 311, 327.

36. Michael Kammen, *American Culture, American Tastes: Social Change and the Twentieth Century* (New York: Alfred A. Knopf, 1999), p. 168; Steven Watts, *The Magic Kingdom: Walt Disney and the American Way of Life* (Boston: Houghton Mifflin, 1997), p. 323; *Saturday Evening Post* 231 (June 27, 1959): 56–57; 232 (May 14, 1960): 60–61; 233 (August 13, 1960): 50.

37. Zora Unkovich, "Take the Family to Gettysburg," *Pittsburgh Sun-Telegraph*, June 7, 1959; Philip Van Doren Stern, "Gettysburg," *Holiday* 11 (June 1952): 141; Phil Hamburger, "Notes for a Gazeteer," *New Yorker* 40 (April 4, 1964): 83; Philip Reaves, "The Shrine of Gettysburg," *Good Housekeeping* 171 (July 1970): 126.

38. *Gettysburg Star and Sentinel*, July 8, 1903; *Gettysburg Compiler*, August 3, 1910, May 19, 1917, *Adams County News*, September 6, 1913.

39. *Gettysburg Times*, January 5, 1921, July 26, 1911; *Canonsburg Daily Notes*, September 4, 1915, GNMPA clipping file, vol. 6, pp. 167–69.

40. *Gettysburg Times*, May 10, 1922, October 31, 1924, February 10, 1926; *Gettysburg Star and Sentinel*, August 3, 1935.

41. *Gettysburg Times*, October 27, 1925. According to Unrau, *Administrative History* tourist numbers dropped nearly 75 percent, from 727,395 in 1928–29 to 195,696 by 1933–34 (p. 150).

42. Bloom, *A History of Adams County*, pp. 395, 403; *Gettysburg Times*, January 15, 1926, April 3, 1948; "Gettysburg: The Heart of the New America" (Gettysburg: Gettysburg Chamber of Commerce, [1925]), Map Collection, Newberry Library, Chicago.

43. *Gettysburg Times*, January 26, 1925, January 15, 1926; "Gettysburg Is the Mecca of Thousands of Tourists Annually," and "Greater Gettysburg Area: Where History Comes Alive" [1967?], both pamphlets in Folder 150, "Tourism," Adams County Historical Society (hereafter cited as ACHS).

44. *Gettysburg Times*, January 15, 1926, February 15, 1926, May 1933, GNMPA clipping file, vol. 9, p. 12, June 23, 1938, June 28, 1938; July 5, 1938; *Philadelphia Inquirer*, July 3, 1938, July 5, 1938. Beginning with the Virginia monument in 1917, many Southern states erected monuments to their troops in subsequent decades.

45. *Gettysburg Times*, June 28, 1938; Kammen, *Mystic Chords of Memory*, pp. 460–62; John S. Patterson, "From Battle Ground to Pleasure Ground: Gettysburg as a Historic Site," in *History Museums in the United States*, ed. Warren Leon and Roy Rosenzweig (Urbana: University of Illinois Press, 1989), p. 140.

46. *Gettysburg Times*, November 11, 1925; Bloom, *History of Adams County*, pp. 394–95; Kathleen Georg, "Longstreet's Headquarters Reexamined," Research Report, GNMP, February 19, 1981, GNMPL vertical file, Folder 1–27; *Gettysburg Times*, March 24, 1987. These structures included Lee's Headquarters, the room where Lincoln "wrote" the Gettysburg Address, and the Dobbin House.

47. *Gettysburg Times*, June 28, 1938, July 1, 1939, August 19, 1977.

48. *Harrisburg Sunday Patriot News*, December 23, 1984; *Harrisburg Sunday News*, June 21, 1989; *Harrisburg Evening News*, November 18, 1970.

49. *The Harrisburg Sunday News* June 21, 1989; Cross and Szostak, *Technology and American Society*, p. 270; Karal Ann Marling, *As Seen on TV: The Visual Culture of Everyday Life in the 1950s* (Cambridge: Harvard University Press, 1994), pp. 5–6, 112–26.

50. Unrau, *Administrative History*, pp. 263–64; Kammen, *Mystic Chords of Memory*, pp. 534, 608; Memo from Superintendent, GNMP, to Regional Director, Region 5, August 26, 1961, RG 79, E 411, Box 9, Folder A-8215, NARA; "Greater Gettysburg," p. 6; *Gettysburg Times*, June 5, 1963; "Report on Centennial Activities at Gettysburg," Kittridge Wing, Superintendent, to Regional Director, NE Region, July 5, 1963, RG 79, E 411, Box 4, Folder A-8215, NARA.

51. *Gettysburg Times*, July 2, 1941; Memorandum from J. Walter Coleman, Superintendent, to Director, NPS, August 9, 1941, RG 79, E 411, Box 39, General Correspondence Folder, NARA; *Gettysburg Times*, May 17, 1945. Helen Longstreet's memorial project failed, but another plan to memorialize the general succeeded in the 1990s.

52. Gettysburg Centennial Commission news releases, May 22, June 4, June 25, 1963, RG 79, E 411, Box 4, Folder A-8215, NARA.

53. "Greater Gettysburg," p. 6; *Gettysburg Times*, January 7, 1960; *Harrisburg Sunday Patriot-News*, July 15, 1990.

54. *Gettysburg Times*, January 19, 1996; *Harrisburg Sunday Patriot-News*, December 23, 1984; "Jennie Wade Museum," ACHS, Folder 145; *Grit*, August 25, 1974.

55. "Help Stop This . . . and Preserve This at Gettysburg" [photocopy of 12-panel brochure] (Gettysburg: Gettysburg Battlefield Preservation Association, [1959?]), Newberry Library, Chicago; *Gettysburg Times*, September 14, 1959, November 23, 1959, December 21, 1959.

56. Stephen S. Fehr, "A Study of the Economic Impact of the Gettysburg National Military Park and Tourism on the Gettysburg Area" (Harrisburg: Pennsylvania Department of Community Affairs, 1975), pp. xiv, 137–41; Bloom, *A History of Adams County*, pp. 397–99.

57. *Harrisburg Sunday Patriot-News*, June 10, 1973; *National Observer*, September 6, 1971; *Richmond News Leader*, September 13, 1971; *Philadelphia Inquirer*, July 30, 1971; *Gettysburg Times*, July 25, 1972.

58. "When Washington Moves to Gettysburg," *U.S. News and World Report* 39 (October 14, 1955): 22–24; "Little White House," *Newsweek* 46 (November 21, 1955): 28–29.

59. "The White House Moves to Gettysburg," *U.S. News and World Report* 39 (November 25, 1955): 58, 60; "Ike Comes to Town: And What's Happening to Gettysburg," *Newsweek* 46 (July 11, 1955): 21–25; "When Washington Moves to Gettysburg," *U.S. News and World Report* 39 (October 14, 1955): 24; "New Battle of Gettysburg," *Time* 69 (May 20, 1957): 28; "About the Battle," *Time* 78 (September 22, 1961): 26; Rowland Moriarty and Frederick McCord, "Ike, Mamie and the Neighbors," *Saturday Evening Post* 229 (November 3, 1956): 114.

60. Thomas Hine, *Populuxe* (New York: MJF Books, 1986), pp. 6–8.

61. *Gettysburg Times*, July 8, 1946; Wat Arnold, Radio Script [July 1947], Wat Arnold Papers, 1947–48, Western Historical Manuscript Collection, University of Mis-

souri, Columbia: Bruce Catton, "Gettysburg: Place of Limitless Vistas," *New York Times Magazine* (December 11, 1955): 71.

62. Catton, "Gettysburg," pp. 9, 71.

Chapter Six: "Dad Got Us There in a Day": Automobiles and Family Touring

1. James R. Murphy to National Park Service, Washington, D.C., June 25, 1964, RG 79, E 414, Box 1, Folder 3415, National Archives and Records Administration (herafter cited as NARA).

2. Harlan D. Unrau, *Gettysburg: Administrative History* (Washington, D.C.: GPO, 1991), p. 278; *Gettysburg Times*, January 7, 1970; Robert Bloom, *A History of Adams County, Pennsylvania, 1700–1990* (Gettysburg: Adams County Historical Society), p. 399.

3. John A. Jakle, *The Tourist: Travel in Twentieth-Century North America* (Lincoln: University of Nebraska Press, 1985), pp. 121, 146–49.

4. Warren J. Belasco, *Americans on the Road: From Autocamp to Motel, 1910–1945* (Cambridge: MIT Press, 1979), pp. 20–24, 30–39.

5. Woodrow Wilson quoted in Jakle, *The Tourist*, p. 102; John P. Nicholson to the Secretary of War, March 3, 1904, RG 92, E 11, Box 1, General Correspondence File, NARA; *Gettysburg Compiler*, March 13, 1912.

6. Unrau, *Administrative History*, pp. 91–93, 101; James J. Flink, *The Car Culture* (Cambridge: MIT Press, 1975), pp. 156, 7–8.

7. Gettysburg National Park Commission, *Annual Report of the Gettysburg National Park Commission to the Secretary of War, 1905* (Washington, D.C.: GPO, 1905), pp. 5–6; *Jenkintown Times-Chronicle*, July 2, 1913, Gettysburg National Military Park Archive (hereafter cited as GNMPA) clipping file, vol. 7, p. 96; *Gettysburg Times*, March 5, 1945; *Gettysburg Compiler*, August 7, 1907, March 30, 1904; *Gettysburg Star and Sentinel*, June 6, 1906.

8. *Gettysburg Times* [1916?], GNMPA clipping file, vol. 7, p. 240; *Gettysburg Times* [1914?], GNMPA clipping file, vol. 7, pp. 152, 224; a number of undated squibs from different newspapers in volume 7 concern speeding in the park. *Gettysburg Compiler*, September 25, 1907; *Gettysburg Times*, April 1933, May 1933, GNMPA clipping file, vol. 9, p. 6; U.S. National Park Service, Gettysburg National Military Park, *Superintendent's Annual Report for the Year 1934–1935*, pp. 6–10.

9. *Gettysburg Compiler*, April 1, 1902; *Adams County News*, May 16, 1916; Gettysburg National Park Commission, *Annual Report of the Gettysburg National Park Commission to the Secretary of War, 1905*, pp. 5–6; *Gettysburg Times*, August 6, 1921, July 15, 1922.

10. *Adams County News*, July 6, 1912; September 11, 1915; *Gettysburg Times*, July 6, 1921; *Gettysburg Times*, August 8, 1922; July 18, 1922; "Gettysburg" brochure published by George Buohl, service station owner, ca. 1925, Adams County Historical Society (hereafter cited as ACHS) folder 150, Tourism; Jakle, *The Tourist*, pp. 146–49, 152–56; John A. Jakle, Keith A. Sculle, and Jefferson S. Rogers, *The Motel in America* (Baltimore: Johns Hopkins University Press, 1996), pp. 31–39.

11. Belasco, *Americans on the Road*, pp. 86–87; postcard from "Mrs. Brower" to Mrs. J. E. Hagey, Henrietta, Pennsylvania, September 16, 1916, author's collection.

12. Pierce Furber, "Gettysburg," journal account of a trip to Gettysburg, May 30–31, 1930, 11 leaves, photocopy of original owned by Frances Furber.

13. *Adams County News*, September 6, 1913; *Gettysburg Compiler*, June 24, 1916; September 12, 1936; *Gettysburg Times*, October 9, 1924.

14. *Adams County News*, March 3, 1916, July 1, 1916, August 11, 1916, Sepetember 9, 1916; Belasco, *Americans on the Road*, pp. 16–17, 28–29.

15. Belasco, *Americans on the Road*, pp. 30–34; *Adams County News*, August 5, 1916; George Stevens and James Larmer, *Transcontinental Trip in a Ford* (Detroit: Joseph Mack Printing House, 1915).

16. David Gregg McIntosh, "A Ride on Horseback In the Summer of 1910 Over Some of the Battlefields of the Great Civil War with Some Notes of the Battles," [1910?], Travel Manuscripts, p. 115, Virginia Historical Society.

17. David Glassberg, "Monuments and Memories," *American Quarterly* 43 (March 1991): 146; Louise Hale, "We Discover the Old Dominion," *Harper's Magazine* 33 (August 1916): 406; Colonel W. R. Gibson to H. Gerow, September 26, 1929, cited in Unrau, *Administrative History*, p. 129.

18. *Canonsburg Daily Notes*, April 4, 1915, GNMPA clipping file, vol. 6, pp. 167–69; Axel Axelson, "Visiting Old Battle Fields," *Confederate Veteran* 34 (November 1926): 416; Memorandum from Regional Historian Roy Appleman to Regional Director, November 4, 1946, RG 79, E 411, Box 47, Folder 620–46, NARA.

19. *Gettysburg Star and Sentinel*, October 8, 1946; Unrau, *Administrative History*, p. 181.

20. Loren Baritz, *The Good Life: The Meaning of Success for the American Middle Class* (New York: Harper and Row, 1982), pp. 76–82; Gary Cross, *A Social History of Leisure since 1600* (State College, Penn.: Venture Publishing, 1990), pp. 179–80; Warren Susman, "The Thirties," in *The Development of an American Culture*, ed. Stanley Coben and Lormar Ratner (New York: St. Martin's Press, 1983), pp. 190–191.

21. Flink, *Car Culture*, pp. 156–58; Elizabeth D. Sergeant, phone interview with author, April 26, 1998; *Harrisburg Evening Telegraph* [1933?], GNMPA, vol. 9, p. 8; *Gettysburg Times*, June 13, 1938.

22. Michael Kammen, *Mystic Chords of Memory: The Transformation of Tradition in American Culture* (New York: Alfred A. Knopf, 1991), pp. 338–40, 460–62; Jakle, *The Tourist*, pp. 286–289, 300; Robert Littell, "Ghosts Speak at Gettysburg," *Reader's Digest* 33 (July 1938): 54.

23. Jakle, Sculle, and Rogers, *The Motel in America*, pp. 23, 31–39; Bloom, *A History of Adams County*, pp. 394–95; *Gettysburg Times*, February 18, 1930, May 27, 1938; *Gettysburg Star and Sentinel*, May 19, 1945.

24. Belasco, *Americans on the Road*, p. 33; Brown, *Inventing New England*, pp. 209–10.

25. William E. Leuchtenburg, *A Troubled Feast: American Society since 1945*, updated ed. (Boston: Little, Brown and Company, 1983), pp. 4–6, 39–40, 58–59, 62–63; "The Good Life," *Life* 47 (December 28, 1959): 62; Elaine Tyler May, *Homeward Bound: American Families in the Cold War Era* (New York: Basic Books, 1988), pp. 25–26, 165–70.

26. Cross, *A Social History of Leisure*, pp. 191–94; Otis Wiese, "Live the Life of McCall's," *McCall's* 82 (May 1954), p. 27. By the mid-1960s, 95 percent of American homes had a television, as compared with less than 10 percent in 1950. In 1959, thirty-two Westerns were offered by the networks to viewers on the suburban frontier (Cross, *A Social History of Leisure*, p. 270).

27. Leuchtenburg, *A Troubled Feast*, pp. 59–60; May, *Homeward Bound*, pp. 166, 171–72, 225; Jakle, *The Tourist*, pp. 186, 286; Kammen, *Mystic Chords of Memory*, pp. 551, 657; Steven Watts, *The Magic Kingdom: Walt Disney and the American Way of Life* (Boston: Houghton Mifflin, 1997), p. 323.

28. Flink, *Car Culture*, p. 213; John Bodnar, *Remaking America: Public Memory, Commemoration, and Patriotism in the Twentieth Century* (Princeton: Princeton University Press, 1992), pp. 195–96.

29. Robert Lawrence, E-mail to author, March 15, 2000; Judith Green, letter to author, April 1998; Jakle, *The Tourist*, p. 305.

30. Bloom, *A History of Adams County*, p. 395; Robert Lawrence, E-mail to author, March 15, 2000.

31. Jakle, Sculle, and Rogers, *The Motel in America*, pp. 41–45, 120–21, 138–42, 324, 329; Sylvia Miller, letter to author, April 28, 1998.

32. Incomplete letter on congressional stationery to Stewart Udall, July 6, 1964, RG 79, E 414, Box 1, Folder 3416, NARA; Anne Markle to the Department of the Interior, August 20, 1960, RG 79, E 411, Box 2, Folder A-3815, NARA.

33. Johanna Guzik, "At Gettysburg Battlefield," *Motor Travel* 44 (July 1971): 6; James Warren, postcard to author, June 6, 1998; Jay Purdy, E-mail to author, November 10, 1999.

34. John Dynia, posting to Gettysburg Discussion Group (GDG) Listserv, October 23, 1997; Judith Green, letter to author, April 1998; Joan Berghey, letter to author, April 27, 1998.

35. Judith Green, letter to author, April 1998; John Dynia, posting to GDG Listserv, October 23, 1997.

36. John Dynia, posting to GDG Listserv, October 23, 1997; Jack Lawrence, E-mail to author, March 15, 2000; Carol Ann Theuer, letter to author, April 27, 1998; Terry Thomann, posting to GDG Listserv, October 23, 1997.

37. George Stafford, E-mail to author, October 22, 1997; Judith Green, letter to author, April 1998; Martha Whitmore, letter to author, April 24, 1998.

38. Guzik, "At Gettysburg Battlefield," p. 6.

39. Hamburger, "Notes for a Gazeteer," p. 94; Superintendent, GNMP, to Regional Director, NE Region, "Report on Centennial Activities at Gettysburg, July 1, 2, and 3, 1963," RG 79, E 411, Box 4, Folder A-8215, NARA; Terry Thomann, posting to GDG Listserv, October 23, 1997.

40. Vera Culver, interview with author, October 6, 1997.

41. *Gettysburg Times*, [August 1959], Jackie White scrapbook; *Gettysburg Times*, July 20, 1959.

42. Pat Beyer, "A Trip Through Fantasyland," *Blair County Motor News* (April 1960): 3; *New Oxford Item*, March 23, 1961, Jackie White scrapbook; *Gettysburg Times*, [August 1959], Jackie White scrapbook; Mrs. Donald Coe to Fantasyland, September 1, 1965, Jackie White scrapbook.

43. "'Caroline' Goes to Fantasyland, Gettysburg, Pa.," promotional booklet, 10 leaves, colored illustrations [1964?]; *Reading Eagle*, August 2, 1967.

44. *Richmond News Leader*, September 13, 1971.

45. *New York Times*, June 14, 1959; *Gettysburg Times*, June 1, 1963; Richard Martin, letter to Fantasyland, n.d., Jackie White scrapbook.

46. *Gettysburg Times*, December 18, 1949; *Gettysburg Star and Sentinel*, April 6, 1946; *Gettysburg Times*, October 18, 1941, October 26, 1946.

47. Bloom, A History of Adams County, pp. 394–99.

48. Unrau, Administrative History, pp. 243, 268–69; Mr. and Mrs. Joesph Bowling to President D. D. Eisenhower, November 17, 1960, RG 79, E 411, Box 2, Folder A-3815, NARA; Battle Lines 6 (Summer 1998): 5; Bernadette Sumen to President Eisenhower [1961] RG 79 E 411, Box 2, Folder A-3815, NARA; Terry Dayton to President Eisenhower, January 18, 1961, RG 79, E 411, Box 2, Folder A-3815, NARA.

49. Superintendent, GNMP, to Regional Director, May 9, 1945, RG 79, E 411, Box 47, Folder 620–46, NARA; Mrs. R. G. Cheffey, letter to author, May 4, 1998.

50. Leonard H. Dore to Conrad Wirth, October 4, 1958, RG 79, E 414, Box 1, Folder 3415, NARA.

51. Kammen, Mystic Chords of Memory, pp. 590–91; Ned J. Burns to Mr. Kahler, Memo, July 27, 1945, RG 79, E 411, Box 47, Folder 620–46, NARA; Bloom, A History of Adams County, pp. 396–97; Battle Lines 7 (October 1999): 5–6.

52. "Let's Not Surrender Our Battlefields," Saturday Evening Post 231 (September 19, 1959): 37; R. C. Gregory, letter to editor, Saturday Evening Post 231 (October 24, 1959): 8; Gary Wills, "Battles of Gettysburg Are Not Over Yet," Philadelphia Inquirer, August 29, 1972.

53. Ernest B. Ferguson, "Just Another Honky Tonk," Baltimore Sun, July 4, 1972.

Chapter Seven: A Future in the Past

1. Gettysburg Times, January 4, 1988; Rhode Island Westerly Sun, August 28, 1988; York Daily Record, July 3, 1988; Gettysburg Times, June 28, 1988, July 20, 1988.

2. Gettysburg Times, February 19, 1988; York Sunday News, November 27, 1988; "125 Years Ago," Americana 16 (May–June, 1988): 51, 53; "Paging Through," Civil War News 16 (July 1990): 2.

3. Gettysburg Times, July 7, 1988; Lebanon Daily News, July 3, 1988; Gettysburg Times, July 9, 1988.

4. Michael Kammen, American Culture, American Tastes: Social Change and the Twentieth Century (New York: Alfred A. Knopf, 1999), p. 259; Tom Engelhardt, The End of Victory Culture: Cold War America and the Disillusioning of a Generation (New York: Basic Books, 1995), pp. 3–15.

5. Quote cited in Kammen, American Culture, American Tastes, p. 259; David Frum, How We Got Here, the Seventies: the Decade That Brought You Modern Life (New York: Basic Books, 2000), pp. xv–xxiv, 73, 58, 353–55.

6. Michael Elliott, The Day before Yesterday: Reconsidering America's Past, Rediscovering the Present (New York: Simon and Schuster, 1996), pp. 21–31, 165–84; Joseph Turow, Breaking Up America: Advertisers and the New Media World (Chicago: University of Chicago Press, 1997), p. 193.

7. Michael Kammen, Mystic Chords of Memory: The Transformation of Tradition in American Culture (New York: Alfred A. Knopf, 1991), pp. 12–13, 559–60, 618–32, 645; David Lowenthal, Possessed by the Past: The Heritage Crusade and the Spoils of History (New York: Free Press, 1996), pp. xi, 3–6, 121, 170; Christopher Lasch, The Culture of Narcissim: American Life in an Age of Diminishing Expectations (New York: W. W. Norton, 1979), pp. xv–xviii, 87; John Sears, Sacred Places: American Tourist Attractions in the Nineteenth Century (New York: Oxford University Press, 1989), pp. 214–15.

8. Robert Hewison, The Heritage Industry: Britain in a Climate of Decline (London: Methuen, 1987), pp. 24–32, 46–47, 132; Time-Life quote cited in Lowenthal, Possessed

By the Past, p. 100; Dean MacCannell, *The Tourist: A New Theory of the Leisure Class* (New York: Schocken Books, 1976; reprint, Berkeley and Los Angeles: University of California Press, 1999), pp. 2–3, 13–14, 145–48.

9. David Lowenthal, *The Past Is a Foreign Country* (London: Cambridge University Press, 1985), pp. xvi–xviii, 230–31.

10. Jim Cullen, *The Civil War in Popular Culture: A Reuseable Past* (Washington, D.C.: Smithsonian Institution Press, 1995), p. 154; Engelhardt, *The End of Victory Culture*, pp. 259, 266–68.

11. Jay Luvaas and Harold W. Nelson, eds., *Guide to the Battle of Gettysburg* (Lawrence: University Press of Kansas, 1994).

12. Neal Gabler, *Life the Movie: How Entertainment Conquered Reality* (New York: Alfred A. Knopf, 1998), pp. 95–97; Kammen, *American Culture, American Tastes*, p. 194; Celia Lury, *Consumer Culture* (New Brunswick, N.J.: Rutgers University Press, 1996), p. 103; Kammen, *Mystic Chords of Memory*, pp. 667–70.

13. Quoted in Desmond Ryan, "The Cinematic Enigma behind *Gone with the Wind*'s Success," *Philadelphia Inquirer*, June 28, 1998; Terry Burger, *Gettysburg National Military Park and Eisenhower National Historic Site: Economic Impact on Gettysburg and Adams County* (Gettysburg: Friends of the National Parks at Gettysburg and Gettysburg-Adams County Area Chamber of Commerce, 1998), p. 27; Lowenthal, *Possessed by the Past*, 127–39; Cullen, *The Civil War in Popular Culture*, pp. 144–48.

14. Turow, *Breaking Up America*, pp. 2–9, 70, 184–97.

15. *Hanover Evening Sun*, April 18, 1993, August 2, 1995.

16. Kathryn Jorgensen, "Gettysburg Is More Than Just Home for Thomas Publication," *Civil War News* 25 (November 1999): 46.

17. "Census 2000: The New Demographics," *Wall Street Journal*, May 15, 2001.

18. Russell Belk, *Collecting in a Consumer Society* (New York: Routledge, 1995), pp. 53–55, 64, 94–95.

19. Turow, *Breaking Up America*, pp. 2–8, 90–91.

20. *York Sunday News*, April 9, 1989; *Gettysburg Times*, February 15, 1990; "Friends of the National Park at Gettysburg" (newsletter hereafter cited as FNPG); FNPG, Summer 1991, p. 3; "The Friends of Gettysburg Quartermaster, 1996–1997," newsletter insert; "Friends of the National Parks at Gettysburg Major Accomplishments, 6/1989–6/1996," newsletter insert; interview with Vicki Greenlee, executive director, FNPG, October 6, 1997; "The Vanguard!" (letter and insert, n.d., received 1999); Turow, *Breaking Up America*, pp. 128–40.

21. See FNPG, esp. Summer 1995, Winter 1996, Summer 1996, Winter 1997, Winter 1998, Spring 1999, Summer 2000; "Friends of the National Parks at Gettysburg" (form letter to members, n.d., received 1999).

22. *Gettysburg Times*, April 30, 1990; FNPG, Spring 1990, p. 2; see FNPG, Spring, Summer, Winter, 1998; "Accomplishments of the Friends of the National Parks at Gettysburg," (publicity handout, n.d., received 1999); Gettysburg National Military Park, *Draft General Management Plan and Environmental Impact Statement* (Gettysburg: Gettysburg National Military Park, 1998), pp. 108–31.

23. *Hanover Evening Sun*, August 21, 1994, *Gettysburg Times*, July 18, 1995.

24. See FNPG Winter, 1997, Spring 1999; *Gettysburg Times*, August 24, 1992; Turow, *Breaking Up America*, pp. 110–14; Belk, *Collecting in a Consumer Society*, p. 111.

25. Michael D. Eisner, *Work in Progress* (New York: Random House, 1998), pp. 319–24; *Gettysburg Times*, May 28, 1994.

26. *York Daily Record*, May 12, 1994; Eisner, *Work in Progress*, pp. 326–28.

27. *Gettysburg Times*, October 13, 1994; Lisa Miller, "Historic Villages Take a Page from Disney," *Wall Street Journal*, August 22, 1997.

28. *York Sunday News*, February 14, 1982.

29. "The Second Battle of Gettysburg," *U.S. News and World Report* 71 (October 18, 1971): 67; Borough Manager Charles Kuhn cited in *Harrisburg Evening News*, July 10, 1973; *Hanover Sun Shopper's Guide*, February 20, 1974; *Gettysburg Times*, June 2, 1993; Walter Powell quoted in *York Sunday News*, June 20, 1993; Neal Beach, quoted in *Gettysburg Times*, November 21, 1972.

30. Martin E. Marty, "Looking Backward into the Future," *New York Times*, February 2, 1975.

31. Kammen, *Mystic Chords of Memory*, p. 628; *Hanover Evening Sun*, June 22, 1990; Philip Magaldi quoted in *York Sunday News*, June 27, 1993.

32. *Gettysburg Times*, March 22, 1991; "Main Street Gettysburg," four-page publicity handout, n.d., p. 1; Gettysburg Historic Pathway Task Force, *Gettysburg Historic Pathway Plan* (Gettysburg: The Task Force, [1990?]), pp. 5–7; *Gettysburg Times*, May 12, 1989.

33. Economic Research Associates, *Feasibility Study and Plan for an Interpretive Center, Gettysburg, Pennsylvania* (n.p.: Economics Research Associates, 1995), p. II-3.

34. "Main Street Gettysburg," pp. 3–4; "Gettysburg: Main Street Vision. A View from Gettysburg's Historic Pathway" (6-page newsletter, [1999?]: p. 4; *Gettysburg Times*, October 6, 1994; *York Sunday News*, September 21, 1997.

35. "Gettysburg: Main Street Vision, A View from Gettysburg's Historic Pathway," pp. 2, 4; Economic Research Associates, *Feasibility Study*, p. V-1.

36. *Weekend Entertainment Guide*, November 13, 1994, Gettysburg National Military Park Archive (hereafter cited as GNMPA) clipping file, vol. 38, p. 11; Economic Research Associates, *Feasibility Study*, pp. IV-3, IV-14, VI-10, V-5; Philip Magaldi quoted in *Hanover Evening Sun*, January 19, 1993; *Hanover Evening Sun*, August 9, 1994.

37. Historic Pathway Task Force, *Gettysburg Historic Pathway Plan*, p. 6; "Gettysburg: Main Street Vision"; Don Long, "The Boyle Group: Developer Planning Outlet Punch beside Famous Civil War Park," *Outlet Retailer: A Supplement to Shopping Center World* (August 1995): 1–2.

38. Kammen, *Mystic Chords of Memory*, pp. 618–19.

39. Bruce Catton, "The Irrepressible Centennial," speech delivered at Gettysburg College, November 19, 1962, RG 79, E 411, Box 5, Folder A-8215, NARA; *Richmond News-Leader*, July 21, 1961.

40. *Philadelphia Inquirer*, June 2, 1974; *Gettysburg Times*, August 21, 1972; February 19, 1974; *Harrisburg Sunday Patriot News*, July 23, 1972, September 3, 1972; Frank Barnes, "Making History Come Alive," speech to NPS Northeast Region, 1964, GNMPA, Frank Barnes folder; Memo to Superintendent, GNMP, July 23, 1973, GNMPA, Frank Barnes folder.

41. *Lincoln Sun Newspaper*, May 31, 1978, GNMPA clipping file, vol. 21, p. 120; *Gettysburg Times*, July 7, 1973; *Harrisburg Sunday Patriot News*, July 30, 1978.

42. *Gettysburg Times*, October 10, 1985; FNPG (Spring 1997): 1, 4; *Battle Lines* 5 (Summer 1997): 2.

43. *York Dispatch*, October 29, 1987; *Civil War News* 21 (August 1995): 16; *Civil War News* 25 (January 1999): 24; *Gettysburg Times*, August 11, 1999; "sixth Annual Gettysburg Music Muster," News Release, National Park Service, August 21, 2000; "2000 Calendar of Events," two-page list of activities, Gettysburg National Military Park, January 2000; Deborah Fitts, "300,000-Plus School Students Interact with Park," *Civil War*

News 26 (June 2000): 53; "GNMP Reaches Classrooms Nationwide," FNPG (Summer 2000): 16–17.

44. Harlan D. Unrau, *Gettysburg: Administrative History* (Washington, D.C.: GPO, 1991), pp. 298–99, 300–316, 440, 489.

45. *Harrisburg Patriot*, July 13, 1982; *Gettysburg Times*, November 21, 1972; *Harrisburg Sunday Patriot News*, November 19, 1972.

46. FNPG (Winter 1998): 9, 20; *Gettysburg Times*, July 17, 1992; *Civil War News* 18 (June 1992): 1; James Myers, GNMP Superintendent, to Region V Director, NPS, May 25, 1961, RG 79, E 411, Box 2, Folder A-3815, NARA; *Portland Press Herald*, March 26, 1994, GNMPA clipping file, v. 38, p. 40.

47. *Gettysburg Times*, March 27, 28, 29, April 6, May 12, August 26, September 2, 1995; *New York Times*, November 18, 1990.

48. See Gettysburg National Military Park, *Draft General Management Plan and Environmental Impact Statement* esp. pp. 266–80; Robert Kinsley in *Washington Post*, November 7, 1997; "Gettysburg General Management Plan Is Now Final," News Release, National Park Service, November 24, 1999; "National Park Service Releases Final Gettysburg Plan," News Release, Gettysburg Public Affairs Office, June 18, 1999; *USA Today*, September 29, 1997; "Gettysburg to Have Improved Visitor Facilities," *National Parks* 72 (March–April 1998): 19–20.

49. Gettysburg National Military Park, *Draft General Management Plan and Environmental Impact Statement*, pp. 122–23, 84; letter from John A. Latachar, *Civil War News* 26 (January 2000): 7; *Civil War News* 26 (February–March 2000): 3; John Latschar quoted in "From the Park," FNPG (Spring 2000): 3; and "National Park Service Releases Final Gettysburg Plan," News Release, Gettysburg Public Affairs Office, June 18, 1999.

50. Gettysburg National Military Park, *Draft General Management Plan and Environmental Impact Statement*, p. 274; *Civil War News* 26 (January 2000): 7.

51. *Gettysburg Times*, June 13, 1975, June 14, 1973, July 10, 1975, June 20, 1995; FNPG (Spring 1999): 3.

52. Latschar quoted in *Washington Post*, August 19, 1998; Belk, *Collecting in a Consumer Society*, pp. 132–33; "National Park Service Holds Public Workshop," News Release, Nartional Park Service, March 3, 1998; "National Park Service Releases Final Gettysburg Plan," News Release, Gettysburg Public Affairs Office, June 18, 1999; Kammen, *American Culture, American Taste*, p. 259; *Civil War News* 26 (January 2000): 7; "Pioneering Effort in Gettysburg," *National Parks* 71 (November–December 1997): 20–21.

53. Unrau, *Administrative History*, p. 274; *Wall Street Journal*, August 27, 1997; "The National Civil War Museum, Harrisburg, Pennsylvania" (pamphlet); Susan G. Davis, *Spectacular Nature: Corporate Culture and the Sea World Experience* (Berkeley and Los Angeles: University of California Press, 1997), pp. 2–4, 236–37.

54. Ada Louise Huxtable, *The Unreal America: Architecture and Illusion* (New York: New Press, 1997), pp. 82–83; Babbitt quoted in "Gettysburg Development Plan Set," *Washington Post*, June 18, 2000.

Chapter Eight: "It's 1863 All Over Again": Heritage Tourists

1. Ed Smothers to gettysburg@arthes.com, September 3, 1997.

2. Joseph Turow, *Breaking Up America: Advertisers and the New Media World* (Chi-

cago: University of Chicago Press, 1997), p. 70; Elaine Tyler May, *Homeward Bound: American Families in the Cold War Era* (New York: Basic Books, 1988), pp. 221–23; Christopher Lasch, *The Culture of Narcissim: American Life in an Age of Diminishing Expectations* (New York: W. W. Norton, 1979), pp. xv–xvi; David Frum, *How We Got Here, the Seventies: The Decade that Brought You Modern Life* (New York: Basic Books, 2000), pp. 58–60.

3. Gary Cross, *An All-Consuming Century: Why Commercialism Won in Modern America* (New York: Columbia University Press, 2000), pp. 214–15, 223–25; Turow, *Breaking up America*, pp. 184–97; Neal Gabler, *Life the Movie: How Entertainment Conquered Reality* (New York: Alfred A. Knopf, 1998), p. 212.

4. See Robert Fogel, *The Fourth Great Awakening and the Limits of Materialism* (Chicago: University of Chicago Press, 2000); Mike Featherstone, *Consumer Culture and Postmodernism* (London: Sage Publications, 1991), p. 95; Robert Hewison, *The Heritage Industry: Britain in a Climate of Decline* (London: Methuen, 1987), pp. 44–45; Christopher Clausen, *Faded Mosaic: The Emergence of Post-cultural America* (Chicago: Ivan R. Dee, 2000), p. 165; Jon Spayde, "A Way Out of Wonderland," *Utne Reader* (July–August 1997), p. 49.

5. David Lowenthal, *Possessed by the Past: The Heritage Crusade and the Spoils of History* (New York: Free Press, 1996), pp. 127–39; Hewison, *The Heritage Industry*, pp. 45–47; Tom Engelhardt, *The End of Victory Culture: Cold War America and the Disillusioning of a Generation* (New York: Basic Books, 1995), p. 259; Richard Miniter, "In the Danger Zone," *Wall Street Journal*, January 5, 2001; Andreas Huyssen, "Monument and Memory in a Postmodern Age," *Yale Journal of Criticism* 6 (Fall 1993): 253.

6. *Miami Herald-Los Angeles Times* [September 1972], Gettysburg National Military Park Archive (herafter cited as GNMPA) clipping file., vol. 15, p. 217.

7. James Yenckel, "In the Footsteps of Lee and Grant," *AAA World* 1 (July–August, 1999): 5.

8. "Advertisers Are Cautious as Household Makeup Shifts," *Wall Street Journal*, May 15, 2001; Cross, *An All-Consuming Century*, p. 234; Friends of the National Parks at Gettysburg Newsletter (Fall 1998): 9 (hereafter cited as FNPG); *Gettysburg Times*, May 15, 2000; Economic Research Associates, *Feasibility Study and Plan for an Interpretive Center, Gettysburg, Pennsylvania* (n.p.: Economics Research Associates, 1995), V-2, 20–21; U.S. Department of the Interior, National Park Service, Gettysburg National Military Park, *Draft General Management Plan and Environmental Impact Statement* (Gettysburg: Gettysburg National Military Park, 1998), p. 191. See also University of Idaho, Cooperative Park Studies Unit, *Gettysburg National Military Park, Eisenhower National Historic Site*, Visitor Services Project Report 73 (Boise: University of Idaho, 1995), pp. 4–6 (hereafter referred to as Visitor Services Project Report 73).

9. *Lancaster Sunday News*, November 21, 1993; Vincent Frontero, "The Hallowed Ground," *New York* 22 (October 9, 1989): 76.

10. Brooke Masters, "The Cold War over Civil War Battlefields," *Washington Post*, September 30, 1991; Florence Palmer Jackson, "History and Terrain Make for Good Skiing," *Philadelphia Inquirer*, February 2, 1979; William O'Donnell, letter to editor, *Civil War News* 19 (April 1993): 3.

11. *Gettysburg Times*, July 13, 1992; Deborah Fitts, "5-K Walk," *Civil War News* 26 (June 2000): 48; *Gettysburg Times*, August 12, 1997; John Fine, "Touring Gettysburg on Horseback," *Pennsylvania Magazine* 22 (May–June, 1999): 22–26; *Hanover Evening Sun*, September 4, 1994.

12. *Gettysburg Times*, May 29, 1985, June 28, 1988; the survey, conducted by four officers at the U.S. Army War College, was summarized in the *Harrisburg Patriot*, October 5, 1987.

13. *Philadelphia Inquirer*, February 18, 1982; Jessica Snow, letter to the editor, *Civil War News 17* (August 1991): 26.

14. FNPG (Winter 1990): 3; *Gettysburg Times*, July 18, 1990; Steve Brizek, letter to editor, *Civil War News 25* (February–March, 1999): 3; John D. Baniszewski to gettysburg@gdg.org, June 19, 1900.

15. *Gettysburg Times*, July 19, 1990; Tim Fisher to gettysburg@appsmiths.com, July 17, 1998; Pati Buford to gettysburg@appsmiths.com, October 24, 1997; Brizek letter, *Civil War News*, p. 3.

16. *Newsday*, April 24, 1983; *Washington Post*, March 29, 1995, October 25, 1986; *Philadelphia Inquirer*, September 1, 1987; *Boston Globe*, February 23, 1999.

17. Jim Ferguson to gettysburg@gdg.org, August 4, 2000; J. Bilby to gettysburg@gdg.org, September 25, 2000; Art Gannet, "Videos for Preservation," *Civil War News 23* (October 1997): 29.

18. Gannet, "Videos for Preservation," p. 29; Mark Hess to gettysburg@gdg.org, August 4, 2000; *Washington Post*, June 11, 1998.

19. Vicki Monrean, "Interview with Wayne Motts," FNPG (Winter 1998): 9; Bruce Trinque to gettysburg@gdg.org, August 13, 2000.

20. Jenna Crowe to gettysburg@arthes.com, September 22, 1999; Chuck Rothlauf to gettysburg@appsmiths.com, September 26, 1997; Gabler, *Life the Movie*, pp. 175–76.

21. *Chambersburg Public Opinion*, July 14, 1994; Richard Page to gettysburg@appsmiths.com, October 23, 1997.

22. According to University of Idaho, Visitor Services Project Report 73, p. 15, the most visited site was the visitors' center (95 percent), followed by Little Round Top (82 percent), and town (76 percent); Bryan Meyer to gettysburg@appsmiths.com, July 28, 1997; Sylvia Sherman to gettysburg@appsmiths.com, August 2, 2000.

23. Thomas Holbrook quoted in *Gettysburg Times*, August 18, 1997; Garry Wills in *Philadelphia Inquirer*, August 29, 1972.

24. *Harrisburg Patriot*, July 1, 1988; *York Sunday News*, June 27, 1993.

25. *Gettysburg Times*, July 21, 1990; Mark Hess to gettysburg@gdg.org, August 2, 2000; FNPG (Spring 1996): 6.

26. *New York Times*, September 16, 1979; *Chicago Tribune*, July 1, 1984; Jack McLaughlin, *Gettysburg: The Long Encampment* (New York: Bonanza Books, 1963), p. v; Patrick King to gettysburg@appsmiths.com, September 8, 1997; Guy Greeneltch to gettysburg@appsmiths.com, September 8, 1997; Barbara Jones to gettysburg@appsmiths.com, January 28, 1998; Arden Williams to author, October 2, 1998; Jan Wehner to gettysburg@gdg.org, October 19, 2000; *Gettysburg Times*, October 30, 2000.

27. Otto Friedrich, "New Age Harmonies," *Time 130* (December 7, 1987): 62–63; "Where the Ghouls Are," *Harper's 289* (October 1994): 24; Gayle Turim, "Hosts of Ghosts," *Americana 17* (October, 1989): 21–24; Joel Schwartz, "Modern Ghosts," *Omni 8* (June 1986): 41; Kathryn Robinson, "Ghost Stories," *Utne Reader 39* (May–June 1990): 119.

28. *Gettysburg Times*, November 11, 1991; *Chambersburg Public Opinion*, October 27, 1991; advertisement in *Civil War News 23* (December 1997): 44.

29. Ty McCauslin, "Supernatural Sojourns," *Car and Travel* (September–October, 1997): 6a; *Gettysburg Times*, January 18, 1995.

30. *Waynesboro Record-Herald*, January 21, 1995; Guy Greeneltch to gettysburg@arthes.com, August 10, 1997; Karen Shaw to gettysburg@arthes.com, August 10, 1997; Margaret D. Blough to gettysburg@arthes.com, September 26, 1999.

31. Battlefield Bed and Breakfast website, www.gettysburgbattlefield.com, February 11, 2000; Thomas Yaglowski, E-mail to author, February 23, 2001; Frontero, "This Hallowed Ground," p. 76; "Eighteenth Annual Civil War Heritage Days, June 23–July 4, 2000" (pamphlet, Gettysburg Travel Council, 2000): 7.

32. Michael Kammen, *Mystic Chords of Memory: The Transformation of Tradition in American Culture* (New York: Alfred A. Knopf, 1991), pp. 631–35, 679; Jim Cameron to gettysburg@gdg.org, July 25, 2000; Cross, *An All-Consuming Century*, p. 227.

33. Flier from Penn State Continuing Education, York Campus, 1981; letter to author from Barbara Reid, June 8, 1998.

34. Virginia Gage to gettysburg@gdg.org, October 24, 2000; Dave Glorioso to gettysburg@gdg.org, October 12, 2000; Virginia Gage to gettysburg@gdg.org, June 8, 2000.

35. FNPG (Summer 1995): 7; letter to author from Barbara Reid, June 8, 1998; Margaret D. Blough to gettysburg@gdg.org, April 16, 2000; FNPG (Fall 1998): 20.

36. Russell Belk, *Collecting in a Consumer Society* (New York: Routledge, 1995), pp. 53–55, 95–96; Jerry Bennett quoted in *Civil War News* 26 (October 2000): 18.

37. Belk, *Collecting in a Consumer Society*, pp. 69–76; Ed Ballam, "Collector's Corner," *Civil War News* 26 (June 2000): 44.

38. Richard Barber, E-mail to author, January 24, 2001; Thomas Hardy, E-mail to author, January 25, 2001; Scott Mingus to gettysburg@gdg.org, August 7, 2000; November 1, 2000.

39. Randall Allred, "Catharsis, Revision, and Re-enactment: Negotiating the Meaning of the American Civil War," *Journal of American Culture* 19 (Winter 1996): 10; Jim Cullen, *The Civil War in Popular Culture: A Reusable Past* (Washington, D.C.: Smithsonian Institution Press, 1995), pp. 198–99; Gabler, *Life the Movie*, pp. 192–211; Roy Turner, "Bloodless Battles: The Civil War Reenacted," *Drama Review* 34 (Winter 1990): 130; "Filming of Antietam Winds Down," *Civil War News* 26 (February–March, 2000): 21; *Philadelphia Inquirer*, August 31, 1992.

40. *Hanover Evening Sun*, September 24, 1992, June 30, 1993, June 22, 1995.

41. *Harrisburg Sunday Patriot-News*, June 26, 1983; Belk, *Collecting in a Consumer Society*, pp. 95–96; Allred, "Catharsis, Revision, and Re-enactment," pp. 11, 10; *Lancaster New Era*, July 3, 1993.

42. Tony Horowitz, *Confederates in the Attic: Dispatches from the Unfinished Civil War* (New York: Pantheon Books, 1998), p. 278; Jim Morgan to gettysburg@appsmiths.com, August 27, 1997; *Hanover Evening Sun*, July 6, 1992, June 30, 1993.

43. Randy Phiel, "More Enjoyment This Year," *Civil War News* 25 (July 1999): 2a; Allred, "Catharsis, Revision, and Re-enactment," p. 5; Dennis Hall, "Civil War Reenactors and the Postmodern Sense of History," *Journal of American Culture* 17 (Fall 1994): 10; *New York Times*, May 16, 1999.

44. Allred, "Catharsis, Revision, and Re-enactment," pp. 4, 7; *Westerly Sun* (Rhode Island), August 28, 1988.

45. Christopher Hitchens, "Rebel Ghosts," *Vanity Fair*, no. 467 (July 1999): 42; Barbara Lane, letter to editor, *Civil War News* 25 (February–March 1999): 6.

46. Jim Getz to gettysburg@appsmiths.com, June 18, 1998; Tom Banks to gettysburg@gdg.org, July 27, 2000.

47. FNPG (Fall 1998): 3; *Hanover Evening Sun*, November 1, 1997; Dave Smith, "Civil War on the Internet," *Civil War News* 26 (September 2000): 19; author's interview with Dennis Lawrence, October 12, 1997.

48. K. Paul Raver to gettysburg@gdg.org, December 14, 2000.

49. Tom Townsend to gettysburg@gdg.org, August 9, 2000.

50. John Dynia to gettysburg@appsmith.com, September 26, 1997.

Epilogue

1. Deborah Fitts, "New Group to Interpret Battlefield Events," *Civil War News* 26 (July 2000): 19; JoAnn Bartlett, "Evergreen Cemetery Plans," *Civil War News* 26 (July 2000): 15a; Kevin Trostle, president, Main Street Gettysburg, e-mail to author, June 26, 2000; Deborah Fitts, "Park Boundary Adds Wills House," *Civil War News* 26 (November 2000): 6; "Announcing Gettysburg Remembrance Trust," solicitation mailing from Friends of the National Parks at Gettysburg (FNPG), December 2000.

2. Deborah Fitts, "It's Gone," *Civil War News* 26 (August 2000): 1, 8–10; Joan Moody, "History with a Bang," *Gettysburg Quarterly* 7 (Summer-Fall 2000): 1.

3. Edward T. Linenthal, *Sacred Ground: Americans and Their Battlefields* (Urbana: University of Illinois Press, 1991), p. 92.

4. The material about play, memory, and adult enchantment are ideas developed by Professor Gary Cross and shared with the author during several interviews, most significantly on December 20, 2000.

5. Gary Cross, *An All-Consuming Century: Why Commercialism Won in Modern America* (New York: Columbia University Press, 2000), p. 251.

6. John Latschar quoted in *Gettysburg Times*, May 15, 2000; "Heritagepac E-mail Alert," October 27, 1999 to gettysburg@gdg.org; Allen B. Ballard, "The Demons of Gettysburg," *New York Times*, May 30, 1999.

Index

☆ ☆ ☆ ☆ ☆ ☆ ☆ ☆ ☆ ☆ ☆